A NEW ACCOUNT OF EAST INDIA AND PERSIA BEING NINE YEARS' TRAVELS 1672 – 1681

JOHANNES FRYER M.D.
Societatis Regiæ Lond. Socius.

A
NEW ACCOUNT
OF
EAST INDIA AND PERSIA
BEING
NINE YEARS' TRAVELS 1672-1681

JOHN FRYER

EDITED WITH NOTES AND AN INTRODUCTION BY

WILLIAM CROOKE

IN THREE VOLUMES

VOL. I

Published by

Facsimile Publisher
12 Pragati Market
Ashok Vihar, Ph-2
Delhi-110052
facsimilepublisher.com

Distribution Network
gyanbooks.com
India, USA, Canada, UK, Australia, France

ISBN : 978-93-5324-481-1 (Set)
ISBN : 978-93-5324-482-8 Vol. 1 (HB)
First Published, London, 1909

2nd Impression 2020

Printed at: Gyan Press, Delhi.

A New Account of East India and Persia being Nine Years' Travels 1672 – 1681
Author: John Fryer

A

NEW ACCOUNT

OF

EAST INDIA AND PERSIA.

BEING

NINE YEARS' TRAVELS,

1672—1681.

BY

JOHN FRYER.

Edited, with Notes and an Introduction,

BY

WILLIAM CROOKE, B.A.,

LONDON:

PRINTED FOR THE HAKLUYT SOCIETY.

MDCCCCIX.

PREFACE.

THE task of editing Dr. John Fryer's *New Account of East India and Persia* for the Hakluyt Society's series was originally entrusted to Mr. Arthur T. Pringle, of the Madras Civil Service. He had edited a calendar of the early Madras records, and from his intimate knowledge of Southern India was specially qualified to undertake such a work. A copy of the folio edition of the book was forwarded to Mr. Pringle at Madras, and he probably collected some materials. But his untimely death occurred before he could have made much progress; and, with the usual fate which seems almost inevitable in literary work done by British officers in the East, his library was immediately dispersed. Enquiries, conducted with the kind assistance of the officials of the Secretariat at Madras, have failed to trace any of the notes or other materials which he may have collected.

My personal interest in the book was largely

enhanced when I had occasion to study it with some care in the course of the preparation of a new edition of *Hobson-Jobson*, the Anglo-Indian Glossary of Sir H. Yule and Dr. A. C. Burnell, who had used it extensively as a source for quotations, Sir H. Yule in his Bibliography remarking: "No work has been more serviceable in the compilation of the Glossary." As no one else was prepared to undertake the edition long contemplated by the Hakluyt Society, the Council were pleased to entrust the task to me.

This duty has proved to be more difficult than I anticipated. The ideal editor of Fryer should possess a singularly wide and varied knowledge of the geography, history, archæology, natural productions, languages, religions, superstitions, and customs of India and Persia. It would have been quite impossible for me to prepare the notes to this edition if I had not received generous assistance from many scholars in various fields of knowledge. Mr. W. Foster and Miss E. B. Sainsbury have supplied me with much information from the MS. records in the India Office Library and Record Rooms: Mr. W. Irvine (whose notes on Manucci's *Storia do Magor*, covering this period, have been most useful), has helped me on various points of Muhammadan history and literature; Mr. V. A. Smith on the earlier period; Mr. D. Ferguson on the Portuguese; Sir G. Birdwood, Sir G. Watt, Sir W. T. Thistleton Dyer, Colonel D. D. Cunningham, and Lt.-Colonel D.

Prain on natural history; Professor E. G. Browne on Persia; Mr. F. C. Conybeare on the Armenians; Professor E. Bensly has traced many quotations from classical authors. Many other officers who have served, or are now serving, in the East, have taken much trouble in answering queries, among whom I may note Sir A. T. Arundel, Messrs. A. R. Becher, A. R. Bonus, E. Carmichael, Dr. A. Codrington, Messrs. H. Cousens, W. Francis, J. R. Henderson, J. A. Ismail Gracias, Jadunath Sarkar, P. B. Joshi, J. L. Rieu, W. W. Skeat, and Dr. C. M. Woodrow. I have also to thank Dr. H. M. Butler and Mr. W. Aldis Wright, of Trinity College, Cambridge, Mr. J. A. J. de Villiers, Secretary of the Hakluyt Society, Mr. R. Harrison, Secretary of the Royal Society, Mr. W. Wesley, Assistant Secretary of the Royal Astronomical Society, and Mr. W. T. Lynn, for information on various points.

A book like this offers unlimited temptations for annotation; and I fear that in some cases I have extended my notes beyond reasonable limits. But, as we know little of the history of the work, it seemed advisable to quote the accounts of contemporary travellers in order to allow the reader to judge how far Fryer was indebted to other writers. Further, it contains many adaptations or corruptions of words and phrases in various native languages, the origin and explanation of which is familiar to officers who have served in the East, but of which the European reader requires information. In the case of terms explained in *Hobson-Jobson* I have usually contented myself with a reference to that Glossary. There are also many references to questions connected with religion and social life on which the general reader will require explanation. Some few quotations, in spite of investigation, still remain to be identified, and the same is the case with some words connected with weights and measures.

W. CROOKE.

11*th October*, 1909.

INTRODUCTION.

JOHN FRYER,[1] M.D., F.R.S., the author of this work, eldest son of William Fryer of London, was probably born in that city about 1650. The facts of his career are obscure, and he displays throughout his book a notable reticence regarding his life and family connections. It is probable that some of his relations were connected with the early fortunes of the East India Company. On the last day of the year 1600, Queen Elizabeth incorporated the subscribers, 217 in number, under the title of "The Governor and Company of Merchants of London trading into the East Indies." In this document entitled "A Priuledge for XVteene Yeares, granted by her

[1] It is remarkable that accounts of no less than four men named John Fryer, M.D., are to be found in the *Dict. Nat. Biog.* The first died in 1563, the second "flourished" about 1571, the third died in 1672. The fourth is our author. Practically all the facts of his life, so far as they are known, are given in the life by Mr. Gordon Goodwin, vol. xx, 302 f.

Matie to certaine Adventurors for the discoury of the trade for the East Indies," we find the name of "Iohn ffryre"; and among "Billes of Aduenture sealed" on 22nd July, 1601, appears the entry: "To Iohn ffryer a Bill of Aduenture & Supplies, Li 240-0-0."[1] Nothing more seems to be known of this John Fryer, or whether or not he was a relation of our author. But it was possibly through a connection interested in the affairs of the Company that his namesake obtained an appointment in India.

John Fryer was educated at Trinity College, Cambridge, the entry in the College Register, as transcribed by Mr. W. Aldis Wright, being as follows: "1664, Julii 13° John Fryer, Pension," his Tutor being Mr. Bainbrigg.[2] No information is forthcoming regarding his career at Trinity College; but he must have retained a kindly interest in it, because the Library contains a copy of his *New Account of East India and Persia*, presented in 1699, "*Ex dono Authoris.*" On 22nd July, for some reason unknown, he was transferred to Pembroke College as a Fellow Commoner,[3] and in the same year, "*per literas*

---

[1] Sir G. Birdwood, *The Dawn of British Trade to the East Indies* (1886) pp. 59, 165, 260.

[2] Communications from Dr. H. M. Butler and Mr. W. Aldis Wright, of Trinity College, Cambridge.

[3] The following is a copy of the entry in the College Register:—July 23, 1671. Johannes Friar Guliel: Londinensis filius maximus huc se recepit ē Coll: Stae Trinitatis cū esset Baccalaureus in Medicinâ et admissus est sub tutela, Magri Peechy ad mensam Sociorū.

regias," he obtained the degree of M.B., followed by that of M.D. in 1683. In his obituary, published in the *Gentleman's Magazine,*[1] he is said to have become a member of the Royal College of Physicians; but this seems not to have been the case.

In 1672, the year following that in which he took his first Cambridge degree, he was appointed to the post of Surgeon in the service of the East India Company. The Court Minute, dated 11th September, 1672, states that "The Committee for Shipping are desired to consider the entertainmt of Mr. Frier a Chyrurgeon for Surat, who is recommended by Mr. Canham [a 'Committee'] to be a skilfull and experienced artist in that profession, and to doe therein as they shall find him deserving."[2] Accordingly he was appointed to the post; and on 13th December, 1672, a few days after Fryer sailed from England, the Company wrote as follows to the authorities at Surat: "We have enterteyned Mr. John Fryer as Chirurgeon for Bombay at 50*s*. per month to commence at his arriveall, and have furnished the Chirurgery Chest now sent according to the directions of Mr. Ward."

He sailed from Gravesend in the ship *Unity*, one of the annual fleet starting for the East, consisting of ten vessels, the *London* being the "Admiral," or leading vessel. In the India Office Records is pre-

---

[1] Vol. iii, p. 214.

[2] *Court Minutes*, 11th September, 1672.

served the Journal of Captain William Basse, commander of the *London*, which furnishes materials for comparison with Fryer's account of the voyage.

The fleet consisted of the following ships, of which the names of the commanders, in the spelling of Captain Basse, may be compared with the list given by Fryer at the beginning of his book.

London (Admiral) .	. commanded by	Wm. Basse.
President (Vice-Admiral)	,,	Jonathan Hide.
Sampson (Rear-Admiral)	,,	Anthony Earning.
Cæsar	,,	Thomas Andrews.
Ann	,,	Zachary Browen.
Massinburgh . .	,,	Peter Westlock.
Bombay . . .	,,	George Earwing.
Antelope . . .	,,	John Goulsbrough.
East India Merchant .	,,	Robert Cooly.
Unity	,,	William Cruft.

At least one of these captains, John Goulsbrough, or as Fryer calls him, Captain Goldsberg, was a man of note—Sir John Goldsborough, who died at Chuttanuttee (Chatānatī) in Bengal, in 1693.[1]

The fleet reached the Downs on 27th December, where they found five King's ships and about sixty merchantmen awaiting them. The combined naval force left the Downs on 15th January, 1672–3, and soon after, as Fryer notes, an accident occurred, Westlock in the *Massinberg* making signals of distress, and reporting, according to the log of

[1] Yule, *Hedges Journal*, ii, 155 ff.; and his life, *sub nomine*, in *Dict. Nat. Biog.*

Captain Basse, that "another shipp came foule with him and carried away his head and boulspret." Accordingly Westlock stood in for "the Wight" to repair damages. On the 18th they came up with Captain Munden, who in the *Assistance*, with three "Marchant shippsmen of warr" and two fireships, was bound for St. Helena to convoy home the Company's returning fleet. On the 19th they lost sight of the Lizard, and soon after, as Fryer states, met five ships, three English and two French, bound for London. He remarks that soon after they lost sight of the St. Helena fleet, which, according to Basse, occurred on 25th January. Three days after they sighted Madeira, and on 1st February Munden overtook them, but parted from them on the fourth day. The next land sighted was Bonavista, and soon after Maio, which Basse calls "May." On 9th February they anchored at St. Iago, "the Lapray Road at Ste. Agoe," as Basse styles the place. Fryer gives an interesting account of this island. Here, on the day before the arrival of the English fleet, three Dutch men-of-war had come in; but being surprised by the English fleet, they cut their cables and fled, pursued by Munden. This incident alarmed Basse, who forthwith weighed anchor.

Later in the course of its voyage the fleet met with foul weather, and on 3rd April the *Unity*, Fryer's ship, and the *Cæsar*, parted company, the latter rejoining two days later, having lost her foretop-mast. On the 16th they spoke the *Johanna* and *Barnardiston*, the *Rebecca* having previously passed them—"all bound from the Coast of Cormandell," not from Bantam, as Fryer was led to believe.

On 8th May they sighted Mayotta and Johanna, islands of the Comoro group, and on the 16th they anchored at Johanna. As many members of the crews were suffering from scurvy, they halted here for four days, Fryer getting the chance of landing and collecting some curious particulars regarding the island and its inhabitants.

Thence they passed the Maldives, where the officers of the fleet held a consultation to settle their position by observations. On 16th June they sighted Ceylon, standing off at night to avoid the rocks, and by day taking advantage of the "Terrenhoes" or land breezes. Soon after, as Fryer records, they met three country junks bound for the Maldives. These, according to Basse, were Bengal "pinks." On one of them a Dutch letter of no particular importance was found. Accordingly the Admiral resolved to capture them, and took them in tow. On the 19th one of them proved to be leaky, and was cast off. On the 21st they sighted the Four Pagodas, where a boat from Porto Novo, with one Mr. Harrison on board, delivered a letter to the Admiral informing him that the Dutch, with twelve ships of war and two smaller vessels, were blockading the coast from St. Thomè to Fort St. George. A consultation was held to decide whether they should risk an engagement or go on to Masulipatam. The latter course was approved, because they had treasure of the Company on board, which it was advisable to land in safety as soon as possible. At noon they observed the Dutch flag flying over an English factory north of "Poole Chere" or Pondicherry, where a Moorish junk was riding at anchor. Goldsborough sent a boat to board her, and was informed through Mr. Harrison that another Dutch squadron of eight ships had gone by after their main fleet had disappeared. A French man-of-war had fought her way through five Dutch ships, and was now lying in the neighbourhood with the French viceroy, Delahay, on board.

On the 24th June Basse set adrift the two captured junks, as they delayed the fleet, and on the 26th anchored at Masulipatam Road, where the treasure was disembarked. Fryer took the opportunity of a trip on shore to collect some information on South Indian politics, particularly regarding the kingdom of Golkonda.

On 4th July news reached them that the Dutch fleet of twelve ships was off Diu Point (the "Diere Point" of Fryer's map of "Mechlapatan" or Masulipatam). According to him they stayed at Masulipatam for a month; Basse's log shows that their visit extended from 26th June to 19th July, when being advised by a courier that the Dutch had raised the blockade and sailed for Ceylon, the British fleet started for Madras, and on the 20th they anchored in Madras Roads, where Fryer parted from the fleet under Captain Basse. The latter sailed for Masulipatam on 9th August, and on the 22nd a running fight occurred between the Dutch and British fleets, the former of fourteen and the latter of ten vessels. The result was that one British ship, the *Antelope*, was sunk, and two, the *President* and *Sampson* were captured. Fryer's account of this action may be usefully compared with other contemporary narratives collected by Sir R. Temple in his edition of Bowrey's *Geographical Account of the Countries round the Bay of Bengal*, 1669–79, issued by the Hakluyt Society.

When the damages caused to the remaining ships were repaired, Fryer started, presumably in the *Unity*, for the Malabar Coast to escape the Dutch and the violence of the monsoons. He doubled Cape Comorin, and reaching the Western Coast, landed at Tanore (Tānūr), Calicut, "Cuty Cony," on the Taliparamba River, Honāvar, and Mirja, and passing Goa, arrived at Bombay on 9th December, 1673, exactly a year after his departure from England.

His account of Bombay, prepared eight years after Humphrey Cooke took possession of the Island and its dependencies, and during the Governorship of Gerald Aungier (1669–77), who was the real founder of the modern city, is most valuable. It is, however, curious that he makes no reference to Aungier's famous "Convention," a sort of Domesday Book in which the properties in the Island were registered.[1] Unfortunately

[1] J. Douglas, *Bombay and Western India* (1893), vol. i, 85 ff.

Fryer seems to have travelled little in the neighbourhood of Bombay, and his map of the harbour is incomplete and inaccurate. He did visit the island of "Canorein" or Kānherī, where he examined the Buddhist caves, and he inspected Bassein, then in the hands of the Portuguese.

He also gives a valuable narrative, probably derived from Henry Oxenden, the ambassador, of his mission to the Court of Sivajī, who was enthroned at Rāīgarh in June, 1674.

At the close of the rains, in September, 1674, Fryer, by order of President Aungier, was transferred to Surat. He gives an excellent account of the Factory and its administration, which throws welcome light upon the duties and condition of the Company's officers at this period. This appears in his Second Letter (the first being undated, but apparently dispatched soon after his arrival at Bombay) dated 15th January, 1674–5. He also displayed much industry in collecting information regarding the customs and rites of the native population, and the animal and vegetable productions of Surat and its neighbourhood.

On 4th April, 1675, he returned to Bombay with Mr. Philip Gyfford, who had been reinstated as Deputy Governor of the Island; and on the 23rd of the same month, St. George's Day he was directed by Gerald Aungier, the Governor, to proceed to the fort of "Jeneah" (Junnar) in the present Poona district, the Mughal commandant "having occasion for one of my Function." Passing through "Gullean" (Kalyān) he crossed the range of the Western Ghāts, the difficulty of the route causing him rather unreasonable apprehensions. He gives a careful account of the forts on the Junnar and Shivner hills and the administration of those famous strongholds. Returning by a slightly different route, he reached Thana, near Bombay, on 26th May; and from Bombay he despatched his Third Letter dated 22nd September, 1675.

At the close of the rains of this year, that is about October, Gerald Aungier having no further trouble with the Dutch or with the factions in the Island, left for Surat, appointing Philip Gyfford to act for him at Bombay. About the same time "Curiosity more than Business" tempted Fryer to take a trip along the coast southward in company with the Chief of the Factory at Kārwār, a place situated in the present North Kanara district. After a short visit there he proceeded to Goa, where he arrived on "the Eve of the Natal, or Christmas." In this trip he had as his companion that strange personage, Captain Henry Gary, who had a house near Goa at Panjim. In company with him on "New Year's Day, *stilo veteri*" he returned to Kārwār; and on 2nd February, 1676, in company with one of the Kārwār Factors he made an excursion to Gocurn (Gokarn), a celebrated place of Hindu pilgrimage in the North Kanara district, where he again collected much information on native customs, and acquired by hearsay some facts regarding Deccan politics and the kingdoms of Golkonda and Bījapur. Philip Gyfford, Deputy Governor of Bombay, falling ill, Fryer was recalled to that place. Leaving Kārwar in the *Phœnix* ketch on 6th April, 1676, he met with unfavourable weather, was unable to pursue his voyage and reach his patient. On 11th May he received a courteous invitation to return to Kārwār, which he hesitated to accept until he was informed that "a gentleman there being almost desparate, implored my assistance." Accordingly he returned to Kārwār, where he spent the rains, sailing on the 17th October "in the *Berkly-Castle* with Mr. Oxendine, who was called up to succeed Mr. Gyfford, the deceased Deputy-Governor of Bombaim." The recall of Oxenden seems to have been in anticipation of Gyfford's death; or rather perhaps because the latter had been for some time incapacitated from duty through illness. On his way Fryer again visited Goa, which he left on the Eve of the Feast of St. Francis Xavier, 2nd December, 1676, and arrived at Surat on the 11th of the same month. From Surat soon after his arrival he despatched his Fourth Letter, enclosing with it *A Special Chorography and History of East India*, containing much curious information, including tables of weights, measures, currency, notes on precious stones, and other valuable productions of the East, which he doubtless obtained from the Factory officials on the Western Coast.

In the meantime an order dated 8th March, 1676, was sent by the Company in England to the Surat authorities, directing that "when Mr. Fryer whome we sent out as a Chirurgeon his covenanted time is out he is to have 3*li* per month."[1]

Soon after Fryer's arrival at Surat "the Agent of Persia representing how highly conducing to the Company's Interest one of my Profession would be there," he was "easily won upon to embark on the *Scipio African*, which with the Persian Merchant were sent this year for the Gulf, as well to support the declining Credit of the English there" as to attempt to open up a trade in English cloth and tin. He sailed from Swally-hole at the mouth of the Tapti below Surat, entered the Persian Gulf, and on the 22nd March, 1677, reached Gombroom or Bandar 'Abbās. Of the climate there he gives a most unfavourable account. Thence on 28th June he started on his journey northwards, passing along the regular caravan route *via* "Lhor" (Lār) to "Siras" (Shīrāz), and finally reaching Ispahān on 7th August, thus accomplishing "a tedious journey in the hottest Season of the Year, over desolate parching sands and naked Rocks, through all Persia into the heart of Parthia to Ispahaun, not only the Chief City of this vast Empire, where the present Emperor sets up his Standard, with

---

[1] *Court Minutes*, 14th January, 1675-6.

all his moving Forces, but of Parthia especially." During a halt at Shīrāz he visited the ruins of Persepolis, which he carefully describes. He states that at Ispahān he witnessed an eclipse of the sun on 19th August; but there is apparently some error in the date, and the eclipse to which he refers has not been satisfactorily identified.

While he stayed at Ispahān he was much in company with the Armenians who resided in the Julfa suburb of that city. He describes at some length their beliefs and customs; but his facts require correction in several particulars. He does not specify what his official duties were at Ispahān; he probably acted as medical officer to the small European community. He had some practice among the natives, and he bitterly abuses a Saiyid patient at Shīrāz, a "Varlet of the Race of Mahomet," who cheated him out of his fees.

The climate of Ispahān did not agree with him, and he fell ill in October. Towards the close of the year news arrived of the death of President Aungier at Surat, which had occurred on the previous 30th June. "The Agent of Persia [Thomas Rolt] having left Gombroon to go to fill up the chair at Surat, the Second at Spahaun was obliged to repair thither to take care of the Company's Concerns there; with whom, I being now recovered, on the 10th of January [1678] with a French Chyrurgeon in our Company, in the depth of Winter we set forth for the Persian Gulf."

The party arrived at Gombroon on 15th February. The President sailed, leaving Fryer in Persia. He remained at Gombroon till the middle of April, when a new Agent arrived, "who being sickly, was willing to leave the port with all expedition, to be in Spahaun before the Heats." Fryer set out accordingly in his company on the 30th April, reached Lār on the 8th May, and thence marched to Shirāz. Here an epidemic of fever prevailed, and on the 29th the Agent started for Ispahān, leaving Fryer in charge of a Spanish ecclesiastic, the Father Visitador of the Carmelite Order, who had long suffered from fever. After his patient was well nigh recovered Fryer himself was attacked, and he was obliged to remain at Shīrāz till 6th July, when he marched to Ispahān.

He remained at Ispahān until the cotton was bursting the pod and the barley was still green, but when he reached Shīrāz on his homeward journey the harvest and vintage were over. He left Shīrāz on 8th October, 1678, reaching Gombroom *viâ* Lār on 13th November. After a trip to Congo Bandar on the Gulf, where he investigated the condition of the pearl fisheries, he sailed from Persia in the *Phœnix* on 30th November, and reached Swally-hole, at the entrance of the river Tapti, on Twelfth Day, 6th January, 1678-9. During his voyage he compiled the important paper entitled "The Present State of Persia," which, with his Fifth Letter, he seems to have despatched on his arrival in India.

It is possible to supplement the scanty details given in his letters regarding his official duties by an extract from the India Office Records, which contain a copy of the only letter written by Fryer, besides those which make up his book, which has been discovered. The following comes from the Surat Factory Records.[1]

"Honourable etca Councill. Being forced by sickness to leave Persia, and thereby both myself and servant Daniell Trenchfield[2] becoming destitute of employment (notwithstanding still retained in the Honble Company's service), and at my arrival in India finding Mr. Thomas Pearse Chyrurgion for Surat ffactory returning for England, I thinke myself obliged to proffer myself to your Honr. etca hoping you will consider me, as next person to succeed in that office; wherefore I become your honrs etca Petitioner."

This is enclosed in a "Consultation held on Swally Marine the 24th January 1678-79 whereat were present Thomas Rolt President, Charles James, Cesar Chambrelan & John Child," who remark: "It will be necessary that we next consider of a Chyrurgion; who are left destitute of any by Dr. Ffrryers coming away; whom we have gratifyed with the employment of Chyrurgion of this ffactory; as being one of the Honble Company's immediate

---

[1] Vol. iv, Pt. II, pp. 6 f.

[2] Some details of a person named R. Trenchfield are given by Yule, *Hedges Diary*, ii, 285 ff.

servants; and seeing that the Company are displeased at the Commission and Sallary formerly agreed to be allowed Dr. Thomas Wilson; as Phisitian of Bombay; we doe conclude that for the present (having here no other fitting person) to make Choyce of him as Phisitian there at the Sallary paid Mr. Ffryer."

The arrangement made by the authorities at Surat is somewhat obscure; but Fryer retained the office of Chirurgeon of the Surat Factory. During his term of office he made some excursions in the neighbourhood, being, for instance, summoned to visit Broach to attend one of the Merchants who had fallen sick. Of his further adventures, up to the despatch of his Seventh Letter from Swally-hole, on 25th January, 1680–1, we know nothing. A year after, on 19th January, 1681–2, he embarked for England in the annual home fleet, taking his passage in the *Massenberg* with Mr. Cæsar Chamberlane, "The Second in India." At the same time the late President, Mr. Rolt, sailed in the *Josiah* with Captain Owen. They passed Madagascar, rounded the Cape of Good Hope, landed at St. Helena and Ascension and disembarked at Folkestone on 20th August, 1682.

Soon after his return to England Fryer married a niece of Rose Desborough, wife of Samuel Desborough, the younger brother of Major-General John Desborough (1608–1680), one of the Parliamentary Generals who brought about the restoration of the Rump Parliament and the deposition of Richard Cromwell. Samuel Desborough was twice married: first, to Dorothy, daughter of Henry Whitfield, of Ockley, Surrey, who died in 1654; secondly, to Rose Hobson, who had been already twice married, first, to a Mr. Lacey, and secondly, to Samuel Penoyer. This latter lady was aunt of Mrs. Fryer, and died in 1698–9.

The Company's records in the India Office supply an account of another incident in Fryer's life. On 19th November, 1684, "J. Fryer, Dr. of Physick, was admitted in the freedom of the Company by Patrimony." In order to effect this, it was necessary that he should be a holder of Stock; and accordingly on the same date William Fryer transfers to John Fryer £225. Fryer did not long remain a proprietor of the Stock, because on the following 17th December he transferred it to Sir John Moore.

He was elected Fellow of the Royal Society in 1697. At the time of his election no record was made of the grounds on which this honour was conferred upon him. He was probably elected in consideration of his professional standing and his sympathy with scientific work. His book bears ample record of his interest in science; in fact, he was evidently well informed both in the scientific literature of his day and in the writings of classical authors. He continued to be a Fellow until 1707; but he seems never to have contributed to the Philosophical Transactions.

He died on 30th March, 1733. In the Letters of Administration granted on 14th April, 1733, to his daughter, Anna Maria Sanderson, widow, he is recorded as late of the parish of All Hallows, Bread Street, London, widower. His portrait, drawn from the life by R. White, forms the frontispiece to the present volume.[1]

In 1698 he published, "printed by R.R. for Ri. Chiswell, at the *Rose* and *Crown* in *St. Paul's* Church-Yard," the book on which his reputation depends. He explains that he now "exposes this Piece to the World" not so much on account of the "Importunity of some, as the Impertinencies of others; there being more than Four hundred Queries now by me, to which I was pressed for Answers, and wherein I found a necessity, if I declined this Work, to appear from other Hands in Print. This then was the first and chief Cause; resting all that while content, that many Foreigners had their Memoirs translated, whereby I thought myself excused this Task; most of whom I had either seen or heard of beyond Sea, but never had read any of their Works, nor knew of their intentions to declare themselves to the World: Finding therefore on my Return, that they had been beforehand with me, I did believe it almost impossible, so many

[1] Burke (*A General Armory of England*, etc.) describes the coat-of-arms there reproduced as follows:—"*Sa.* a chev. betw. three dolphins embowed *ar.* *Crest*—Out of a ducal coronet *or*, an antelope's head *ar.* attired, crined, and tufted of the first."

writing on the same Subject, should not in many, and the most material Points especially, if they followed Truth, relate the same things; which made me still desist, supposing it a lost Labour. But at last, considering these Travellers before me had few of them been in those parts where I had been, or at least not dwelt so long there, I venture to offer some Novelties, either passed over by them, or else not so thoroughly observed."

Here he may be supposed to refer chiefly to the writings of Jean Baptiste Tavernier, of which various translations in English were published between the dates of the commencement of Fryer's travels and the publication of his letters (1672-1698). *A New Relation of the Inner Part of the Grand Seignor's Seraglio*, and *The Six Voyages of John Baptiste Tavernier Baron of Aubonne through Turky into Persia and the East Indise for the Space of Forty Years*, were issued in 1677, with editions in 1678, 1680, 1684, and 1688. Fryer mentions Tavernier at the close of Letter II, as one of the foreign jewellers "who have made good Purchase by buying Jewels here, and carrying them into Europe to be Cut and Set, and returning sell them here to the Ombrahs." From the parallel passages quoted in the notes to this edition there seems little doubt that Fryer must have read Tavernier, particularly his account of Persia.[1]

[1] Other accounts of the East published in English translations about this period were those of Olearius (1662, 2nd ed., 1669);

An English translation of the *History of the Late Revolution of the Empire of the Great Mogul*, by F. Bernier, was published in 1671-72. Fryer was certainly a careful student of Sir Thomas Herbert, whose *Description of the Persian Monarchy now beinge: the Orientall Indyes, Iles and other parts of the Greater Asia and Africk*, was published in 1634. Four years later a new and enlarged edition appeared under the title *Some Yeares Travels into Africa and Asia the Great*; a third in 1664; a fourth in 1677. Fryer refers in his Preface to *The Ingenious Sir Thomas Herbert*, and in his Fifth Letter, Chap. III, in a side-note, he mentions his identification of Gerom (Jahrūm) with Kirjoth-Jerom, Kiriath-Jearim of the Old Testament. He seems to have been indebted to John Huyghen van Linschoten, of whose voyage an English translation appeared in 1598, for his account of seed pearl and mother of pearl.

Fryer's book purports to be a reprint of a series of letters addressed to some unnamed correspondent in England. This was clearly a person of distinction and learning, because Fryer (I, 29) speaks of his "singular favour in seeing me aboard ship;" and (I, 126) speaking of the causes of floods in the Nile and Indian rivers, he remarks: "You

Della Valle (1665); Texeira (1668); G. Vermeulen (1677); Jean Struys (1686); Thevenot (1687); M. Duquesne (1691); Dellon 1698; Sanson (1695). How many of these Fryer may have consulted it is impossible to say.

who have greater Reading and Leisure to digest these Metaphysical Notions, will mightily oblige me to furnish me with your solid arguments."

The question remains whether such letters were really despatched or not; or whether the book was compiled in England from the author's note-books. All doubts on this matter have practically been set at rest by the researches kindly made by Miss Sainsbury in the India Office Records. She finds that in cases where Fryer dates his letters, ships carrying mails were, about those dates, despatched to Europe. Thus, for example, in the case of the Second Letter, dated Surat, 15th January, 1674-5, she finds that "the shippes *Faulcon* and *Mary*, who set saile from Bombay the 18th January last, carried you large advices from us dated 16 Xber and 18 Jan."[1] So with the Third Letter, dated Bombay, 22nd September, 1675, the *Golden Fleece* leaves Bombay for Surat on 30th September, 1675.[2] The Sixth Letter, dated Surat, 31st December, 1679, may have gone by the *Bengalla Merchant*, which sailed on 24th January, 1680;[3] and the Seventh Letter, dated Swally, 25th January, 1681, was probably conveyed by the *Williamson*, *Lancaster*, and *Johanna*, which left on that date.[4] This, of course, only proves that mails for Europe did leave on dates which would permit the conveyance of certain dated letters. That they were rewritten,

---

[1] O.C. 4118, 10th October, 1675.

[2] *Ibid.*, 4118.

[3] *Ibid.*, 4692.

[4] *Ibid.*, 4729.

revised, and extended for publication in 1698 is more than probable.

The peculiarities of Fryer's style immediately strike any reader. He probably kept note-books or a diary in which he jotted down his rough memoranda; his concise, jerky style seems to be largely due to his habit of transcribing *verbatim* from notes of this kind. In part, it was probably modelled on that of Sir Thomas Herbert. He was also a student of Sir Thomas Browne, whose *Religio Medici*, in fourteen editions, was published between 1642 and 1685. With this book he was certainly acquainted, because he quotes from it a denunciation of the Koran in the Thirteenth Chapter of his Fifth Letter.

In connection with this denunciation of the religion of the Prophet, Fryer takes occasion strongly to commend Christianity; and in his Preface he mentions as one of the objects of his book that he desires to reclaim the atheist and inculcate a purer form of belief. He reprehends Puritanism, remarking in the First Chapter of his Third Letter that it was from the custom of the Musalmān Qāzī conducting the marriage rite that "doubtless our Phanaticks borrowed their custom of Marrying by a Justice of Peace"; and he calls the "Hodges" or Muhammadan pilgrims "such strict Puritans, that if they met a Christian, Jew, or Banyan, and by chance his garment brush against them, they hye them home, shift and wash, as if they had been defiled with some unclean thing, a Dog or Hog." While marching in Persia, as he states in the Third Chapter of his Fifth Letter, he fasted on the 30th January, "for the Execrable Death of the Martyr Charles the First," a proceeding which amazed his companion the Carmelite friar, who observed that "on their Fasting days they were allowed a Buccado of Sweetmeats and a Glass of Wine before Noon, and at Noon a small Repast, and so likewise in the Afternoon, but at Night a good plentiful Supper; With the latter part we promised we would agree with him, but for the other we thought there was no great Restraint put upon Nature."

More than one cause prevented Fryer from utilising his great industry and powers of research to greater advantage. In the first place, he had little or no knowledge of the vernacular dialects, and was largely dependent upon a "linguist" or interpreter. His perversions of vernacular words are instructive, and often amusing, and have supplied some of the best examples in the *Hobson-Jobson* of Sir H. Yule. When he quotes passages in Persian, they are often so distorted as to be unintelligible. It must, however, be remembered that, as has been pointed out in a note to this edition, the knowledge of native languages among the British officers of the day was inconsiderable, and they seem generally to have used a sort of "pigeon" dialect, largely composed of corrupted Portuguese, in their business transactions at the trading stations on the coast.

It is, in the second place, unfortunate that his travels were practically confined to the seaboard; and he had no personal acquaintance with the great cities and States situated in the interior The only important journey which he made inland was to Junnar, which as the crow flies is about seventy-five miles from Bombay. He knew little or nothing about the Mughal Empire save from meeting a few of its officials. He had heard the names of "Bonares" (Benares), "Lhor" (Lahore), and "Shaw Juan Abad" (Delhi); but he never visited any of the great cities, even Ahmadābād, Bījapur, or Golkonda. What he knew of these cities, their rulers and politics, was mere gossip current in the marts on the coast. In Persia he merely traversed the caravan track leading from Bandar 'Abbās *via* Shīrāz and Lār to Ispahān.

In spite of these deficiencies, his work is rightly described by Sir G. Birdwood[1] as "the most delightful book ever published on those countries, and invaluable for the graphic descriptions it gives of the factory life and general condition of the people of India in his time." He was versed in all the learning of his age, and was specially interested in all questions connected with the natural sciences, the botany, zoology, geology, and meteorology of the lands which he visited. He paid particular attention to the scientific acquirements of the people of the East; and he

[1] *Report on the Old Records of the India Office*, (1891), p. 238.

naturally investigated with care their knowledge of medicine and surgery. He was a good Latin scholar, and had some knowledge of Greek. Numerous quotations, not only derived from classical authors, but from later and less known writers, are scattered through his work. The task of identifying these has been rendered difficult by the almost complete absence of references. and from his habit of quoting from memory, and often in an incorrect form. The love of quotation was common to the writers of his day; and, though he never names him, it would be a pleasure to believe that he was familiar with one of the most delightful books ever written, *The Anatomy of Melancholy* of Robert Burton, first published in 1621, reprinted four times before the death of the author in 1639, and assuming its final form in the sixth edition, published in 1651-2.

In many respects he was a model traveller, dignified, good tempered, with a keen sense of the humorous, ready to make light of the difficulties and privations which fell to the lot of a European wandering in strange places and among strange races unfamiliar with the white man and his ways. A Londoner by birth and training, he was unaccustomed to mountain travel, and he was wont to exaggerate the difficulties of crossing the Indian Ghats and the hill passes on the road from the Persian Gulf to Ispahān.

It can hardly be said that he was in full sympathy with the peoples of India and Persia.

He felt the contempt characteristic of his day for the religion and manners of peoples whom he regarded as semi-savages and mere idolators. The spread of the new sciences of comparative religion and ethnology has forced us to adopt a different attitude towards the beliefs and usages of the East. But the value of his investigations of their religions, customs, and folk-lore, made at a time when they had been little influenced by the West, cannot be overrated.

His relations with these races seems to have been generally friendly, and his skill in medicine and surgery doubtless earned their respect. On one occasion, at any rate, he admits behaving with brutality to the unfortunate bearers of his litter, who, strange to say, were, he asserts, alarmed at some fire-flies in a bush, a sight with which it is difficult to believe that they could have been unfamiliar. In the Fifth Chapter of his Third Letter he writes: "The *Coolies* beheld the Sight with Horror and Amazement, and were consulting to set me down, and shift for themselves; whereof being informed, I cut two or three with my Sword, and by breathing a Vein, let *Shitan* (the Devil) out, who was crept into their Fancies, and led them as they do a startling Jade, to smell to what their Wall-Eyes represented amiss."

Mr. Anderson[1] charges him with being addicted to excess in the use of intoxicating liquor. "A

---

[1] *The English in Western India*, 2nd ed. (1856), p. 282.

fondness for intoxicating spirits was carried even by superior minds to an astonishing degree of coarseness. Fryer, man of excellent education as he was, could not attend the banquet of a Mussalman officer, without having the bad taste to draw a flask out of his pocket, and qualify his sherbet with the more potent draught to which he was accustomed. This he tells us himself with an evident conviction that he had been knowing and clever." Fryer's account of this transaction does not justify the charges brought against him by Mr. Anderson. He writes in the Fifth Chapter of Letter III: "Having feasted the Fancy, he contends to cloy the Stomach, with loads of *Viands* stowed in Plate, serving me with his own Hands, his Friends and he being content to feed on the desire they had to satisfy me, not to be courted to fall to till I had done; they served me with a Variety of Stews and Baked Meats, but offered me *Sherbet* only for Drink; I had provided against this chance by filling my *Metarrah* with Beveridge, which passed for Water, being drunk out of a Leather Bottle Tipped with Silver, for Travel." Fryer obviously meant no discourtesy to his hosts, nor does it appear that they were offended. Throughout his book there is no evidence that he exceeded in any way.

His pages display many instances of graphic description, terse and vivid narrative; and he can tell a good story with quaint dry humour. His accounts of the island of Johanna, of the caves at Kānherī and Elephanta, are in their way excellent. His sketches of the austerities of the Faqīrs, the customs of the people of Surat, the Banyans and Pārsīs of the West Coast, the Armenians of Julfa, are all admirable.

Many readers will prefer the almost contemporary accounts of the East by Bernier, Tavernier, and Manucci. But to these the work of Fryer will always remain a most valuable supplement.

BIBLIOGRAPHICAL NOTE.

If the interesting nature of the work be considered, it is surprising to find that this is the first full re-print in English of Fryer's *East India and Persia.*

Letters I—IV, being that part of the book relating to India only, appeared in various issues of *The Englishman,* a Calcutta weekly, in the 'sixties of the last century, and were subsequently published in book form, together with the account of some travels by Sir Thomas Roe, in 1873. The title ran :—

> Travels in India in the Seventeenth Century ; by Sir Thomas Roe and Dr. John Fryer. London : Trübner and Co. 1873. Pp. 474.

That issue, copies of which are now very rarely to be met with, was without notes and disfigured by many typographical errors.

A Dutch translation appeared as early as 1700. It is full, and has all the plates (somewhat reduced), and even an extra one opposite the frontispiece. The title runs :—

> Negenjaarige Reyse door Oostindien en Persien . . . In agt Brieven beschreven door d'Heer Johan Freyer, M.Dr tot Cantelberg. 's Gravenhage, 1700. Pp. 566.

The Plates have been reproduced and slightly reduced from those of the Edition of 1698 by Mr. Donald Macbeth.

TABLE OF CONTENTS

VOL. I

VOL. II

VOL. III

LIST OF ILLUSTRATIONS

VOL. I

VOL. II

VOL. III

A

NEW ACCOUNT

OF

EAST-INDIA AND PERSIA,

IN

EIGHT LETTERS

BEING

Nine Years Travels,

Begun 1672, And Finished 1681.

Containing Observations made of the *Moral, Natural,* and *Artificial* Estate of Those Countries: Namely, Of their Government, Religion, Laws, Customs. Of the Soil, Climates, Seasons Health, Diseases. Of the Animals, Vegetables, Minerals, Jewels. Of their Housing, Cloathing, Manufactures, Trades, Commodities. And of the Coins, Weights, and Measures, used in the Principal Places of Trade in those Parts.

By JOHN FRYER, M.D. *Cantabrig.*

And Fellow of the ROYAL SOCIETY.

Illustrated with Maps, Figures, and Useful Tables.

LONDON.

Printed by *R. R.* for RI. CHISWELL, at the *Rose* and *Crown* in St. *Paul's* Church-Yard. MDC XC VIII

TO THE

High Potent, and Noble PRINCE,

John Holles,

Duke of Newcastle,

MARQUIS,

AND

EARL of *CLARE*,

Baron *Houghton* of *Houghton*,

Lord Lieutenant of the County of *Nottingham*,

AND

Custos Rotulorum for the said County and Town of NOTTINGHAM.

These *Nine Years Travels*, out of the profoundest Respect, are most humbly Dedicated,

BY

JOHN FRYER.

---

[1] John Holles, Duke of Newcastle (1662-1711), eldest son of Gilbert Holles, third Earl of Clare: a strong Protestant and Whig, to whom Dryden dedicated the *Spanish Friar* in 1681. He was created Duke of Newcastle in 1694: Lord Lieutenant of Nottinghamshire in 1694. He died on 15th July, 1711, from the effects of a fall from his horse at Welbeck, and was buried in Westminster Abbey, where his daughter erected an enormous monument to his memory (*Dictionary National Biography*, xxvii, 170 f.). His successor in the title, Thomas Pelham Holles, Duke of Newcastle, in a letter of 6th April, 1731, signs himself "Holles Newcastle" (Birdwood, *Report on the Old Records in the India Office*, 32).

THE

PREFACE.

WHAT prompted , after so many Years Silence, to expose this Piece t the World, was not so much the Old Topick, Importunity of some, as the Impertinencies of others; there being more than Four hundred Queries now by me, to which I was pressed for Answers, and wherein I found a necessity, if I declined this Work, to appear from other Hands in Print. This then was the first and chief Cause; resting all that while content, that many Foreigners had their Memoirs translated, whereby I thought my self excused this Task; most of whom, I had either seen or heard of beyond Sea, but never had read any of their Works, nor knew of their intentions to declare themselves to the World: Finding therefore on my Return, that they had been before-hand with me, I did believe it almost impossible, so many writing on the same Subject, should not in many, and the most material Points especially, if they followed Truth, relate the same things; which made me still desist, supposing it a lost Labour.

But at last, considering those Travellers before me had few of them been in those Parts where I had been, or at least not dwelt so long there, I venture to offer some Novelties, either passed over by them, or else not so thoroughly observed.

And indeed, this being the first of this kind I know of, wrote by our own Countrymen, since the Ingenious Sir Thomas Herbert, I hope it may find the more favourable Acceptance; since it bears no other Design than the Good of my Country, setting before them the True State of their Trade in East-India and Persia.

The reclaiming of Atheists, by leading them first to behold the Beauty, Order, and admirable Disposition of the Universe, and then to see if they can so far abuse their Reason, to deny the Author; which if they should, the Indians, how barbarous soever esteemed by them, are to be preferred before them for Men of Sense; who out of the very Principles of Nature, keep to that Law written on their Minds, That there is a God to be ador'd; and rather than be without, will frame themselves one of their own creating; which Depravity of theirs while Atheists deride, they admonish them of as great an Error in owning none.

And lastly, To inform those busy Translators, That the Industry of our own Nation is not fallen beneath that of France, whose Language and Manners we so servilely affect, as to think nothing Excellent or *Alamode*,[1] which has not a French Dress; but that it still is in the Power of the English to retrieve their former Renown both by Pen and Sword: *Tam Marti quam Mercurio.* Nor will any Englishman accuse me of Self-Confidence or Arrogance, when it is a Justice only intended my Country against its Decriers; nor in the least to undervalue the Authors or the Books translated, but to whet our Endeavours to equalize, if not outdo them.

As to the Method I have taken, it is unconfin'd (it being the Privilege of a Traveller) not bounded with the narrow Terms of an Historian, nor loosely extravagant, like Poetical Fictions, but suited both to Time and Place, and agreeable to the Nature of the Relation: And herein I have followed Busbequius; which though it may make

---

[1] Fr. *à la mode*, "in the manner or fashion"; adopted into English in seventeenth century, the first quotation in the *New Eng. Dict.* being from Selden, *Laws of England*, I, lxxi, 198 (1649): "Commanders that are never *à-la-mode* but when all in Iron and Steel."

some Unevenness in the Stile, as where the Ruggedness of the Ways interpose, or the Subject-matter is varied, it must happen, yet the Warp quite through is most of the same Thread ; which being the Clue to so many and intricate Meanders, trodden by a few, I am the more pardonable when I slip : Though I do declare my desire is, To shew my Diligence in collecting, and Sincerity in compiling what may make the Road more easy to the next Adventurers, and satisfy the present Enquirers.

A List of the Ships, Names of the Commanders, Number of Passengers, Soldiers, Seamen, Tuns and Guns.

Ships.	Comman.	Pas.	Sol.	Seam.	Tun.	Gun.	Squadrons.
London	Capt. *Bass*	03	14	120	500	40	Admiral.
Massenberg	C. *Westlock*	09	10	100	560	44	
Bombaim	C. *Erwin*	03	08	083	400	40	
Unity	C. *Craft*	02	08	076	350	34	
President	C. *Hyde*	03	16	120	500	42	Vice-Admiral.
Ann	C. *Brown*	04	12	097	550	36	
East-India Merchant	C. *Cooly*	03	10	090	400	36	
Sampson	C. *Erning*	03	12	100	460	40	Rere-Admiral.
Cæsar	C. *Andrews*	03	03	130	560	46	
Antilope	C. *Golsberg*	03	12	094	460	36	

Qui mare fluctisonum sulcat, curvisque Carinis
Admovet externas vaga per commercia Gentes,
Non ignota illi Divina potentia, nec quæ
Monstrat in immenso miracula sæpe profundo.

Geo. Buchanan, Psal. cvii.

THE

CONTENTS.

LETTER I.

CHAP. I.

Treats of Embarking, and Passage till past St. Iago.

CHAP. II.

Passage to Johanna, *and Relation of that Island.*

West to reach the Cape. The Current of the Sea against the Wind. Cape-Birds. Winter at the Cape. Separated from the Fleet for two days. Soundings off the *Cape Good Hope.* Spoke with some *English* Ships homeward bound. Doubled *Cape d'Angullis* to gain St. *Lawrence.* The *Eastern* Sea. A Whale. We follow the Sun. Lost sight of St. *Lawrence.* Arrival at *Johanna.* Care of the Sick. Situation of the Island. The Inland Inaccessible. The circuit. A Tree fourteen Fathom round the Body. Best Water, next *Thames*-Water. Their Town and Buildings. Two Mosques. The King's Court. Their Nobles. Their Priests. We Present them. Vassals to the *Arabs.* Villages. A pleasant Grove. The Hills fruitful. Temper of the Inhabitants. Their Vessels for Sea. Active at climbing. Slaves, how known. Skill'd in Letters and Astrology. Ape Printing. Their Speech. Religion. Women. Their Children troubled with the Navel-Rupture. Their way of killing Fowls, *&c.* Their Diet. Corn. Want Asses, Mules, and Horses. Fowls for Game. A *Budgee.* Their Hate to the *Mohelians.* We are called aboard to set sail.

CHAP. III.

Declares our Course from Johanna, *to our landing at* Mechlapatan.

We repass the *Equinoctial* Line. The *North*-Star is raised again. The *Maldivæ* Islands. Near *Ceilon.* A couple of Whales. A Fright occasioned by a Mistake in the Night. Sight of *Ceilon. Ceilon* has the best Breed of Elephants. The *Terhenoes.* Three Country Junks. *Catamarans. Sanderaslapatan* on the Main. Resolved to fight the *Flemmings.* Put to Sea again, on Advice from the Agent. Saw a *French* Man of War. Dismissed the Junks. Met the Freshes caused by the Rains. Having quartered the World, anchor at *Mechlapatan.*

CHAP. IV.

Takes up our Stay at Mechlapatan, *to our landing at* Fort St. George.

The Treasure set ashore. The Boatmen described. *Peons* to wait on us. Landing at *Mechlapatan.* The Fort and Town. The Custom-house Keys. Publick Structures. The Bridges. The Story of this Place, and Kingdom of *Gulconda.* At first governed by their Tribes. How alter'd. Their King a *Chias-Moor.* All Noblemens Estates fall to the King. The barbarous Custom of poysoning among the *Eastern* Monarchs. *Gulconda* the Metropolis gives Name to the Kingdom. The Prime Ministers are Eunuchs. Their Wealth, how rais'd. The Army, how paid. The Bigness of the Kingdom. The Governor of

CHAP. V.

Gives a true Narrative of the English, French, *and* Dutch, *on the Coast of* Coromandel, *continuing till we double the Cape for the Coast of* Malabar.

CHAP. VI.

Views the Malabar *and* Canatick *Coasts, up to* Bombaim.

LETTER II.

CHAP. I.

Mentions the Island, and its Possessors.

CHAP. II.

A Survey of the Island Canorein, *near* Bombaim.

CHAP. III.

A Visit to Baçein, *a* Portugal *City in* India : *Our Return by* Elephanto, *&c., with Observations on the Island* Bombaim.

CHAP. IV.

Narrative of an Embassy to Seva Gi, *and Journey to* Rairee, *the Court of the* Raja.

CHAP. V.

Our Passage to Swally, *and Relation of the* English *Presidency at* Surat.

LETTER III.

CHAP. I.

Animadversions on the City and People of Surat.

CHAP. II.

Shews the Tombs, Outwalks, Ceremonies, and Austerities of the Gentiles; *with the Ships and River about* Surat.

carry them to *Pulparra*. The Postures and Severities of the Heathen *Fakiers*. *Paunch Augy*, or the Penance of Five Fires. Whether it be an Imposture? A Devote that had not sat down in sixteen Years. A great Tank. Gardens. Grottoes. The Cotton-tree. Bang. *Alluh*. No great Variety of Flowers. The sensible Plant, and *Arbor de Rais*. Milk-Bushes. Sugar-Canes and Tobacco. The River commodious for Ships. The *Dutch* learn the Natives nothing. Their Navy. The Young King of *Bantam*. His Story. Their Junks and Seamen.

CHAP. III.

Of their Solemnities, Sports, and Pastimes; Marriages; of the Parsies; *their Strength by Land and Sea; their abundant Wealth, and fitness for Trade.*

Their New-Moons. *Ramazan*, or Lent. Grandeur of their Governor and Great Men. The *Moors Æde*. Their mourning for *Hosseen Gosseen*. The Emperor a great Zealot for his Religion. How they behave themselves in Eclypses. Ceremonies in Marriage. *Dually* of the Heathens. The Women have a time of Freedom. Feast of Flies. Hospitable to Dogs. Their Exercise or Recreation. Hunting. Buffolaes and Rams set to fight. The Master-piece of the *Banyans*. Education of Youth. The Sloth of the *Moor* a Whet to the *Banyan*. All the World brings Treasure to *India*. The *Bassa* of *Bussorah*. Their Jewellers may be improved. The City kept nastily. The Diseases. Remedies outward and inward. The Country Physician. The several Tribes how known. The *English* have the respect of their *Ombrahs*. Rarities in the *English* House. Venomous Creatures. The *Surat* Governor forced to comply with the *Dutch*. The *Parsies*. Worship the Sun. They expose their Dead to Ravenous Fowls. Their way of living. Large Milk-white Oxen. A *Buffola*. The Marshes breed Cattel. The Growth of this place. The *Colum*-Bird. Wine and Strumpets set the Soldiers and Seamen by the Ears. Four *Arab* Ships. Left *Surat* and *Swally*. *Mahmud Emir Caun*, son of *Emir Jemla*, Governor of the Province.

CHAP. IV.

Brings me with a New Deputy-Governor from Surat *to* Bombaim, *and sends me to the* Mogul's *General at* Jeneah.

Captain *Shaxton* sent home. A Sea-Tortoise taken. The Fable of its having three Hearts, confuted. The Flesh restorative. Take Boat for *Duccan*. Landing and Reception at *Gulean*. Set forward for *Intwally*. The Countrey all burnt and destroyed. Thence to *Moorbar*. Forced to keep Watch. The Guides lead us about. Come

CHAP. V.

Introduces me to the Nabob's *Presence : My Business with him : A Prospect of the Country*, &c.

LETTER IV.

CHAP. I.

Concerning our Shipping for Carwar ; *of the Factory there* ; *the unsettled Condition of the Place* ; *and our coming to* Goa.

The President goes to *Surat:* I to *Carwar*. *Seva Gi's* Naval Power. His Arms have conquered all round *Carwar*. The Ground our House stands on, granted by the King. *Seva Gi* governs by *Brachmins*. The hard usage of *Seva Gi's* Subjects. Distractions of the Kingdom of *Visiapour*. Their miserable Condition betwixt the *Desy* and *Seva Gi*. Take Barge for *Goa*, whose Passes are well guarded. The Gallantry of the *Portugals*, and neglect of their *Carracks*.

CHAP. II.

Takes a View of Goa ; *makes a Voyage to* Vingula ; *engages with the* Malabars ; *and returns us to* Carwar.

The Archbishop's See. The Provost of the Jesuits. The College of the *Dominicans* the Seat of the Inquisitor. St. *Roch*. *Domo* of *Bon Jesu*. Why the Jesuits are called *Paulistines*. The Convent of St. *Austin*. Several Seminaries. The *Franciscans*. The *Carmelites*. The Spittal. *Sancta Monacha*, a Nunnery. The *Theatini* in the Virge of the Palace. Going to *Vingula* we engage a *Malabar*. They caress us ashore at *Vingula*. Monuments for Women burnt alive with their dead Husbands. Return from *Vingula* to *Goa*. The King's Yards viewed. The Industry of the *Portugal* Ancestry. A well-weigh'd choice of an Harbour. Old *Goa*. *Sancto Pilar* the Seat of the *Capuchins*. The way betwixt Old *Goa* and New *Goa*. Their Prisons and Executions. *Seva Gi* a bad Neighbour. The Power of the Viceroy and Archbishop. The outward Port of the *Fidalgoes*. The Clergy how respected. The Women and Children. The finest Manchet. How the Outguards inform the City. Return'd to *Carwar*.

CHAP. III.

A Pilgrimage to Gocourn ; *where was a great* Gentile *Solemnity* ; *a cursory Discourse of the bordering Princes.*

Anchola Castle supplied with Brass Guns from a *Portugal* Shipwreck. The Country properly *Canatick*. Peace makes people chearful. Our coming to *Gocourn* discovered. It is an University. The *Tomasia* the *Brachmins* Harvest. The *Jattery* or Washing. A Vow performed. *Jougies* or Devotes. A Solemn Procession of their *Duels*

People use Charms, or think they do so. Their Sacrifice for the Fields. Whether these Wretches do work by the Devil or no. The sublime Wit as much in the Wrong as the depressed. No Evasion for the Atheist. I am sent for to *Bombaim*. All Butchers Flesh forbidden at *Goa* in the Heats, but Pork. *Mangoes* good to cleanse the Blood. *Cheruses*. *Ananaes*. I winter at *Carwar*. Bad a final Adieu to *Carwar*, and come again to *Goa*. *Jews* feed on Hogsflesh, for fear of the Inquisition. Left *Goa* on St. *Xaverius* his Eve. In danger of being shipwreck'd at *Bombaim*. Return to *Surat*.

CHAP. VI.

Is a summary Rehearsal of the whole.

The business of *Alexander* and King *Porus* suspicious. The Name of *India* doubtful from what beginning. *India* produces three Harvests in some places. Sunday observed by the *Indians*. How they count the Hours. Their Years divided into Three Seasons. The Mountains. Rivers. The Country rich in Increase. The Desarts. Mines. Wild Beasts. For Game. Fowls of Prey. Fish. Insects. Their Men of Learning. Their Notion of God. The Conceit of Transmigration forcible to Merits. They Write on Leafs. The *Muttanies* and *Jougies*. Jugglers, *&c.* A *Crocus*-colour'd Coat intimates a Resolution to dye or be Conqueror. Opium eaten in quantity. Whether the *Banyan* be a *Jew*. Distinguished by their several painting their Forehead, and Cuts of their Beard. The *Ombrahs*. Petty *Ombrahs*. The Artillery. Their Pride and Luxury. The reason of the Licentiousness of the *Fakiers*. The *Portugals* might have conquer'd *India*, had not the *English* interrupted them: Whereupon the *Dutch* fell upon them. The *English* not much valued. The *Parsies* expose their Dead to the Fowls of the Air. The Women of the same Species with others, the Position of their Veins being the same. Few crooked or deformed. The Cause of their Blackness left in suspense. Their Houses built for Conveniency. They live to a good Age, by care of their Diet, and Cleanliness. Their Washers and other Craftsmen work well for little Money. The World Peopled after the Flood from *Scythia*.

CHAP. VII.

The last Observable is the Weights, Coins, and Precious Stones; a Collection whereof follows:

Rupees. Mamoodees. Pice. Maund. Sear. Candy. Coved. Tuss. Tolla. Mass. Valls. Gudianus. Ruttees. Tanks. Cruzado. Dollar. Chequeen. Duckra. Juttals. Pagods. Carrack. Miscallis. Vassael. Mangore. Larees. Zerephins. Rues. Tuccas.

LETTER V.

CHAP. I.

Of our crossing the Sea to the Persian *Gulph : Arrival at* Gombroon, *and stay there.*

CHAP. II.

Our setting forth from Gombroon, *and leaving* Lhor.

CHAP. III.

We Measure the utmost Bounds of the Province of Lhor *and* Gerom, *to the City of* Siras.

CHAP. IV.

Of Siras, *and the Ancient* Persepolis; *and our journeying quite through* Persia.

CHAP. V.

Our Progress into Parthia, *Entrance into* Spahaun, *and Reception there.*

CHAP. VI.

Carries us to Jelfa ; *where is treated of the* Gabers, *the* Armenians, Georgians, *and* Europe *Artizans.*

CHAP. VII.

Gives us a Sight of the Palace, and *Rarities there. Our Entertainment by the* French *Artizans in the Emperor's Service. The Diversions of the Place ; and its Product : And the Close of the Year, With its Seasons.*

CHAP. VIII.

CHAP. IX.

CHAP. X.

A Voyage to Congo *for Pearl: A Discourse of their Generation. Departure from* Persia, *and Return to* India.

We come to *Congo*. A Dearth in the Water as well as on Land. We come again to *Bunder Abassee*. The Pearl. The Adulteration. Its Names. The kinds of Pearl. *Cheripo*, or Seed-Pearl. *Chanquo*, or Mother of Pearl. Scallop: Its Properties. Its Dignity and Value. The Prices and Sizes. We undergo difficulties in our passage back to *India*, through Negligence of the Pilots.

The Present State of PERSIA.

CHAP. XI.

Gives the various Names, Situation, &c.

Its Names, Situation, and Bounds. Temper of the Air. High Mountains. Their Four-footed Beasts: Wild-Fowl: Fishes. The Valleys made fruitful by the Snow from the Hills. Plants. Tobacco. Manufactories. *Persian* Pearls the best. *Gombroon* Earthen Ware the best, next to the *China*. *Lapis Lazuli*. *Tutiæ*. *Manatæ*. *Bole*. Marble. *Naptha*. Minerals. Rivers. Springs. Little Rain. Showers of Sand. Dew turn'd to *Manna*. Cities. Houses. *Spahaun* proposed as a Patern of their Politicks. *Shaw Abas* well advised in the choice of it for the Imperial City. The *Cauns*. *Etimundoulet*, or Chancellor. A *Janiseen* Deputy-*Caun*. The *Droger*. The *Calenture*. The *Cadi*, or *Cazy*. *Spahaun* the chief Empory. The Citizens humbled. Courtiers and Soldiers great. Their Caravans. No Priority at Church, Bath, or Caravan. The *Gelabdars* not so esteemed in *Persia*, as the *Caphala Bashee* in *Turkey*. Their Temples, Colleges Hummums, or *Balneo's*. The Coffee-houses.

CHAP. XII.

Of the present Inhabitants, &c.

The present *Persians Scythians*. *Jews* here ever since the Captivity. On the Death of the Emperor, the new one causes his Brothers and near Relations Eyes to be put out. Nobles by Birth among the *Persians*. The Government Hierarchical: Whereon is grounded the Emperor's Security. His Wealth. His Course of Life. His Name and Genealogy. The *Suffees* introduced, from whom *Spahaun* is called

Suffahaun. Oppositions made by the *Turkish* Sect. The *English* sack *Ormus* by Surprize. Articles of Agreement between the *English* and the *Persians.* Vengeance pursues the Enterprizers. *Shaw Abas* kills his Son *Mirza.* The present Emperor given up to Debauchery. The way of receiving Ambassadors. The Procession of the *Seraglio*, or *Haram.* The Cruelty of the Black Eunuchs. The Cavalry. Their Arms, and manner of fighting. The *Suffees* Church-Militants. Their Order created to check the *Saieds.* Their Habit, and the *Persians* Standard White and Red. Their Privileges. Other Knights. The Watchmen. The Navy.

CHAP. XIII.

Of their Book-men and Books. Of their Religion, and Religious Worship. Of their Notions in Philosophy: Of Heaven and Hell. Their Astronomers, Physicians, and Lawyers.

A Learned Clerk rare. The School-Language. Their Books written with a Pen, not printed. Pens made of Reeds. Education of Youth. Preposterous way of learning. Emulation in gaining Disciples. Logick. Their Physicks: Metaphysicks. Books in esteem. *Mahomet's* Revelations: Assisted by *Sergius* the Monk. His blasphemous Opinions. *Friday* his Sabbath. Polygamy. The *Mufti*: His Revenue: His Authority. The *Talman*, or *Mullah.* Their Funerals more pompous than the *Turkish* Sects are. Their Tribes clarified by Pilgrimage. Their Names given by the Parents. No Garb to distinguish their Clerks. How they are maintained. Their Limners. Historians. Alchymy. Mathematicks. Necromancy. Astrologers. Astronomy. A *Pithonissa.* Several sorts of *Dæmons.* Longitude and Latitude. Dialling. Musick. Medicks. Anatomy rejected. The *Suffees* Death required of his Physician. Their Prescripts. What Purges approved. What Authors in esteem. They are unskilful in Chyrurgery. Endemial Diseases. Large quantities of Opium eaten at a time. Their Lawyers. The *Cadi.* A Corrupt Judge. *Lex Talionis.* Drubbing on the Soles of the Feet. They buy their Wives. Are often divorced. All Contracts made before the *Cadi.* Usury forbid by *Mahomet*: Yet his Disciples are cruel Extortioners. The *Cheik.* The *Codre.* Guilty of Bribery and Injustice. Their Paradise. Their Hell. The Progress of their Religion. The Souls of Men superior to Brutes: Cannot embrace a Carnal Religion, but an Holy, Pure, and Spiritual; which is no where to be found but in Christianity. Success no Argument.

CHAP. XIV.

The Appellations of the Warrior and Scholar; of the Merchant, Mechanicks, and Villains. Of their Garb, Civility of Manners, Facetiousness, Revellings, Sports, Weddings, Cleansings, and Burials. Of their Women; and License of Curtezans. The Eunuchs, &c.

The Merchant. Cheats in all Professions, make the Brokers necessary. The Villany of a Droger. The *Persian* in his City Dress. The Drover. The Herdsman. The Husbandman. The Dervises. Vinedressers. Slaves made of the Old *Persians*. The Eunuchs. The Old Women. Their Women. Their Excellencies. The Mark of a Whore. Curtizans: Their Children provided for. Lyings in and Purifyings. Widows reckoned Mutes. Sodomy. Addicted to Pleasure. Corruptness of the Courtiers. Women made use of to Complain. The *Persian* places Felicity in Prosperity. Their Recreations and Exercises. They Hunt a long time together. How treated on their Return. Immoderate in their Feasting. Their Religious Feasts. Foot-Racing. Their Valour, whence it proceeds. Their Urbanity. The Custom of carrying Aves. Their Virtues. Vices. How far beholden to Constitution of Body and Air. Their Diet. *Cabob. Pulloe. Dumpoke.* Stews. *Cookoo Challow.* No good Confections. Sherbets. The *Persians* Spit as much as other Folks. Their happiness of Body. Commutative Justice.

LETTER VI.

CHAP. I.

Takes notice of Broach: *The Change of Governors at* Surat. *Intestine Broils of the Empire. Rencounter of the* English; *and Portentous Accidents of this Year.*

The Author sent for to *Broach*. Different Modes of Travelling in *India* from that of *Persia*. Their Chariots for Travelling. *Bereaw. Uncliseer. Broach* City. What Profit to the *Mogul*. *Rama Jessinsin* defies the Emperor. The Confederates make Disturbance. *Morad Beck* made Governor of *Surat*. Great Inundations by the Rains. The *Mogul* prepares to Chastise the *Pagans*. The Return of the *Juddah* Fleet. *Seva* Seizes *Henry Kenry*. The *Barbarians* Relieve it. Their Fleet drove into *Tull*. The Eldest Son of the *Mogul* brings an *Army* to *Brampore*. Two Portents.

LETTER VII.

CHAP. I.

Continues the General Occurrences, with Remarks.

The *Syddy* and *Seva* left to contend for *Henry Kenry.* The *English* Reproach'd. The *Mogul* inflicts a Double Poll. *Seva Gi* Dies. Heats about Succession. The *Mogul's* Eldest Son sent to the Post. Withdraws his Army. An Example on Treason. The *Mogul's* Secretary's Reasons to dissuade the Emperor from his Persecuting the Heathens. A Drought feared. The First Interloper. A Comet.

LETTER VIII.

CHAP. I.

Concludes with my Return to England.

We set Sail for *England.* A Young Man lost over-board. We Sail on the back side of St. *Lawrence.* We weather the Cape of *Good Hope.* Land at St. *Helena.* The Story of the Island and Islanders. Of *Ascension,* and Catching of Tortoises. Foolish Birds. Isle of St. *Thomas.* A bold Act of an *Algier* Slave. The *Azores. England.* We Land at *Folkstone* near *Dover.*

A

NEW ACCOUNT
OF
INDIA AND PERSIA:
IN EIGHT LETTERS.

LETTER I

Containing a Twelve Month's Voyage through Divers Climates.

CHAP I.

Treats of Embarking and Passage 'till past St. Iago.

SIR,

FOR your singular Favour, in seeing me Aboard ship (which might reasonably be supposed the last kind Office to a departing Friend, considering the various Chances of so long a Voyage, as well as the Uncertainty of my Return) I must keep to that Promise, whereby you obliged me to give you an account not only of my Being, but of what Occurrences were worth my Animadversion.

You may remember, It was the 9th of *December*, in the Year of our Lord 1672, when by virtue of an Order from the Honourable *East-India Company*, I being received on

Board the *Unity*,[1] we took of each other a long Farewel ; the ship then breaking ground from *Graves-End*, to fall down to the *Buoy in the Nore*.

The *London*,[2] our Admiral, lay expecting our whole *East-India* Fleet there, which were Ten in Number ; to whom his Majesty, Charles II. was pleased to grant Letters of Mart : Which impowered them to wear the King's Jack, Ancient and Pennant, and to act as Men of War (the *English* and *French* at this time being at open Defiance against the *Dutch*).[3]

When they were altogether, their Commands were to go over the *Flats* ; which, notwithstanding the Hazard to Ships of their Burthen, was thought securer now than to venture about the *King's Channel*, where they might be exposed to the Attempts of the *Hollanders* : By which means, together with the unsteadiness of the Weather, it was the day after *Christmas* before we arrived at the *Downs* ; where rode a rich and numerous Fleet of Merchants, with their respective Convoys, designed for their several Places of Traffick, when the Wind should present.

Here, as we ended the Old Year, so we began the New with a desire of prosecuting our intended Voyage : But a *South-West* Wind prevented our Course, and held us there Three Weeks ; when an *East* Wind made a general delivery and a clear *Downs*.

Being at Sea, we make easy Sail, that our Ships might have the liberty that Night to single themselves from the Crowd of the other Ships ; notwithstanding which Proviso, we had a shrewd Suspicion ; for Night hastening on (and in such a swarm of Vessels of greater bulk, not so readily

---

[1] See list of ships (p. 7) and Index.

[2] See list of ships (p. 7) and Index.

[3] The secret treaty with France, known as the Treaty of Dover, was signed on 20th May, 1670. War with Holland was declared in March 1672 ; and, on 28th May following, the Duke of York met De Ruyter in a naval action at Southwold Bay.

manageable as smaller) we beheld three Lights out of the Poop of a goodly Ship, the same unfortunate signs our Directions bound us to take notice of; which made us conclude the Damage on our side, as indeed it proved by the next Morning-song; for having cast our Eyes abroad to look what Ships we had in company, running over a great many (that had shrowded themselves under our Protection and of Six Men of War more, Captain *Munday* Commander in chief (whereof Two were Fireships) sent for to meet the *East India* Fleet at *Sancta Helena*, for their better Defence homeward-bound, and to prevent their falling into the Enemies Hands, who had lately possessed themselves of that Island[1]) we at length missed the *Massenberg*,[2] on whom (it seems) a small Pink falling foul, had carried away her Head and Boltsprit, and 'tis to be feared had disabled her this Voyage; we saw her afterwards make for *Portsmouth*.

Off the *Land's End* we met with Four *English* Merchant Ships, Two *French* Men of War their Convoys, laden from *Cales*, bound for *London*.

In Four Days, from the *Downs*, we were losing *England* on our Backs, reckoning the *Lizzard* the most extreme part *South* to bear *North and By East* 14 Leagues; from whence hereafter we were to fetch our *Meridian Distance*: It lies in the Latitude of 50 deg. 10 min. *North*.[3]

Thus relinquishing the *British Seas*, we make our selves Possessors of the *Western Ocean* for a while: 'Till following our Compass more *South*, we contend with the troublous Wind and tempestuous Waves for some part of the *Bay of*

---

[1] The Dutch withdrew from St. Helena in 1651; but, on two occasions (1665 and 1673), managed to expel the forces of the East India Company, which had at once seized the abandoned island. The Company regained possession on 16th December, 1673.

[2] See list of ships (p. 7) and Index.

[3] 49° 57′ 30″ N. lat.

Biscay, whose Mountain Seas we are to cut through to the Main *Atlantick*. What makes these Seas in such a constant Turmoil is imputed to the falling in of the whole Force of the *Western Ocean* into this *Sinus* without any Impediment, 'till it recoils against its Shores; so that in the calmest Season here are always high swelling Billows.

About the Latitude of 41 the Men of War, that came out with us, determining to make the *Madera Island*,[1] went away more Easterly, and the next day were out of sight.

Two days after we espied one Sail to the Leeward under a main Course, steering very doubtfully; after she had had her full view of us, she made from us too nimble for us to follow; we supposed her to be either an *Algerine* Pirate, or a *Dutch* Privateer. We still directed our Course *South*, and in Twenty four Hours ran One hundred and seventeen Miles by our Log-board for some days together, the Weather not allowing us to observe with the Quadrant; but as soon as we could take the *Sun's* Altitude, we found our selves to be in the Latitude of 36 deg. 2 min. *North*, Longitude 7 deg. 26 min. *West*, an hundred Miles in four Days more than we judged our selves to be; which sufficiently proves the little credit to be given to the former way of reckoning.

The following day maintaining the same Course, we past by the Mouth of the *Streights* of *Gibraltar*, one of *Hercules's Pillars*, farthest Point *South* of all *Europe*.

Here we began to drop the rest of our Company, some striking *East* for the *Streights*, others *West* for the *Canaries*, *Virginia*, &c.

At Noon our Admiral fired a Gun, and hoisted his Ancient, whereby we understood he saw Land, which we thought to be *Porto Porto*,[2] bearing off us *East*. An hour

---

[1] Madeira.

[2] Perhaps Porto Santo, the second inhabited island of the group.

more being hardly run, we in like manner made the *Madera* Island, the largest of the whole *Atlantick*, being *South East* some twelve Leagues, too great a distance to take a perfect Landschap, it being only discernible to be Land, and confirmed to be so by this days Observation, which was 33 deg. 17 min. to the *Northward* of the *Equator*, in Latitude and Longitude from the *Lizzard* as before, we having neither raised nor depressed it. Where the Trade winds begin to offer themselves, the Mariner relaxes his anxious care of Sailing, and is at more leisure to Repose; he not being so often called upon to shift his Course, or hand his Sails; which has yet this inconvenience, giving him leave now to fall into those distempers Idleness contracts, *viz.*, the *Scurvy*, and other ill Habits; unless rouzed by an Active Commander, either to Sports, or more useful Employments: Although the perfect knowledge of these Trade-winds (which are more constant within the Tropicks) are of such importance as to make our Modern Navigators perform that in six Months, which took up the Pains and Travels of as many Years from the first Discoverers, they keeping all along the Shore, whereupon they became not only liable to unaccountable Changes, as they met with Land briezes, Head-lands, or Contrary Winds; but were many times disappointed either to go on, or return, by the several Accidents they encountered thereupon; which these more experienced and bold Adventurers by standing off to Sea, and study of their Compass by a more accurate Computation of their Way by the Quadrant and Azimuth, and a strict enquiry of the commencing and terminating of these Winds, avoid.

In this short space we have almost out-ran the *Northern Winter's* Blasts, and begin to be sensible of a more vigorous Clime, whose temperate Warmth adds Spirits to our frozen Limbs: Yet, in this forward Spring (for such it seemed to us) we cannot escape some Lashes of that cold *Nemesis*;

for Night being come, she sends a Storm of Rain and Hail with an high and bleak Wind, in which appeared the Sailors Deities, *Castor* and *Pollux*, or the same it may be gave light to those Fables, they boding fair Weather to Seamen, though never seen but in Storms, looking like a Candle in a dark Lanthorn, of which there were divers here and there above the Sails and Shrowds, being the *ignes fatui* of the Watery Element; by the *Portugals* christned *Querpos Santos*,[1] the Bodies of Saints, which by them are esteemed Ominous. But I think I am not too positive in relating them to be a Meteor-like substance exhaled in the Day, and at Night (for except then, they shew not themselves) kindled by the violent Motion of the Air, fixing themselves to those parts of the Ship that are most attractive: For I can witness they usually spent themselves at the Spindles of the Top-mast-heads, or about the Iron-hoops of the Yard arms, and if any went towards them, they shifted always to some Part of the like Nature.

The succeeding Morning had not long withdrawn this black Vail, and brought us tidings of a more serene Day, when we beheld our Frigots that had left us, busking after us with all the winged speed they could, and about Noon

---

[1] Port. *Corpo Santo*, "a fiery meteor: Castor and Pollux, which at sea seems sometimes sticking to a part of the ship, in form of balls" (Vieyra, *Dict.*, ed. 1773). "The same night we saw upon the maine yarde, and in many other places a certaine signe, which the Portingalls call Corpo Santo, or the holy body of brother Peter Gonsalves, but the Spaniards call it S. Elmo, and the Greekes (as ancient writers rehearse, and Ovid among the rest) used to call it Helle and Phryxus. Whensoever that signe sheweth upon the Maste or Maine yarde, or in any other place, it is commonly thought, that it is a signe of better weather: when they first perceive it, the maister or the chiefe boteswaine whistleth, and commandeth every man to salute it with a Salve Corpo Santo, and a misericordia, and with a very great cry [and exclamation]. This constellation (as astronomers doe write) is ingendred of great moysture and vapors, and sheweth like a candle that burneth dimly, and skippeth from one place to another, never lying still" (Linschoten, ii, 238 f.). "We had some thunder and lightning or *corpo santos*, such as seeme good Omens to the superstitious *Portugalls*" (Herbert, 9).

they gained us, keeping on the same Course as we, but missed of their design of touching at the *Madera's*.

Being blessed with a prosperous Gale, in fifteen Days from *England* we were to the *Southward* of the Tropical Circle of *Cancer*, which lies in 23 deg. and ½ *North*, and passeth through *Barbary*, *India*, *China*, and *Nova Hispania*; we making at Twelve at Noon, Latitude 22 deg. 16 min. *North*, Longitude 8 deg. *West*, when we must be 1 deg. 14 min. *South* of the Tropick.

A *Guinea* Merchant-man bound for the River *Gamboa* kept us Company hither, but his Voyage requiring a more Easterly Course, was the last Merchant Ship took leave of us.

We holding on still *South*, the frequent Noise of Thunder, the sultry Rains, quiet Seas in respect of what we had before, were assured tokens of our drawing nigher to that Fountain of Heat, the *Sun*.

By reason whereof it was familiar to behold, the sportful Fishes greedy of their Prey raise whole Flocks of that Scaly Nation.[1] For those whom Nature has placed in the vast Deep, defenceless of themselves, and innocent to others of a more powerful Greatness, so as many times they become their Prey, she has not altogether left them unprovided; either out of her abhorrency of Idleness, resolving every thing should labour for its Belly, or else out of a

[1] ". . . we had such shoales of flying fishes as darkened the glorious Sunne by their interposing multitude; a fish most excellent in its eyes, which flame like a rolling Dyamond; the body is equall to a well fed Herring, big enough for those complementall wings (or fins) Nature has provided it to avoid the swift chase of Sea Tyrants, Sharks, Albicores, Dolphins, Bonetaes and such as feed upon small fishes; but alas! a *Scilla* in *Charibdin*; no sooner taking advantage of her wings (imitating a bird 200 paces, a dozen yards high from the face of the Ocean, so long as she keeps moisture) when an Armado of starv'd birds and hawks greedily prey upon them; by this, becoming the most miserable of all creatures, blest with 2 shifts, but neither availeable, in the water not so full of bravery as upon the wing, yet that becomes the only gin and cause of her destruction" (Herbert, 33). Also see Pyrard de Laval, i, 9; Ovington, 36.

peculiar respect towards every individual Species for their Preservation as well as Production; furnishing these with Fins of larger size and double use for swifter conveying them under Water, as also for soaring into the Air when they are too closely pursued. Of these sort we saw good store flying from *Bonetos*[1] and *Albecores*,[2] who were hunting them. Some of these flying Fish (for no other Name they have as I can learn) were so put to it, that after often dipping their fishy Wings in the briny Water (without which genuine Artifice they could not use them) chose rather to make our Ship their Sanctuary, than to yield themselves to the Jaws of their devouring Adversaries: By which means you have their more exact Description, they being as large as a River Perch bedeckt with Silver-spangled Scales, and long Fins as before.

Not many days after, two of the lesser Off-spring of the great Leviathan, (the Weather being calm, these sort of them else not visible, being of no swift motion) came sailing after us; our Men as eager of them as they of their Prey, hastned their Engines for to take them; which no sooner in the Water, but each of them guided by some half a dozen delicately coloured little Fishes, which for their own safeguard perform the Office of Pilots,[3] (they never offering to satisfy their Hunger on them) who lead them to the Baits; when they turning their Bellies up, seize upon them on their Backs, hook themselves in the Toils, beating the Sea into a Breach, and not without a great many Hands are drawn over the sides of the Ship; which seen by the poor silly little Fishes (as conscious of their

---

[1] Port. *bonito*, "fine"; the *thynnus pelamys* of Day (Yule, *Hobson-Jobson*, 104).

[2] A similar fish, *thynnus albacora* or *macropterus*: probably Arabic *al-bukr*, "a young camel, heifer"; Port. *bacoro*, "a young pig" (Yule, *Hobson-Jobson*, 10; *Gray's Note on Pyrard de Laval*, i, 9).

[3] The pilot fish, *naucrates ductor*, of the family of Horse Mackerels.

Error) they swim to and again, and hardly forsake the Ship; but being within Board, the Ship's Company armed with Hatchets presently divide the Spoil. They are not scaly, and therefore imagined to be a kind of Whale, being finned like them, with a great Fin on their Backs near their Tails, (which dried is used instead of a Slate) of a darkish grey Colour on their Backs, lighter on their Sides, and white under their Bellies; their Snout on the same Plain with their Mouths, but their Mouth within that a great way; the cause why they turn their Bellies when they take their Prey. The Mouth of one of them extended, is two Spans wide, armed within with three Tire of sharp pointed Teeth on both Jaws, so piercing that Needles exceed them not, and of such strength that a Leg or an Arm, Bone and all, is but an easy Morsel; wherefore called Sharks by the Seamen, on whom they are bold enough to fasten, and dismember if not shunned when they wash themselves: They are of a rank smell, and not good to eat but by stout Stomachs; of Length they are ten, sometimes fourteen Feet.

By this time we had got into 17 deg. 19 min. *North* Latitude, Longitude 9 deg. 10 min. *West*, when our Men of War thinking to birth themselves before us at St. *Iago*,[1] (where our Ships were permitted to refresh, being otherwise tied up by Charter-party not to put in any where unless for absolute necessity) made all the Sail on head they could.

Our Commanders were well enough content with their proffer, knowing the danger of a many Ships going in there together: The day ensuing plying to the *West*, we discovered *Beunovista*[2] bearing full *West* ten Leagues, but at Noon were within two Leagues of it.

---

[1] Santiago, Cape Verde Islands.

[2] Bõa Vista, the most easterly of the Cape Verde Islands.

It is one of the Islands of the *Gorgades* or *Cape Verde*, because situate over against that Promontory on the Land of *Negros*.

They are said to be Nine in Number. *Beunovista, quasi* good sight, it deserving that Appellation from four Hills,[1] which raising themselves to an Eminency above their Fellows, yield a fair Prospect at a distance; but approaching nigher it is not unlike the crawling of a Snake, it's various Hills and Vallies fluctuating as it were, seem to borrow that riggling Shape, the two remotest Mountains figuring her Crown and Head.

The succeeding day, *South-East* of us, we saw the Isle of *Maijo*,[2] another of the *Gorgades*,[3] plentiful in nothing more than Salt, whither our Traders in that Commodity often send Ships to fetch it, which is brought down to them in Barrows blowed by the Wind, they having Sails fitted for that purpose.

In two and twenty days from the *Lizzard*, early in the Morning we were close under St. *Iago*,[4] another Island of the same Knot; whose interwoven barren Mountains are as impossibly exprest as *Stonehing* numbred.[5] Towards

---

1 The loftiest peak attains the height of 1260 ft. (*Ency. Brit.*[9], v. 52).

2 Maio, 35 miles from Bõa Vista, the inhabitants of which still depend on the exportation of salt. *Ency. Brit.*, v, 52. "The three faire daughters of *Hesperus*, were the honest Ilands in the West, adjoyning this garden; their names *Aeglae*, *Arethusa*, and *Hesperthusa*; now new named *Mayo*, *Sal*, and *Bonavista*" (Herbert' 8). "7th May came to anchor at Mayo, a place not worth staying at, it yieldeth no water, but poor lean goats, as many as we will take" (Danvers, *Letters*, i, 9).

3 So called because they were supposed to be the abode of the Gorgons. Pliny *N. H.*, vi, 36 (31) tells how Hanno, the Carthaginian General, brought from thence the hairy skins of two Gorgons, possibly those of some ape.

4 San Thiago, the largest, but also the most unhealthy island of the Archipelago. The port is Villa da Praia, at the south extremity of the island. The highest peak is Pico de Antonio, 4500 ft. in elevation (*Ency. Brit.*[9], v, 52).

5 The same story is told of the Rollright Stones in Oxfordshire and of other stone circles (*Folk-Lore*, vi, 26).

the *South-West* they are very high and burnt ; but steering to loof about the Bay, we found it empty, and the Men of War missing ; for all that we came to an Anchor about ten a Clock in the Forenoon in the Bay of St. *Iago.*

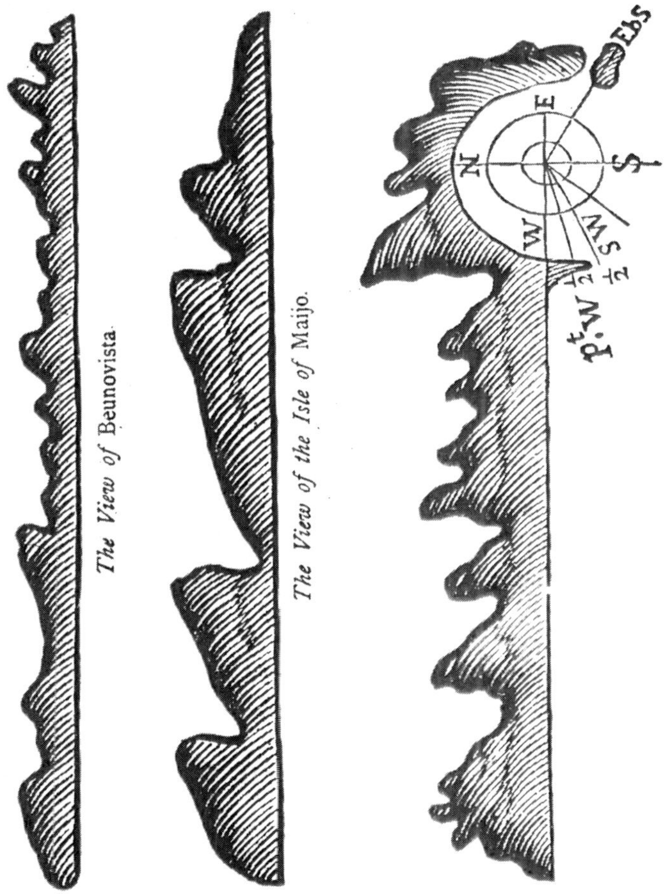

The View of Beunovista.

The View of the Isle of Maijo.

The View of the Bay of St. Iago.

The Ground was covered with Corral of all sorts, under which it was Sandy of a duskish Colour. Having discovered three Buoys, our Commander sent his Boat to seize on one, which proved to be the Mark to a special good Anchor of 2400 weight, with a Cable seven Inches Diameter; the rest of the Fleet shared the other two. The Bay the Ships rode in was smooth Water, the Wind coming from the Shore; in Figure a Semicircle, in which it might contain four Miles, the weathermost Point bearing *South-West*, and half a Point *West*, the other Point to which was an Islet, *East* and by *South*, and *South*.

Of the Island of St. Iago, *one of the* Cape Verde *Islands*.

In the Afternoon I went ashore, which was near two Miles from the Ship, where was a convenient watering place, which emptied its fresh Current into the Salt Sea; the Beach was sandy, and easy going ashore. Here met us whole Troops of the Natives with their several Wares, some offering us Cocoes, others Oranges and Limes; some brought Jackanaps's,[1] such green Ones as are commonly seen in *England* to be sold; and all at the price of a cleanly Rag, or a Bunch of Ribbons.

Before us in a Valley was a most stately Grove of Cocoes[2] and Oranges (through which ran the Stream our Men filled their Casks with Water) surrounded with a Wall.

The first of which Trees, so much celebrated for its usefulness, deserves as much for the pleasure it affords the Sight. It grows with an upright, tall, and slender Body, the Bark of an Ash colour, loricated; not sending any Branches forth till it come to its chiefest Summit, where it spreads its shady Branches with some resemblance to our

---

[1] Jackanapes, "an ape or monkey," a word of which the origin is uncertain (*New Eng. Dict.*, *s. v.*).

[2] The coco-nut palm, *Cocos nucifera*. For various theories regarding the origin of the name, see Yule, *Hobson-Jobson*, 228; P. della Valle, i, 181; Fryer (Letter V, chap. II) repeats the statement that it produces fruit and boughs with every moon.

a. Represents ye young Plant as it appears first above ground Springing from ye Nut under ground
b Shews ye shape of ye Tree with that of its branches near ye top, the under & more ripe being fallen off & leaving the Signes of their roots on ye bark of the Stock
c. The shape of ye Branches with their stemms & feet as they grow from ye Tree, extending sometimes from ye foot to ye tip longer 5 & yards in length fringed or gathered on both sides with long narrow leaves
d. The Purse or Sheath containing ye branch of flowers
e. The branch of Flowers &c when fallen leaves ye young nutts
f. One of the branches grown more ripe
g. One of those Nutts full ripe. h. The Coco Nutt shell intire, ye outward Pill or husk being fallen off
i. The Roots & blade peircing through ye holes of ye Shell
k. The Kernell of ye Nut half ye Shell being taken off
l. Represents ye intire tree of an older & longer standing
m. Represents ye manner how they fasten a gourd to collect ye liquor

To face 2

Osmond[1] Royal Fern, but more like the Palm ; and under these protects its weighty Fruit ; which hang very thick round about the Tree, to which it yields but one Stalk, but that fit to support its ponderousness ; every Moon produces a fresh Harvest both of Fruit and Boughs ; the first being gathered, the others being thrust off when sapless by the young ones : If the Juicy ones be wounded, there distills an heady Liquor, which they preserve in Earthen Pots fitted to receive it, but that spoils their bearing Nuts. Next to the Stalk it bestows a Calix, not differing (only in bigness, and that it is smoother) from that of our Acorn ; from which proceeds the Rind of a lighter Green, under which a fibrous substance presents its self, which might supply them with Utensils, for Roaps and Sails; beneath which appears a spacious brown Shell, proper for many Necessaries, big enough for a Drinking Cup, a Ladle, and many more ; serving them for the chief part of their Householdstuff : Enclosed in this is a delicious Meat, white in Colour, cloathed with a pithy matter, as our Hasle-nuts, and not inferiour to them in Taste ; this they chuse for their ordinary Nourishment. Nor does it afford them a less grateful emulsion, contained in the Nut to the quantity of a Pint, or Pint and half ; in colour like Whey, and of that consistency, but in relish far excelling.

When the Meat of the Nut grows rancid, they express an Oyl serviceable for their Lamps.

Thus abundantly has Providence furnished them from this one Root. The figure of the Fruit, take it intire, is oval, and as big as the largest Melons.

On the other Fruits it's needless to insist, as Oranges, and the like, being planted nearer home, and therefore not such strangers.

---

1 A name formerly given to various ferns ; now the "Flowering Fern" (*Osmunda regalis*). It is Med. Lat. *Osmunda*, of doubtful origin (*New Eng. Dict.*, *s. v. Osmund*).

Having observed enough here, we entred a Door which gave us admittance to a Court in the same Valley, whose party Wall made of Mud and Stone, separated it from the Grove.

Here lay at the Foot of the ascending Mountain, in a careless posture, one Company of their Militia, raised on this occasion, having rested their Arms, as Muskets, and Pikes, with their Colours of White Silk, with a Green Cross athwart, and the Arms of *Portugal* in the midst of it, against the Wall, but Breast high; which could not have held up the Pikes, had not some adjoining Trees contributed to their aid.

They saluted us with the civility of the Hat, and Congeed[1] to the ground; those of them that walked about, had Javelins in their hands, and long Swords tied to their Backs.

Labouring to reach the top of the Mountain, which was very steep, some we met on foot, others mounted on Asses, with Jackanaps's behind them, passed us with no small Grandure and Ceremony of the Cap; and which was wonderful, to see them ride these creatures over Precipices, only Goats and they could clamber on.

At last gaining the highest part another Wall accosted us, over which a Gate, and upon that a Cross. On the left hand, as soon as we were in, was either a Prison, or a Guard-house. Not many Paces from it, on the same side, a Row of Houses, one Story high, thatcht with the Branches of the Cocoe, and Windows with wooden Shutters. but no Casements, built with Mud and Stone, as all their Buildings were which I saw; the insides visible enough, for the biggest of them had not four yards Front, and half that, for the greater state, was taken up by the Door: Their Furniture is answerable to the splendour of their

---

[1] Fr. *congé*, "a bow"; Lat., *commeatus.*

Habitations; but because we will not refuse the Courtesy of their Entertainment, see in what a manner they present us with their viands.

They invite us with an Hubble-bubble[1] (so called from the noise it makes) a long Reed as brown as a Nut with use, inserted the body of a Cocoe-shell filled with Water, and a nasty Bole just pressing the Water, they ram Tobacco into it uncut, out of which we may suck as long as we please, but for any thing else they tell us as the Poet did,

> *Vina mihi non sunt Gazetica, Chia, Falerna,*
> *Quæque Sereptano palmite missa bibas.*[2]

Their Common Drink being only Water; and their Food as plain, being only the Fruits of the Earth.

But to keep on our way, which here we found easy and plain; on the right stood another Cross, propped with a four-square Pillar raised on steps, and half a Stone's cast from it, a Chappel, not proud enough to brag of any great elegancy for its Architecture (being but the Rural Seat of one of their Black Padres). Not much beyond it the *Corps de Guard*, from whence they supplied their Sentinels, which were placed in a Military Order here and there: Nearer the water-side, on the brow of the Precipice which overloo'k the Haven, in a well-appointed place, were planted half a dozen small Pieces of Ordnance, which spake Thanks for our respect paid when we came to an Anchor; not far from hence another Guard and House regarding the Main, which gave notice to the rest of what Vessels they saw at Sea.

And now we began to think of returning, when we met with some had happen'd to see the glory of the Day; who told us, our Admiral had sent to the Deputy-Governour, residing here, to be certified about the Anchors; who first

---

[1] The *hookah* or water-pipe. (Yule, *Hobson-Jobson*, 428.)

[2] Sidonius, *Carm.*, xvii, 15.

claimed those Anchors of our Emissaries with the Majesty effential to that Nation he represented (being a White *Portugal*) for his Master, being slipped in Port; and then informed them, that they were left there the Afternoon before we came in, by Three great *Holland* Men of War, who were separated by foulness of Weather, from the Squadron of Admiral *Eversdon*,[1] who was sent to vex the *English* Plantations at *Virginia*: Who at the sight of our Men of War, had put to Sea in great confusion, leaving some of their Crews behind them, who went off in their Shallops, but could not reach their Ships; keeping therefore the Shore on board, they put in at St. *Iago* Town, where they now remain: From whence this Morn by fresh Advice he was assured only six Ships were seen to ply to windward; which must be our Fleet striving to regain the Island, which is difficult by reason of the Trade-winds, it being beside their Commission to pursue them. Thus being alarm'd to our Ships, that Night we weighed.

In the dusk of the Evening came into this Bay a *Sattee*[2] of *Portugal*, laden from *Madera* with Wine, some of which we purchased, but restored not the Anchors.

The Country without is rocky and mountainous, the Island but small; what Towns it has of note, our small stay would not permit the Enquiry: It is said to be pleasant within the Country; well watered and furnished with all things necessary for the life of Man; discovered for the King of *Portugal*, Anno 1440.[3] Well peopled by the *Portugals*, and a Colony of their Plantation from *Ginea*.

---

[1] Probably the Dutch admiral Evertsen, who fought so bravely at the Battle of Beachy Head (Macaulay, *H. of England* (1855), iii, 604).

[2] "Wee had sight of a sayle . . . and comming neere unto us we espied it to bee a sattie, which is a ship much like unto an argosey, of a very great burthen and bignesse" (Taylor, 1630) in Nares, *Gloss. s. v.*

[3] Cape Verde Islands, partially discovered in 1441 by an expedition fitted out by Dom Henrique of Portugal, under Antonio and Bartolomeo di Notti. Settled after the voyage of Cada Mosto in 1456.

In respect of the Heavenly Bodies, it lies in *North* Latitude, 15 deg. 25 min. Longitude from the *Lizzard* 12 deg. 10 min. *West*, the length of Days altering very little.

The People are of a comely Black, their Hair frizled. Tall of stature, cunning and Thievish: they staring one in the Face, and in the mean time cut a Knot from the Shoulder, or steal an Handkerchief out of the Pocket.

Their Speech is broken *Portugal*, as also is their Habit, imitating therein the *Portugals*; though few of them so well clad as to hide their Nakedness so, but that either Leggs, Shoulders and Back may be seen, and in some all. If they get an old Hat with a Bunch of Ribbons, two White Sleeves, a Waistband, or a Coat slasht to hang back to shew their Sleeves, or an old Pair of Long Breeches to their Buttocks; an unsizeable Sword to their Backs, a Javelin in their Hands, without either Hose or Shooes (as if cut out for Sir *John Falstaff's* Humour)[1] they shall have them strut, and look as big as the greatest Don in *Portugal*.

The Women are not so handsome as the Men, Blubber-lipp'd, more corpulent, and shorter; notorious also for their Levity. Their Head-geer a Clout rowled up like our Water-bearers; their Backs, and Breasts (which were large, and hanging down) bare, as also to their Wasts, from whence a thin Cloath, in fashion of a Petticoat, down to their Feet, which are bare likewise. Some of the best of them adorn'd with Bracelets about their Arms and Necks, false Jewels in their Ears, with a kind of Vail from their Head to their Knees, with a Close-bodied Coat with Hanging-sleeves.

By Religion they are Christians of the *Romish* Church.

Their Governour is from *Portugal*.

Nothing more observable in this little time, but that at Night on Shipboard, we had the sight of *Del Fogo's*

---

[1] Shakespeare. 1 Henry IV, iv, ii.

Flames ;[1] it being an Island of Fire, the Smoak of which is also apparent at Noon-day ; which is of the same Batch with the rest, we seeing only these Four Islands of the Nine belonging to the *Gorgades*.

CHAP. II.

Contains our Passage from St. Iago *to* Johanna, *and Relation of that Island.*

THUS forsaking these *African* Islands, and being forsaken of all but our own Fleet, with a brisk Gale we gave our Ships head to the *Eastward* of the *South* ; whereby we came nearer to the Coast of *Africa* ; the *Northern Monsoons* (if I may so say, being the Name imposed by the first Observers, *i.e. Motiones*)[2] lasting hither ; they (springing from the pressure of the Winter's Snow, Clouds or Vapours lodged on the *Artic* Mountains, and now beginning to be dissolved) leave us to struggle with those moving with the Sun, between the Tropicks *East* and *West*, as those without do *North* and *South*, mostly or collaterally to those Cardinal Points. And therefore we are forced to steer more *Easterly*, either to fetch a Wind to cross the *Æquator*, or gain a Side-wind from the constant ones to carry us to *Brasil*. For which cause those Ships bound for St. *Helen's* from *Europe*, must come into the Latitude of 28 deg. *South*, and sometimes to the *Cape of Good Hope*, before they can bend their Course thither, though in a direct Line it would cut off three quarters of the way.

When we were in four degrees of the Line, and Longi-

---

[1] Fogo, thirty miles distant from San Thiago, with a volcanic cone 9150 ft. high, which produced fire uninterruptedly from 1680 to 1713, and intermittently since that time (*Ency. Brit.*[9], v, 52).

[2] This ingenious derivation is inaccurate. The word comes from Ar. *mausim*, "season." (Yule, *Hobson-Jobson*, 577.)

tude from St. *Iago* 7 deg. 22 min. *East*, (renewing thence our Meridian) we became subject to the most parching Heat of the Torrid Zone; whose Effects were so much the more outragious, by as much as the Winds shrank upon us from off the Coast of *Ginea* (which we drew nigh to) and had left us at a stand, the usual Treatment hereabouts, imputed to the scarcity of Mountains on that vast Tract of ground: Insomuch, that we lay wholly at the mercy of the two unruly Elements, Fire and Water; the one assailing us with flashy Lightnings, and horrid Noises, breaking forth the Airy Region; the other pouring on us whole Streams of unwholsome and dangerous Flouds, when they fall in Spouts, (which are frequent here:) Nay the kindest and the softest downfal on our Bodies is productive of Vermin, such as Flies, and Maggots, if our Cloaths be not quickly dried and shifted; (these Seasons the Seamen term the *Tornados.*)[1]

But above all, when these had played their parts, the scorching *Sun* making towards us with his fiery Face made us almost breathless: In this remediless Condition we lay, till Heaven pitying our languishing under this burning Fever, dispatched to our Relief an *East South East* Wind, which leading us *West* and by *South*, brought us to the *South* of the Equinoctial Line, depressing our Longitude to 5 deg. 55 min. *East.* And now we were to the *Northward* of the *Sun* four degrees, with whom circling a little *East*, in nine days time we were in a Perpendicular, whereby our Quadrants became of small use, we not being able to make an Observation for their want of Shade, but by an Astrolabe at Night: The *Sun* passing over our Heads, and we being to the *Southward* of the Line, the first fair Wind made us out-sail the *Northern* Polar Star, it not being to be seen in this Horizon.

---

1 Span. Port. *tornada*, *tornar*, "to return or go back."

Steering now by the *Crosiers*,[1] a *South* Constellation, taking its Name from the Similitude of that Pastoral Staff; as also supplied by the *Magellanian* Clouds,[2] in number Two, (averred to be such by those that use this way continually) fixed as the *North* Star; but to me they seem no other than a *Galaxia*, caused by the Reflection of the Stars.[3]

Being to the *Southward* of the *Sun's* Declination, it is obvious to note, a *North Sun* makes the same time of Day a *South Sun* does on the contrary side.

An Epidemical Distemper, by the Sea-Chyrurgions termed a Calenture[4] (a malignant Fever with a Frenzy, so that if not watched, they leap into the Sea) raging in the Fleet, many were thrown over-board.

Where the *Atlantick* (washing the Shores all along from the *Streights* of *Gibraltar*) mixes with the *Æthiopick* Ocean, there the Meridian Compass varies very much, so that the

---

[1] Span., *crucero*, "cross-bearer," the constellation known as the Southern Cross. "At the same time sighted the Southern Constellation, or Antartic Pole, otherwise called the *Croisade*, from being composed of four stars in the form of a cross, though it is distant 27° from the Pole" (Pyrard de Laval, i, 9). "This [South] pole is a constellation of four stars the mariners call the *crosiers*; these stars appear near one another, like a cross, and almost equidistant" (Terry, 31). Elsewhere (p. 70) Fryer calls them "crociers."

[2] The remarkable group of nebulæ, known as the Nubeculæ or Magellanic Clouds, in the southern heavens. "These resemble the Milky Way in aspect, but on telescopic examination are found to consist, not of stars alone, like the Milky Way, but of stars mixed with nebulæ. Within the Nubecula Major, Sir J. Herschel counted 278 nubulæ, besides more than 50 outlying nebulæ. The Nubecula Minor is not so rich in nebulæ, but still deserves to be regarded as an aggregation of these objects" (*Ency. Brit.*[9], ii, 821).

[3] "The *Magellan* Cloudes first appeare, and they keep their course with the Polar Starre, alway equidistant, 11 or 12° the most southermost. They are streamy and glaring, whyte, like the Galaxia" (Sir T. Roe, i, 5).

[4] Fever, with delirium; Fr., *calenture;* Lat., *caleo*, "to be hot." "The weather increast from warme to raging hot, the Sunne flaming all day, insomuch that *Calentures* began to vexe us" (Herbert, 7).

Wind being at *South-East* and by *East*, lays out a *South* and by *West* way, but corrected by the Magnetick Azimuth (which gives the *Sun's* Amplitude) it differs two Points and an half, which with Leeway allow'd, makes a *South-West* Course, which we held on till we were on the Coasts of *Brasil*, when we were at distance enough to take the Altitude of the *Sun*, which made 14 deg. 40 m. *South* Latitude, Longitude 2 deg. 24 min. *East*.

Being between *Brasil* and several Islands, as *Trinidado*,[1] *Isl. de Picos*, *Sancta Maria*,[2] &c., we met with Winds carried us to the *South* of the Tropick of *Capricorn*, which crosseth *Æthiopia Inferior*, and the midst of *Peruviana*.

Before we leave this Ecliptick Circle, we must observe at the Æquator, the *Sun* becomes twice Perpendicular ; at each Tropick but once ; beyond them never ; because hence may naturally be collected all the Seasons of the whole Year ; unless some accidental Cause, as the Interposition of Mountains, Headlands, Lakes, or such like intervene.

But in his Solar Progress Through the twelve Signs, the *Sun* always carries Rain along with him, its Heat otherwise could not be endured ; for which reason, the first Contriver and Former of all things, has ordained the wet Season a *Winter*[3] to those inhabit here, and to them as dreadful as our cold Seasons to us (which we shall evidence more experimentally when we come to live among them) : On this account is it, that under the Line two *Winters* and two *Summers* alternately succeed, but not above three

---

[1] An uninhabited island in S. Atlantic ; lat. 20° 35′ S. ; long. 29° 30 W.

[2] "The Isles of Acores, or the Flemmish Islands, are 7, that is Tercera, Saint Michael, S. Mary, S. George, Gratiosa, Pico, & Fayael" (Linschoten, ii, 276). The Azores are divided into three distinct groups : the S.E., Saõ-Miguel, or St. Michael's, and Sta. Maria; the central and largest, Fayal, Pico, Saõ Jorge, Terceira, and Graciosa ; the N.W., Flores, Corvo (*Ency. Brit.*[9], iii, 169).

[3] The rainy season (Yule, *Hobson-Jobson*, 970).

quarters of that length as the one at each Tropick, they continuing four Months together; to wit, four Months *Winter*, as many *Summer*, and the other four Months moderate or cold Weather; though nearer the Line, the Rule holds not good as to the cool Weather, for that cause more frequently visited with Wet than the Sunshine.

Our Men at length tired with salt Provisions, began to be studious for fresh; Necessity having taught them an Invention, by counterfeiting those formerly mentioned Flying fish, with a white Rag stuffed to hide the Hook, and Feathers pricked in instead of Fins, to catch their Enemies at their own game, and so they did; providing for themselves and us too, *Bonetos* and *Albicores*;[1]. the latter bigger than the former, in length two Feet, in thickness one, of a brave shining Colour, with spiked Fins; but the other preferred by the Palate, bearing the make of our Jacks; both of them a good Repast at Sea, where it is denied to be curious in our choice.

The Dolphin is extolled beyond these, which they strike with a Fisgig:[2] They are swift and strait when they swim, and for Composure surpass all others in neatness, as well as for variety of Colours, for which it seems to vie with the Rain-bow, or *Juno's* darling Bird, the Peacock.

There is another Fish they call a *Stone-Bass*,[3] which eats better than it looks, it being of a Colour sandy, but has a Relish equal to our *Soles*.

Hitherto having kept mostly a *South-West* Course, furthered in it by Gales from the Coast of *Ginea*, we are now to expect *Westerly* Winds to carry us to *Cabo da boa*

---

[1] P. 36, *supra*.

[2] Fizgig, fishgig, "a kind of harpoon" (*New Eng. Dict.*, *s. v. fizgig*).

[3] A term applied to various fishes of the genus *Labrax*, especially *Polyprion cernium*; very rare in British seas, but common in the S. Atlantic.

esperança ;[1] near the Latitude of 30 deg. *South* we had a promising *Fresco*,[2] but somewhat dulled by too frequent Calms, yet here not so vexatious as before, we going retrogade with the *Sun*.

It is observable here, that the Sea had a contrary Course with the Wind, presumed to proceed from its blowing so long in one Quarter ; and now not altered so long as to be powerful enough to turn the Current of the Waters.

Gaining upon the *East* with a slow pace, we met with those feathered Harbingers of the Cape, as *Pintado*[3] Birds, *Mangofaleudos*,[4] *Albetrosses* ; the first remarkable for their painted Spots of black and white ; the last in that they have great Bodies, yet not proportionable to their Wings, which mete out twice their length.

Three Months being near consumed, we were at last accompanied with long lookt for *Western* Blasts, and now we fly afore the Wind : But by the way take notice a *South-West* Wind becomes as bleak here, as a *North-East* in *England*. So that all the Seasons of the Year being undergone in this time, we may begin to calculate our

---

[1] Cape of Good Hope, named by Diaz (1486) *Cabo de todas los tormentos*; renamed by John ii *Cabo de Buena Esperanza*.

[2] Port. *Fresco*, "a cool wind."

[3] The Cape pigeon or Pintado (Port. *pintado*, "painted") Petrel, *Daption capensis*. "Those who voyage from or to Australia, whatever be the route they take, are certain to meet with many more species" (*Ency. Brit.*[9], xviii, 712). ". . . being off to sea we perceiv'd a storme intended us, happy in sight of a small black bird, long wingd (injustly by seamen call'd the Divells bird) an Antimalago never seene but against stormy weather : doubtlesse it is a warning from God rather, as be the Pantado birds (like Iayes in colours) who about these remote seas are ever flying and give seamen an infallible incouragement (when neither sounding nor observation from Sunne, Moone nor Planets for many days are had) they are upon this Coast, these birds and Sargasus or Trumbaes (eradicated by stormes) being never seen in such quantity in any other part of the universe, upon these for 50. leagues into the sea seldom failing our intelligence" (Herbert, 20).

[4] Port. *Mangas de velludo*, "velvet-sleeves." Mandelslo (*E. T.*, 248) speaks of "Mangas de valeudo, a kind of sea-mews, being white all over the bodies and having black wings." Various references to this bird will be found in Pyrard de Laval, i, 21.

Ephemeris afresh; and as a fit Platform, *Easter* Holy-days bring with them such Weather as is essential to Christide.

But bidding Adieu to these Fancies, the Wind that till now seemed to dally, proves in good earnest, and begins a frowning *April*, driving the trembling Sea on heaps, and on them piling more, till the swelling Surges menace the lowering Skies, leaving a Hollow where they borrowed their Gigantine vastness, as if they were intended to exenterate the Treasures of the Deep. At top of which 'twas dreadful to behold the angry Surface of the foaming Billows, descending down beneath no less uncomfortable, when the Vans of the next Ships (though groveling with a neighbouring Wave) could not be discerned.

This tossing Condition lasted long, and was taken kindly too, as long as we spooned before the Sea, and kept from running foul of one the other; but when a Fret of Wind rowled the Waves athwart our Quarters, it made our Ship shake, proving the soundness of her Sides, where had she given way never so little, we must have sunk without Bail or Mainprize. Still the Tempest encreases, and brings with it Gusts of Rain and dismal darksome Weather, whereby we were separated from the rest of our Fleet: For all, we put our Lights abroad as did they, yet in the badness of the Night we lost them, and were left alone to shift with the boisterous Winds.

At last the Morn appears, but with the Symptoms of a blowing Day. She had not wasted many Hours, but on the advantage of a rising Wave, we spied a Sail to Leeward with her Fore-top-mast by the Board, which at Noon we knew to be the *Cæsar* crowding under all its Sails.

In this Encounter we shipped many a perilous Sea, (not without being well-drenched our selves): Such was the force of this Nights Storm, that our Boat, and some of our Men, were not without difficulty restrained from being carried over-board. In this pickle we reeled out this Day, and out-stretching the *Cæsar*, we made what Sail we durst, and by the next Light had sight of our Fleet, who shortning Sail, we came up with them, to whom we declared the misfortune of the *Cæsar*, and that it bore *South-West*; wherefore they lay by, (the Wind slackning) and in half an hour we saw the Hull, and presently after it made up our Company compleat again.

Near the middle of this Month we could have made that known Cape, the *Cape of Good Hope*, being in the Latitude of 36 deg. 14 min. *South*, and Longitude from St. *Iago* 37 deg. 19 min. *East*. But the *Dutch* having some Forts there, it was thought no good Policy; wherefore veering to the *South*, the Cape bore *East-North-East*, some thirty Leagues off us; for heaving our Dipsy-lead[1] we were in soundings eighty Fathom depth, which the Pilots note to be in that distance.

Here we made two Sail to Leeward, and one to Windward, who directed her Course with us; but the Wind from the Shore coming *East*, they Tacked, and she passed without speaking to her: But the Leeward-most came up boldly to us and the *Ann* (we being the nearest and ready to receive them); but making them *English* built by their Galleries, we only shewed them our Colours (which they answered by St. *George's* Cross) and fired a Gun; when they brought to, and we bearing up, our Commander went Aboard one of them, the *Johanna*, a Ship of 700 Tuns laden from *Bantam*, who told us, That five more were in Company with them from the Coasts, but dispersed by Tempests; the other Ship was the *Bernardiston*; that which escaped us, the *Rebecca*.

They also inform'd us, The *French* had worsted the *Flemmings* in *India*, taken and demolished a Fort on the Island *Ceilon*; and that they had beat the *Moors* out of

---

[1] Deep sea lead; see *New Eng. Dict.*, *s. v.*

St. *Thomas*:[1] That on our side never a Ship was lost, as they heard. So likewise giving them an Account of what we knew, with some Instructions communicated on both sides, we left them to take their Course, which served them for St. *Hellens*, the *Antartick Monsoons* favouring them directly thither, and the Squadron under Captain *Munday*, if they have raised the *South* Latitude of 28. may be there a little before to expect them.

We kept on *South-East*, till we had doubled the most *Northern* Promontory of the Cape, *Cape de Angullis*,[2] (which Course would lead us to *Bantam*) when bending to the *North*, we held on till we came betwixt St. *Lawrence*[3] or *Madigascar*, and the Main, reckoned one of the four biggest Islands in the World, *viz. Sumatra*, *Java*, St. *Lawrence* and *Britannia*. The most traded Empories here, are St. *Augustine*[4] on the Island, and *Mosambique* on the Main; frequented by the *Portugals* for Elephants Teeth, Gold, Camphire, and Ambergreece. Why we creep in between this Island and the Main, Is to borrow from the Land-

[1] In 1672, on the outbreak of war between Louis XIV and the United Provinces, a French squadron under Admiral De la Haye seized Trincomalie; and the Dutch, in their panic, abandoned Cottiar and Batticaloa (Tennent, *Ceylon*.[3], ii, 60). In the same year De la Haye landed troops, and in July stormed St. Thomé, then occupied by the Musalman forces of the King of Golkonda. The French surrendered to the Dutch on 26th August, 1774 (Wheeler, *Madras in the Olden Time*, i, 75 ff.).

[2] Cabo das Agulhas, "Cape of the Needles," the most southern point of the African continent; Lat. 34° 51′ 30″ S.; long. 19° 56′ 30″ E. See Pyrard de Laval, i, 21. It is mentioned again, Letter VIII, cap. I.

[3] The name of Madagascar during the Portuguese period; so called because it was visited, after Soares, who arrived on 1st February, 1506, by d'Abreu on St. Laurence's Day, 10th August, of the same year. "Madagascar, so called by the natives: by *Ptolomy*, *Menuthyas*; by *M. Paulus Venetus*, *Magaster;* by *Thevetus*, *Albagra;* by *Mercator*, *Do Cerne*; (both unwisely); by *Tristan d'Acuna*, the *Portuguise* (who discovered it *Anno Dom.* 1508), Saint *Lawrence;* that day he first viewed it" (Herbert, 20). Also see Pyrard de Laval, i, 29 n.; Linschoten, i, 19 n.

[4] St. Augustine's Bay, on S.W. of the island, the estuary of the Onilahy River.

briezes assistance against the general stated Winds settled for these Months between the Cape and this Island.

The Sea here takes the Name of *Oceanus Orientalis*, beginning from the Cape till it joyn with the *Indian*, *Red*, and *Arabian* Seas.

Here it was we had a notable Fish stretched its self along our sides for the space of an hour: Some called it a Grampos; but those that pretended skill, would have it a young Whale: it might be in length forty Feet and upward, bolting out of the Water with a great Surf; the Mouth large, but not responsible to so large a Body, the form whereof was a Pyramid inverted, the Basis of which from Gill to Gill near five Feet in breadth, the Conus terminating with a narrow Snout; where his Mouth opening, he suckt in a huge quantity of Water, and with that same eddy his Prey, which he retains within his Jaws, but spouts the Water out with the same spurting noise our Engines make, and as immense an heighth from an hole in his Neck, opening after the fashion of a Mouth or Slit; at the performance of which Action it contracts its self into an Orbicular Figure, and again dilates its self in its Diastole: The Back is of a dark Gray without Scales, sixteen Feet over, leaping as other Fishes, but in a more Majestick manner, moving but slowly, whereby we had the sight of his Head and Neck first, (all one Rock, and as impenetrable, it being proof against the Prongs of the sharpest Harping-Iron); his whisking Tail last, near which a ridge of Fins, the true mark of Distinction for a Whale: The extreme part of his Tail extended is very broad and finny, which is the Rudder to this great Leviathan, wherewith, and two Fins more proceeding one from each side, he guides himself through his watery Territories.

May had now began, when making after that glorious Charioteer, the *Sun*, we were once more spirited with milder Weather; the Mariners casting off their wet Cloaths, cared not for any more than would slightly cover them.

We being in sight of five Small Islands off St. *Lawrence*, for fear of the Tides driving them on shore, some of our Ships anchored; by which lingring we lost two of our Companions for two days; but we steering something *West*, and lying by a-nights to prevent falling on St. *Christophers* and *Juan de Novo*,[1] both Low Lands, they had time to reach us: Being becalmed, it was the middle of the Month before we lost sight of St. *Lawrence*.

The day after we had *Meoty*[2] on our Larboard Bow, bearing *North-East* 20 Miles, High Land.

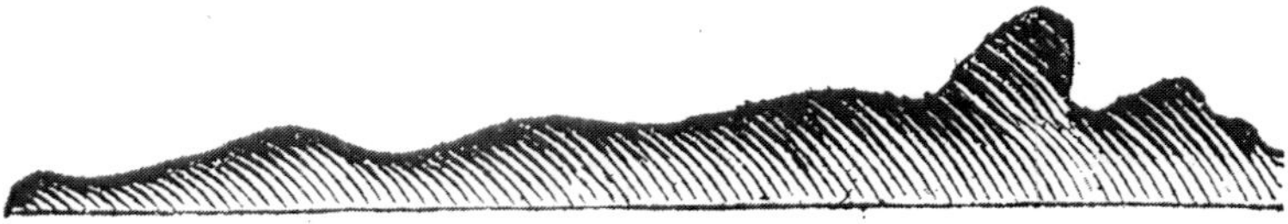

The View of Meoty.

At Night we had sight of *Mohelia*,[3] *Johanna*,[4] and *Meoty* together.

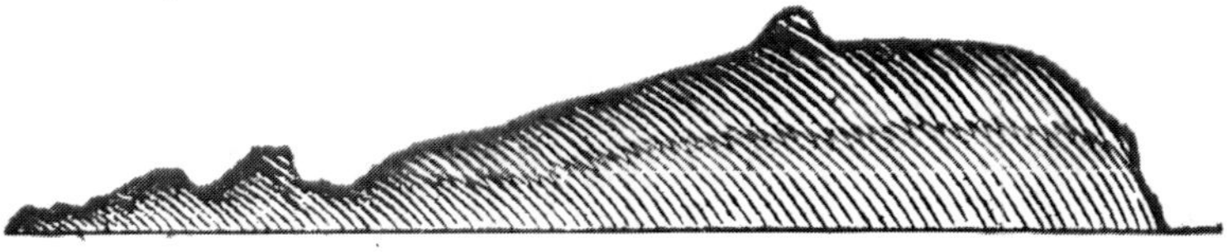

The View of Mohelia.

---

[1] St. Christopher and Juan de Nova, in the Mozambique Channel, between Madagascar and the mainland. "These Iles (call'd the Iles of *Cumro*) be 5; either because *Chumro* (or *Cumr-yne*, the *Welshmen's* Ile) is greater than the rest, or that it was first discovered: named *Cumro*, *Meottis*, *Ioanna*, *Mohelia*, & *Gazidia*; by others thus: *St. John di Castro*, *Spirito Sancto*, *Sancto Christofero*, *Anguzezia*, and *Mayotto*" (Herbert, 25). Also see Terry, 50 f.

[2] Mayotta, one of the Camores or Comoro Islands, lying between Madagascar and Cape Delgado (*Ency. Brit.*[9], vi, 220).

[3] Mohilla, the smallest of the Comoro group (*Ib.*, vi, 221). See Herbert, 27; Sir T. Roe, i, 17.

[4] Johanna "rises in a succession of richly-wooded heights till it culminates in a central peak upwards of 5000 ft. above the sea, in 12° 14′ 17″ S. lat., and 44° 27′ 34″ E. long." (*Ib.*, vi, 220). See the account by Sir T. Roe, i, 18 ff.; Grose, 19 ff.

The History of Johanna.

The Morning following we came under the *Westward* part of *Johanna*, where opposed us a lofty Ridge of Mountains, one of which advanceth its aspiring Head up to the towring Clouds: Over against which lies the Island called *Mohelia*, at the same distance *Calice* is from *Dover*; the better Island of the Two, though not so big, nor quite so Mountainous; it being more plentifully, as 'tis said, stored with Provisions; but not furnished with so safe an Harbour

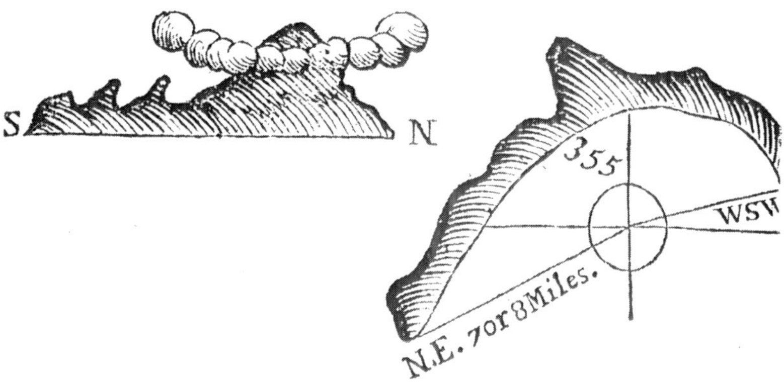

The View of Johanna.

for Ships as *Johanna*: The only difficulty here being the Weathering the Point, in which, notwithstanding several Ships have been driven off to Sea, not being able to recover the Island again, the Winds descending in desperate Gusts drive them into the Trade-winds, which here commence again. But our Ships were blest with better success, and came all safe to Anchor under a Lee-shore, which sufficiently protected them from the Winds by the highth of the Mountains. A Blessing not to be passed by without a grateful Commemoration, when half the Fleet were disabled by Distempers acquired by Salt Meats, and a long Voyage without Refreshments; and must have suffered too for want of Water, had not they met with a seasonable Recruit.

The first care then was to send the Sick Men ashore which it is incredible to relate how strangely they revived in so short a time, by feeding on Oranges and Fresh Limes, and the very smell of the Earth ; for those that were carried from the Ships in Cradles, and looked upon as desperate, in a days time could take up their Beds and walk ; only minding to fetch them anights, that the Misty Vapours might not hinder the kind Operation begun on their tainted Mass of Blood, by these Specifick Medicines of Nature's own preparing.

We had Leisure now joined to Security of the *Dutch*, for that no Ships from *India* can readily return this way into *Europe* at this time of the Year ; and the *Hollanders*, after having touched at the *Cape*, usually go first to *Batavia*, before they coast *India* ; which gave us free leave to dedicate our selves to all the Pleasure this Place could afford ; which for its Excellencies may deserve to be called Happy, as well as any the Ancients bestowed the Name of Fortunate, *Macaria* or *Fœlix* on. It lies in 12 deg. *South* Latitude, Longitude 62 deg. 4 min. It is one of the Islands of *Africa*, though lying in the *Eastern* Sea ; yet because the Coasts of *Africa* extend themselves to the Line on this *North* side of the *Cape*, we must take these Adjacent Isles in the same Account : On the *South-East* lies *Meoty*, *North-West* *Mohelia*, and *North-East* *Comero*, all Four Colonies of the *Moors* or *Arabians*, or at least in subjection to them.

But to return to *Johanna* ; the innermost part we suppose to be fruitful, by what the Verge of it declares ; for to be satisfied in that Point would be hardly worth the while, the Mountains requiring more pains to conquer than would quit cost, they being altogether inaccessible, or their Passages unknown to us.

The Relation therefore to be expected, must be of that lies lowest and nearest the Sea. The Circuit I imagine to be almost an 100 Miles, all along which, it is variously cast into Hills, and furrowed into Vales; as if Nature had plowed them on purpose for encrease. The outwart Coat of which is embroidered with *Thamarind Palmetto*[1] (from the Tree distills a Wine intoxicating, and an Oil medicinable, externally applied to Bruises, Strains, *&c.*) It yields also some store of Pine Apples, Ananas, growing on Shrubs like Artichokes. But above all, there is a Tree famed for being 14 Fathom compass, it resembles most a small Ivy Leaf; the Body seems to be many smaller incorporated into one huge one, of no other use than to be admired, *Hederâ formosior albâ*,[2] unless in opposition to the Heathen, who adore it, they throw the Dead Bodies of their Slaves under it, when Justice is executed on them, to expose them for Terrour to others, many Bones of Humane Bodies lying there at this time.[3] There is also a Gourd esteemed of them more for the large Shell than Meat; it will hold a Pailful, in Figure like a Man's Head, and therefore called a *Calabash*.[4]

Rivers they have not many, but Rivulets good store; and of such Water, that next our *Thames*, it is the best, which is justly preferred, (I mean our *Thames* Water)

---

1 Lt.-Col. D. Prain, who kindly made enquiries, has been unable to identify this tree.

2 Virgil, *Ecl.*, vii, 34.

3 Probably the Baobab (*Adansonia digitata*). "The bodies of men denied the honour of burial are often suspended within the hollow of the trunk, and these become dry and mummified" (Watt, *Econ. Dict.*, i, 107). Two of these at Bijapur were, under the native government, the trees of execution (Meadows Taylor, *Tara*, ch. 45). There is an enormous Baobab at Junnar in the Deccan, the circumference of which is 47 ft., with a hollow large enough to stable a pony in (*Indian Antiquary*, iv, 66).

4 Sir J. Murray (*New Eng. Dict.*, *s. v.*) connects it with Pers. Hind. *Kharbuza*, *Kharbûza*, "water-melon": it is an American "humorous name for the head; cf. Pg. *cabaça* = *calabaça* with *cabeça*, head."

because it bears a Body beyond others, and therefore kept till the last to be spent, always reserving a stock thereof to serve them home ; for though it stink like Puddle-water when opened first, and have a Scum on it like Oil (which the Coopers affirm they are as cautious to strike with their Adds on the Cask for fear of taking fire, as of Brandy it self) yet let it stand unbunged on the Deck twenty four hours, it recovers its goodness, and is the only Water they rely on in an *East India* Voyage and therefore they are careful to save it till the last.

Towns some few they are Masters of, but for Sumptuous Fabricks none will be found here.

Their Chiefest Town bears the Name of the Island, which is seated along the Strand, under an high Hill ; on one side refreshed with a gentle gliding stream ; on the other side recreated with a fine Plain, prodigal of its Fertility. The Town it self is to look on, an heap of Ruins, nothing remaining but the Marks of former Industry (probably the *Portugals*) here being left Walls of an huge thickness, composed of Stone, and cemented with Lime : To every House a Portal, but miserably defaced with Age ; the Planks of their Doors sewed together, their Buildings not exceeding one Story ; against these, Laziness has suggested them to lean their Flaggy Mansions : Flags especially in their Villages (by them called Cajans,[1] being Co-Coe-tree Branches) upheld with some few Sticks, supplying both Sides and Covering to their Cottages. They commonly order their Model so, as to make a Quadrangle with only one Entrance, all the rest being closed outwards without any Windows ; in which every House of Note on the Right-hand has a shady Contrivance, like the Walks to our Tennis-Courts, but not so long ; on the upper end of

---

[1] The leaf of the palm, especially that of the Nipa, used for thatching or matting : Malay, *Kajang* (Yule, *Hobson-Jobson*, 139).

which sits the Master of the Family on a Bed of Rattans, a kind of Cane: Here he, with the Steward of his House, are observed by his Slaves (who stand aloof) to spend the heat of the day.

Among these, but at some remoteness from any of their Dwellings, are two Mosques, or places for Devotion, built after the manner of our Churches (but for Magnificence much like their other Structures) with Isles and Naves walled up to the very top; within them only a place left for entrance at the West end. They are decently Matted on the Floor, though not hung so much as with a Cobweb on the Walls; which they keep (and in that to be commended) very clean. In the Piatzos[1] (for such their Porches had) stands on the Right-hand a square Stone Cistern, full of Water; and the whole without any Doors always open. The Nobler of the Two has at the West-end a round Tower, not very high; to this likewise belongs a more spacious Yard, filled with Tombs reared Man's heighth, covering them with a falling Ledge atop, leaving open a Port-hole at the North-end, where the Head lies, for a Lamp: To inrich them they are bestuck with *China* Ware of good value.

Having given you the Description thus far, I must crave leave for my Error, in not giving it the Style of Regal before now: For it proves to be the Seat of one of their Kings, which I had almost forgot, had not my greedy Eye espied a House more eminently seated, and more decently covered than the rest, but the Materials not much different; only they have allotted him a little more Air to breath forth his swelling Title, King of *Johannah* Town. Wherefore after a small Enquiry, it was manifest it was the Palace Royal; nor did I much doubt it, after we had

[1] A colonnade, "covered gallery, or walk," = piazza; see *New Eng. Dict.*, *s. v.* "... the *Meidan*, or great Piazza of the City" (Tavernier, 22).

gained admission; where did sit the King in state, at the upper end of such a Place as before was taken notice of, on a Cott, or Bed, strewed with a Quilt. On a Bench at each Elbow were placed two of his Nobles by him: We being introduced, instead of Kissing his Majesty's Hand, he took us one after another most graciously by the Fist, and by the Mouth of his Interpreter pronounced us heartily welcome, and bad us take our Seats according to our Qualities; which, after we had put our Hats on, we did; and the Interpreter with great Respect took his on the Floor crouching in the midst of us. In this manner, without show of dread or fear of being misconstrued, we talked freely of matters relating to both our States; as he first examining if we had any Gunpowder or Compass-Glasses to spare him? We seconded his Demands with what regarded Provisions for our Voyage; for which License our Captains are obliged to make him Presents of Scarlet-cloth, and other *Europe* Rarities, that they may unmolested buy the Bullocks, Cows, Goats and Hens of his Subjects. Both being at length out of Discourse, or not very well understanding one another, he speaking *Arabick*, we as good *English* as we could; we had liberty in this interval to survey the Gorgeousness of his Attire. On his Head he wore a large White Turbat, and had as good a White Shirt on his Back; from his Girdle half way his Legs, a Blue Silk Vest fringed with Purple, without Shooes or Stockins to his Feet, which he often pulling up into his Cott or Couch, would smilingly cross them, and with his Nails claw off the Dirt. By him lay a Purple Silk Robe, attended with a Black-guard of some a Dozen Slaves; compared with whom he looked great, and was a comely well Limb'd Person, though a Woolly-pated Coffery.[1]

[1] Ar., *Kāfir*, "an infidel, an unbeliever in Islām"; applied by the Arabs to pagan negroes, adopted by the Portuguese, and from them by our countrymen (Yule, *Hobson-Jobson*, 140 ff.).

His Nobles (because we are not to meet with many of them) pray take them in their best Liveries. On their Crowns they wear Caps of *Arabian* Needle-work intermixed with divers Colours; which notwithstanding no bigger than Skull-caps, they move not to the best Man in the Company; it being their Custom only to *Salam*, giving a bow with their Hands across their Breasts: Their Bodies clad in White also; about their Loins Cloth of *Arabia*, Checquered as our Barbers Aprons, but not so good (*pace tantorum virorum*) over all a thin Robe; both King and Princes encourage their Beards to their full growth.

Their Priests, one of which attended, are habited in fashion not much different, had not the Colour inclined to Black; and on their Heads a Leather Coif lined with Fur.

When we took our leaves, we Presented him and his Peers with a few Brass Rings with False Stones, with which they seemed to be well pleased.

What Towns they have of Note we could not learn; but Towns they have, if not Cities, within the Country. And certain it is, their Chief Governour is an *Arabian* Lord.

This *Johanna* Town is about Three quarters of a Mile in length, and may contain Two hundred Houses; their Streets being no broader than our Allies.

Villages are very thick, and Cottages disperst in every place.

Every Valley makes a delightful Grove, one of which exceeding all the rest; was cooled with two dainty Currents, decked with a continual Spring, charming the Senses with the real Sweets of any the most exquisitely feigned Paradises; to see Limes grow on Shrubs, Leafed and Thorned like our Crabs, Oranges, (of which there is a pleasing sort, though small, not giving place to our *China* ones) tempting the Sight from a more exalted, and less suspicious Tree. Over which the lofty Cocoes with unparallel'd straitness stretch forth their Boughs, disposed in Ranks, as if ordered by the Skilfullest Planter.

Lower than these, but with a Leaf far broader, stands the Curious Plantan, loading its tender Body with a Fruit, whose Clusters emulate the Grapes of *Canaan*, which burthened two Mens Shoulders ; below which, an odoriferous Plant seizes the Smell ; and winding through its subtile Meanders, revives the Faculties of the Brain : Here the flourishing Papaw[1] (in Taste like our Melons, and as big, but growing on a Tree leafed like our Fig-tree), Citrons, Limons, and many more, contend to indulge the Taste ; the warbling Birds the Ear ; and all things, as if that general Curse were exempted, strive to gratify the Life of Man.

Neither has Nature so played the Wanton here, as to be unmindful of the Ascending Hills, which in other places by chance are productive, but here they abound, and liberally bestow on the humble Valleys : Notwithstanding the Clime it is situate under, bears the reproach of that uninhabitable *Zone* ; yet that Aspersion is blown off by those admirably tempered Breizes of the Mountains.

The Inhabitants are black, though not so black as at St. *Iago*, as well Limb'd, and as well Featur'd ; neither so tall, nor so proud as they, but more honest : Whether out of fear of Punishment, or natural Integrity, may be left to conjecture : For our Fleet lying as now at an Anchor, some years passed, they filched some slight things from the *English* ; as likewise some Sailers from them ; the Grievances on both sides known, and the Parties detected.

---

[1] "This word seems to be from America, like the insipid, not to say nasty, fruit which it denotes (*carica papaya*, L.)" (Yule, *Hobson-Jobson*, 670 f.). Span. and Port., *papaya*, *papayo*, from a Carib dialect (*New Eng. Dict.*, *s. v.*). The Portuguese probably brought the word to the Malay Peninsula (see Mr. J. Platt, 9th Ser., *Notes and Queries*, iv, 515).

Our Commanders had their Men slashed publickly on Shore, when they cut the Throats of theirs.

To proceed; They are like the Country they live in, innocent; for as the one produces nothing hurtful, so they have always had the Character of being harmless. They are courteous to Strangers, but above all to the *English*;[1] punctual in their Words, and as ready to tax for breach of Promise: Lazy above measure, despising all Mechanical Arts; and in them Necessity compels them to employing their Priests; as in building Boats, making Mats. Yet in one thing to be wondred at, for making Old Iron, which they covet mightily, into Knives, or Tools, as sharp as Raisors; in other things rudely imitating, but not deserving the name of Artists.

The while we were there, they had a great Vessel on the Stocks; Stocks like the Checks[2] to our Long Boats; the Keel of it was a whole Tree, no otherwise fitted than it grew, only the Branches lopped off. To it, for Stem and Stern, were fastened two others, shorter; on both sides Planks sewed to the main Timbers, with the Thread of the Cocoe-nut, each Hole stopped with Pitch. Thus had they raised it to the capacity of Thirty Tuns: When it will be finished, at the rate they work, will be hard to guess.

They are Owners of several small Provoes,[3] of the same make, and Canooses,[4] cut out of one intire piece of Wood; poised with Booms to keep them from over-setting; in these they paddle with broad Sticks, not row as we with Oars.

They are very active at Climbing, Running like Jacka-

---

[1] "*Joanna* has courteous people and such as readily help strangers in necessity" (Herbert, 25). They are still friendly to foreigners, particularly to Englishmen (*Ency. Brit.*,[9] vi, 220).

[2] Boat-chocks, "clamps of wood upon which a boat rests when stowed on a vessel's deck" (Smyth, *Sailor's Word-Book*, *s. v.*).

[3] Prow, a small craft, galley (Yule, *Hobson-Jobson*, 733).

[4] A seventeenth-century form of *canoe* (*New Eng. Dict.*, *s. v.*).

napes[1] up their Cocoe-nut Trees, which they do by twisting a Band to keep close their Feet, as they raise their Bodies by their Arms grasped about the Trees.

They are not solicitous for much to cover them, only a Clout to hide their shame, trust with a String round about their Waists, in which they stick their Knives, in a readiness to cut down their Food from the Trees.

Their Slaves have a dejected Countenance, distinguished by boreing their Ears: They sit on Stones, or low Seats, their Arms folded like Monkies.

However, they are not so abject, but that they have the use of Letters, and some science in Astrology, by what I can testify: For walking the Country, and almost tired, I stept into an House, where I saw a Man writing with a Pen made of a Cane, in the bottom of a Bowl besmeared over with black; considering-a-while, at length I observed he made *Arabian* Characters, and aimed to draw a Scheme, which when he had done, he poured Water upon, and stirring it round with his Finger, wiped it out again, and as he did this, muttered seriously to himself, doing so thrice.[2] I watched what he intended, and found that a Woman lay sick there, and this Charm was her Physick.

---

[1] An ape; see p. 40.

[2] The custom of using charms for disease in this way is common. "These magic squares are, for all purposes, written on a white porcelain plate, or on paper; the inscription is then washed off with water, and the latter drank" (Herklots, *Qanoon-e-Islam*², 238). "The most approved method of charming away sickness or disease is to write certain passages of the Kur-ân on the inner surface of an earthenware cup or bowl; then to pour in some water and stir it until the writing is quite washed off; when the water, with the sacred words thus infused in it, is to be drunk by the patient" (Lane, *Mod. Egypt.*⁵, i, 320, 189). In South India bowls of mixed metal, engraved both on the outside and inside wi ' texts from the Qurân, are taken or sent by Muhammadans to Mecc where they are placed at the head of the tomb of the Prophet, and blessed; they are much valued, and used for the administration of medicine or nourishment (Thurston, *Ethnographic Notes*, 357). Also see *Relation of the Grand Seignor's Seraglio* in Tavernier, p. 73; Layard, *Nineveh and Babylon*, 511, 526; *Id.*, *Early Adventures*, i, 370; ii, 332.

Besides this, I have it on report from some that saw their Schools for Education of their Youth, where they teach them to write, and by Bundles of Characters tied together to Ape Printing. What they make their Impression on, I cannot inform you; but Paper is no despicable Commodity among them.

That *Arabick* is their Speech, is without contradiction; with what purity I am no competent Judge.

The Religion among them is *Mahometism*; their Priests not so much exercised in Learning, as the Labour of their Hands.

Their Women are fat and short, not so big Breasted as those at St. *Iago*, better clad than the Men, wearing a course Sheet about them from their Breasts below their Knees; about their Heads they wear an Hairlace,[1] or somewhat instead of it, not to tie their Hair up, which is short enough; but it may be, as our Dames in *England*, to keep the Wrinkles out of their Foreheads: In their Ears Mock-Jewels; about their Necks and Wrists trifling Bracelets of Beads, Glass, or Wire of Brass; about the small of their Legs Brass Chains, and on their Fingers Rings of the same Metal. Seemingly fearful of a White Man, as are their Children, who are much troubled with the Navel-Rupture (*Hernia umbilicalis*), either from the Windiness of their Food, or Ignorance of their Midwives in cutting the Navel-string, when they design to make the Boys good measure; which succeeds in these, for their *Penis* is of the larger shape. The Wives are very obsequious to their Husbands, seldom stirring abroad, doing the Drudgeries of the House.

They dress Fowls very well, but kill them very barbarously, pulling first their Feathers off to the Wings, then

---

[1] An obsolete term for "a string or tie for binding the hair: a fillet, headband" (*New English Dict.*, *s. v.*, where the latest quotation is from Swift, 1738).

by degrees raise the Skin, after which Torture they as slowly cut their Throats, till they have finished a short Litany, which is the Priest's Office, if at hand;[1] otherwise the Good Man of the House says Grace; they butchering their Goats in as *Jewish* a manner.

Their usual Diet is the Fruits of the Earth, not caring much for Flesh, though they have great store of Pullen, Goats, and Kine; which last but small, and not very good Meat, their Fat cleaving to the roof of the mouth; not so big as our *Welsh* Beasts, yet have this peculiar, a Bunch of Fat betwixt their Shoulders, which eaten tastes like Marrow.

Their Pasture, for want of Agriculture, rather Reeds than Grass; they have Rice in the Low-lands, and a Pease called *Garavance*:[2] On the Sand near the Sea grows *semper vivum maximum*, from whose Juice comes *Aloes*, the best from *Succotra*:[3] Here-grows *Cow-Itch*[4] in abundance, and all sorts of *Saunders*,[5] which the Seamen cut for firing to bring aboard. Destitute of Asses, Mules, and Horses, but that want compensated by a richer Commodity, *Ambergreece*,[6] for which the *Arabian* is the greatest Merchant and Sharer.

---

[1] No animal, except fish and locusts, is lawful food unless it be slaughtered according to Muhammadan law, by drawing the knife across the throat, and cutting the windpipe, the carotid arteries, and the gullet, with the words *bi'smi 'illāhi*, *Allāhu akbar*, "in the name of God; God is great" (Hughes, *Dict. of Islam*, *s. v.* Food).

[2] Calavance, Span. *garbanzos*, the bean *dolichos sinensis* (Yule, *Hobson-Jobson*, 144).

[3] Aloe socrotina or succrotina, for a full account of which, see Watt, *Econ. Dict.*, i, 184 ff.; Yule, *Hobson-Jobson*, 16.

[4] The irritating hairs of the pod of *mucuna pruriens*, the name being a corruption of the Hind. *Kewānch* (Yule, *Hobson-Jobson*, 268; Watt, *Econ. Dict.*, v, 286).

[5] Red sandal wood, the produce of *pterocarpus santalinus*; Port. *sandalo* (P. della Valle, i, 99; Watt, *Econ. Dict.*, vi, Pt. i, 359 ff.)

[6] Probably a concoction formed in the stomach or intestines of the spermaceti whale, *physeter macrocephalus*. Many fabulous accounts of this substance are given by the earlier travellers. See Barbosa, 165; Pyrard de Laval, i, 229 *n*; Linschoten, ii, 92; Tavernier, ed. Ball, ii, 138 f.; *Āīn*, i, 77 f.

Fowls for Game they have several, the best of which is the *Guinney* Hen, Turtle Doves; Crows with White Breasts, Buzzards, and Bats bodied like and near as big as a Weasel, with large Wings wove upon strong Gristles.

They have a sort of a *Jackanape* they call a *Budgee*,[1] the handsomest I ever saw.

Honey and Mullasses they have good store.

Having thus taken a Survey of them, one would think Ambition banished hence, and that Discord should have little countenance from Subjects so alike contemptible. Such is the growth of that Seed, that no Ground comes amiss to it: Here, where neither care nor Toil is burthensome, are they vexed with continual War by their opposite Neighbour the *Mohelian*, whom formerly they used to engage on Planks at Sea, casting Stones and Darts; since, by a better Instinct, they have provided themselves of securer Vessels, and as at this time devising greater, they adventure with better force, and in shrewder Battels, beginning to enquire after Swords and Guns, with the first of which the *English* do supply them: For which, and a former Courtesy of a Vessel lent them to land some Men on the Enemies Coasts, proceeds their more than ordinary love for the *English*.

How these behave themselves in War, or with what Discipline, is not in me to tell: Some Marks of their Valour many of them bear about them, as the Badges of their greatest Honour, who have their Limbs distorted, or Flesh beaten in. What the ground of these Feuds are, we cannot learn; unless the bad Influence of some malignant Planet,

---

[1] Mr. D. Ferguson suggests that this word represents Port. *bugio*, "an ape" (10 Ser., *Notes and Queries*, x, 253). Another writer (*Ibid.*, 10 Ser., x, 137) identifies the animal with that described by Ogilby from De Flacourt's account of the island: "Monkies or baboons are of several sorts. . . . A third, and the most common, called Varii (Virgis), are grey and long-nosed with great shaggy tails. These may be tamed without difficulty if taken young." In the Index he gives: "Virgees or Varii, a species of lemur."

or else that Make-bate of the world, whose greatest business is Contention, should insinuate it into them. The *Arabian* Lords of each do strive to reconcile them; which if they do for a time, it breaks out again in open War: And probable it is, that these Animosities have rendred them liable to the Subjection they are now in; whose very Islands else, with an united Force of Stones and Arms to bear them, were able to defend them.

Four days being spent in this sweet Wilderness, our Admiral by firing a Gun, and loosing his Fore-top-sail summoned us aboard.

CHAP. III.

Declares our Course from Johanna, *to our landing at* Mechlapatan.

A Fresh Gale and a fair Wind soon set us once more to the Norward of the *Equinoctial*, accompanied with soaking Showers, Thunder, and Cloudy Weather, which with the continuance of the Winds did us a kindness; for following the heels of the Sun, we were got within Twelve Degrees of him, when we sailed into the *Indian Sea, East North East*, the *Maldive* Islands being *South-East*, the *Red Sea West North West*, and the *Arabian North by West*, without labouring under that irresistible Heat we did before; by reason of which adjunct Heat, the Rains however became ntemperate; not but that they mitigated the Heat *in actu*, tho as to its effects, it proved more virulent, impregnating the Air with a diseased Constitution, whereupon we had many hung down their Heads.

About the third Degree of *North*-Latitude we lost sight of the *Magellanian* Clouds and the Crociers,[1] and raised our *Northern* Polar Director.

---

[1] See p. 48.

Having 8 deg. 53 min. *North* Latitude, we left the Sun to run his Race to the *North*; and steering *East* to raise our Longitude, we fell into a Channel between the *Maldivæ*[1] (a Concatenation of Islands from the *Eqator* hither, and here only parted by this Channel, the rest of them lying scatteredly to the 10th deg. of *North* Latitude) which makes us lye by a-nights, (signified by One Light out of the Main-Top of our Admiral[2] (which he always carries at Night), and another out of the middle Lanthorn on the Poop, answered by all the rest with one at the same place), for fear of falling foul of them, the Weather continuing wet, dark, and tempestuous.

After which we shaped our Course *East South-East*, when the Admiral fired a Gun, spreading St. *George*'s Flag in the Mizen-shrowds for a Consultation, knowing we began to draw near *Ceilon*, an Island in the *East-India*, divided from Cape *Cory* by *Ptolomy*,[3] *Comory* by our Modern Authors, by a narrow, swift, and unnavigable Current, where the *Flemings* have nested themselves in the *Portugals* Castles at *Columbo*, *Point de Gaul*,[4] and elsewhere; so that if at all, we are to meet with them hereabouts, they commonly having a Fleet of Ships in these Seas: We out of necessity are forced to make this Land, and were it peaceable Times should sail all along in sight of it, till we came upon the Coast of *Cormandel*.[5]

---

[1] The Maldive Archipelago, extending from Lat. 7° 7′ N. 0° 42′ S., a space of 540 miles. The classical account of the group is that of Pyrard de Laval, i, 93 ff.

[2] As elsewhere, the leading ship of the fleet.

[3] Κομαρία ἄκρον καὶ πόλις—Ptolemy VIII, i, § 9. On Cape Comorin see Yule, *Hobson-Jobson*, 238.

[4] See Temple's note on Bowrey, who has "Point de Gala" (p. 75) where the other forms of the name are collected; also Yule, *Hobson-Jobson*, 360. Colombo was captured by the Dutch in 1656; they held Galle from 1646 (Tennent, *Ceylon*³, ii, 44 f.). Also see Bruce, *Annals*, i, 24 f., ii, 39, Manucci, iv, 81.

[5] Choramandala, the Chola country: the East Coast (Yule, *Hobson-Jobson*, 256 ff.).

Wherefore our Commander returning on board, after assigning every one his Post, to be ready on any surprize, he found a Chearfulness in all to obey him.

Here two Whales, bigger than the former, shewed themselves.

In the dead of the night a lamentable Outcry was caused by some of our Men on the Forecastle, who looking out thought they had seen a Rock, with which these Seas abound, whereupon they cried out, *A Breach, A Breach*; which made the Mates leap out of their Cabins with the same grisly Look as if going to give up their last Accounts: Here was Doomsday in its right Colours, Distraction, Horror, and Amazement had seized on all, one commanding this, another acting quite contrary; the Breach surrounding us, every one expected the fatal stroke, when the Ship should be dashed in pieces. In this Panick Fear, had any had so much heart as to have ventured a Composition for his empty Noddle by looking over-board, he might have discovered the Jig: For at length it was evident that only a Chorus of Porpoises had taken the Sea in their Dance; which Morris once over, the Seas were quiet, and our Men left to repose themselves with a shorter Nap than they thought themselves like to have.

Five days after our Summer Solstice we had soundings 14 Fathom, and at break of day had sight of *Ceilon*, when we altered our Course to *East North-East*; it bore from us *North by West* 12 Leagues, the out-Land low, but rarely enriched with Woods of Cinamon, from whence only it is brought.[1]

[1] The true Cinnamon is a native of the Ceylon forests, but now cultivated on the West Coast of that island; it is also to be met with in the forests of Tenasserim, and is now being experimentally cultivated in S. India (Watt, *Econ. Dict.*, ii, 324). For the trade, see Hakluyt, iii, 223.

This is the first Shore presented its self in *India*: The Inland hath a Prospect over the Sea: It lies in *North* Latitude 6 deg. 3 min. and Longitude from *Johanna* 37 deg. 10 min. *East.*

This is the Island where (if true) the Elephants are bred, who, transported, exact Homage from all Elephants of other places, and they withal, by prostrating (as it were) their Necks between their Feet, submissively acknowledge it.[1]

At Nights we stood off to Sea to escape the insidious Rocks, a-days we made for the Land, to gain the Land-Breizes, which are not felt far off at Sea, by reason of the Constancy of the Trade-Winds: They begin about Midnight, and hold till Noon, and are by the *Portugals* named

The View of Ceilon.

Terrhenoes;[2] more *North* they are more strong, and hardly give way to the Sea-Breizes, which sometimes succeed the others twelve hours, but not always on this Coast.

Two Days passed after we made Land, we discovered three Country Junks a-head, and coming up with them we commanded their Skippers on board: examining their

---

1 "It [Ceylon] hath also yron, Flaxe, Brimstone, and such like ware, also many Iuorie bones, and divers Elephantes, which are accounted far the best in all India, and it is by daylie experience found to be true, the Elephantes of all other places and countries being brought before them they honour and reverence those Elephantes" (Linschoten, i, 80 f.). The same story is told by Tavernier (ed. Ball, ii, 317), where the editor remarks that Tennent (*Ceylon*[3], ii, 380) has misunderstood the remarks of the traveller. Mirkhond (Elliot Dowson, *H. of India*, ii, 454 f.) calls the Ceylon elephants Muslim, or faithful to Islām, because they bowed as Muhammadans do at prayer.

2 Port., *terrenho vento*, the "land-wind" of S. India, the "along-shore" wind of Ceylon (Yule, *Hobson-Jobson*, 503; Tennent, *Ceylon*[3], i, 57.

Cockets,[1] they produced *English* Passes, the Masters of two of them being *Portugals*, the other a *Moor*, from whom was taken a Packet of *Dutch* Letters: Their Crew were all *Moors*[2] (by which word hereafter must be meant those of the *Mahometan* Faith), apparell'd all in white, on their Heads white Scull-caps, their Complexions tawny: Their Junks had three Masts, wearing an *East-India* strip'd Ancient, and might contain an 100 Tuns apiece.

They managed their Sails but aukwardly, and are unskilful in Maritime Affairs; wherefore in any long Voyage they employ *Europeans* to navigate their Vessels.

Coasting along, some *Cattamarans*[3] (Logs lashed to that advantage that they waft off all their Goods, only having a Sail in the midst, and Paddles to guide them) made after us, but our Ships having fresh way, we were unwilling to tarry for them; besides, at that instant we espied under the Shore a mighty Vessel, with her Yards and Top-Masts lower'd; but they continuing to follow us, the *Anne* lay by for one of them, who affirmed that a Fleet of 24 Sail of *Batavians* were passed to retake St. *Thomas* from the *French*. The *East-India* Merchant and *Antelope* by this were up with the Vessel under shore, who proved to be a great Junk of the *Moors*: Overagainst where she rode, a fair *Pagod*[4] or Temple of the *Gentus*, beleaguer'd with a Grove of Trees (excepting that it was open towards the Sea) cast a Lustre bright and splendid, the Sun reverberating against its refulgent Spire, which was crowned with a Globe white as Alabaster, of the same tincture with the whole.

---

[1] "A document sealed by the officers of the custom-house, and delivered to merchants as a certificate that their merchandise has been duly entered and has paid duty (now disused)" (*New Eng. Dict.*, *s. v.*).

[2] A Muhammadan, particularly a person of that faith inhabiting India (Yule, *Hobson-Jobson*, 581).

[3] Rafts formed of three or four logs of wood lashed together, used on the S. Indian Coast (Yule, *Hobson-Jobson*, 173).

[4] For an account of this difficult word, see Yule, *Hobson-Jobson*, 652 ff.

Nearer the Point we descried a Town, in which a Castle overawing it, and upon the highest Pinacle *Dutch* Colours, which high Noon gave us to be *Sandraslapatan*,[1] a Factory of theirs, our Staff having as much as together with the Sun's declination made 11 deg. 50 min. *North* Latitude, but 10 Leagues to the *South* of *Fort St. George*, where our Commanders were to touch first, according to their Charter-Party.

Whereupon we put abroad our Jacks, Ancients, and Penants, and running out all our Guns, it was unanimously consented to fight our way through the *Flemish East-Indians*, had we not seen a *Mussoola*[2] hailing our Admiral, which came off with Advice from the Agent: This Afternoon therefore we lay by, the Admiral calling a Council aboard him; and at night our *Mercury* was waited on

The View of Sandraslapatan.

towards the Shore by the *Bombaim*: All this while we lay in sight of *Sandraslapatan*, whose Soil is Fat and Opulent, like their *Netherlands*.

The Water here ran smooth and discoloured: Till once again committing ourselves to the Sea, we ploughed deeper Water, *North-East*, of a *Cærulean* dye.

The next day we saw a *French* Man of War, and he us, but would not trust us. We knew him to be *French* by our Intelligencer, who laid out his Station, where he had encountered five *Batavians*, and discomfited them.

---

[1] Sadras (Tamil, Shathurangappattanam, "City of the four arms. *i.e.*, infantry, cavalry, elephants, chariots"), 40 miles S. of Madras, The Dutch factory was established in 1647; and the place was captured by the British in 1765 (*Madras Adm. Man.*, iii, 775; Welsh, *Military Rem.*, i, 139 f.).

[2] The surf-boat of S. India: properly a fishing-boat (Tamil, *māsūlu*; Hind., *machhlī*, "a fish") (Yule, *Hobson-Jobson*, 602).

This Day's observation made 30 m. to the *North* of *Fort St. George*. We were beating now against the Wind (which blows fiercely from the Shore) and a strong Current, which had set us 14 deg. 20 min. *North* in three days time, when the *Junks* we compelled with us hither, had the liberty to make the best of their way for the Bay of *Bengala*; for which the Winds served them well enough, though full in our Teeth, who laboured for the Land.

However, in four days time we met with the *Freshes* off the Shore caused by the Upland Rains:[1] The Sea despising to defile its purer Azure with their Muddy Green. The same Antipathy was held betwixt the lively Fishes and their slimy Brood, they intermixing with such unfriendly Concord; for playing in whole Shoals about the Edges, they would not exceed the Limits the jarring Torrents had won upon each other. So the fierce *Tigris* in his swift Career neglects the scorned *Arethusa*, and she with the like disdain retaliates his unkindness, neither Stream mixing either Fish or Water.

Thus quartering this Sublunary Globe, out of *Europe* into *Africa*, from thence cruising on the Coast of *Brasil* upon the *American* Seas, till joining with the *Ethiopick*, we double the *Cape of good Hope* into *Africa* again, at last we came in sight of the *Asian* Shores; and the latter end of *June* we cast Anchor in *Mechlapatan* Road;[2] which was composed of Shoals and Deeps, where we found three *Portugal* Ships riding.

---

[1] Compare the account of Bowrey (171 f.) of the floods in the Ganges.

[2] Masulipatam (Telugu, Machlīpattanamu, "fish-town"), Lat. 16° 11′ N., Long. 81° 10′ E. An English Agency was established in 1611; a factory in 1621, which was removed to Armegaim in 1628: re-established under the *farmān* of the King of Golkanda in 1632. It then became the centre of English trade in those parts, being the chief seaport of Golkanda, which was not subdued by the Mughals till 1687 (Hunter, *H. of British India*, ii, 74). The Dutch in 1660, and the French in 1669, also established factories. The Portuguese, as Fryer states, also had an establishment (Birdwood, *Report*, 88, 178).

Our Fleet expressed their joy by the roaring of the wide-mouth'd Cannon, and the sounding of the shriller Trumpets; which the *English* Factory, welcomed by displaying their Flag (being allowed no Ordnance, but what they privily plant for their own security) as being under the Tutelage of the Natives, as also are the *Portugals* and *Flemmings* (who each have here their Staples) so in like manner all they have any Commerce with: No act of Hostility, either on Shore, or in the Road, being tollerated without leave first obtained; those on Shore being the Pledges forfeited on the breach of Peace.

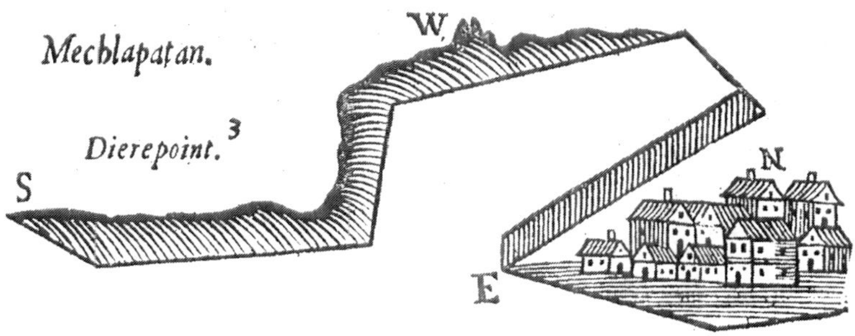

Bar Town.

The firm Land was plain and nothing elevated beyond the Trees, unless Edifices of the *European* erection.

---

[3] A misprint for Dievi Point, Divy or Divi (Skt., *Dvīpa*, "an island"), being the headland at the mouth of the river Kistna (Lat. 15° 57′ N., Long. 81° 13′ E.), 16 miles from Musulipatam. Bowrey (pp. 55, 110) calls it point Due. A. Hamilton (*New Account*, i, 371) speaks of "firewood from the islands of Diu, a low point of land that lies near Matchulipatam." In 1713-14 the Company engaged with Khwāja Sarhad to "get the grant of Dew Island near Metchlepatam" (Wilson, *Early Annals*, ii, 158).

CHAP. IV.

Takes up our stay at Mechlapatan, *to our Landing at* Fort St. George.

THE next Morning the Second of the Factory (the Chief) being at *Fort St. George*, visited the Admiral, and ordered the Treasure to be set on Shore.

That if the empty *Hollander* should be so hardy as to face us, their small hopes of Plunder might abate their Courage; which otherwise might tempt them to attack us with greater vigour.

The Boat-men that came for it were of a Sun-burnt Black, with long black Hair, tied up in a Clout of Calicut Lawn,[1] girt about the Middle with a Sash, in their Ears Rings of Gold; those that were bare-headed, were shorn all to one Lock, which carelessly twisted up (some have foolishly conceited) to be left for *Perimel*[2] (one of their Prophets) to hold fast by when he should haul them to Heaven;[3] but more truly to preserve them from the *Plica*

---

[1] Calico (Yule, *Hobson-Jobson*, 147).

[2] Perumāl, "the great person," the most common appellation of Vishnu in the Tamil country (Ziegenbalg, *South Indian Gods*, 83). Tavernier (ed. Ball, ii, 190), speaking of the belief in God, the Creator, writes: "They call him in some places Permesser [Paramesvara], in others Peremael, as, for example, towards the coast of Malabar; and Vvistnou [Vishnu] in the language of the *Brahmins* who inhabit the coast of Coromandel." The name appears in the title of Cherumān Perumāl, the last Hindu ruler of Chera, who, on his conversion to Islām in the ninth century, sailed as a pilgrim to Mecca (Barbosa, 102; Linschoten, i, 71; Rowlandson, *Tohfut-ul-Mujahideen*, 55 ff.; Logan, *Man. of Malabar*, i, 195).

[3] Here he seems to apply to Hindus the common Muhammadan belief that the scalp-lock is retained by them in order that by it they may be pulled up to Heaven. Lane (*Mod. Egypt*[5], i, 35), speaking of the *Shūshah*, writes: "This last custom (which is almost universal among them) is said to have originated in the fear that if the Muslim should fall into the hands of an infidel, and be slain, the latter might cut off the head of his victim, and, finding no hair by which to hold it, put his impious hand into the mouth, in order to carry it: for the beard might not be sufficiently long: but it was probably adopted from the Turks:

Polonica,[1] which attends long Hair not cleanly kept, and to which these People are incident.

Among these, some more modish than the rest, as going in a Garb more Civil, Coiling Calicut about their Heads, Turbat fashion, on their Bodies light Vests, underneath long loose Breeches, and swadled about the Waist with a Sash; offered their Service for a small Pension, to execute our Affairs on Shore, or wait on us Aboard.

These spake *English*, and acquainted us, how the *French* had set fire to four Vessels of the *Moors*, and made Prize of four more, as they were in this Road not two Months ago; that they had constrained some *Dutch* Factories to run on score to supply their wants with Victuals, and other Necessaries; whose Credit, by these Emergencies, and their Cash failing, begins to sink: Money being here not only the Nerves and Sinews, but the Life it self of Trade.

Being sent for on Shore by the desire of the Factory, by one of the Country Boats, I was landed at *Mechlapatan*: These Boats are as large as one of our Ware-Barges, and almost of that Mould, sailing with one Sail like them, but padling with Paddles instead of Spreads, and carry a great Burthen with little trouble; outliving either Ship or *English* Skiff over the Bar. Which by the rapid motion of the Waves driving the Sands into an Head, makes a noise as deafning as the Cataracts of *Nile*, and not seldom as difficult a Downfal. Over this the Land shuts us up on

for it is generally neglected by the Bedawees; and the custom of shaving the head is of late origin among the Arabs in general, and practised for the sake of cleanliness." The traditional explanation of the custom is given by Burton (*Ar. Nights*, i, 284: ix, 152: cf. Terry, 126).

[1] A loathsome disease of the scalp, prevalent in Poland, due to a fungus of the genus *Trichophyton*. Bernier (p. 316) says of the Jogis: "Some have hair hanging down to the calf of the leg, twisted and entangled into knots, like the coat of our shaggy dogs, or rather like the hair of those afflicted with that *Polish* disease, which we call *la Plie*."

both sides, and the stiller Waters contentedly do part their Streams to embrace the Town.

Near which a Fort or Blockade[1] (if it merit to be called so) made of Dirt, hides half a score great Guns; under the command of which several *Moors Junks* ride at Anchor. A Bow-shot from whence the Town it self, environed with a Mud Wall, entrenched with a stinking Moras, and at some time Moated with the Sea, creates a spacious Prospect; it is of Form oblong.

Their *Bank Solls*,[2] or Custom-House Keys, where they land, are Two; but mean, and shut only with ordinary Gates at Night.

The High-streets are broad, set forth with high and lofty Buildings, the Materials Wood and Plaister, beautified without with folding Windows, made of Wood, and lattised with Rattans, entring into Balconies shaded by large Sheds covered with Tiles:[3] Within a Square Court, to which a stately Gatehouse makes a Passage, in the middle whereof a *Tank* vaulted, with a flat Roof above, and on it Terras Walks are framed, the one to wash in, in the heat of the day; the other to take the Air in the cool of the day; the whole Fabrick intire within its self, covered atop Taber-like.

The poorer, of which multitudes are interspersed, both in their High-streets and Allies, are thatched, cast round as Bee Hives,[4] and walled with Mud; which in the Summers drought often take fire, and lay the taller equal with the ground.

---

[1] An earlier instance of the word, and used in a sense not recorded in the *New Eng. Dict.*

[2] Bankshall, a warehouse, of which the origin is doubtful (Yule, *Hobson-Jobson*, 61).

[3] Bowrey (p. 106) speaks of Masulipatam as "the great Bazar of these parts for above 100 miles in circuit."

[4] For these primitive round houses in India, see Crooke, *Things Indian*, 257.

For publick Structures their principal Streets present sundry Mosques, one Custom-house, one Court of Judicature, and that but mean.

For Places of resort there are three *Buzzars*, or Market-places, crowded both with People and Commodities.

On the *North-East* a Wooden Bridge, half a Mile long, leading to the *Bar* Town ; on the *North-West* one, a Mile Long, tending to the *English* Garden, and up the Country.[1] Each of which have a Gate-house, and a strong Watch at the beginning, next the Town : Both these are laid over a Sandy Marsh, where Droves of People are always thronging.

The present Incumbents are the *Moors*, *Persians*, *Gentiles*; Sojourners *Armenians*, (who maintain their Correspondence over Land) *Portugals*, *Dutch* and *English* ; and some few *French*.

For the Story of it, and with it of the Kingdom ; the *Gentues*, the *Portugal* Idiom for *Gentiles*, are the *Aborigines*, who enjoyed their freedom, till the *Moors* or *Scythian Tartars* (whether mediately from *Persia* or immediately from that overflow of *Tamerlane* into these Parts, is not material, since the both pretend to the same Extract, and that will be fitter declared in another place) undermining them, took advantage of their Civil Commotions. For one Cast or Tribe (by the Chief of which they were ruled) clashing with another, overturned all ; which that we may the better understand,

These Tribes were distinguished by their occupations,

---

[1] Streynsham Master mentions two bridges in Masulipatam in 1677 : "The Towne of Metchlepatam stands about half a mile from the sea, a small creek with a bar to it going up to it, and every spring tide the water overflows round about the towne soe that there is no goeing out but upon two wooden bridges" (*Temple's Note to Bowrey*, 63). "Round the fort stretches a vast expanse of waste land, swamp during the rainy season but firmer in summer, over which a causeway about two miles in length, running in a westerly direction, leads to the native town" (*Imp. Gaz.*, xvii, 215).

espousing therefore Vocations as well as Kindred; and thereby, as one was a more honourable Calling than the other, so they stood upon their Nobility in that Imployment, never marrying out of it.

As the Head were the *Brachmines*, the Ancient *Gymnosophists*; out of whom branched their Priests, Physicians and their Learned Men.

Next in esteem were the *Rashwaws*, *Rashpoots*,[1] or Souldiers.

But the most insolent were the Artificers; as the Engravers, Refiners, Goldsmiths, Carpenters, and the like; who behaved themselves not only disrespectfully to their Superiours, but tyranically to those of a viler Rank; as the Husbandmen and Labourers. Whereupon they jointly conspired their Ruin, and with that their own Slavery; taking the *Moors* to their assistance, who not only reduced the Usurpers to Composition, which was, That they should be accounted the Off-scum of the People, and as base as the *Holencores*[2] (whom they account so, because they Defile themselves by eating any thing, and do all servile Offices) and not be permitted to ride in a *Palenkeen* at their Festivals or Nuptials, but on Horseback, which they count an high Disgrace; but they also took the Power into their own hand; which though Despotical, the *Gentus* endure, rather than endeavour the recovery of their former Liberty, and to subvert it from a Monarchy into an Aristocracy.

Their King reigning is a *Moor*, raised to the Throne from the lowest ebb of Fortune.[3]

---

[1] The old British traders meant by Rājput the squalid, "military" retinue of the petty chiefs and dignitaries of the country (Yule, *Hobson-Jobson*, 754; Bowrey, 19, 83 f.).

[2] Hatālkhor, "one who eats food slain according to the Muhammadan ritual"; a term applied euphemistically to the sweeper or scavenger caste (Yule, *Hobson-Jobson*, 409).

[3] This is a confused account of the revolution at Golkonda, of which a narrative is given by Ovington (pp. 525 ff.), under the title of "The History of the Late Revolution in the Kingdom of Golkonda."

For it being in the breast of the Regent to appoint his Successor, his Predecessor, on defect of his own Children, raised him; by the practice of *Siegmanjaffa*, his Chief Eunuch (who are made in this Kingdom the prime Ministers of State) partly to strengthen his own Interest by ingratiating with the Heir Apparent, and partly out of gratitude to the Young man's Father, a Great Man, and of the Bloud-Royal, who, when alive, was the promoter of *Siegmanjaffa*: This same Prince of the *Chias*,[1] or *Sophian* Extract, was raked out of the Embers of Oblivion.

Where you must note, That though his Father expired a Blazing Comet in the Court, yet at the death of any Nobleman, his Wealth falls all into the King's hands; whereby this poor Gentleman for a long time lived an obscure and miserable Life, no one taking his word for the Victuals he put into his Belly: But upon the old King's importunity for one to sway the Scepter after him of his own Line, *Siegmanjaffa* urged him; and placed him poor and lean as he was, where the King might see him, but not he the King.

At first the King rejected him, as having no promising look; still *Siegmanjaffa* interceded, and desired his Lord to allow him like a Gentleman, and see to what use he would expend his Money; Which condescended to, a *Brachmin* (who are become the Farmers of the King's Rents) was dispatched to offer him the Loan of Money,

---

Mr. Irvine suggests that "Siegmanjaffa" represents Sayyid Muzaffar, the minister who procured the accession of Abū,'l Hasan to the throne in 1672. But he was not a eunuch. The eunuch concerned with him in these transactions was Sīdī Musē Khān, the Mahāldār or head eunuch, a Habshī or Abyssinian. "The chiefest persons about the King were *Moso Cawne*, *Siud Meer Zapher*, and *Mushuke*" (Ovington, 529 f.). Mr. Irvine refers to Khāfī Khān, *Muntakhab-ut-tawārīkh*, vol. iii (unpublished), B. M. Addl. MS. 26265, fol. 418 a. D. Havart, *Op en ondergang van Cormandel*, Pt. II, p. 214, calls him "Seyid Muzaffer." See Manucci, iii, 132, iv, 444.

[1] Shī'ah, called "Sophian" because connected with the Sūfī or Ṣafavī dynasty of Persia.

which he willingly accepted of, and therewith put himself into an handsome Equipage, both for Apparel and Attendants, (which specious Shews recommend here more than profoundness of parts) and withal Fed and Whored (which is a great point of Manhood) as well as the best of them. Wherefore after a short time he was again brought into the King's Presence, who now began to have some hopes of him; and therefore to try him farther, he gave him a constant supply of Money; and bad *Siegmanjaffa* put him on some laudable Enterprize in his Army, of which *Siegmanjaffa* was General; which he undertook with much Alacrity, and behaved himself with that Gallantry, that at length the Old King sent him a Tipstaff with a Royal Robe, requiring him to come to Court in one of the King's own *Palenkeens*: At which he was dismay'd, Saying he should never return to his House again.

However, by *Siegmanjaffa's* encouragement he apparelled himself, and rode on the King's *Palenkeen*: His jealousy was grounded on a barbarous Custom of the *Eastern* Monarchs, who when any Subject becomes suspected, send them alike honourable Presents with those in Favour, which in their receit only shall testify to the World the King's Displeasure, though they whom they are designed for, live not to know the cause, being poysoned by them before they can plead for themselves. But he was assured no ill Intentions were towards him when speaking with the King face to face, he declared him his Successor to the Crown, which not long after he was established in by the Death of his Master.

His residence is at *Gulconda*, the Metropolis, and bearing the Name of the Kingdom, fifteen days journey *West* from hence.

Under him *Siegmanjaffa* orders the whole Realm, amassing great Treasures (though he himself pays Homage to the *Great Mogul*) exacting every Man's Estate when he pleases, mulcting them at his own Will, squeezing the common People to perfect Penury: Besides the Reversions of Great Mens Estates, he has large Revenues from his Diamond Mines, which he lets out yearly to those bid most.

His Expences are inconsiderable, his Subjects in their distinct Provinces maintaining his Soldiers, of whom he has a standing Army of an Hundred thousand Horse and Foot, when all together; besides Two hundred Elephants in continual readiness, which are provided for by the Farmers of his Revenues.

All that he consumes is on his Voluptuousness, with which he is swallowed up.

The Kingdom of *Gulconda* extends from 10 deg. *North* Latitude, to 19 deg. ½ along the Coasts of *Coromandel*, and up into the Country Three hundred *Course* (which is a Mile and a quarter) though in some places thinly inhabited.[1]

The next in Dignity to *Siegmanjaffa*, is the Governor of *Mechlapatan*, an Eunuch also, and a Slave to *Siegmanjaffa*, who came through the Town while we were here, waited on by a Noble Train, besides Soldiers and Followers; having an Elephant led before his *Palenkeen*, which none presume to do, unless the King honour them therewith;

---

[1] The Kingdom of Golkanda extended from the territory of Bījapur and Ahmadnagar east as far as the opposite coast: roughly from 78° to 82° E. Long.; from Chanda on the N. to the Kistna river on S. Its eastern boundary was the Godāvarī (Grant Duff, 36; *Bombay Gaz.*, i, Pt. II, 584). "The most powerful of the Kings of Decan, next to Visiapour, is the King of Golconda. His Kingdom borders on the East side, upon the Sea of Bengala; to the North upon the Mountains of the Countrey of Orixa; to the South, upon many countries of Bisnagar, or Ancient Narsingue, which belongs to the King of Visiapour; and to the West, upon the Empire of the Great Mogul, by the province of Balagate, where the village of Calvar is, which is the last place of Mogolistan on that side" (Thevenot, Pt. III, 93). For the Course or Kos, see Yule, *Hobson-Jobson*, 261. Fryer's estimate of the length is very low. Elsewhere (Letter III, chap. IV) he states that three "course", equal 7½ miles.

nor to ride on any but Females, unless of the Royal Family, who may only mount a Male to ride in State through their Cities. His Substitute here is a *Chias Moor* who takes charge of the Keyes every Night.

Over the *Gentues* they keep a strict hand, entrusting them with no Place of Concern, using them as Mechanicks and Servitors, to few of them attributing the Title of Merchants; though in this Town of *Moors* and *Persians* there are many Owners of good Trading Vessels.

The *Persians* have planted themselves here through the Intercourse of Traffick as well as Arms, being all of them at their first coming, low in Condition; but inspired by the Court-Favour, and making one of their own Nation always their Executors, they arrive to Preferment. Nor are any of these so exempted when they grow too rich, to be deplumated by the same hand.

Their way of living is truly Noble, having a Retinue which bespeaks their Greatness as they rise in Fortune or the King's Grace.

Magnaque est Comitum æmulatio quibus primus ad Principem locus, & Principum cui acerrimi & plurimi Comites. Hæc dignitas, hæ vires, magno semper electorum juvenum globo circumdari; in pace decus, in bello præsidium.[1] Each contending to have the most numerous and handsomest Fellows for Attendance; their Pride at home, and abroad their Safeguard.

However, for the *English* Honour be it spoke, none of them surpass the Grandeur of our *East-India* Company, who not only command, but oblige their utmost Respect; none of their Servants showing themselves in Publick without a Company answerable to theirs, and exceeding them in Civility of Garb and Manners. When the Chief made his Entry at his Return from the Fort, it was very

---

[1] Tacitus, *Germania*, 13.

Pompous, all the Merchants of Esteem going to meet him with loud *Indian* Musick and Led-Horses: Before his *Palenkeen* an Horse of State, and two St. *George*'s Banners, with *English* Trumpeters; after him the Factors on Horse-back, and lusty Fellows running by their sides with *Arundells*,[1] (which are broad Umbrelloes held over their heads,) Soldiers and Spear men Two hundred at least, and after these a Row of *Palenkeens* belonging to *English* and other Merchants.

At Meals their Domesticks wait on them with Obeisance suitable to great Potentates, enclosing their Tables, which are strewed liberally with Dainties served up in Plate of *China*; *Nam nulla aconita bibuntur fictilibus*, says *Juvenal*,[2] which crack when poysoned; which whether true or false (since it is so much practised in this Country by way of Revenge) is but a necessary Caution by all means to avoid.

They fan the Air with Peacocks Tails set in huge Silver Handles,[3] and chiefly now, because the busy Flies would cover the Table, were they not beaten off. Abroad shading their heads with broad Targets held over their heads; washing and rubbing them in their *Tanks*; wanting in no Office may render them acceptable to their Masters.

But not to detract from the Inhabitants, their Solemnities

---

[1] A state umbrella, as contrasted with Sombrero, which was usually applied to the Chinese kind, made of paper (Yule, *Hobson-Jobson*, 770).

[2] Sat., x, 25. The Anglo-Indian of the seventeenth century shared in the belief current in many parts of India to the present day, that a peculiar composition of china, when brought in contact with poison of any kind, cracks, and thus betrays the danger arising from the food. The Lepchas of the Himalaya "drink out of little wooden cups, turned from knots of maple or other woods. . . . Some are supposed to be antidotes against poison, and hence fetch an enormous price; they are of a peculiar wood, rarer and pale-coloured. I have paid a guinea for one such, hardly different from the common sort, which cost but 4*d.* or 6*d.*" (Hooker, *Himalayan Journals*, 90; Huc, Gabet, *Travels in Tartary, Tibet and China*, ed. Hazlitt, ii, 144).

[3] The *Chaunri* (Yule, *Hobson-Jobson*, 214).

are very Courtly, commonly performed by Night with the noise of Drum, Shawm, and Fife; especially at their Weddings, when the meanest (excepting those protested against) of the *Gentues* must not be denied his Week's Jollity in a *Palenkeen*, and a Guard of Targets, Swords, and Javelins, and others bearing the Ensigns denoting the Honour of their Tribe. If any of the subjected Tribes (as they count them) assume the Honour (though the Governor connive) they fall together by the ears, and drag him shamefully by the Hair of the Head to the place he first set forth.[1]

They are array'd in White Vests, girt with Sashes, small Turbats on their Heads, long Breeches to their Heels; the *Gentues* barefoot mostly; The *Moors* and *Persians* shod with Sandals, and over their Shoulders a Silk Mantle of what colour they fancy.

The *English* keep their fashion, though cloathed in white: The *Armenians* like the Inhabitants.

The *Moors* are very grave and haughty in their demeanor, not vouchsafing to return an Answer by a Slave, but by a *Deubash*,[2] who is the Interpreter. Their chiefest Delight and Pride is to be seen smoking Tobacco cross-legg'd in a great Chair at their doors, out of a long Brass Pipe adapted to a large Crystal *Hubble-bubble*,[3] fixed in a Brass Frame, their Menial Servants surrounding them.

All of this Robe's way of Salute is by lifting their Hand to their Head, except the *Armenians*, who move their Turbats as we our Hats.

The *Moors* are by Nature plagued with Jealousy, cloistring their Wives up, and sequestring them the sight

---

[1] The use of the palanquin is a mark of dignity (Yule, *Hobson-Jobson*, 660).

[2] Hind. *dubhāshiyā*, "a man skilled in two languages" (Yule *Hobson-Jobson*, 328).

[3] See p. 43.

of any besides the *Capon* that watches them. When they go abroad, they are carried in close *Palenkeens*, which if a Man offer to unvail it is present death; the meanest of them not permitting their Women to stir out uncovered; of whom they are allowed as many as they can keep.

Their Matches are contrived by their Parents when young; at Seven Years the Son being taken from the Mother, the Sister from the Brother, and not a Father, though Fourscore and ten, suffered the Interview of his Daughter; every Dwelling having Apartments allotted for this Confinement.

The *Gentues* observe not that strictness, both Sexes enjoying the open Air. Their Women are manacled with Chains of Silver (or Fetters rather) and hung with Ear-rings of Gold and Jewels, their Noses stretched with weighty Jewels, on their Toes Rings of Gold, about their Waste a painted Clout, over their Shoulders they cast a Mantle; their Hair tied behind their Head (which both in Men and Women is naturally very long); a-top a Coronet of Gold beset with Stones; compleatly bodied, and so flexible that they are excellent Dancers, and good at Feats of Activity: I having seen them hold Nine Gilded Balls in play with their Hands and Feet, and the Muscles of their Arms and Legs, a long time together without letting them fall:[1] They are clearer complexion'd than the Men.

As for their dealing in the World, they are well skill'd,

---

[1] Tennent (*Ceylon*[3], ii, 185) describes a juggler: "Keeping a series of brass balls in motion by striking them with his elbows, as well as his hands. Balancing on his nose a small stick with an inverted cup at top, from which twelve perforated balls were suspended by silken cords, he placed twelve ivory rods in his mouth, and so guided them by his lips and tongue, as to insert each in a corresponding aperture in the ball, till the whole twelve were sustained by the rods, and the central support taken away." Forbes (*Oriental Mem.*[2], ii, 78), speaking of jugglers in W. India, writes: "The most conspicuous was generally one of those women mentioned by Dr. Fryer, who hold nine gilded balls in play, with her hands and feet, and the muscles of her arms and legs, for a long time together, without letting them fall."

and will arithmetize the nicest Fractions without the help of Pen or Ink; much given to Traffick, and intelligent in the way of Merchandize, if not fraudulent; having an accomplishment in the Art of Staining Calicuts here beyond any other place in the *East-Indies* (for that they are upon washing rather clearer and livelier than at first, and this is it that makes this Port so much frequented) which is painted with the Pencil by little Children as well as elder grown, they stretching the Pieces on the ground, and sitting upon them, run them over with a dexterity and exactness peculiar to themselves.[1]

They are all of them of Disposition timerous, so that Twenty four *English*-Men armed kept the *Bank Solls* against them on a late Demur; and thereupon at the coming in of our Ships they were all packing up to be gone, notwithstanding 200000 Souls receive here their daily Sustenance: And as Tyrranous when they get the uppermost; an instance whereof the Occasion of this Demur presents: For our Factory protecting one of the *English* Nation from their Fury, who too incautiously had to deal with some of their Women, they set a *De-Roy*[2] on the Factory (which is a Prohibition in the King's Name for any one to have any thing to do with them till that be taken off) whereby they were debarred Wood and Water; and all other Necessaries, till they had their Revenge on the

---

[1] Masulipatam was renowned for its chintz (Birdwood, *Report*, 225). "They are prized for the freshness and permanency of their dyes, the colours being brighter after washing than before. There is still a great demand for them in Burma, the Straits, and Persian Gulf; but Manchester goods threaten to destroy also this immemorial industry of India" (Id., *Industrial Arts of India*, 257).

[2] Mahr. *durāhī*, "an exclamation or expression used in prohibiting in the name of the Rājā or other high authority; implying an imprecation of his vengeance in case of disobedience" (Molesworth, *Mahr. Dict.*, *s. v.*). "I s[ai]d these are ye men and I charged him with the Shaw Sollyman de Roy" (*Travels of Richard Bell*, ed. Temple, p. 36). "Then they laid the King's *deroy* upon it and seized upon it for the company's use" (Wilson, *Early Annals*, i, 15). Fryer uses the word again (Letter III, chap. 1).

Aggressor, which terminated not till Death had expiated the Fact: For having intrapped him by deluding Speeches into their merciless Power, they cut him in pieces before the Factory Gate: Whereupon the *English* drew out some Field-Pieces, and scowred the Streets, when they fled and left the *Bank-Solls* to their possession, which were not resigned till the *De-Roy* was taken off, which was not done till within a little of our Arrival; when the thing being fresh, and thinking us not only able by such a Fleet to demand Satisfaction, but resolved so to do, they were all shifting for themselves: According to the true nature of Cowards, who when Peril is far from them, strike all with Lightning; but when it appears on equal terms, presently discover the wonted Paleness of an unsound Virtue.

Of Complexion the *Gentues* are blacker than the *Moors*, the *Moors* than the *Persians*.

Their executing of Justice in Capital Cases is sudden, either cutting them in pieces (which for Murder is always begun by the next Relation, who must be both Prosecutor and Executioner, and then seconded by the Rabble[1]) or Impaling them on Stakes.[2]

---

[1] The *lex talionis* of the Muhammadans (*Koran*, ii, 173) is identical with that of the Jews (*Exod.* xxi, 24). Tavernier (48 f.) describes how a Cafer (*Kāfir*) killed a camel-man in a squabble: "When the rest of the kindred came with the *Cafer* to *Schiraz*, the *Kan* did all he could to persuade the widow to take Money; but not being able to over-rule her, he was forc'd to give the *Cafer* into their hands; and how they us'd him I cannot tell." In India Haibat Khān, a slave of Sultān Balban, while intoxicated, slew a man. "The dead man's friends brought the matter before the Sultán, who ordered that Haibat Khán should receive five hundred lashes in his presence, and should be given to the widow. Addressing the woman, he said: 'This murderer was my slave. I give him you; with your own hands stab him with a knife till you kill him.'" Haibat Khān secured his release by paying 20,000 tankas (Elliot-Dowson, *H. of India*, iii, 101). The rule prevailed among the Mongols (Elias, *Tārīkh-i-Rashidi*, 43, 383).

[2] Impalement of criminals prevailed in Assyria, the stake being driven into the body immediately below the ribs (Layard, *Nineveh and Babylon*, 355; *Nineveh and its Remains*, ii, 374; Maspero, *Struggle of the Nations*, 639). It was used by the Hindus of Sind.

The punishing of their Great Ones, because not in force in our *Western* Empires, may deserve to be mentioned.

Upon an Offence they are sent by the King's Order, and committed to a place called the *Post*[1] (from the Punishment inflicted), where the Master of the *Post* is acquainted with the heinousness of the Crime; which being understood, he heightens by a Drink, which at first they refuse, made of *Bang*[2] (the Juice of the intoxicating sort of Hemp), and being mingled with *Dutry*[3] (the deadliest sort of *Solanum*, or *Nightshade*) named *Post*, after a Week's taking, they crave more than ever they nauseated. *Ad illorum vicem qui degustato Sardonum graminum succo feruntur in morte ridere*; making them foolishly mad. Then are they brought into the Inner Lodgings of the House, in which Folding Doors open upon delicious

---

and by Fīroz Shāh (Elliot-Dowson, *H. of India*, i, 129; iii, 233). Jahāngīr ordered the impalement of three hundred adherents of his son Khusru (*Ibid.*, vi, 268; Manucci, i, 131). It was a Mongol punishment (Elias, *Tarikh-i-Rashidi*, 258), and in Egypt (Burton, *Nights*, xii, 190). In quite recent times criminals were punished in this way in Malabar (Thurston, *Notes*, 429).

[1] The poppy-head or capsule (Pers. *post*, Skt. *pusta*, "covered"). The custom of the Mughal Emperors sending State prisoners to Gwalior, where they suffered a slow death from doses of an infusion of poppy, is described by several travellers. Tavernier (ed. Ball, i, 63) attributed it to Shāh Jahān. The case of Murād Bakhsh, to which he refers, is also quoted by Hamilton (*New Account*, i, 172). Bernier (p. 106) writes: "This *poust* is nothing but poppy-heads crushed, and allowed to soak for a night in water. This is the potion generally given to Princes confined in the fortress of *Goualeor*, whose heads the Monarch is deterred by prudential reasons from taking off. A large cup of this beverage is brought to them early in the morning, and they are not given anything to eat until it be swallowed; they would sooner let the prisoner die of hunger. This drink emaciates the wretched victims, who lose their strength and intellect by slow degrees, become torpid and senseless, and at length die." Also see Elliot-Dowson, *H. of India*, vii, 131.

[2] Hind. *bhang*, the dried leaves and stalks of hemp (*cannabis indica*) (Yule, *Hobson-Jobson*, 59).

[3] Thorn-apple (*datura stramonium*). It is still used by road-poisoners in India (Chevers, *Man. of Medical Jurisprudence*, 179 ff.) For this drug see Watt, *Econ. Dict.*, iii, 29 ff.; Burton, *Anatomy of Melancholy*, ii, 286; Yule, *Hobson-Jobson*, 298.

Gardens, where Apes and Cats, Dogs and Monkeys are their Attendants, with whom they maintain their Dialogues, exercising over them their Humour of an Assassin, Usurper, Miser, or what their *Genius* led them to, whilst themselves. After this manner are they imprison'd during the King's Pleasure, or he order their Cure, to restore them to their Senses again ; which otherwise, after their Spirits are tired by a restless Appetite of doing, and in the mean time have not a suitable recruit, they linger by a lasting Leanness into the Shades, which alive they represented.

As for their Law-Disputes, they are soon ended ; the Governor hearing, and the *Cadi*[1] or Judge determining every Morning.

Religions of all Inventions are licens'd. The *Moors* are *Mahometans* of the *Arabian* Sect : The *Persians* as much deluded by *Mortis Ali* or *Hali*,[2] accused therefore of Heresy by the *Moors*. The Natives are Idolators worshiping many *Penates* or Household-Gods, yea, the Devil too for fear :[3] Yet they acknowledge but one Supreme God ;[4] and the various Representations or Shapes adored, are but so many different Attributes. After every day's Devotion they dawb their Foreheads with Paint, and as Principles

---

[1] Ar. *qāḍī*, "a judge" (Yule, *Hobson-Jobson*, 177).

[2] Ar. *murtaza*, "the chosen, the approved" : a title of 'Alī, cousin-german and adopted son of the Prophet. The Shī'ahs hold that, on the death of the Prophet, he was entitled to the Khalifate, as opposed to the Sunnī claim on behalf of Abū Bakr, 'Umar, and 'Usmān. He is the Mortada or Mortadi of Ockley and other writers of his day.

[3] "All the reason they give for worshipinge the Devil is, they hold that God Ordained the Devil to Governe this World and to torment all mankind, and that God himselfe resteth in the heavens, wherefore Upon Earth they worship Gods of much deformitie, as partly to please the Devil whom they say is of no less deformitie, and the Other reason is, they say that theire prayers are to God to Deliver them from such Satyricall Creatures" (Bowrey, 15). On such rites in S. India, see Caldwell, *Dravidian Grammar*[2], 585 f. ; Burnell, *Devil Worship of the Tulavas*.

[4] On S. Indian Monotheism, see Dubois, *Hindu Manners, Customs, and Ceremonies*, 406.

of Zeal, abominate eating with any, unless of their own Cast, when they strip and wash themselves before Meals.

They have a due command of their Appetite both as to Time and the Matter they feed on, to wit, Roots, Herbs, Rice, and *Cutchery*,[1] all manner of Fruits, but nothing that has had Life, or likely to produce Vital Heat, as Eggs, which they will not eat; but they will drink Milk and boil'd Butter, which they call *Ghe*.[2]

For their Easements both Men and Women keep a set hour, and go with every one a purifying Pot in their hand (for to take up Water to wash after their occasions) to some Publick *Tank* or Pond; the Men apart from the Women; neither of them concerned for Passengers, keeping their back-sides towards them till they have done their Business.

Among them all it is common to make water sitting,[3] as when they evacuate the other way; and it is a shame for any one to be seen to do otherwise, they sarcastically saying, Such a one pisses like a Dog (which is held unclean) standing.

Their Doctors of Divinity are the *Brachmins*, who instruct them in their Law, to preserve all Creatures that are beneficial, and teach them the old *Pythagorean* Μετεμψύχωσις,[4] Transmigration of Souls out of one body into another; as a Tyrant into a Tygre, a Covetous Man or Cruel into a Boar, a fearful Man into an Hare, and so on: If they see a Tree twined about with another (as most Bind-Weeds will), they tell you that in this life, when Human, the Soul got into that Tree was a Debtor to the

---

[1] Hind., *khichrī*, rice cooked with lentils, butter, flavoured with spices, shred onions, etc. (Yule, *Hobson-Jobson*, 476).

[2] *Ghī*, "boiled butter" (*Hobson-Jobson*, 370).

[3] Herodotus (ii, 38) notes this habit in Egypt. See Herbert, 243; *Mishcat-ul-Masabih*, tr. Matthews, i, 84 f.; Burton, *Nights*, i, 238.

[4] On this doctrine among Hindus of S. India, see Dubois, *Hindu Manners*, 564 ff.; Bowrey, 28, 205; Tavernier, i, Pt. II, 167.

other, and therefore it is held fast by the other. The Soul of a Good Man is believed to depart into a Cow, wherefore 'tis Sacrilege with them to kill a Cow or a Calf; but highly piacular to shoot a Kite,[1] dedicated to the *Brachmins*, for which Money will hardly pacify.

Their Religious Worship consists most in washing and purifyings; more of which hereafter.

They marry very young, not knowing their Wives though till at riper years they come to consummate their Hymeneal Rites.

Their Language they call generally *Gentu*:[2] They write on the Leaf of a *Cocoe*[3] with a sharp Iron Instrument. The peculiar Name of their Speech is *Telinga*.[4]

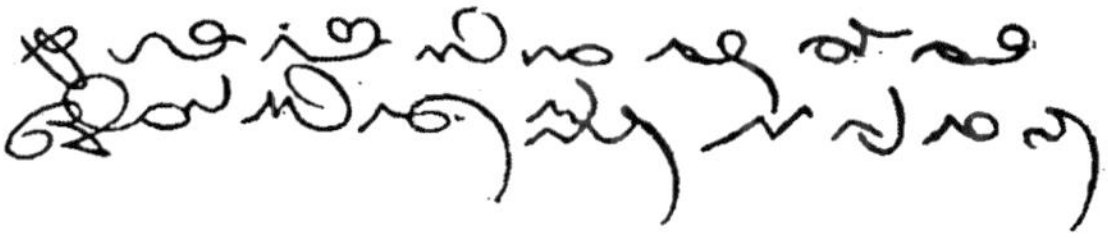

The *Telinga* Character.

The *Mahometans* bury their dead; the *Gentues* burn them; and in the Husband's Flames the Wife offers her self a Sacrifice to his *Manes*, or else she shaves and turns Whore for a Livelihood, none of her Friends looking upon

---

[1] The so-called "Brahminy Kite" (*Milvus Pondicerianus*) (Yule *Hobson-Jobson*, 112).

[2] Port. *gentio*, "a gentile": a term used for Hindus, as opposed to Moors or Muhammadans (Yule, *Hobson-Jobson*, 367).

[3] Commonly called Ollah (Yule, *Hobson-Jobson*, 636); cf. Bowrey, 24 f.

[4] The country E. of the Deccan, and extending to the coast (Yule, *Hobson-Jobson*, 912). The word represents the original Tri-Kalinga. This, with the other example of S. Indian script (Letter I, chap. VI), has been submitted to the best scholars in England, and both were photographed and sent to Mr. E. Thurston at Madras. No one has been able to interpret them satisfactorily. They are probably corrupt transcripts of what is known as the Ollah writing, done on palm-leaves, which is read only with the greatest difficulty. The Curator of the Government Oriental MSS. Library, Madras, is unable to interpret the passage. He states that it is really in Malayālam characters used about three hundred years ago.

her; hers, not her Husband's Acquaintance, thrusting her upon it; to which end they give her *Dutry*; when half mad she throws her self into the Fire, and they ready with great Logs keep her in his Funeral Pile.[1]

The *Armenians* are settled here on account of Trade (whose History is reserved for a fitter place); they are Christians of a separate Communion.

The *Portugals*, of the *Romish* Church.

The *English*, of the Orthodox Episcopacy.

The *Dutch*, most *Calvinists*.

The Coin current here is a *Pagod*,[2] 8 *s.*; *Dollar*, 4 *s.* 6 *d.*; *Rupee*, 2 *s.* 3 *d.*; *Cash*, 1 *d.* ½; a *Cash* ¼.

Staple Commodities are Calicuts[3] white and painted, *Palempores*,[4] Carpets, Tea; Diamonds of both Rocks, the Old and New; Escretores,[5] and other Knick-knacks for Ladies, because far-fetch'd and dear-bought.

Beasts they have, Wild Lions,[6] Leopards, Bears, Boars, Tygers, Antelopes, Spotted Deer.[7]

---

[1] On the subject of Suttee (*Sati*), see Dubois, 359 ff.; Crooke, *Things Indian*, 446 ff.

[2] For the history of this difficult word see Yule, *Hobson-Jobson*, 652. Accounts at Madras, down to 1815, were kept in pagodas, fanams, and cash. 80 cash = 1 single fanam; 42 single fanams = 1 pagoda. In the above-named year the rupee was made the standard coin. Many varieties of the pagoda are described in *Madras Admin. Man.*, iii, 643. For cash, see *Hobson-Jobson*, 167.

[3] Calico.

[4] A term for a chintz bed-cover; the origin of the word is doubtful. (*Hobson-Jobson*, 662.)

[5] Writing-desks; Fr. *escritoire*, *écritoire*; Lat. *scriptorium*. "Metchlipatam Affordeth very good and fine Commodities, vizt., all sorts of fine Callicoes, plaine and coloured, more Especially fine Palampores for Quilts, divers sorts of Chint curiously flowred, which doth much represent flowred Sattin, of Curious living Colours, as also Chaires and tables of that admirable wood Ebony, Chests of Drawers, Screetores finely wrought inlaid with turtle Shell or ivory." (Bowrey, 71.)

[6] The lion was formerly widely distributed in N.W. and Central India, where a few specimens still survive in the Gir forest of Kāthiāwār. But it is almost certain that it could not have existed so far south as Masulipatam in Fryer's time (Blanford, *Mammalia*, 566).

[7] *Cervus axis* (Blanford, 546).

For Service, Oxen, Buffola's, Camels, Asses which they use for burthen, to carry Packs, Water in great Leathern Sacks about the Town for every Family, and any other Slavery: But their Horses, which are small and hot-mettled, they put to no such drudgery, but use them with all the kindness and fair speeches imaginable.

With these (without disparagement to that Image God has stamp'd on that *Enchiridion* of his Handywork, Man) we might recite the *Coolies*, *Duties*,[1] and *Palenkeen* Boys; by the very Heathens esteemed a degenerate Offspring of the *Holencores*;[2] and in earnest (excepting the Shape) they come nigh to Brutes. These are the Machines they journey by: On the Shoulders of the *Coolies* they load their Provant, and what Moveables necessary. The *Duties* march like Furies, with their lighted *Mussals*[3] in their hands (they are Pots filled with Oyl in an Iron Hoop, like our Beacons, and set on fire by stinking Rags). Ambling after these a great pace, the *Palenkeen*-Boys support them; four of them, two at each end of a *Bambo*, which is a long hollow Cane, thick, light, and strong, arched in the middle (which is done in Cases while it is growing),[4] where hangs the *Palenkeen*, as big as an ordinary Couch, broad enough to tumble in; cieled with Silk, and Bosses pendent to raise withal, and others at each Corner, as our Coaches have; underneath it is laced with strong broad Girts, over which a Quilt, Skin of a Tyger, or Hide to lye upon, and round Pillows of Silk or Velvet, to bolster their Heads. At every

---

[1] Hind. *diutī*, properly "a lampstand"; here "a link-bearer" (Yule, *Hobson-Jobson*, 307).

[2] See p. 82.

[3] Ar. *mash'al*, "a torch" (Yule, *Hobson-Jobson*, 601).

[4] The habit of bending the bamboo, while growing, for use as a palanquin-pole, is referred to by many old travellers. Tavernier (ed. Ball, i, 46) says that some cost 200 *écus*, and he paid 125 for one. See P. della Valle, i, 183; Pyrard de Laval, i, 330; Ives, *Voyage*, 481; and the illustration in Bowrey, Plate vii.

Angle turn'd Staves, and overspreading it a Scarlet Coverlet of *London* Cloath.

A Set of these Rascals, who are eight, in a Week's time with this Load shall run down their choicest Horses; and bait them generously shall stage it a Month together.

For War, Elephants: For to eat, Sheep, poor, fleeced rather with Hair than Wool, their Aspect bewraying as much Goat as Sheep: Goats; Hogs low and black, unclean to the *Mahometans*: Cows, sacred to the *Gentues*, as *Serapis* to the *Egyptians*; Conies, Hares.

Reptiles, Snakes, Serpents, the *Amphisbena*[1] and other kinds; all which they pretend to charm, carrying them up and down in Baskets to get Money of the People, as well as Strangers; when they strike up on a Reed run through a Cocoa-Shell, which makes a noise something like our Bag-Pipes, and the subtle Creatures will listen to the Musick, and observe a Motion correspondent to the Tune;

---

[1] The real *Amphisbœna* is found only in S. America and the W. Indies; but the name has been applied to some Asiatic snakes. Tavernier (ed. Ball, ii, 287) writes: "There are there [in Siam] some snakes which are 22 feet long and have two heads, but the head at the extremity which answers to the tail, and where the snake ends, does not open the mouth and has no movement." Fra Paolino (248), writing of S. India, says: "The *Irutala Kuszali* is a snake with two heads, whatever Charleton and others may say to the contrary. In Portuguese it is called *Cobra de duas cabeças*, and in Latin *Amphisbœna*. M. Rosier, the commandant at Collam, showed me two snakes of this kind, which he preserved in a glass jar. I saw one of them also in the mountains of *Melcatur*. It is a palm or a palm and a-half in length; has the colour of withered leaves; and does not, like other snakes, creep straight forward, but always rears one of its heads, and makes an arch with its body when it moves. Its bite always occasions a tumour filled with venom; but the poison acts very slowly, so that it is seldom or never too late to apply a remedy." In N. India such snakes are known as *domunhā*, "two-mouthed"; and the name is often applied to the *dhāman* (*Ptyas mucosus*). The Marathas apply the name *dutonde* to *Eryx johnii*. *Russ.*; and snake-charmers frequently mutilate its short, thick, rounded tail, in order to give it the appearance of a second head. It is quite harmless, avoids wet ground, and prefers sandy plains, in which it can burrow with ease. In the Deccan it is known as *māndul*. (*Bombay Gaz.*, xviii, Pt. i, 80 f.; Rice, *Mysore*[2], i, 188; Tennent, *Ceylon*[3], i, 194 f.). Fryer was probably acquainted with Sir T. Browne's account (*Works*, i, 294, ff.).

a Generation of Vipers that well deserved to be stiled so, knowing when the Charmer charms wisely.[1]

Fowls of all sort belonging to *India* are plenty, but chiefly tame Geese.

Fishes in abundance, from whence the Town derives its Etymology, *Mechlapatan* signifying the Fish-Town.

For Corn, they have Rice the Staff of the Land, some Wheat.

Fruits to variety.

The Water they drink they dig for; not that they are without Rivers, but they are brackish. It lies in 15 *deg. North* Lat. 40 *min.* From the *Lizzard* 96 *deg. East.*[2] By reason of the Multitude of People and ill Site it is unhealthy; though it agree with the Natives, who live to a good Old Age.

The *English* for that cause, only at the time of shipping, remove to *Medapollon*,[3] where they have a wholesome Seat Forty Miles more *North*.

Rain they have none from *November* to *May*, all which time the Land-Breezes (which blow one half the day and off the Sea but faintly the other) torment them with a suffocating Heat; so that the Birds of the Air as they fly, often drop down dead, the wind coming as hot as the Steam from an Oven, by the reflecting of the Sun upon the Sands, which are hurled about the Marshes. When they feel themselves freest from Sickness, though all Perspiration through the Pores by Sweat is dried up:

---

[1] See the account of snake-charming in Bowrey (59 f.) and his drawing. Plate vi.

[2] Lat. 16° 11′ N.; Long. 81° 8′ E.

[3] Madapollam (Tamil, Madhavayyapālemu, "fortified city of Madhava"), about 45 miles N.E. of Masulipatam, in the Godavari District. An English factory was established in 1679 in part of the present town of Narsapur (*Madras Adm. Man.*, iii, 440). For Narsapur see Bowrey (p. 98), where his editor gives numerous extracts from records to show that Madapollam was at this time a flourishing shipbuilding and manufacturing centre, as well as a health-resort (*Ibid.*, 100 f.).

From the beginning of *May* they are refreshed with cooling Showers, which at length with the overflowing Sea cause an Inundation; in which space, the Air growing foggy, *Empyema's* and Fluxes are rifest; and Swarms of Ants, *Muskeetoes*, Flies, and stinking *Chints*,[1] *Cimices*, *&c.* breed and infest them: This Season we experimented; which though moderately warm, yet our Bodies broke out into small fiery Pimples[2] (a sign of a prevailing *Crasis*) augmented by *Muskeetoe*-Bites, and *Chinces* raising Blisters on us.

To arm themselves against this Plague, those that live here have fine Calicut-Lawn thrown over their Beds, which though white as Snow when put on, shall be in an hour besmear'd all over, which might be tolerable, did not their daring Buzzes continually alarm, and sometimes more sensibly provoke, though cloath'd with long Breeches to their Toes,[3] and Mufflers on their Hands and Face, and a Servant to keep them from them with a Fan, without which there is no sleeping.

Notwithstanding these provisions, yet there is another Insect more disturbing than these, and not to be escaped but by this Device, and that is the Ant, which creeps up to all their Quarters, and between their Beds, if the Bed-Posts were not set in Pans of Water to hinder their Progress. *Chinces* stick among the Cotton, and in rotten Posts, whose bitings wheal most sadly, and if they strive to take a Revenge for that abuse, and chance to squeeze them, they leave a stink enough to choak them.

The Air so bad here, that it agrees with few new Comers; removing Three Miles up the Countrey it is an infallible Cure for the Diseases of this place, provided it be done in

---

[1] Port. *chinche*; Lat. *cimex*, "a bug" (Yule, *Hobson-Jobson*, 201).

[2] The common "prickly-heat" (*lichen tropicus*) (Yule, *Hobson-Jobson*, 731).

[3] The "long-drawers" of other writers (Yule, *Hobson-Jobson*, 518).

time: Where the *English* have a Garden for Divertisement; where also is a Burial-place graced with Monuments both of Antique and Modern Workmanship.

Half a Mile beyond, a Dozen of the King's Elephants are stabled. When we came they were feeding out of their Houses on Sugar-Canes fresh gathered and administred by their Keepers: Alighting from our *Palenkeens*, they loosed one which was Fourteen Feet high,[1] and the Black clawing his Poll with an Iron Engine,[2] he stooped down for him to get up, and being upon his Back guided him as he listed. His Body is a Symetrical Deformity (if I may so say); the Hanches and Quarters clapt together seem so many heaps; his Neck short, flapping Ears like Scates, little-Eye'd, a broad Face, from which drops his *Proboscis* or Trunk, thrusting it out, or shriveling it in, as he chuses; through its Hollow he sucks his Liquor, and with two Fingers, as it were, reaches the Fodder, shaking off the dirt against his Thigh, or Vermin, such as Mice, which he abhors, he brings it under to his Mouth, from whence proceed two huge Tusks of Ivory for Defence, not Mastication, for which he is supplied within with others; his Tail is curt: He shuffles an end a great Pace, moving all the Joints of his Legs, though the Motion of his Hinder-Legs imitate Human Progression, having a *Patella* or Knee-Pan afore, not articulated behind as other four-footed Beasts are.[3]

---

[1] This was a mighty beast. The average height of the elephant is 9 ft. In the Indian Museum at Calcutta is a skeleton of an animal which must have been nearly 12 ft. high (Blanford, *Mammalia*, 463 f.)

[2] The *ānkus* or *gajbāgh* of N. India (*Āīn*, i, 129). Tennent (*Ceylon*[3], ii, 382 *n.*) remarks that this implement has retained its shape from remote antiquity, being figured on coins of Caracalla in the identical shape in which it is used at the present day. In connection with it, Linschoten (ii, 2) exhibits an extraordinary theory regarding the anatomy of the animal.

[3] The straightness and apparent want of flexibility in their limbs, an effect produced by the greater nearness of the knee and elbow to the ground, produced for centuries the belief that they were jointless, or to have such joints as could not be used. "The elephant hath joints, but

When he stands, his Legs appear so many Columns scollop'd at bottom, being flat-hoof'd.

The She's have their Paps under their Bowels afore, as *Laurentius* truly relates.

Their Modesty in ingendring has given matter for dispute, though doubtless they perform it after the manner of other Beasts. They are of a Mouse-Colour. With their Trunks they strike a violent Blow, and are taught to sling Iron Links, to the destruction of their Enemies.[1] That they draw their weighty Cannon is certain; but that they engage with smaller on their Backs, I am no Eye-Witness.

After a Month's Stay here, a *Patamar*[2] (a Foot-Post) from *Fort St. George*, made us sensible of the *Dutch* being gone from thence to *Ceilon*: The Treasure was reshipped, and we in less than a Week, through contrary *Monsoons* and Ill Weather (the Sun being in his *Zenith*, and encountring the *Dog-Star* over our heads) arrived there.

When sliding by four *French* Men of War at Anchor under St. *Thomas* (of whom the Admiral[3] the *Brittoon* was a Ship of 1200 Tuns, 68 Brass Guns; the second had 50 Brass Guns; the other two were less; and the Platform of the City mounted with Brass Pieces, that slung their Shot an incredible way), we against all probability found the *Massenberg* there, having ventured alone, and but the day before us came into the Road under our Fort; there

---

none for courtesy; his legs are legs for necessity, not for pleasure" (Shakespeare, *Troilus and Cressida*, ii, 3). On this ancient fallacy, refuted by Sir T. Browne (*Works*, i, 219 ff.), see Tennent (*Ceylon*[3], ii, 292 ff.). *Hāthī kē dānt khānē kē aur, dikhānē kē aur*, "the elephant has one set of teeth for use, another for show," is a common proverb.

[1] In the battle between Aurangzeb and Shuja', the elephants of the Saiyids of Bārha, "each of them dashing about with his trunk a chain of two or three *mans* weight, and overthrew and crushed everyone who came in their way" (Elliot-Dowson, vii, 235).

[2] A courier, a word of which the origin is obscure (Yule, *Hobson-Jobson*, 687).

[3] Here, as in other writers of the day, admiral means the flag-ship (Linschoten, i, 9, 41; ii, 178; Tavernier, ed. Ball, i, 313).

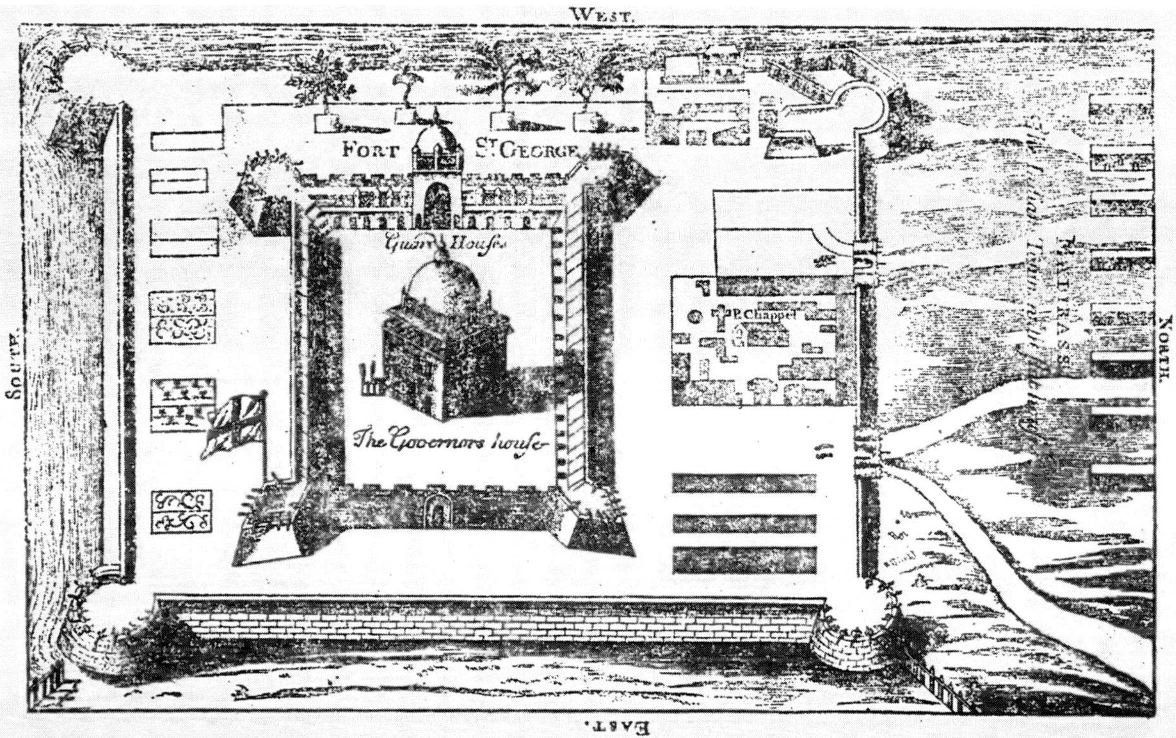
West.
Fort St George
Guard House
The Governors house
R. Chappel
Madrass
North.
South.
East.

(To face p. 103)

also rode two *Portugal Junks.* The Colours the Fort shewed us, was St. *George*'s Flag ; it bore from us one League *West,* Low-Land : St. *Thomas* one League and an half *South-West,* High-Land behind it ; *North-Lat.* 12 *deg.* 30 *min.* *Long.* from the *Lizard* 96 *deg. East.*[1]

CHAP. V.

Gives a true Narrative of the English, French *and* Dutch *on the Coast of* Coromandel, *continuing till we double the Cape for the Coast of* Malabar.

I WENT ashore in a *Mussoola,*[2] a boat wherein ten Men paddle, the two aftermost of whom are the Steers-men, using their Paddles instead of a Rudder : The Boat is not strengthened with Knee-Timber, as ours are ; the bended Planks are sowed together with Rope-yarn of the Cocoe, and calked with *Dammar,*[3] (a sort of Rosin taken out of the Sea) so artificially, that it yields to every Ambitious Surf, otherwise we could not get ashore, the Bar knocking in pieces all that are inflexible : Moving towards the Shore, we left St. *Thomas,* which lies but Three Miles to the *South* of *Maderas,* and *Fort St. George* ; in the midway *Maderas* River[4] in great Rains opens its Mouth into the Sea ; having first saluted the Banks of *Fort St. George* on the *West* : Towards the Sea the Sand is cast up into a Rampire, from whence the fluid Artillery discharges it self upon us, and we on the Shoulders of the Blacks must force our way through it.

---

[1] Madras is situated in lat. 13° 4′ N., long. 80° 15′ E.

[2] Telugu *māsūlā*, a fishing-boat ; Hind. *machhlī*, Skt. *matsya* "fish."

[3] Malayo-Javanese, *damar* (Yule, *Hobson-Jobson*, 294).

[4] The Cooum (Tamil, *Kūvam* ; Skt., *kūpa*, "a well"), rising at Sriparmatur about thirty miles from Madras, and falling into the sea S. of Fort St. George.

Though we landed wet, the Sand was scalding hot, which made me recollect my steps, and hasten to the *Fort*.[1] As it looked on the Water, it appeared a Place of good force. The Outwork is walled with Stone a good heighth, thick enough to blunt a Cannon-bullet, kept by half a dozen Ordnance at each side the Water-gate, besides an Half-moon of Five-Guns. At both Points are mounted twelve Guns eyeing the Sea, *Maderas*, and St. *Thomas*; under these in a Line stand Pallisadoes, reaching from the Wall to the Sea; and hedge in at least a Mile of ground. On the *South* side they have cut a Ditch a sufficient depth and breadth to prevent scaling the Wall, which is a quarter of a Mile in length afore it meets with a third Point or Bastion, facing St. *Thomas*, and the adjacent Fields; who suffer a Deluge when the Rains descend the Hills. From this Point to the Fourth, where are lodged a Dozen Guns more than grin upon *Maderas*, runs no Wall, but what the Inhabitants compile for their Gardens and Houses planted all along the River parallel with that, that braves the Sea. From the first Point a Curtain is drawn with a *Parapet*; beneath it are two Gates, and Sally Ports to each for to enter *Maderas*; over the Gates five Guns run out their Muzzels; and two more within them on the Ground.

Over all these the Fort it self lifts up its Four Turrets, every point of which is loaded with Ten Guns alike: On the *South-East* Point is fixed the Standard; the Forms of the Bastions are Square, sending forth Curtains fringed

---

1 "The site was a marshy plain where the Coôum and what was known as the North River met. It was gradually enlarged and improved until it reached its present dimensions" (*Madras Man. Adm.*, iii, 446, which gives an account of the Fort in its present state). Fryer's plan seems to be largely a fancy sketch, if we compare other descriptions of the place in its original condition (Wheeler, *Madras in the Olden Time*, i, 48 f.; Bowrey, 3 f.), and the plan given by Orme (*H. of Military Transactions*, vol. iii, Madras reprint of 1862). For an account of the Fort at various times, see Mrs. F. Penny, *Fort St. George, Madras* (1900).

with Battlements from one to the other; in whose Interstitiums whole Culverin are traversed. The Governor's House in the middle overlooks all, slanting diagonally with the Court. Entring the Garrison at the Out-gate towards the Sea, a Path of broad polished Stones spreads the way to pass the Second Guard into the Fort at an humble Gate; opposite to this, one more stately fronts the High-street; on both sides thereof is a Court of Guard, from whence, for every day's Duty, are taken Two hundred Men: There being in pay for the Honourable *East India* Company of *English* and *Portuguez* 700 reckoning the Montrosses[1] and Gunners.

The Streets are sweet and clean, ranked with fine Mansions, of no extraordinary Height (because a Garrison-Town) though Beauty, which they conciliate, by the Battlements and Tarras Walks on every House, and Rows of Trees before their Doors, whose *Italian* Porticos make no ordinary conveyance into their Houses, built with Brick and Stone.

Edifices of common note are none, except a small Chappel the *Portugals* are admitted to say Mass in.

Take the Town in its exact proportion, and it is Oblong.

The true Possessors of it are the *English*, instated therein by one of their *Naiks* or Prince of the *Gentues*, 90 years ago,[2] 40 years before their total subjection to the *Moors*;

---

[1] An obsolete term for an inferior class of artillery-man; Germ. *matrose*; Dutch *matross*; Fr. *matelot*; "a sailor" (Yule, *Hobson-Jobson*, 562).

[2] Fryer's chronology is incorrect. In March, 1639, Francis Day, Chief of the settlement of Armagon, obtained a lease of a narrow strip of land north of the Portuguese monastic village round the shrine of St. Thomas. The grantor was Sri Ranga Raya of Chandragiri, who was in this outlying district the representative of the decadent power of the dynasty of Vijayanagar, which had been shattered in the battle of Talikot in 1565. The consideration for the lease was a yearly rent of 1200 pagodas, or, roughly speaking, about £600 (Wheeler, *Early Records*, 49 f.; *Madras in the Olden Time*, i, 19 f.; Bruce, *Annals*, i, 368 f., 377 f.).

who likewise have since ratified it by a Patent from *Gulconda*, only paying 7000 *Pagods* yearly for Royalties and Customs, that raises the Mony fourfold to the Company; whose Agent here is Sir *William Langham*,[1] a gentleman of Indefatigable Industry and Worth. He is Superintendent over all the Factories on the Coast of *Coromandel*, as far as the Bay of *Bengala*, and up *Huygly* River (which is one of the Falls of *Ganges*)[2] Viz. *Fort St. George* alias *Maderas*, *Pettipolee*,[3] *Mechlapatan*, *Gandore*,[4] *Medapollon*, *Balisore*,[5] *Bengala*,[6] *Huygly*, *Castle Buzzar*,[7] *Pattanaw*.[8] He has his Mint, and Privilege of Coining; the Country Stamp is only a *Fanam*, which is 3 *d.* of Gold;[9] and their *Cash*,

---

[1] Sir William Langhorn, Governor of Madras, (1670-77). For an account of his administration, see Wheeler, *Madras in the O. T.* i, 68 ff.; Wilson, *Early Annals*, i, 43.

[2] The westerly, and for commercial purposes the most important channel by which the waters of the Ganges enter the Bay of Bengal.

[3] Telugu Peddapalli, "great village," now known as Nizāmpatam, in the Kistna District. The factory was established in 1611 by Capt. Hippon, commanding the Seventh Voyage; it was re-established in 1633, but abandoned on account of a pestilence in 1687. Bowrey (p. 53) calls it "a very pleasant and healthy place, and very well populated by the Gentues, of whom many are very wealthy" (*Madras Adm. Man.*, iii, 593; Birdwood, *Report*, 209; Hunter, *H. of British India*, ii, 70, 72).

[4] Gūdūr (Telugu Gūdūru, "good village"), about 4 miles N.W. of Masulipatam. Bowrey (p. 62) speaks of the bridge which "reacheth from the great gate of Masulipatam over to Guddorah, which is one English mile in length and of a considerable breadth, and is called by the Name of Guddorah bridge."

[5] A port in the district of the same name in Orissa, on the right bank of the Burābalang River. The name is properly Balīsvara, "strength of God." The right to establish a factory was granted in 1642, and in 1645-6 the privileges were extended on account of the services of Surgeon Gabriel Broughton to Shāh Jahān and his viceroy, Sultān Shuja' (Birdwood, *Report*, 92; Hedges, *Diary*, iii, 147 ff.: Hamilton, *New Account*, i, 396).

[6] This apparently means Chittagong (Yule, *Hobson-Jobson*, 85).

[7] Cossimbazar, Kāsīmbāzār, now a decayed town in the Murshidābād District of Bengal, where a factory was established in 1658 (*Ibid*, 263).

[8] Patna.

[9] The fanam was originally worth about 1¼ rupees; later, it was coined of silver or base gold. According to the old Madras monetary system, which prevailed till 1818, a Madras fanam was worth about 2*d.* (*Madras Adm. Man.*, iii, 293; Yule, *Hobson-Jobson*, 348).

twenty of which go to a *Fanam*. Moreover he has his Justiciaries; to give Sentence, but not on Life and Death to the King's Liege People of *England*; though over the rest they may. His Personal Guard consists of 3 or 400 Blacks; besides a Band of 1500 Men ready on Summons: He never goes abroad without Fifes, Drums, Trumpets, and a Flag with two Balls in a Red Field; accompanied with his Council and Factors on Horseback, with their Ladies in *Palenkeens*.

The *English* here are Protestants, the *Portugals* Papists, who have their several Orders of Fryers; who, to give them their due, compass Sea and Land to make Proselytes, many of the Natives being brought in by them.

The number of *English* here may amount to Three hundred; of *Portuguez* as many Thousand, who made *Fort St. George* their Refuge, when they were routed from St. *Thomas* by the *Moors* about ten years past, and have ever since lived under protection of the *English*.[1]

Thus have you the Limits and Condition of the *English* Town: Let us now pass the Pale to the Heathen Town, only parted by a wide Parrade, which is used for a *Buzzar* or Mercate-place.

Maderas

Then divides it self into divers Long Streets, and they are checquered by as many transverse. It enjoys some

---

[1] In the Fort and Town "Many Portugals are admitted to dwell, beinge Subject to our English Goverment, many of which are very Eminent Merchants, and are admitted a free trade, payinge Custome, vizt., 4 per cent. to the English in and out for theire goods; many of them alsoe beare arms in the Honourable East India Company's Service as private Centinels, but not otherways, none of them beinge raised to any place of Office; and although their Sallary be Smal, yet they live very well of it, being paid monthly as all the English Soldiery are, and provisions with cloths well befittinge Suche a climate very Cheape and Good" (Bowrey, 3). St. Thomé was captured by the King of Golkanda on 1st or 2nd May, 1662 (Manucci, iii, 126).

Choultries[1] for Places of Justice; one Exchange, one *Pagod*, contained in a square Stone-wall; wherein are a number of Chappels (if they may be comprehended under that Classis, most of them resembling rather Monuments for the Dead, than Places of Devotion for the Living) one for every Tribe; not under one Roof, but distinctly separate, though altogether, they bear the name of one intire *Pagoda*. The Work is inimitably durable, the biggest closed up with Arches continually shut, as where is supposed to be hid their Mammon of Unrighteousness, (they burying their Estates here when they dye, by the persuasion of their Priests, towards their *viaticum* for another State) admitting neither Light nor Air, more than what the Lamps, always burning, are by open Funnels above suffered to ventilate: By which Custom they seem to keep alive that Opinion of *Plato*, in such a Revolution to return into the World again, after their Transmigration, according to the Merits of their former living.[2] Those of a minuter dimension were open, supported by slender straight and round Pillars, plain and uniform up to the top, where some Hieroglyphical Portraicture lends its assistance to the Roof, flat, with Stones laid along like Planks upon our Rafters. On the Walls of good Sculpture were obscene Images, where *Aretine*[3] might have furnished his Fancy for his Bawdy Postures: The Floor is stoned, they are of no great altitude; stinking most egregiously of the Oyl they waste in their Lamps, and besmear their Beastly Gods with: Their outsides shew Workmanship and Cost enough, wrought round with monstrous Effigies; so that *oleum &*

---

[1] A shed or place used for public business; Telugu, *chāwadi*, "a place where four roads meet" (Yule, *Hobson-Jobson*, 211).

[2] He possibly refers to the well-known passage in the Phædrus (P. 249 A), though it is difficult to suppose that Plato or the later Greeks believed the doctrine of the metempsychosis (*Ency. Brit.*[9], xvi, 106 f.)

[3] Pietro Aretino, Italian wit and satirist, 1492-1557.

operam perdere, Pains and Cost to no purpose, may not improperly be applied to them. Their Gates are commonly the highest of the Work,[1] the others concluding in shorter Piles.

Near the outside of the Town the *English Golgotha*, or Place of Sculls, presents variety of Tombs, Walks and Sepulchres; which latter, as they stand in a Line, are an open Cloyster; but succinctly and precisely a *Quadragone* with Hemispherical Apartitions; on each side adorned with Battlements to the abutment of every Angle, who bear up a Coronal Arch, on whose *Vertex* a Globe is rivited by an Iron Wedge sprouting into a Branch; paved underneath with a great Black Stone, whereon is engraved the Name of the Party interred. The Buildings of less note are Low and Decent; the Town is walled with Mud, and Bulwarks for Watch-places for the *English* Peons; only on that side the Sea washes it, and the Fort meets it. On the *North* are two great Gates of Brick, and one on the *West*, where they wade over the River to the Washermens Town.

Its Map renders it a *Trapezium* by an Oblique Stroke of the River on that Corner, and another next the Sea thus.

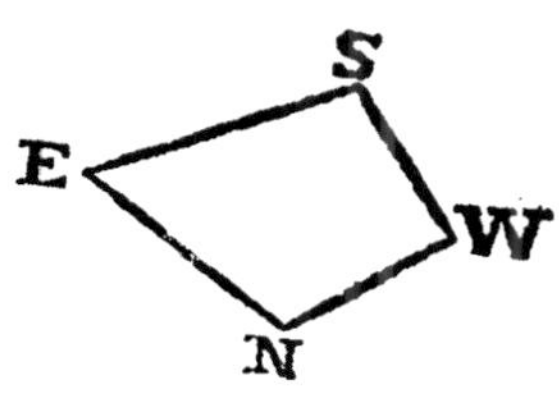

The Figure of Maderas.

[1] The gate pyramids (*gopuram*) are, in the Dravidian style of architecture, the principal features in the quadrangular enclosures, which always surround the temple itself (*vimána*) (Fergusson, *H. of Indian and E. Arch.*, 325). "The entrance, vizt., the Great Gate of Some of these Pagods, I have Often Observed, are most rare and Admirable worke, vizt., a man on horsebacke cut out in one entire piece Set upon each Side one full as bigge or bigger than any naturall ones; all of marble" (Bowrey, 7).

Without the Town grows their Rice, which is nourished by the letting in of the Water to drown it: Round about it is bestrewed with Gardens of the *English*; where, besides Gourds of all sorts for Stews and Pottage, Herbs for Sallad, and some few Flowers, as Jassamin, for beauty and delight; flourish pleasant Tops of Plantains, Cocoes, *Guiavas*,[1] a kind of Pear, *Jawks*,[2] a Coat of Armour over it like an Hedg-hog's, guards its weighty Fruit, Oval without for the length of a Span, within in fashion like Squils parted, *Mangos*, the delight of *India*, a Plum, Pomegranets, *Bonanoes*,[3] which are a sort of Plantain, though less, yet much more grateful, *Beetle*;[4] which last must not be slipt by in silence: It rises out of the Ground to twelve or fourteen Feet heighth, the Body of it green and slender, jointed like a Cane, the Boughs flaggy and spreading, under whose Arms it brings forth from its pregnant Womb (which bursts when her Month is come) a Cluster of Green Nuts, like Wallnuts in Green Shells, but different in the Fruit; which is hard when dried, and looks like a Nutmeg.

The Natives chew it with *Chinam*[5] (Lime of calcined Oyster-Shells) and *Arach*,[6] a *Convolvulus* with a Leaf like the largest Ivy, for to preserve their Teeth, and correct an unsavoury Breath: If swallowed, it inebriates as much as Tobacco. Thus mixed, it is the only *Indian* Entertainment, called *Pawn*.

These Plants set in a Row, make a Grove that might delude the Fanatick Multitude into an Opinion of their being sacred; and were not the Mouth of that Grand Impostor Hermetically sealed up, where Christianity is

---

[1] The Guava, *Psidium Guayava* (Yule, *Hobson-Jobson*, 399).

[2] The Jack, *Artocarpus integrifolia* (*Ibid.*, 440).

[3] The Banana, *Musa paradisaica* (*Ibid.*, 56).

[4] *Piper betel* (*Ibid.*, 35, 89), the well known *pān*.

[5] *Chunam*, fine prepared lime (*Ibid.*, 218).

[6] Areca-nut.

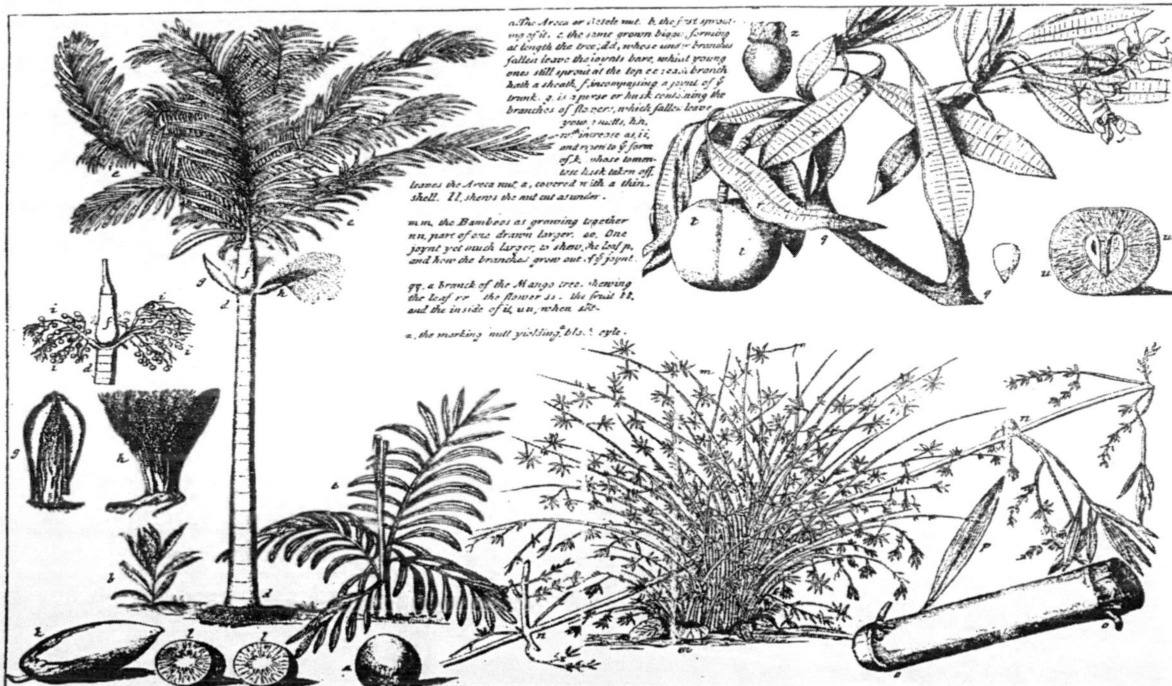
a. The Areca or Betele nut. b, the first sprout-
ing of it. c, the same grown bigger, forming
at length the tree; d d, whose under branches
fallen leave the joynts bare, whilst young
ones still sprout at the top e e; each branch
hath a sheath, f, incompassing a joynt of ye
trunk. g, is a purse or husk containing the
branches of flowers, which fallen leave
young nutts, hh,
wch increase as ii,
and ripen to ye form
of k, whose tomen-
tose husk taken off,
leaves the Areca nut, a, covered with a thin
shell. ll, shews the nut cut asunder.
m m, the Bamboos as growing together
n n, part of one drawn larger. oo, One
joynt yet much larger, to shew the leaf p,
and how the branches grow out of ye joynt.
qq, a branch of the Mango tree, shewing
the leaf rr the flower ss. the fruit tt,
and the inside of it, uu, when slit.
w, the marking nutt yielding a black oyle.

(To face p. 110)

spread, these would still continue; as it is my Fancy they were of old, and may still be the Laboratories of his Fallacious Oracles: For they masquing the face of Day, beget a solemn reverence, and melancholy habit in them that resort to them; by representing the more inticing Place of Zeal, a Cathedral, with all its Pillars and Pillasters, Walks and Choirs; and so contrived, that whatever way you turn, you have an even Prospect.[1]

But not to run too far out of *Maderas* before I give you an Account of the People; know they are of the same Nation with *Metchlapatan*, have the same unbelieving Faith, and under the same Bondage with the *Moors*, were not that alleviated by the Power of the *English*, who command as far as their Guns reach: To them therefore they pay Toll, even of Cow-dung (which is their chiefest Firing) a Prerogative the *Dutch* could never obtain in this Kingdom, and by this means acquire great Estates without fear of being molested. Their only Merchants being *Gentues*, forty *Moors* having hardly Cohabitation with them, though of the Natives 30000 are employed in this their Monopoly.

The Country is Sandy, yet plentiful in Provisions; in all Places Topes of Trees, among one of which, on the top of a withered Stump sate perching a *Chamelion*,[2] *Græce* Χαμαιλέων, clasping with its Claws its rotten Station, filling himself with his Aerial Food, *ex tali satietate facile est parare famem*; a Banquet which most other Creatures else arise an hungred from: But to be confirmed in the truth

---

[1] The virtues of Pān are described by many early travellers: Barbosa, 73; Linschoten, i, 212 ff.; ii, 62 ff.; Pyrard de Laval, ii, 362 ff.; Abd-er-razzak, *India in Fifteenth Century*, 32; Ovington, 122. Also see the account in the *Āīn*, i, 72 f. Fryer compares the conservatory made of mats hung on poles, on which it is grown, to a cathedral. Such places are believed to be semi-sacred, no one in a state of ceremonial impurity being admitted, as the plant is supposed to be most susceptible to spirit influence (Crooke, *Popular Religion and Folk-Lore of N. India*[2], ii, 303 f.)

[2] The Indian variety is *C. zeylanicus*.

of what we have only by Tradition, I caused a Black who had a Bow there, to fell him with an Earthen Pellet,[1] which when he had, after a small time he revived, and making a Collar of Straw for his Neck, he carried him to my Lodgings, where I dieted him a Month on the same Provant. That he changes his Colours at a constant time of the Day, is not to be contradicted; but whether he live by the Air alone, I will not stand to it, unless there were a Dearth of Flies in the Countrey; though for my part I never did see him eat any. In Shape he comes nearest a Newt; with his Lungs his Body does agitate its self up to its Neck; he crawls on all Four, and has a Tail longer than his Body, which altogether was no more than half a Foot; he has Teeth, and those sharp, which makes me think him an *Anti-beel-ubian.*

Nine Days spent here, our Ships set sail again for *Mechlapatan*, leaving us behind them.

In this Interim we have leisure to say something, if not a plenary Panegyrick,

Of the French *Transactions in the* East-Indies.[2]

Of late Years, that stirring King *Lewis* the XIVth (who was well instructed first by *Mazarine*, and since having been no bad Proficient under so expert a Master) has made himself to be taken notice of in *Europe* by his Conquests and Attempts upon *Flanders* and the *Low Countries* by Land; and has also by his Foreign Expeditions, acquested

---

[1] The common pellet-bow, Hind. *gulel* (Yule, *Hobson-Jobson*, 386).

[2] For the operations of the French squadron, under the command of Admiral De la Haye, on the coasts of India, see the account in Wheeler, *Madras in the Olden Time*, i, 73 ff.; Bruce, *Annals*, ii, 44. Bowrey (p. 65 f.) gives an interesting contemporary narrative, where his editor, Sir R. Temple, quotes further details from Delestre, *Relation ou Journal d'un Voyage fait aux Indes Orientales*, Paris, 1677, pp. 34, 59, and gives extracts from the local records.

the World's admiration, by his speedy Growth in Maritime Power.

Insomuch that at his Infant Entrance upon the Watry Stage he was so audacious to join with the *Belgians* against his Royal Patron of *Britain*; having his Ends of those he pretended to succour, his wary Policy taught him another Lesson, that caused him to mediate a Triple Alliance.

About which time enjoying full Coffers, he ruminated on great Designs, as the raising an Army against *Spain*; to the same intent it was necessary for him to think of the continuing a Supply of Money: He therefore (omitting other ways of enriching his Exchequer) put in a Stock with his Merchant Adventurers, fitting out a Fleet of Twenty Sail of lusty Ships, to settle a Trade in *India*, committing them to the Charge and Conduct of a Viceroy; who coming safe about the *Cape*, touched at St. *Lawrence*, where they did but little besides burying their Viceroy, and dispatching four Ships into *Europe*.

In the stead of the Viceroy deceased, the now reigning succeeded.

From thence they sailed to *Surat*, where the *Great Mogul* endowed them with Immunities of Traffick.

In the mean while a second War betwixt *England* and *Holland* was fomented, in the which the *French* threw off the protecting the *Dutch*, and sided with his Majesty of *England*. When neglecting his newly-hatch'd Factory at *Surat* (whether out of its not answering his expectations, or his earnestness in prosecuting the *Hollanders* by Sea as well as by Land, may be known by those that are more intelligent in his Affairs at Home), sense of Honour, obliged his Fleet in the *East-Indies* to New Adventures; and want of Money, the Merchants at *Surat* to Trade upon the Credit of the *French* King.

With fourteen Sail of Ships they roved on the Coasts of *Malabar*, and at last came to the Island *Ceilon*, setting upon the *Dutch* at *Trincomalai*, and forced it; but being destitute of Provisions forsook it, after the loss of abundance of their Men, and four of their Ships.[1]

From whence they passed along the Coast of *Coromandel*, and with Ten Sail came before St. *Thomas*, demanding Victuals of the *Moors*; but they denying, they brought their Ships to bear upon the Fort, and landing some small Pieces they stormed it, driving the *Moors* to the search of new Dwellings.

After they had taken it, they broke up their weather-beaten Vessels, and brought ashore their Ordnance, keeping their Trenches within, and mounting it with the Sea without; they still maintain it maugre all the great Armies the King of *Gulconda* has sent against it.[2]

Till now the 18th Month of its Siege, and the fourth year of their leaving *France*, the *Dutch* of *Batavia*, in revenge of the Inroads the *French* have made on their Countrey at home, undertaking to waylay them, that no Sustenance might be brought to them by Sea, came against it with 20 Sail, 15 Men of War, great Ships, some of 72 Brass Guns apiece, well mann'd.

For all that, the Viceroy, who had then been gone out with four Sail, but returning alone, got betwixt them and the Fort with his single Ship in the Night: The Device this; He left his Light upon a *Catamaran*, so that they thought him at an Anchor without them, when the next

---

[1] In 1672, "on the outbreak of war between Louis XIV and the United Provinces, a French squadron made its appearance at Trincomalie, commanded by Admiral De la Haye. They were eagerly welcomed by the Emperor as unexpected allies, likely to aid him in the expulsion of the pestilent Hollanders. The French took instant possession of Trincomalie, and the Dutch in their panic abandoned the forts of Cottiar and Batticaloa, but the inability of the former to maintain their position in Ceylon, and their sudden disappearance, sufficed to allay the apprehensions of the Dutch" (Tennent, *Ceylon*³, ii, 60).

[2] Compare this account with that of Bowrey and Delestre, quoted by Sir R. Temple, Bowrey, 46 ff.

Morn he play'd upon them from under the Fort: This Exploit, and the bruit of our Approach, made them withdraw to the *Southward* for fresh Recruits of Men and Ammunition.

Which gave the *French* encouragement to sally out upon the *Moors* (they before being beaten from their Works near the City, had decamped Seven Miles off St. *Thomas*), and with an handfull of Men pillaged and set fire to their Tents, foraging the Countrey round about, returning loaden with Spoils.

Three days after our Ships departed, the *Batavians* came again, and cast Anchor over-against St. *Thomas* with their Flags flying; in the afternoon they received some Shot from the *French* Fort and the Ships that lay in the Road: The next day all but five weighed, who tarried not many days before they followed the rest to *Policat*,[1] a Strong-hold of theirs, but 50 Miles *North* of us: Where we leave them to the landing 700 Men, to join with the *Moors* by Land, and their Ships to wait upon ours, upon their repair for *Fort St. George*: And at a distance (because too near an Intrusion would but exasperate the enraged *Moors* to enhanse the Price of our Curiosity) we will take a Survey

Of St. Thomas.

It is a City that formerly for Riches, Pride, and Luxury, was second to none in *India*; but since, by the mutability of Fortune, it has abated much of its adored Excellencies.

The Sea on one side greets its Marble Walls, on the other a Chain of Hills intercepts the Violence of the inflaming Heat; one of which, called St. *Thomas* his Mount, is famous for his Sepulture, (in Honour of whom a

1 Pulicat (Tamil, Pazhavērkkādu, "old acacia forest"), in the Chingleput District, 24 miles N. of Madras. Its great breakwater, or Pulicat Lake, formed a safe haven. The place is described by Hamilton, *New Account*, i, 372; Bowrey, 51.

Chappel is dedicated, the Head Priest of which was once the Metropolitan Bishop of *India*), and for a Tree called *Arbor Tristis*, which withers in the Day, and blossoms in the Night.[1]

About this Mount live a Cast of People, one of whose Legs are as big as an Elephant's; which gives occasion for the divulging it to be a Judgment on them, as the Generation of the Assassins and Murtherers of the Blessed Apostle St. *Thomas*,[2] one of whom I saw at *Fort St. George*.[3]

Within the Walls seven Churches answer to as many Gates; the Rubbish of whose stupendious Heaps do justify the truth of what is predicated in relation to its pristine State.

The Builders of it were the *Portugals*.

---

[1] *Nyctanthes Arbor-tristis*, the flowers of which open towards evening, and fall to the ground on the following morning, the *harsingār* of N. India, the coral Jasmine. The tree has been described by many writers: Linschoten, ii, 58 ff.; Pyrard de Laval, i, 411; ii, 362; P. della Valle, ii, 406; Bowrey, 49 f.; Fanny Parkes, *Wanderings of a Pilgrim*, i, 312. Also see Watt, *Econ. Dict.*, v. 434 f.; Yule, *Hobson-Jobson*, 34 f.

[2] The legend of the visit of St. Thomas to Southern India is discussed by Yule, *Marco Polo*[3], ii, 353 ff.; Rae, *The Syrian Church in India*, 15 ff., the latter remarking (p. 59) that, "according to this apocryphal story, which is almost the only post-canonical information we have regarding St. Thomas, the apostle died and was buried in that India west of the Indus to which he went on receipt of his commission. In that India he preached, and performed miracles, and established churches. From the date of his arrival in the country to the date of his death he never left it. That, and that alone, is the India of which he was the apostle." Also see *Indian Antiquary*, xxxii; *Journal Royal Asiatic Society*, April, 1905; Medlycott, *India and the Apostle St. Thomas*; *Manual of Travancore*, ii, 136 ff.

[3] Elephantiasis results from thread-worms, some of which cause serious disorders of the lymphatic system, resulting in this hideous disease, which is probably communicated by the agency of the mosquito (*Ency. Brit.*[10], xxxi, 120). The traditional account of its origin, in connection with St. Thomas, is shown in the Portuguese name, *Pejo de Santo Thoma*. It is repeated by Hamilton, *New Account*, i, 328, and by Linschoten, i, 88, 288. Terry (p. 424) discredited the belief. Also see Pyrard de Laval, i, 392; Tavernier, ed. Ball, ii, 395; Ives, *Voyage*, 193; Buchanan, *Journey*, i, 48; Bowrey, 50.

The Confounders the *Moors*, who surprized them wallowing in their Wealth and Wantonness.

The present Competitors are the *French*, who are very unlikely to keep it (not for want of Valour, but for that few and unprovided, are not able long to resist multitudes) the *Moors*, and thirdly, the *Hollanders*, whose Interests are to destroy the *French* in *India* ; Which the *French* foreseeing, had wisely solicited a Truce with *Gulconda*, and had hopes of that King's complying, till the Arrival of the *Dutch*, when they could not be heard. For considering a Kindness extorted not so obliging as that freely offered, and his Honour attainted by their Swords being still in their hands, he closed with the Hatred of the *Hollanders*, for their final Extirpation.

Before which be accomplished, he may chance to find it an hard Task, especially had the *French* any hopes of Succours : For now they are 600 strong in the Fort and Ships, all stout Fellows, every Soldier fit to be a Commander. Their greatest scarcity will be of Food, with which had not the *English* privately befriended them, they could not have subsisted hitherto. Though the *English*, should they have War with *France*, would find them to be an Annoyance to their Trade : So that were the City again in the hands of the *Moors*, or even with the Ground, it were better for us.

Here it may be queried, Why *Gulconda* being a Potent Prince, should permit Garisons to be in the hands of Aliens? To this may be answered, That this of St. *Thomas* was founded when the *Indians* were naked and unarm'd. But this satisfies not the Question, since that the *Moors* having conquered it, they again offered it the *Portugals*, who slighted the Propositions, unless they would restore them their Guns which they carried away with them. The true reason then is this, That *Gulconda*, as all the *Indian* Princes are, is weak at Sea ; therefore it is a Maxim among them to commit their Strong-holds on the Sea-Coasts to those they can call their Friends, for not only preventing Invasions at the Charge and Courage of Foreigners; but they (not being Absolute, but subject to the Authority of the *Great Mogul*) upon any Defeat, have these Places as sure Asylums of Retreat.[1]

Amidst these Scenes of Affairs, what next offers to our View, is odd in itself, To find an Aptness in these People to improve all Gainful Arts, and not to have advanced one footstep from the false Rudiments either of Religion or Customs of the Old World; for they do in my mind more than imitate, pertinaciously holding their Antiquities of *Pan*, *Ceres*, and *Flora*; as may appear by this and other following Farces.

Towards the latter end of *August*, when their Corn was in the Blade, and they were expecting a plentiful Crop, the *Gentues* of *Maderas* held a Feast in Memory of some of their Saints of the Devil's canonizing.

Their Ceremonies were usher'd in with Tumult; in the middle of them were carried their Gods in State, garnished with the Riches of the *Orient*; they were cut in horrid Shapes; the reason of which, *Divina assimulatio est causa diversitatis in rebus*; though I should allow the diversity of Creatures in all Orders of the World, hath no other aim but to represent the Divinity, by whatsoever Image, yet I cannot imagine such Deformities could ever be invented for that end. Before them went the *Brachmins*, making a Noise with their loud Musick; after them their dancing Wenches (who always Morning and Evening tumble afore their Gods, which with some Mimical Gesture is all their Dancing) with Ephods of Silk and Gold upon their Breasts: With these in a Ring hand in hand, were the Dancing

[1] Compare the suggestive remark on the command of the sea, Letter III, chap. III.

Boys, all naked but a Clout about their Privitics, like the *Bacchanalian* Youths that used to revel it with *Flora's* Strumpets through the Streets of *Rome*.

Thus went they in Procession, till they came to a Pageant, whereon was pictured their Gods; from whence over a cross Piece of Timber, hung a Cocoa Nut which the Hinds in Yellow Caps, and Clouts about their Wastes, striving to hit with a great Club, are Washed by a Shower of Water, by the *Brachmins* placed on purpose; after a long Trial of their Patience, they suffer one to bear it away in Triumph.

All the time of their Sport, *Beetle* and *Cocoa Nuts* are scattered among the People, for which they scramble as earnestly as if they were Medals at Coronations.[1]

On a Pageant over-against the Pagod they had a Set of Dancers handed like Puppits, to the amusing of the Mobile.

Then setting open the Gates of the Pagod, they received all the unsanctified Crew, and shut them in; where how they conclude their Rites, is not to be divulged, Ignorance with them being the Mother of Devotion.

---

[1] This rite may be compared with another in which coconuts are used, described by Fryer elsewhere (Letter II, chap. IV). Welsh (*Military Reminiscences*, ii, 73 f.) describes a festival at Tellicherry on 26th August. "Under the Fort of Moilan, there are some large rocks jutting into the sea. . . . On one of these projecting eminences, we took our stand, and other Brahmins on another, surrounded on three sides by the principal natives of all castes. The head Brahmin then squatted down on the side towards the sea, with a dish of rice, and a whole cocoa-nut, gilded over, in the centre. He muttered a prayer, and having distributed the rice with the finger and thumb, threw the cocoa-nut into the sea; which was immediately followed by some hundreds from the crowd that surrounded him. A number of men and boys dashed into the water at the same time to catch the cocoa-nuts, and a scene of amusing confusion followed, in which the exertions of the boatmen were now and then requisite, particularly when any young gentleman got a crack on the sconce, with a cocoa-nut. Thus ended this extraordinary ceremony, and returning home we got wet through, as if to prove the fallacy of the sacrifice to put a period to the rains." In the rite as described here by Fryer the dousing of the youths seems to be intended as a piece of mimetic magic to secure abundant rain (Fraser, *Golden Bough*[2], i, 211).

At *Triblitore*,[1] four Miles *North* of *Maderas*, is a Pagod transcending both in respect of Building and Antiquity; there being Characters, the Expounders of the *Gentu* Language or Holy Writ understand not: To this Mother-Pagod, at certain Seasons of the Year, long Pilgrimages are set on foot, at what time there is an innumerable Concourse, whereat some of the Visitants count it meritorious to be trod to death under a weighty Chariot of Iron made for the carriage of their Deities; and with themselves lay their Wives and Children to undergo the same Self-martyrdom.

In one of their open *Pagods* or Chappels, stands a Venerable Sir at the upper end, with the Attendants of Lamps and Bats, to whom they pay a world of Worship: Who this should be, unless that *Periomel*,[2] from whose Head the *Brachmins*, Pallas-like fable their origination, I am yet to seek.

In the way hither are store of *Antilopes*,[3] not to be taken but by a Decoy made of Green Boughs, wherein a Man hides himself, and walking with this Bush upon his Back, gains so near on them, while grazing or browzing rather on Shrubs or Bushes, as to hit one with an Arrow, when it may be run down with Dogs, the rest of the Herd shunning it: They are of a delicater shape and make than a

---

[1] Trivettore (Tamil Tiruvottiyūr, "village sacred to Siva"), a place of pilgrimage in the Chingleput District. There is an ancient Śaiva temple, at which an annual festival is held in the month of February (*Madras Adm. Man.*, iii, 900). Bowrey (p. 7 f.) refers to "the figure of the Pagod called Tressletore, 5 and ½ miles to the northward of Fort St. George." Other contemporary forms of the name are Trivatore and Trevitore.

[2] See p. 78.

[3] These may be the Black Buck (*Antilope cervicapra*); and to this Bowrey's account of the animal (p. 59) and his drawing (Plate x) seem rather to point. But it seems now to be found in most of the Madras Districts, except on the West Coast (*Imp. Gaz.*, xvi, 244). If he does not refer to the Black Buck, the animal may be the Indian Gazelle (*Gazella bennetti*), (Blanford, *Mammalia*, 526).

Deer, their Horns not jagged, but turned as an Unicorn's; not spread into Branches, but straight, and long, and tapering, rooted on the *Os frontis*, springing up on both sides.

At the end of *August* one of the *Portugal* Junks, we found in the Road, set Sail for *Achein*; where is Gold, and the Island thought by some to be *Solomon's Ophir*; and the Queen thereof, by whom it is constantly governed,[1] confidently reported to be the Queen of the *South*, *Achein* being on the Island *Sumatra* in the *South* Seas.

The first of *September* only Seven of our Ten Ships returned from *Mechlapatan*, with their wounded Men and torn Hulks, who had met the *Hollanders*, and tried their Force; two days after they were dispatched from *Mechlapatan*, in *Pettipolee* Bay,[2] where as soon as Day began to peep, a Thicket of Twenty Sail of our Enemies were discovered stemming the flowing Tide at an Anchor.[3] Our Fleet might have passed them without giving Battel; but that the undaunted *Britains* scorned to fly, chusing rather to lye a Battery for them, than cowardly to flinch: Wherefore they braced their Sails to the Masts, and being to

[1] There was a belief current that Achin was always ruled by a queen. Bowrey (p. 295) says that a queen had then reigned for a considerable time. Sir R. Temple (note *in loco*) shows that there were Kings of Achin from 1521 to 1641, when, on the death of the King, a tyrant, a queen succeeded, and reigned long enough to establish the legend.

[2] See p. 106.

[3] The Dutch fleet, under Rickloff van Goens, the Dutch Governor-General of India, was cruising along the Coromandel Coast. Van Goens laid siege to St. Thomé, and endeavoured to wrest it from the French, but failed. This fleet of fourteen vessels encountered the English Company's homeward fleet of ten ships on its passage from Bengal. "A running engagement took place on the 22nd August, 1673, of which no details appear to have been preserved, but in which one ship was sunk by the enemy, and two fell into his hands. The remainder escaped to Madras, and after being repaired, were enabled to proceed on their way to England" (Wheeler, *Madras in the Olden Time*, i, 76 f.). Bruce (*Annals*, ii, 345) gives a similar account. Hunter (*H. of British India*, ii, 199) speaks of it as "an honourable engagement which English patriotism has recounted in somewhat florid terms." Sir R. Temple (Bowrey, 92 *n.*) quotes narratives of the fight by Basse and Earving, Purser's Mate of the *Sampson*, which seem to show that Captain Cruft, who commanded the *Unity*, the ship in which Fryer sailed to India, behaved with some lack of energy.

Leeward, stayed for the Wind which favoured the *Hollanders*; who coming up with our Fleet, made as if they would have gone by them; but were intercepted by the headmost of ours: Which perceived by the forwardest of theirs, they sent their Shallops aboard their Admiral for Orders, for *vis consilii expers mole ruit suâ*, Strength void of Counsel sinks with its proper weight; which was but too truly the fault of our Commanders, over-confident of their own Conduct, and lightly regarding the Authority of their General

When they came back again, they brought their Fleet up in a Body, and after the Signal given, it thundred and hailed Bullets till Night.

The first that felt the warmth of the Showres, was the *Bombaim*; who after an hours hot dispute almost board and board with one of their biggest Ships, bore off hardly able to keep above water, and never came in again, having received 80 Shot in her Hull, and some between Wind and Water, so that in the Hold there was four Feet and an half Water; besides innumerable in her Rigging, Masts and Sails, from those that pelted at a distance.

The next Ship that behaved her self stoutly, was the Admiral's; who lost 34 of her Men by the Scurvy Accidents of Powder 17 of them were slain outright.

But the Three fatal Ships were the *Antilope*, Captain *Golsbery*; the *Sampson*, Captain *Ernnig*, Reer-Admiral; and the *President*, Vice-Admiral Captain *Hide*, whose rigid Fortune saved the drooping honour of the *English*, which is not less conspicuous in Adversity than in Prosperity. For having sustained the Brunt of the day, they left not off when they were penned in by the Enemy, and deserted by their Friends: For by Five in the Afternoon the *London* bore away to stop her Leaks, the rest were glad to follow; and left them to maintain so unequal a Fight. The Vice-Admiral was seen to blow up his Decks several times, distributing the *Hollanders* as Doles to the Fishes, and left not off till Night parted the Fray ; so that what became of them our Ships could give us no account.

Six days since this, a Thousand Men under *Dutch* Colours, with a dozen Carriages with great Brass Pieces, marched by out of shot of our Leaguers, and fixed their Standard with the *Moors* in sight of St. *Thomas.*

The next day was sent from *Mechlapatan* hither, the Copy of a Letter from Captain *Hide*, which assured us of his being alive, but wounded, his Ship as it is, at the disposal of the *Dutch* ; as also Captain *Ernnig's*, though he was killed first : That Captain *Golsbery* sunk his, rather than it should go to *Batavia* ; that he, and what Men could shift for themselves, were safe.

It may be wondred why the *French* did not assist us, they being as much at odds with the *Dutch* as we ; the reality is, they offered their Devoirs, but we must equip their Ships ; for which our Commanders pretended lack of Orders as well as Money and Materials : Though the plain truth was, they despised their kindness, thinking it beneath them to be beholden to them for their help.

The Factories of the *Hollanders* on this Coast, are *Ceilon*,[1] *Jaffnapatan*,[2] *Sandraslapatan*,[3] *Negapatan*,[4] *Policat*,[5] *Mechlapatan.*

---

[1] For the Dutch occupation of Ceylon, see Tennent, *Ceylon*³, ii, 32 ff. Their connection with the island began on the arrival of Admiral Spilberg in 1602. In 1658 they finally expelled the Portuguese on the capture of Jaffna.

[2] At the extreme north of Ceylon ; held by the Portuguese from 1617 to 1658. It is the Japhonapataõ of Manucci (i, 335) ; the Japhnapatam of Bowrey (181). See Tennent, ii, 540 f. ; A. Hamilton, *New Account*, i, 342 : Yule, *Hobson-Jobson*, 445.

[3] See p. 75.

[4] Tamil, Nāgappattanam, "snake-town," in the Tanjore District, one of the earliest Portuguese settlements on the Coromandel Coast, from whom it was taken by the Dutch in 1660. It became, in subordination to Bantam, the headquarters of the Dutch trade in this part of India (*Madras Adm. Man.*, iii, 580 f.). The place is described by A. Hamilton (*New Account*, i, 345) and by Welsh (*Mil. Rem.*, i, 19).

[5] See p. 115.

The *Danes* have a few, the *French* less.

In the *South Sea*, under the Agent of *Bantam*, the *English* have Factors at *Pegu*, *Siam*, *Jambee*:[1] The *Dutch* have *Batavia*,[2] and the *Moluccos*, from whence Nutmegs, worth more alone than all we have in *India*; they being as powerful for Men, Riches and Shipping in *Batavia*, as in *Europe*; which is grounded on a different Principle from our *East India* Company, who are for the present Profit, not future Emolument.

These, as they gain ground, secure it by vast Expences, raising Forts, and maintaining Souldiers: Ours are for raising Auctions, and retrenching Charges;[3] bidding the next Age grow rich as they have done, but not affording them the means.

Our Ships that were left, were no sooner repaired, than fraited with their *Salt Peter* and Fine Cloth; and had leave to make the best of their way for the *Malabar* Coast in less than a Fortnight's time, when it was determined to keep off to Sea, as well to escape the *Hollanders*, as the Violence of the *Mossoons*; who being upon the point of shifting their Quarters, are most dangerous near the Shore.

These *Mossoons* or *Monsoons*, are the Winds and Rains customary to all *India*, varying here only in respect of the Mountains.

Therefore on these Coasts the *South Winds* blow for Eight Months, four of which are *May*, *June*, *July*, *August*. Then the Sun is so strong, that it would be uninhabitable,

---

[1] On the N. coast of Sumatra, in the Province of Palembang. The Dutch had a factory here in 1607 (Birdwood, *Report*, 186). For descriptions of the place, see Milburn (*Oriental Commerce*, ii, 349); Bowrey (295); A. Hamilton, *New Account*, ii, 123 f.

[2] In 1619 the Dutch acquired the sovereignty of Java, and on the 12th August of that year laid the foundations of the city of Batavia or Jacatra, which replaced Amboyna as the seat of their Supreme Government (Bruce, *Annals*, i, 211; Birdwood, *Report*, 187).

[3] On the Company's policy of economy, see the remarks of Hunter, *H. of British India*, i, 237 ff.

did not there fall at Night those Vapours which the Sun draws up in the Day; and by declining of his exorbitant Heat, leaves them to be condensated at Night; when the Air is more gross, and the Earth is cooled either by thick Mists, or a more palpable Moisture (which you may call pouring Showres) and thereby made fertile, which otherwise would be insupportable and barren.

That which makes this the more plausible is, That the *Asiatick India intra Gangem*, is a *Pene Insula*, and the Seas lie near round the Land.

But about the Sun's retiring to his *Southern* Tropick, the Winds take their *Northern* Course, the Rains do cease, and the Sea alters its Current to the *South*, when by the innate coldness of these Blasts the Clime becomes more habitable, unless where the Sands cause a reflection of heat, as at *Mechlapatan*; where they keep close all Day for three or four Months together, (though then the *North Wind* begins to abate its impetuosity, and the *South Winds* prevail) repelling the Heat by a course wet Cloath, continually hanging before their Chamber-windows; which not only resists the Ambient Air, but by the afflux of Nitrous Particles from within, does cast a Chilness over the Room; without which, the Walls, that for that intent are plastered, would be so hot, you could not abide your Hand on them; the same way they have of cooling their Liquors, by a Wet Cloth wrapped about their Gurgulets[1] and Jars, which are Vessels made of a porous kind of Earth; the best of *Mæcha*, reasonable good from *Goa*, which are carried with them in this nature wherever they travel.

Before we dismiss this Discourse, it may be noted, That the Rains on this Coast are more intermitting than on the

---

[1] Port., *gorgoleta*, "an earthen and narrow-mouthed vessel, out of which the water runs and gurgles"; another form of the word is goglet. See Linschoten, i. 207; Pyrard de Laval, i, 329, ii, 74; Yule, *Hobson-Jobson*, 382.

Malabar Coast, so that they can loose hence their Ships for *Persia*, *Mæcha* and *Juddah*, and to the *South Seas* in those Months they are Wind-bound on the other Coast: for having the Land-Breezes to carry them off to Sea, the *Mossoons* are more favourable.

Concerning the Regularities of these Winds, perhaps some others may give patter Guesses than my self; who am not conceited enough to dogmatize.

Among the many that be alledged, I am not fond of any, though this have won a little upon my Opinion; That the Sun may be as well the reason why these Winds should observe his Annual Circumrotation; as that the Ebbings and Flowings of the Sea, by the Moon's meer depression of Air, should be ascribed to her Monthly Revolutions.

And here one thing may be worthy our Curiosity, That after the Seasons of the Heats and Rains, the Rivers *Indus* and *Ganges* are said to swell their Banks, and thereby abundantly to encrease the Bordering Countries, where these Rains are less frequent: Whence, it may be, some insight may be had for the Overflows of *Egypt*, which has set so many Wits on the Tenterhooks, where it is reported it never rains: But in the Countreys near the supposed Source of *Nile*, it does to Excess.

But you who have greater Reading and Leisure to digest these Metaphysical Notions, will mightily oblige me to furnish me with your solider Arguments.

Among which I would intreat you to consider the Variety of the Loadstone in the common Chart: For what the incomparably Ingenuous *Des Cartes* has wrote on that Subject, acquiesces only in modest Hypotheticks, not any ways informing the Understanding to a clear Apprehension; but after he has brought it through the Maze of Probabilities, he parts with it at the same Predicament it entred.

Not to deviate any longer, we are now winding about the *South-West* part of *Ceilon*; where we have the *Tail of the*

Elephant[1] full in our mouths; a Constellation by the *Portugals* called *Rabo del Elephanto*, known for the breaking up of the *Munsoons*, which is the last Flory this Season makes, generally concluding with *September*, which goes out with dismal Storms.

Yet so good is Providence, as to warn us here, when all is obscured, by *Water-Snakes*,[2] of our too near approach to the Land; which are as sure Presages on the *Indian* Coasts, as the *Cape*-Birds are there.

Here the Mountains running *East* and *West*, the Winds are to the *East* of the *South*, and to the *West* of the *North*; else quadrating with those on *Coromandel*; only here in *April* and *May* the Winds are variable, and then they hasten to leave these Coasts for *Persia*, the *Red-Sea*, and *South-Seas*, or those make in that are to return hither; otherwise they run an hazard of losing their Voyage, when the *South* to the *South-East* Wind is fixed, which continues to the latter end of *September*, or beginning of *October*: Then

---

[1] The name of the lunar asterism, which ushers in the end of the rainy season, the name of which the Portuguese adopted from the Hindu *hasta*, with the same meaning. "Suddenly from the west arose a great storm, known as *fil tofani*" (*Travels and Adventures of Sidi Ali Reis*, 17).

[2] "The sign by which those who come hither by sea know they are nearing land is their meeting with snakes, which are here of a black colour, not so long as those already mentioned, like serpents about the head, and with eyes the colour of blood" (*Periplus*, cap. 55, in M'Crindle, 136). "Wee found ground at forty fadomes, many snakes swimming about our ship, which (with the waters changing colour) assured us we were neere the shoare" (Herbert, 34). The same phenomenon was noticed by Linschoten (i, 35, with Burnell's note): also see Foster, *English Factories* (1615-21) 272. Maclean (*Guide to Bombay*[21] (1896) 191) writes: "Perhaps steamers have driven the serpents away; at all events, we seldom hear of them now, although Capt. Dundas, of the P. and O. Co., states that what old travellers have said on the subject is not altogether wrong. The serpents are seen during the S.W. monsoon, a season in which alone voyages used to be made to India. In Horsburgh's 'Sailing Directions,' shipmasters are warned to look out for the serpents, whose presence is a sign that the ship is close to land. Capt. Dundas says the serpents are yellow or copper-coloured. The largest ones are farthest out to sea. They lie on the surface of the water, and appear too lazy even to get out of a steamer's way."

from the *North* to the *North-West* sets in again; and this Course is observed mostly on all the *Indian* Shores, only some few days different in the beginning and ending, which happen to the *South*, and in Lands commonly earlier than to the *North*, and break up later when they are more severe, but the Intervals are milder; the middle Months clearing up in the day time; but from the first setting to the going out towards the *North*, the Sun hardly shews his Face, unless a Fortnight after the Full Moon in *May*, and a Fortnight before the *Elephanto*.

On the Coast of *Surat* from { *Gemini* to *Libra*.

This happens in the Sun's *Ecliptick* Road.

On the Coast of *Coromandel* from { *Taurus* to *Scorpio*.[1]

And thus much may be said in general; only the Land and Sea-Breezes in particular, on this Coast of *Surat* and *Malabar*, when the Rains are over, keep exactly Land-Breezes from Midnight to Mid-day, and Sea-Breezes from the Noon of Day to the Noon of Night.

Making Land, we beheld it all a Flame, they burning their Stubble for Soilage, the Forerunner of the ensuing Rain; notwithstanding a *Kingfisher* flew aboard us with the flattering Coaks's[2] of Halcyon days; but like an unskilful Augur was deservedly reproached with the Ignorance of her own Destiny, to dye in Captivity; which fatal Necessity made her elect, rather than suffer with whole Flocks of little Birds blown from the Main, who not able to

---

[1] "The primary fact in the meteorology of India is the alternation of seasons known as the south-west and north-west monsoons." The subject is too wide for treatment in a note. It is fully discussed in the *Imperial Gazetteer* (1907), i, 109 ff.

[2] Obsolete form of *coax*; see *New Eng. Dict.*

stem the boisterousness of the Winds, were hurried thence to perish in the Sea.

And now we were begirt with Land: The *Maldivæ* Islands lying *South*; Cape *Comerin*[1] *North and by West*; the *Malabar* Islands *West*, (whose Inhabitants have no relation with those on the Coast); whence is brought great quantities of *Ambergreece*; *Ceilon*, *&c.*

The Land our Master took for a *Malabar* Island proved a mistake; for by a strong Current we were lock'd in between the Island *Ceilon*, and the *North-East* side of the Cape, within that desperate Canal we before described. Our Error was first corrected by some Fishermen busy at their Nets, who brought aboard plenty of Fishes, all new to us, who never had seen such coloured ones, some gilded like Gold, others with Vermilion, varied by several Intermixtures.

Whilst we were lost in admiration, our Mates nd themselves no less at a loss in their accounts, wher they understood they were drove 30 Leagues to Leeward of the Cape, by the broken *Portugueze* spoken by these Men, and that we could not sail much farther than *Tutticaree*,[2] a *Portugal* Town in Time of Yore, where they had a Citadel, and two famous Churches; and before us, which was the Lure, a Ketch of the *Dutch's* (which we chased for hopes of Prize) was sailing to that Port, and presently after anchored: We were then in seven Fathom Water.

This is the place where they drag Pearl.[3]

---

[1] Cape Comorin; Tamil, *Kumari*; from the temple dedicated to Kumārī, the maiden Durgā (Yule, *Hobson-Jobson*, 238). The temple, known as Kanniyāmbāl, is one of the most important places of pilgrimage in S. India.

[2] Tuticorin (Tamil, Tuttukkudi, "place of scattered houses"), in the Tinnevelly District. The Portuguese founded a settlement here about 1540, which in 1658 was captured by the Dutch.

[3] The pearl fisheries on the Gulf of Manār (Tamil, Mannār, "sandy village") are the most important in India. On the Ceylon side the banks lie from 6 to 8 miles off the W. shore, a little to the S. of the

All along here the Top of *Gates* is seen above the Clouds, the Ground beneath it Fair, Low, and Sandy.

Tutticaree is now in the hands of the *Dutch*, running the same Risco with *Columbo*, over-against which it lies; we being now in the very Jaws of our Enemies, might have here concluded our Voyage, had their Fleet been nigh us.

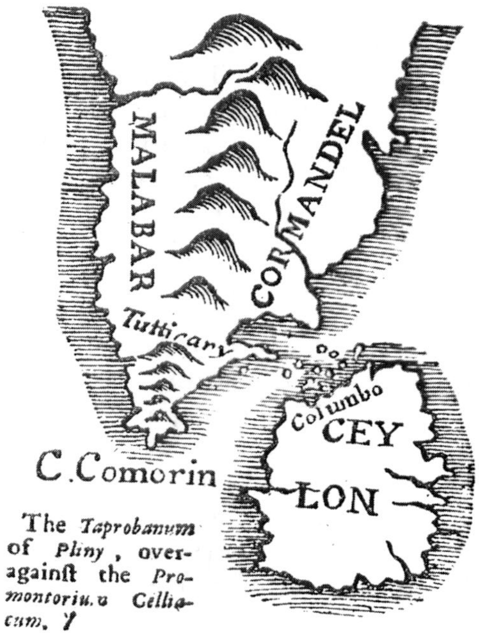

Cabe Comeri.

---

island of Manār; while those on the Madras side are situated off Tinnevelly and Madura. For accounts of this fishery see Watt, *Econ. Dict.*, iv, Pt. I, 120; Hakluyt, iii, 224 ff.; Linschoten, i, 80; Tavernier, ed. Ball, ii, 211; Tennent, *Ceylon*[3], ii, 560 ff.

[1] Pliny (N. H., vi, 24 (22)): "They further said that the nearest point of India is a promontory called Coliacum, a few days' sail distant from the island, and that midway between them lies the island of the Sun." "Kōlis is a name by which Pomponius Mela and Dionysios Periēgētēs designate Southern India. Pliny's promontory *Coliacum* is Cape Kōry, the headland which bounded the Orgalic Gulf on the south. The two names are variant forms of the Indian word

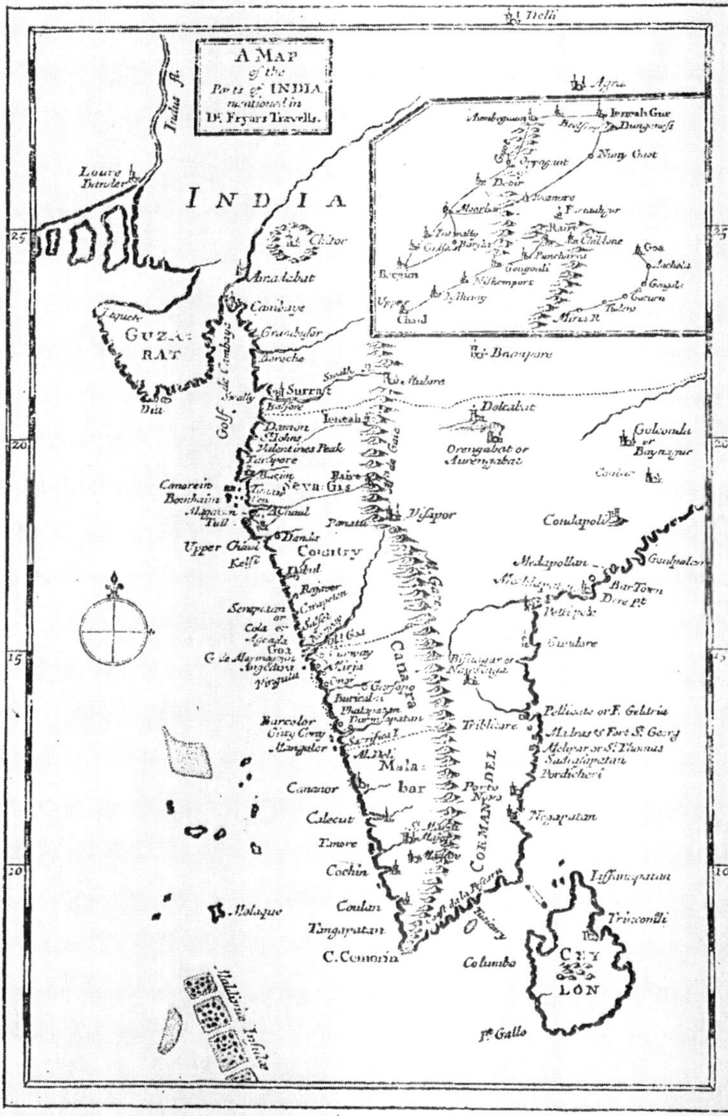
A MAP of the Ports of INDIA mentioned in Dr. Fryars Travells.
INDIA
Delli
Agra
Indus fl.
GUZARAT
Golf of Cambaya
Surrat
Goa
Canara
Malabar
Cormandel
Ceylon
Cochin
Calecut
Cananor
C. Comorin
Columbo
Pt. Gallo
Golconda
Orengabat or Aurengabat
Doltabat
Visapor
Maldivie Insulae

(To face p. 131)

The next day we were becalmed, and thereby carried into the midst of the Stream; and although in the Afternoon we had an humming *Frisco*, it ran with such Violence that we lost more than we gained: This Mistake cost us a Fortnights time before we could compass the Cape, besides Fears and Jealousies both of our Falling into the Torrent, and our Enemies hands.

The Cape lanches into the Sea with Three Points, running into a Campaign several Miles together, till it grows big with Mountains, procreating their prodigious Race 400 Leagues, severing the Coast of *Coromandel* and *Malabar*, *East* and *West*; Latitude 8 *deg.* 50 *min. North*; Longit. 96 *deg. East.*[1]

CHAP. VI.

Views the Malabar *and* Canatick *Coasts up to* Bombaim.

TO prevent the mischief of ingulphing again by the Current, we anchored a-nights; when a Pitchy Blackness was interposed betwixt us and the Skies, and not a Star to be seen: The *Plebs Squammosa* beneath the Surface of the Salt Ocean, gathering their little Fry (which proved to be Pilchards[2]), either by the Repercussion of the Saline Bodies of the Waves, which is frequent, or by the more apt Position of their Glittering Scales, through that Medium

---

Kōti (in Tamil Kōdi, which naturally becomes Kōri or Kōry), which means *end* or *tip*" (M'Crindle, *Ancient India as described in Classical Literature*, 104).

[1] The chain of the western Ghāts runs N. from Cape Comorin, which is situated lat 8o° 5′ N., long. 77° 33′ E.

[2] The true pilchard (*Clupea pilchardus*) does not seem to be an Indian fish; but *C. fimbriata*, *ilisha*, *longiceps*, and *variegata* appear in Day's lists (Watt, *Econ. Dict.*, iii, 378 f.). "The flesh of the Malabar swine is very difficult of digestion, and has a disagreeable taste. This is owing to their being too much fed with pilchards, which are found on the sea-coast in the utmost abundance" (Fra Paolino, 212, 239).

to refract the hovering Light benighted in the Atmosphere, dispersed a Lustre as bright as Day; insomuch that a small Print might easily be read by it.[1]

Taking advantage of the Land-Breezes and the Tides, we scudded along the Shore, which was Woody, and well stock'd with Trees, the Ground even for many Leagues together; the Mountains peeping up behind a great way in the Country.

Being against *Carnopoly*,[2] a *Portugal* Friar boarded us: It is some Miles to the *North* of *Caulam*,[3] formerly inhabited by the *Portugals*, and from them taken by the *Dutch*, who have built a Castle there, and Lord it over the Natives, so that at *Carnopoly* the *Dutch* exact Custom for all the Goods they carry off to Sea, though there live but one Boy and two *Dutchmen*. The *Portugals* have only Five Persons here. The *English* had also a Factory for Pepper, but they are gone both from hence and *Purcat*,[4] 20 Miles more *North*; the Cause we are unacquainted with, but believe the *Dutch* will leave nothing unattempted, to engross the Spice-Trade; for none has escaped them but this of Pepper; Cinamon, Cloves, Mace, and Nutmegs, being wholly theirs; and by the Measures they follow, this also in time must fall into their hands.

Nor indeed are Pretentions wanting, they holding here

---

[1] Sea phosphorescence is due to the animals which inhabit it, except in a few cases when it has been ascribed to putrescent matter. It is most commonly caused by the luminous animalcule, *Noctiluca miliaris* (*Ency. Brit.*[9], xviii, 813 ff.)

[2] Karngapalli in Constable's *Hand Atlas*; Mal. Karunāgappalli, "black snake village": in Travancore, about 15 miles N. of Kaulam. It is the Carnoply of early writers (Birdwood, *Report*, 233).

[3] Quilon of modern maps (Mal., Kovilagam, "King's palace"), in Travancore. The Portuguese established a factory in 1503; but were expelled by the Dutch in 1661-64 (Birdwood, *Report*, 189).

[4] Porakād of Constable's *Hand Atlas*; Mal. Purakkātu, "outside forest"; on the coast of Travancore. It is the Porca and Porcai of early travellers (Tavernier, ed. Ball, i, 241; Varthema, 154). Under the names Porca and Porqua it occurs repeatedly in the English records (Birdwood, *Report*, 85, 174, 190, 233).

their Right by Conquest (a fairer Claim than undermining), they boasting they have in a manner subdued the Natives; which is no hard matter, since this Region of *Malabar* (in which general Name I reckon as far *South* as the *Land's End*, and *Phalapatan*[1] *North*) is divided into several Petit Signiories, or Arch-Rebels against the *Zamerhin*[2] of *Calicut* only paying some slight Acknowledgments of his Supremacy, as their Chief Bishop, and joining with him against the *Great Mogul*; else striving to supplant each other; having a Government most like Aristocracy of any in the *East*, each State having a Representative, and he to act according to the Votes of the *Nairos*[3] Gentry in full Assembly; which as they interfere with one anothers Interests, the weakest have always been ready to call in help: For which reason the *Dutch* were first permitted to rear Castles to secure the Sea-Coasts; which they have

---

[1] For this place, see p. 145. "The limits usually assigned to Malabar are Mount Dely on the north, and Cape Comorin on the south (Yule, *Cathay*, 450; Barbosa, 101; Fra Bart., *Eng. Trans.*, 103). Barros (*Dec. I*, liv. IV, cap. vii) puts the northern boundary at Carnate, near Dely; De Couto (*Dec. XII*, liv. I, cap. xviii) puts it at Cananor; others, erroneously, as high as Goa. Linschoten (i, 65) and Mandelslo (p. 87) agree with Pyrard in assigning Barcelor (*Bārkūr*) in S. Kanara, as the northern limit; and if we go by language, as Pyrard does, they are right, as this is the northern limit of Malayālam" (Gray, on Pyrard de Laval, i, 369). Dalboquerque (ii, 77) writes: "The Province of Malabar commences at the port of Maceirão, close to Mangalor, and reaches as far as the Cape of Comorim in the interior country, bounded by the great Kingdom of Narsinga."

[2] The Zamorin; Mal. Sāmūtiri, a Sanskritized translation of his Mal. title—Kunnalakkon, "King of the hills and waves" (Yule, *Hobson-Jobson*, 977).

[3] The Nāyar or ruling caste in Malabar. It is curious that their remarkable marriage customs did not attract Fryer's attention. Few castes in India have been more often described; as, for instance, *Tohfut-ul-Mujahideen*, ed. Rowlandson, 62 f.; Barbosa, 105, 124 ff.; Hieronimo di Santo Stefano (*India in Fifteenth Century*, cap. iv, 5); Pyrard de Laval, ii, 218 ff., 361; Ovington, 80. For modern accounts, see Buchanan, *Journey*, ii, 408 ff., 573 ff.; Welsh, *Military Reminiscences*, ii, 107; Burton, *Goa and the Blue Mountains*, 215 ff.; Logan, *Man. of Malabar*, i, 131 ff.; *Madras Museum Bulletin*, iii, No. 3; Gopal Panikkar, *Malabar and its Folk*, 38 ff.

made so good use of, as to bring them under their Yoke; the *Greal Mogul* not discouraging them in the least.

Keeping on our Course we left *Cochin*[1] to the *Southward*, once a famous Mart of the *Portugals*, since wrested from them, and made impregnable by the *Dutch*.

At this place we bad adieu to all our bad Weather, though not the Practices of the *Dutch*, who had prevented the *English* at *Panana*[2] also; so that here neither being any Pepper, we had nothing else to do but hoist Sails for *Tanore*,[3] where we touched the first of *November*, the Natives having hardly shaken off the fear of the *Dutch*: For a Boat with Sails of Mats (all their small Boats making them their Sails) came to take a Survey of us, and made towards us uncertainly; when after several Fetches to and again, at last they were within Call of us: We saw two *Sumbrero's*[4] (a Mark for some of Quality) held up in the Boat-stern, and a Man stand up and wave his Hat, which

---

[1] Mal. Kochchi, "small place," in the Malabar District. This was one of the first places in India visited by Europeans, a legend connecting it with St. Thomas. A Portuguese factory was established by Vasco de Gama, on his second voyage, in 1502. Dalboquerque built here the first European fort in India, in 1503 (Danvers, i, 99). In 1616 the English, under Keeling, proposed to found a factory, which was erected some years later with the permission of the Portuguese. In 1663 the town and fort were captured from the Portuguese by the Dutch, and the English retired to Ponany (Birdwood, *Report*, 189 f.; *Madras Adm. Man.*, iii, 194). For early notices of the place, see Barbosa, 156 f.; Linschoten, i, 68 f.; Pyrard de Laval, i, 433 ff.; Dalboquerque, i, 5 f.; Hakluyt, iii, 221 f.

[2] Ponani, Mal. Ponnāni, "a gold coin"; a port in the Malabar District. Barbosa (or his editor) (p. 153) calls it Pananx, "another city of the Moors, amongst whom a few Gentiles live. The Moors are very rich merchants, and own much shipping. The King of Calicut collects much revenue from this city." Varthema (p. 275) says it was the headquarters of a fleet. Pyrard de Laval (i, 398) erroneously speaks of it as an inland town. Linschoten (ii, 169) describes the erection, in 1585, of a fort by the Portuguese, which was soon abandoned.

[3] Tānūr (Mal. Tānūr, "village of the *terminalia bellerica* tree"), a port in the Malabar District. It is an old place, mentioned by Barbosa (p. 153); the Tananor of Pyrard de Laval (i, 425). It is described by A. Hamilton (*New Account*, i, 322). It is now a decayed place, a centre of the Moplas (*Madras Adm. Man.*, iii, 697).

[4] Port. *sumbreiro*, "an umbrella" (Yule, *Hobson-Jobson*, 851).

made our Master stretch his throat to know what he was whereupon down went the *Sumbrero's* held up in the Boat stern, the Boat cleverly tacked, and the Men tugged stoutly at their Paddles, and we as roundly sent seven Shot after them, and the *London* as many; but they were more scar'd than hurt; for after we had mann'd three Boats after them, they return'd with their Labour for their Pains, the Boat getting safe from them. At Night another boat with an *Englishman* came to ask what Ships we were: Whom when we answered *English*, he boarded us, and told us our unadvised Salutes were level'd at an *English* Merchant sent off by the Chief, who notwithstanding he presented two Pistols at the Breasts of the Boatmen, could not beat out of them the suspicion they were possessed with of our being *Dutch*: which shews how strangely they are awed by them; and the rather, they being solicitous Blazers of their own good Fortune upon us, and our Defeat by them; which they had taken care to publish, to bring us into Disrepute, which commonly waits on Ill Success, before we could come to tell our own Tale.

At our arriving ashore the Natives flocked about us, and gazed upon us as if they would have stared us through; amidst a Lane of whom we were ushered by a few *Portugals* to their Chappel, at the Door whereof stood the *Padre* to receive us, and through it to conduct us to his House.

From whence I went to observe the Town, which is miserably poor and straggling, though in the heart of it a double Row of Cottages opened their Shops of Wares, which consisted of *Pepper*, *Turmerick*, *Ginger*, *Cassia Lignum*,[1] the lesser *Cardamoms*, *Bunco*,[2] i.e. Tobacco, and

---

[1] *Cassia lignea* or *C. tamala*, Cassia cinnamon, of which the leaves, oil, buds, and bark are used in manufactures and medicine (Watt, *Econ. Dict.*, ii, 319 ff.)

[2] Buncus, an old word for a cheroot; Malay *bungkus*, "a wrapper" (Yule, *Hobson-Jobson*, 126).

Hubble-bubble[1] *Canes*, the Product of this Coast, as are also *Beetle-Nuts* the greatest Gain from this place to *Surat*, to be reaped by them.

Amongst whom were *Shroffs*,[2] or Money-changers. On one side in a square place was their Fish-Market, through which we came into another Lane, at whose end there was a Mosque.

Their Houses are little Hovels or Hogsties, the best of them scarce worthy the Name of a Booth. The *English* House is in the fashion with the rest, covered all over with *Cajans*,[3] and seated (which they mightily affect) under Trees. The People are Tawny, not Black. Their Language *Malabar*.[4] Here is a Specimen of their Character.

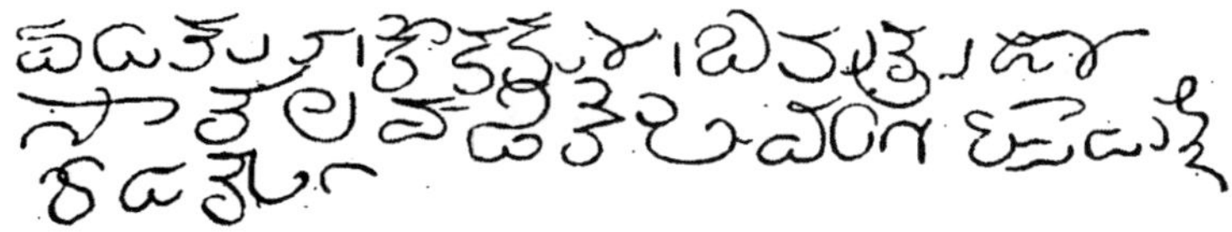

They are subject to the *Zamerhin* of *Calicut*, who sent hither his Delegate to welcome us, and invite us to a Continuance of Trade: He gave our Fleet seven Guns, which were planted near the Water-side; which Compliment was returned by the Fleet.

The Nation is distinguished by Three Ranks. The Priests make the first; they come abroad in several distracted Postures, sometimes all naked, plaister'd over with Ashes, their Hair plaited like an Horse's Tail; at other times appearing less barbarous, being covered, but as Stoical in their Behaviour.

---

[1] See p. 43.

[2] Ar. *sarrāf* (Yule, *Hobson-Jobson*, 831).

[3] See p. 60.

[4] This passage was referred to the Curator Oriental MSS. Library, Madras, who, as in the case of the script (p. 95), is unable to interpret it. He describes it as really written in "Telinga characters, bearing a marked resemblance to Kanarese."

The second Form is that of the *Nobiles*, who are all bred Soldiers, and therefore called *Nairo's*; the one part of them wearing naked Swords rampant in one hand, and a Target made of a Buffola's Hide lacquer'd and curiously painted in the other, with which they defend themselves as assuredly as with an Iron Shield; the rest of them walk with a spiked Lance barbed, as long as a Javelin, and poised at the But end with Lead; at darting of which they are very expert.

The last and lowest are the Artizans and Tillers of the Earth, of which here are no great store, being ever negligent in that they reap the least Benefit by; wherefore their Vassals are commonly employed in that service, they being Drudges both to their Masters and Prince, who here as in all *India* is sole Proprietor of Lands;[1] allowing the Occupiers no more than a bare Subsistence, and not that when a bad Year fills not the Publick Granaries; drubbing the Poor Hinds till their Bones rattle in their Skins, they being forced often to sell their Children for Rice, which is the best here on this Coast of any place else in the whole World.

In Habit they excel not one another; the Peer as well as Peasant, wrapping only a *Lunga*[2] about his Middle, and thence reaching to his Knees. Only their Men of Honour that have deserved it from the *Zamerhin*, have their Wrists

---

[1] On the theory that the land in India is the property of the State, see Elphinstone, *H. of India*[6], 23: "Whatever may have been the precise date to which the right of the State to be considered superior owner of the soil may be carried back, it is certain that no ancient Hindu authority can be quoted for it; nor is it consistent with the genuine principles of the Muhammadan law. On the other hand, by the beginning of the eighteenth century, and in some cases of conquest long before that, all the rulers of the Muhammadan States, and all the local Rajas, who were conquerors and mostly foreigners, were found *de facto* to claim the superior ownership of every acre of their dominions. And this right is asserted by the Native States to the present day" (Baden-Powell, *The Indian Village Community*, 209).

[2] A waist-cloth; Hind. *lungī* (Yule, *Hobson-Jobson*, 519).

rounded with thick golden Bracelets, illustrated with Precious Stones.

Their Women are nearer White than the Men, of an Olive or Sallow Colour, cloathed as they on *Coromandel*, stretching their Ears with Gold and Gems.[1]

In Manners the Natives are slovenly enough, if not brutish. In Religion most Heathens, though the Infection of *Mahometism* is contagious among them.

They have Hospitals here for Cows ;[2] and are Charitable to Dogs, providing for them abroad, but not suffer them to defile them within Doors ; being more merciful to Beasts than Men.

Of Christians here are not an inconsiderable number. Here are also those Elephant-Legged St. *Thomeans*,[3] which the unbiassed Enquirers will tell you chances to them two ways : By the Venom of a certain Snake, for which the *Jangies*[4] or Pilgrims furnish them with a Factitious Stone (which we call a Snake-stone[5]) and is Counterpoyson

---

[1] The habit of distending the ears, which sometimes, from the weight of the rings, hang almost down to the shoulders, is common in many parts of India. "The Nairi and their wives use for a braverie to make great holes in their eares, and so bigge and wide, that it is incredible, holding this opinion, that the greater the holes be, the more noble they esteeme themselves" (Hakluyt, iii, 223). The same custom in S. India is noticed by Grose (p. 387) ; Pyrard de Laval (i, 377) ; Burton, *Gôa and the Blue Mountains*, 232 f. ; Bowrey, 34 f. It appears in an exaggerated form in the later images of Buddha, and in the figures in the Caves of Elephanta (*Bombay Gaz.*, xiv, 83, 329). It is prevalent among the wilder tribes of Assam (Gurdon, *The Khasis*, 23). In 1583 Fitch remarked it among the women of Ormus (Harris, *Voyages*, i, 207). The historian Sulaimān (850 A.D.) noticed it as a peculiarity of the Balhara King of the Konkan (Elliot-Dowson, *H. of India*, i, 3).

[2] This is the well-known Pinjrapol or animal hospitals of W. India, which date from the days of Asoka Maurya (Smith, *Early History*[2], 172 ; Hamilton, *Description of Hindostan*, i. 718 ; Crooke, *Things Indian*, 371 f. ; Yule, *Hobson-Jobson*, 713).

[3] See p. 116.

[4] The well-known Jogī ascetics. The word should be "Jaugies."

[5] The constitution and qualities of this curious form of remedy are fully discussed by Yule, *Hobson-Jobson*, 847 f. ; Tennent, *Ceylon*[3], i 197 f.

to all deadly Bites; if it stick, it attracts the Poyson; and put it into Milk, it recovers it self again, leaving its virulency therein, discovered by its Greenness: As also by drinking bad Water (to which, as we to the Air, they attribute all Diseases) when they travel over the Sands, and then lying down when they are hot, till the Earth at Night is in a cold sweat, which penetrating the rarified Cuticle, fixes the Humours by intercepting their free concourse on that side, not to be remedied by any *Panacea* of their *Esculapian Sectators*; it is not much unlike the *Elephantiasis Arabum*.[1]

Their Coins are of Gold; a St. *Thomas*[2] 10 *s.* a *Fanam*,[3] 7 and ½ of which go to a *Dollar*, or *Petacha*:[4] These are Gold. Of Copper, a *Buserook*,[5] 20 of which make a *Fanam*.

The Country is inticing and beautiful, Woody in the Plain, up the Country Mountainous, where grows the Pepper: It is a Berry that is brought forth by a Bindweed, wedded to a Tree, which it hugs as affectionately as the Ivy does the Oak; it is first Green, when dried it is black, and husked white: Long Pepper grows on a Shrub leaved and stalked like our Privet.[6]

Their other Trees and Fruits are common with the rest of *India*; Rice is their chief Grain.

Beasts and Fowls, Tame and Wild, are not scarce.

---

[1] See p. 116.

[2] "So called from the figure of St. Thomas on the reverse (see cut in G. da Cunha, *Indo-Port. Num.*, pl. 2). It was first coined by Garcia de Sá, 1548-9. According to Manoel Barbosa (*Rem. Doct.*) it was worth 10 tangas, or 600 reis, in 1618 (*i.e.*, about 9*s.*)." Gray, *Note on Pyrard de Laval*, ii, 69.

[3] See p. 106.

[4] Ital. *patacco* (Yule, *Hobson-Jobson*, 683; Manucci, ii, 383).

[5] Can. *bajāra-rokkha*, "market-money"; a low value coin made of copper, tin, lead, etc. (Yule, *Hobson-Jobson*, 121).

[6] Black pepper, *piper nigrum*; long pepper, *piper officinarum* and *piper longum* (Yule, *Hobson-Jobson*, 697 f.; Watt, *Econ. Dict.*, vi, Pt. i, 258 ff.; Linschoten, ii, 72 ff.).

The first Blackamore Pullen I ever saw, were here; the outward Skin was a perfect *Negro*, the Bones also being as black as Jet; under the Skin nothing could be whiter than the Flesh, more tender, or more grateful.[1]

After two Nights cold and disquieted Lodging on the Ground (though under covert of the *English* House) and an Hellish Consort of *Jackalls* (a kind of Fox),[2] with the Natives singing and roaring all Night long; being drunk with *Toddy*,[3] the Wine of the Cocoe: I was desirous to go Aboard; when, it being Evening, the Sea Breezes began to drive the Waves with a great surf upon the Shore; insomuch that our Men could not carry me to the Pinnace, riding at the Grapling without; wherefore hiring a *Canoo*,[4] the Blacks played the Charon, and I narrowly escaped with my Life (being overset); finding by sad Experience, that Cold Nights affect even in these Hot Countries, as sensibly as under the Frozen Bear: Leaving off to wonder at the Natives quivering and quaking after Sun-set, wrapping themselves in a *Comby*,[5] or Hair-cloath, and the better sort with Quilts, and making good Fires: For being well drenched in the Sea, the Wind blowing very high, I was almost nummed to death before I could reach the Ship. The reason of this coolness anights is because the Rains have lately cooled the Air as well as Earth, which also may be ascribed to the Sun's Ecliptic

---

[1] Fryer does not fall into the error of Linschoten (i, 25) and Pyrard de Laval (ii, 231), who say that the flesh is black. Such fowls are commonly known as "nigger fowls" or "Japan silkies." Bernier (p. 251) saw them at Delhi; Forbes (*Or. Mem.*[2], i, 205) says they abound in Calicut; Tennent (*Ceylon*[3], ii, 160 *n.*) in Colombo. De la Loubere (*New Hist. Rel.*, 37 f.) describes them in Siam.

[2] Though classed with wolves and jackals, they differ sufficiently to be entitled to generic distinction (Blanford, *Mammalia*, 147).

[3] Hind. *tārī* (Yule, *Hobson-Jobson*, 927).

[4] Canoa was another form of the word used about this time (Bowrey, *Intro.*, xxxix).

[5] A blanket; Skt. *kamala* (Yule, *Hobson-Jobson*, 279).

distance, as well as the length of the Nights, which are but little longer than the Days ; but chiefly to the soaking Mists bedewing the Earth after Sun-set.

Tanore lies in 10 deg. 30 min. *North* Latitude.[1]

Having taken in what Bales of Pepper this Place afforded ; we weighed by Two in the Morning, and by Four in the Afternoon Anchored against that Anciently Traded Port of *Calicut*,[2] in the Latitude of 11 deg. 30 min. *North*.

Of Calicut.

A Shore the first House facing us was the *English* ; near it were placed six small Pieces, resounding our Salutes at our Entry.

On the back-side lay two great Guns, dismounted, of Brass, all that is extant of the *Portugal* Town and Castle (which ran out as far into the Sea as our Ships now ride, near four Miles) overflowed by Water ; nothing remaining of it but only what is taken upon Chronicle.[3]

What is also left of *Calicut*, is not equivalent to what might be expected from the gleaning of so many Ages of Traffick ; unless, as Antiquaries esteem, most of those things are Moth-eaten by Time, which Vermin has been plaguy pernicious here : For the City that stood upon Stilts is tripped up, for down it is gone ; and the Temple, whose Marble Pillars durst compare with those of *Agrippa's* in the *Roman Pantheon*, is Topsy-turvy.[4] And if any one

---

[1] Properly 10° 58′ N. lat.

[2] Mal. Kōzhikkōtu, "cock foot," from a legend that all the area within cock-crow was ceded to the Zamorin. It is situated in N. lat., 11° 15′ E., long., 75° 49′.

[3] There is a modern legend of a town built by the Portuguese lying under water (*Madras Man. Adm.*, iii, 118).

[4] Writing of Calicut, Linschoten (i, 68) says: "But when the Portugals began to prosper and to get possession of the countrey, and so became maisters of the sea, Calecat beganne to decay, and to lose both name and traffique, and now at this time [*c.* 1598] it is one of the towns

that comes after me, make you believe it to be not above Four Miles in length, and in that not an House befitting a Christian; here and there a Mosque, and Burying Places and Tanks: A good long *Buzzar* with Trash, and Ripe Fruit; another with *Opium*, and Spices of this Coast; Changers and Jewellers, unfenced and rude in Building; he tells you but the truth. Indeed it is pleasantly situated under Trees, and it is the Holy See of their *Zamerhin* or Pope.

The Citizens are urbane, being trained up to Commerce; but the Trade gone to *Goa*, along with the *Portugals*; who at their first arrival into this Bay, found more Ships by 500 than we did, without either Chart or Compass, who most of them transported their Commodities to the *Red Sea*, along the Coasts; or to the Gulph of *Persia*; and thence they were carried over-land to *Scanderoon*, *Aleppo*, or *Constantinople*, unto the Hands of the *Venetians*, from whom we were served with them; and by that means they gained for themselves the Power and Greatness of their State.

Since by the Prosperous Attempts of the *Portugals* about the *Cape of good Hope*, we are taught to bring them home at a cheaper Rate, whereby these *Indian* Hugsters begin to decline.

For a long time the *Portugals* kept in with *Calicut*, and drew a great resort hither, as well over-land as by Sea; till the *Zamerhin*, not brooking them as Inmates, ruined their Fortifications, (which occasioned their remove to *Goa*), and with them the Fame of *Calicut*.

---

of least accourt in all Malabar and Cochin to the Contrarie, their King being very rich, and richer than the Samoriin." In 1510 Dalboquerque attacked the town, burnt the Zamorin's palace, and wrecked the place; but the natives, rallying, drove him back to Cochin with great loss. Three years later, the Zamorin made peace with the Portuguese, who at once erected a factory, the origin of the present establishment (*Madras Man. Adm.*, *u. s.*; *Comm. of Dalboquerque*, ii, Intro., lxiii ff.; for the building of the fortress, with an illustration of it, *Ibid.*, iv, 71 ff.)

Their Coin admits no Copper; Silver *Tarrs*,[1] 28 of which make a *Fanam*, passing instead thereof.

They have yet a correspondence with *Persia*, as may appear by their *Abseés*,[2] a Sixteen penny piece of Silver, current among them.

Their Trade in common with *India* is mostly for Beetle Nuts, and Cocoe Nuts, for Oyl, which latter they dunging with (*Bubsho*)[3] Fish, the Land-Breezes brought a poysonous Smell on board Ship caused by their putrifying.

Breaking ground hence, the Mountains were grown to that height, that they seemed to be the Partition Walls betwixt this World and the Sphere of Fire;[4] for the Sun was a long while after he had gilded the Canopy of Heaven, before he could drive his Steeds over those *Olympick* Towers with his blazing Orb: Which I take notice of, because the Sun and Stars ascend the *Horizon* to the *Meridian* directly in the *Torrid Zone*, and so descend; whereby there is little or no Twilight, as there is nearer the Poles, where they ascend and descend more obliquely.

At *Mangalore*,[5] the *Dutch* have a Fort, and 6 Miles to the *North* the *French* have a Flag flying; within a League off which a Grey Rock extols its hoary Head eight Fathom above Water, navigable on all sides, justly

---

[1] Mal. *tāram*, possibly from Skt. *tāra*, "star" (Yule, *Hobson-Jobson*, 901).

[2] A coin which is said to take its name from Shāh 'Abbās ii. Herbert (p. 231) fixes its value at 16*d.* (Yule, *Ibid.*, 389).

[3] *Baushē*, *baushem*, a Konkani term for fish fry, still in use in Goa and Kanara (*Bombay Gaz.*, xxvi, Pt. I, 253*n.*).

[4] Fryer, as elsewhere, exaggerates the height of the mountains above Calicut. Dodabetta, the highest peak of the Nilgiris, is 8647 ft. high.

[5] Can. Mangalūru, "village of Mars"; in S. Kanara District: Lat. 12° 52′ N., long. 74° 53′ E. The Dutch factory and French outpost do not seem to be mentioned elsewhere.

called by us *Sacrifice Island*;[1] in remembrance of a bloody Butchery on some *English* by the Pirate *Malabars*,[2] who are the worst *Pickeroons*[3] on this Coast, going in Fleets, and are set out by the Great Men ashore; the Chief of whom lives at *Durmapatan*,[4] where we took in fuller and larger Pepper than any yet: They are stronger here in Shipping than the rest; they housing several *Junks* of Burthen, drawn up on the Banks of the River, not yet lanched since the Rains; which they always do when they set in, keeping them dry all the Winter with the Thatch of *Cajans*.

Parting from hence, the Mountains above, and the Valleys below were covered with Woods, only now and then Hills of Red Earth were interspersed (which our Dawbers use for Painting) that held on their pace till we were up with *Canamore*,[5] another Fortress of the *Dutch*: From whence they spake Defiance by spending three Shots unregarded by us.

---

[1] Sacrifice Rock, off the Malabar coast: Lat. 11° 29′ N., long. 75° 34′ E., 23 miles N.N.W. of Calicut. "There is a rock lies off Cottica, about 8 miles in the sea, which bears the name of Sacrifice Rock. . . . How it came by its name is uncertain; but common tradition tells us that when the Portuguese first settled at Calicut, which is about 7 leagues south-east of this rock, Cottica cruizers surprised a Portuguese vessel, and sacrificed all the prisoner on the rock, which gave name to it" (A. Hamilton, *New Account*, i, 307). Forbes (*Or. Mem.*[2], i, 203) says that the crew of an English ship were massacred there by pirates in the beginning of the seventeenth century. He adds that the rock is famous for its edible bird-nests.

[2] For Malabar Pirates, see p. 164.

[3] Span. *picaron*, *picaro*, "roguish." See *New Eng. Dict.*, *s. v. picaroon*.

[4] Dharmapatam, "City of piety," in the Malabar District: Lat. 11° 49′ N., long. 75° 30′ E. It is the Dehfattan of Ibn Batuta; Darmaftan of the *Tohfut-ul-Mujahideen* (p. 52); Tormapatani of Varthema. It lies 41 miles N.N.W. of Calicut (*Madras Man. Adm.*, iii, 269).

[5] Cannanore, Mal. Kannūr, "beautiful village," in the Malabar District: Lat. 11° 52′ N., long. 75° 25′ E., 50 miles N.N.W. of Calicut. In 1656 the Dutch settled here, and built the present fort, which they held until 1766, when it fell into the hands of Mysore troops. The Bībī or Moplah chieftainess of Cannanore is well known in Anglo-Indian history (Buchanan, *Journey*, ii, 553; Welsh, *Mil. Rem.*, ii, 34).

From *Durmapatam*, five Leagues *North*, lies *Phalapatan*,[1] where I took Boat, and sailed up the River with the *Lascars*, or Sea-men of the Country ; of whom I shall say no more at present, than, that they are a shame to our Sailors, who can hardly ever work without horrid Oaths and hideous Cursing and Imprecations ; and these *Moormen*, on the contrary, never let their Hands do any Labour, but that they sing a Psalm, or Prayer, and conclude at every joint Application to it, *Allah*, *Allah*, invoking on the Name of God.

On each side upon the Teaming Banks are homely Villages, a plain Dress becoming Art, the Servant, where her Mistress, Nature, is so coruscant, here being whole Armies of Trees surprisingly beautiful. Besides these Benefits for Delight, there flow no less for Profit ; they improving the Commodiousness of the River (which is Sailable round to *Durmapatan*) by a Free Trade. Six miles up stands *Phalapatan*, of Building base ; it is overgrown with the Weeds of *Mahometism*, the *Moors* planting themselves here ; whose King I was so lucky to see out of my Boat, my *Lascars* entreating me to give them leave to go ashore to provide Victuals in the *Buzzar*.

His Meen was Patriarchical, his Head gray, his Beard, Snowed with Age, his Raiment white in the *Eastern* Mode. His Son and Heir, a Child, followed him ; as he passed, the People payed him humble Respect ; he was without a Guard, it being needless where Subjects are Loyal-hearted.

The River was full of *Aligators*, or Crocodiles, which lay basking in the Sun in the Mud on the River's side, whom the Natives are fearless of ; conceiting the *Brachmines* have power to lay a Spell upon them, that they do

[1] Beliapatam of Constable's *Hand Atlas*: Lat. 11° 56′ N., long. 75° 24′ E., 4¾ miles N. of Cannanore. The river he sailed up is that formed by the junction of the Beliapatam and Taliparamba. Fra Paolino (p. 145) describes it as "formerly a large and considerable mart of trade, but at present a very obscure town."

no harm.[1] Which, whether true or false, 'tis certain they as seldom do harm in the Water, as the Tigres in the Woods, over whom they fancy their Priests have the same prevalency.

A Mile more up was *Cutty-Cony*,[2] the fair Palace, as it signifies in *Malabar*; but though it do in their Language,

---

[1] Stevens (*H. of Persia*, 133 f.) tells a curious story of a native at Malacca, "who going sometimes to the Bank of the River of St. *Jerome* . . . utter'd some words, which drew the crocodiles thither, then he pronounc'd some others, and taking one or two of them, threw a Rope about their Necks, and so led them about the City, being come to the Governor's House, he commanded them to make their Obeysance which they did; then he conducted them back to the Shore, when he dismiss'd them, and they went away very gently." One day he seems to have forgotten the charm, and one of the animals struck him on the head with his tail, "whereof he dropt down dead." Manucci (ii, 94) tells of a man on the Ganges, who caught crocodiles by sorceries. "They take a pot and throw into it some flowers, repeating a spell over the pot. Then they place the pot in the river, and it moves of itself against stream. They follow it leisurely in the boat until the pot arrives of itself where there is a crocodile. Thereupon the sorceror orders the crocodile to give a paw, and it obeys. This paw is made fast; then he asks for the other, and it, too, is fastened. Then the brute is dragged to shore as if he were quite meek, or merely an old woman. They kill him with their spears in perfect security."

[2] Mr. W. Francis, Collector of Malabar, has kindly sent me a very interesting note on the identification of this place. It is Kotta-Kunnu, which means "fort hill"; but below it is a little valley called Eripuram, "shining hamlet," and Fryer may have confounded the two. "This Kotta-Kunnu tallies closely with Fryer's description, and is such a particularly beautiful spot (even for this beautiful district) that it is not surprising that it should have earned itself special mention. South lies the Taliparamba river, even now fringed with 'a wood of Jamboes, Mangoes, Cocoes'; east, another laterite plateau (now almost bare, but doubtless once 'a gravelly forest with tall benty grass'); north, pepper-gardens are still in existence; and west the heights of Mount Deli 'do bound the sight.' These last are the strongest arguments in favour of this identification of 'Cutty-Cony', for they are the only hills of any size on the whole coast of Malabar." On Kotta-Kunnu still stands a little temple in ruins. But it is difficult to reconcile Fryer's distances with local conditions. Mr. Francis suggests that Fryer confounded "Phalapatan" with Palayangādi, which "may have been known as Palayampatam, or 'old town,' from whence 'Phalapatan' is not a long step. It is almost exactly six miles up from the mouth of the Baliapatam river, and was a very ancient Musalmān settlement. Kotta-Kunnu is not so much as a mile above the present bazaar; but one cannot be sure from what points Fryer took his distances."

it would not make the Interpretation good in *English*, it agreeing but in one particular, that is, the Site. It having the advantage of an Hill, has an easy Prospect over the Water, as broad here as our *Thamesis*; and over the Verdent Meadows, which spread themselves *Westward*, till Hills of *Cardamoms* do bound the sight, running from thence *North* by *East*, while they meet with Mount *Sephir*[1] (all along unchristned *Gate*) these are the minor *Cardamoms*,[2] and the best, if not the only in the World: On the *East* a gravelly Forest with tall benty Grass, offers, besides its taking Look, diversity of Game; as Hares, wild Boars, Tigres, and wild Elephants, which are dreaded by Travellers, they striking all down before them, Trees as well as Animals: The like Terror is conceived by the crashing noise among the Woods made by the wild Bulls;[3] for all which, 'tis the practice of the Woodmen to dig deep Pits, and cover them with Sads, laid over with Boughs, to entrap them in their headstrong and unwary Course. Monkeys with white Ruffs, and black shagged Bodies, looking very gravely, are brought from hence.[4]

On the *South* a Wood of *Jamboes*,[5] *Mangoes*, *Cocoes*; on the *North* a Grove of Pepper.

The Place is now resigned to the *English*, though the *Gentiles* were unwilling to desert it, it being an Arch-*Brachmine's* Seat, where was a small *Pagod* standing in the middle of the Yard well endowed, till they had robbed their Gods of their Gold and Silver; and now they are

---

[1] See Letter III, chap. IV.

[2] *Eletarria cardamomum*, the lesser Cardamom, indigenous in the rich, moist forests of the hilly tracts in S. India (Watt, *Econ. Dict.*, iii, 288 ff.).

[3] He probably means *Bos gaurus*, the Gaur, the Bison or Indian Bison of European sportsmen (Blanford, *Mammalia*, 484 ff.).

[4] Probably one of the varieties of the S. Indian Langūr; *semnopithecus priamus*, *hypoleucus*, or *johni* (*Ibid.*, 31 ff.).

[5] The rose-apple, *Eugenia jambos*; Skt. *jambū* (Yule, *Hobson-Jobson*, 448 f.).

said to be dumb and sullen because of the *English*. But without any prejudice to Truth, we may believe the Usurers Faith and theirs to be both under one Lock and Key; *Quantum nummorum habet in arcâ, tantum habet & fidei.*[1]

It is walled about by the *English* with Mud, except the two round Points towards the Land, whose Foundations and Bastions are of Stone. They have Fourteen small Guns mounted; here are twenty two Soldiers, besides Factors: The Air so salubrious, that never any *English* are remembred to lay their Bones here. The Fort is a *Tetragone* from Corner to Corner.

Without, besides the *English*, there are a select Company of *Nairoes*, who are stout, ready, and resolute for any Action: Their Weapons are Bows and Arrows, with Falchions by their sides.

By these the Countrey is inhabited; among whom if a Man fall single, salvage Beasts are more compassionate; but if you have but a Boy with you of their Cast, you may travel secure enough.[2]

Beyond the Outworks live a few *Portugals Mustezoes* or *Misteradoes*;[3] among whom are Stews and Brothels; the Women of this Coast being the most professedly Lewd of any; being said to instruct the Men to be Patients, while they act the Masculine Part in their Lascivious Twines.

---

[1] "Quantum quisque suâ nummorum servat in arcâ, Tantum habet et fidei" (Juvenal, *Sat.*, iii, 143).

[2] The institution of guides in S. India dates from very early times. "The Kingdom of Dakshina is out of the way and perilous to traverse, There are difficulties in connection with the roads; but those who know how to manage such difficulties [Giles has "those who know the way," which is better], and wish to proceed, should bring with them money and various articles, and give them to the King. He will send men to escort them. These will (at different stages) pass them on to others, who will show them the shortest routes" (*Travels of Fa-hien*, tr. Legge, 97). For these guides in later times, see Pyrard de Laval, i, 339, with Gray's note; Yule, *Hobson-Jobson*, 450, *s. v.*, *Jancada*.

[3] Port. *mestiço*, "half-caste" (Yule, *Hobson-Jobson*, 604 f.).

Sixteen *Tarrs*[1] here make one *Fanam*; Nine *Fanams* one *Piece of Eight*; four *Cash* are the eighth part of one *Rupee.*

Outstretching the *Malabar* Coast, we sailed along by *Batticalai*[2] on the *Canatick* Coasts; and the next Morning, between two Islands we saw sculking Six *Malabar Proes* waiting their Booty; but making use of their Oars as well as Sails, soon outstripped us.

The Day after we came to an Anchor at *Onor*,[3] the Land Hilly and Barren, which I went to see; it is in 13 *deg.* 10 *min. North.* We passed to it through a narrow Bite, which expatiates into a wide Swallow, and then thrusts us up the River. On the *North* side a Bow and Arrow Castle overlooks it, while it runs peaceably to the Town. Where we landed, the *Dutch* had a House, and a new *Junk* lanched, with her Colours furl'd: One end of the Town stands in an hole; over a Rocky Hill stands the other part, upon which the Castle with its Stone Wall faces an Heath a great way, yet looking asquint on the Under-

---

[1] See p. 143.

[2] Here Fryer passes from what is now the Madras Presidency to that of Bombay. Batticalai is BhatKal, in N. Kanara District. Lat. 13° 59′ N., long. 70° 34′ E. The name is probably derived from the circle of hills surrounding it. Mahr. *vatkal*, "round town." It is probably the Batycola of Linschoten (i, 66). A. Hamilton (*New Account*, i, 283) calls it Battacola; and he describes the massacre by the natives of John Best and seventeen other Englishmen, slain because a bull-dog belonging to them killed a sacred cow. For other references to the place see Yule, *Hobson-Jobson*, 71; *Bombay Gaz.*, xv, Pt. II, 266 ff.

[3] Honāvar, "golden village," a seaport in N. Kanara District; Lat. 14° 16′ 30″ N., long. 74° 29′ E. The river on which it stands is the Shirāvatī or Girsappa, on which are the so-called "Grasshopper Falls" (Yule, *Hobson-Jobson*, 394). The fort stood on a flat-topped laterite hill, precipitous to the river, and more or less scarped to the W. Nothing now remains of it except a trench, isolating the extreme point of the hill. Fryer does not mention the sacred hot spring with its tame fish, described by P. della Valle (ii, 205) and A. Hamilton (*New Account*, i, 279 ff.). For the famous defence of the place by Major Torriano in 1783-84, see Forbes (*Or. Mem.*[2], ii, 455). There is a full account of the place in *Bombay Gaz.*, xv, Pt. II, 305 ff.

woods. It is built after the exact Rules of Ancient Fortifications, with a Drawbridge, and a Moat round, now a dry Ditch, the Castle without Soldiers, falling to decay. It was built by the *Portugals*, seized by the *Canareens* by the help of the *Dutch*, between whom and the *Portugals*, the Town of poor Buildings is divided: Many of the Natives have receiv'd the Christian Faith. Though those that continue in their Paganism are the most impiously Religious of any of the *Indians*, being too too conversant with the Devil.

The *Nairoes* have no footing here, nor have the *Moors* much.

They live in no diffidence of one another, nor Strangers of them, journeying among them without a Guide, in Broad Roads, not in By-Paths, as in the Nations properly called the *Malabars*: They have well-constituted Laws, and observe them obediently.

From hence we came to *Mirja*[1] in the same Dominions. I went to view the Place; the Boat that carried me was *Brigantine* built.

At the Entry into the Harbour only a Rock withstands the Washes, but on the Shore huge craggy Mountains are drawn up for a second Onset, all of Black Stone, yet somewhat undermined by the beating of the Sea, where it works its self into a *Syrtes*; on the other side of which the Fragments of the Town are shelter'd. At my Landing, one of their Princes was the first that welcomed me ashore, (who here as well as in *Italy* scorn not to be Merchants); he was seated under a shady Tree, on a Carpet spread upon the Sand, and his Retinue standing

---

[1] Mirjān, about 20 miles N. of Honāvar, in N. Kanara District, at the S.E. end of the Tadri estuary or back-water. Fryer visited it again in 1675 on his way from Gokarn (Letter IV, chap. III). From the N. an encircling chain of wooded hills approaches, until on the S.E. its base is scarcely a mile distant. Fryer usually exaggerates the height of hills. The place is described in *Bombay Gaz.*, xv, Pt. II, 330 ff.

about him; he it seems was expecting the Protector of *Canara*[1] (the *Raja* being in Minority), who came anon, with his Lords and Guards, armed with Swords and Gantlets, Partizans adorned with Bells and Feathers, as also were the Horses that carried his *Luscarry*[2] or Army, with such Trappings as our finest Team-Horses in *England* wear.

He ventured off to Sea to see our Ships; he was rowed by a Gang of 36, in a great deal of Pomp; his Musick was loud, and with the Kettle-drums made a Noise not unlike that our Coopers make on their Hogsheads driving home their Hoops: He went aboard two or three Ships, who entertained him with their Guns and Chears of their Men, presenting him with Scarlet-Cloath.[3] He is a *Gentile*, as are his Subjects.

Our Lading here was *Pepper*, *Salt-Petre*, and *Beetle Nut* for *Surat*.

In our way from *Mirja* we met with a Man of War Pink, commission'd from the President for the scowring these Seas, which had 22 Guns, and seventy odd Men, the Name, *The Revenge*.

Near *Carwar* is the Island *Angediva*,[4] Fam'd for the Burial of some Hundreds of our Countreymen.

Carwar[5] was the Chief Port of *Visiapour* on this Coast,

---

1 This personage was apparently Bhadrappa Nāyaka (1671-81), eldest son of Sivappa Nāyaka, the greatest chief of the Bednūr house, who defeated the Jain Rājas of Tuluva, and acquired Kanara (Buchanan, *Journey*, iii, 126; Sewell, *List of Inscriptions*, 177 f.).

2 Pers. *lashkar*, "an army."

3 Here, as in other writers of the time, the reference is to the woollen stuff known as Suklāt, for which see Yule, *Hobson-Jobson*, 861.

4 Anjidiva: Lat. 14° 45′ N., long. 74° 10′ E., 5 miles S.W. of Kārwār, and 2 miles from the mainland, a Portuguese possession The name is probably derived from Mal. *añju-dīvu*, "five islands' (Yule, *Hobson-Jobson*, 28). For the mortality of Englishmen, see p. 163. The island is described in *Bombay Gaz.*, xv Pt. II, 249 ff.

5 Kārwār, port and town, headquarters of N. Kanara District: Lat. 14° 50′ N., long. 74° 15′ E. It is the only first-class harbour between Bombay and Colombo. In 1665, after his attack on Barce-

but a Grand Traytor to that King *Seva Gi*, is now Master of it, and the adjacent Countrey as far as *Guzerat*; having well nigh forced our Factory, and done other Outrages on us, which would ask our Fleet a longer time to require Satisfaction, if they were able, than they could stay; unless they would lose their Passage round the *Cape of Good Hope*, and content themselves to winter at the *Mauritius*, which all Ships that outstay their time are forced to. For the Sun being almost at his *Southern Solstice*, at his return he leaves a sharp Winter (which we proved), and adverse Winds in those Seas, they lying without the Tropick, which spurs them on for expedition. What this *Seva Gi* is, and the reason of his Usurped Power, a longer Duration in the Countrey must declare, who is every where named with Terror, he carrying all before him like a mighty Torrent.

The Shore is Hilly, and indifferent Woody; near it Islets are scattered to and again.

The People partly *Moors*, partly *Gentues*, under the King of *Visiapour*, who was, till this turbulent *Seva Gi* drove all into a Commotion, a perfect Monarch, hardly paying the *Mogul* Tribute, when *Duccan* and *Visiapour* were united into one Kingdom.

Hence it is Hilly up to *Guzerat*; though *Gates*[1] hold

---

lore, Sivaji dismissed his fleet, and "having divided his troops into parties, scoured the whole country, and acquired immense booty from several of the rich mercantile towns in that neighbourhood; Carwar stood on the defensive, and Sivajee had only time to exact a contribution," of which the English factory paid £112 (Grant Duff, 90 f.; Anderson, 162). In 1673, the year of Fryer's visit, the Faujdār or Governor appointed by Bījapur, revolted, seized the loyal subordinate officers, and laid siege to the English factory because the factors would not supply him with ammunition (*Bombay Gaz.*, xv, Pt. II, 321 f., quoting Orme, *Hist. Fragments*, 35-40). The hills mentioned by Fryer are a spur of the Kārwār range running W. to the sea, and rising at Kārwār Head to a height of 640 ft. above the sea. The islets are Devgad and Kurmagad, forming a natural break-water.

[1] The range of the Western Ghāts.

on where the Coasts of *Guzerat* begin and outstretches them.

Fifteen Leagues to the *Norward* of *Carwar* lies *Goa*,[1] the only place of consequence the *Portugals* retain of their first Discoveries.

The City lies up the River, out of our sight on Shipboard, though we could discern the River to be thwacked with small Craft; without the Bar a great *Carrack* unrigg'd, and on both sides the River Magnificent Structures. The Soil Fat, Level, and fit for the Share many Miles together, the Hills keeping a wide distance from them.

About two days after we passed *Goa*, a Ship with a *Portugal* Flag at the Main Top-Mast Head weathered our Admiral, and after seeing what we were, lay by for a Fleet of six more good Ships, one Hoy, and half a dozen *Proes*, being their *Northern Armado*;[2] they fitting out one for the *South* also; the one against the *Arabs*, the other against the *Malabars*.

The beginning of *December* the *North West* Wind blew bitter cold upon us, and would hardly give the Sun leave to be Master in his own home; though a Cloud in the day time, ever since the Rains cleared up, could hardly vapour betwixt him and the Earth.

At Nights we had hospitable Lights shewed us from the Shore, to mark out the Rocks, which lye very thick along to intrap the unwary Pilot.

---

[1] Goa is about 60 miles N.W. of Kārwār.

[2] "The Portuguese and the Viceroy of Goa are wont every year at the beginning of summer [*i.e.*, at the close of the monsoons or "winter"], which is in the month of September, to equip two fleets of a hundred galeots, along with three or four large galleys. Half of the fleet they send to the north, as far as Diu or Cambaye, and thereabouts, to guard the coast, and hold their power over the sea, and prevent any one from sailing there without their passport. The other half they send south, as far as Cape Comorin, for the same purpose, but principally to purge the seas of the Malabar Corsairs" (Pyrard de Laval, i, 439 f.). These fleets were called respectively *Armada do Norte*, that north of Goa, and *Armada do Sul* or *Malavar*, south of that port (Fonseca, *Goa*, 38).

In 17 *deg.* 20 *min.* *North*, lies *Rajapore*,[1] a *French* Factory now, formerly *English*.

Twenty Miles to the *Northward*, *Choul*,[2] a Fortress of the *Portugals*, lay fair in sight.

And having the Latitude of 18 *deg.* 40 *min.* *North* *Bombaim* opened its self; the Tide being spent, we came to an Anchor without the Bay, not having our Bearings right; and *December* the Eighth we paid our Homage to the Union-Flag flying on the Fort of *Bombaim*.

The BAY

Is indented a vast Circumference, in which it is able to contain 1000 of the best Ships in *Europe* in safe Harbour from Wind and Weather. As we passed up the Bay, two of the *Mogul's* Men of War, each 300 Tun, with bloody Colours out, rode before *Kerenjau*.[3] Under the Castle, besides innumerable little Vessels, as Hoys, Ketches, and the like, lay Three Men of War with their Top Armour out, Waste-Cloath and Penants at every Yard-Arm; to wit, The *Revenge*, 22 Guns: The *May-boon*, taken from the *Dutch*, 220 Tuns: The *Hunter*, 14 Guns.

The Castle is seated towards the bottom of the Bay, commanding it in every way from the Points and Flankiers.[4]

---

[1] Rājāpur, port in Ratnagiri District: Lat. 16° 37′ 50″ N., long. 73° 22′ 22″ N. Courten's Association founded a factory here in 1637-8 (Bruce, *Annals*, i. 358, 444; Birdwood, *Report*, 216, 27). Tavernier names it, with Dabhol and Kareputtun, as one of the three good ports of Bījapur (ed. Ball, i. 181). A. Hamilton (*New Account*, i, 246) mentions both the English and French factories. The place must be carefully distinguished from Dhanda Rājāpur or Janjira. Fryer, however, seems to make this confusion in speaking of the French factory, which he probably heard of at the other Rājāpur.

[2] Here, again, he seems to have misunderstood his information, if he refers to the Cheul, Chaul, or Revdanda in the Kolāba District: Lat. 18° 33′ N., long. 73° E., about 30 miles S. of Bombay. He may have been thinking of Dhanda Rājāpur.

[3] See p. 159.

[4] "A fortification projecting so as to flank or defend another part, or to command the flank of an approaching enemy" (*New Eng. Dict.*, *s. v.*).

At Evening the next day I was sent for on Shore, and received by the Honourable *Gerald Aungier*,[1] Governor both for the King and Company, and President of all the *East-Indies*.

Thus after a plenary Anniversary, this Voyage was accomplished ; and just that Day Twelvemonth you left me Aboard Ship at *Gravesend*, I set foot on shore at *Bombaim*, where for this Shipping I remain

Yours,

J. F.

---

[1] His name does not appear in the *Dict. Nat. Biog.* He was brother of the Earl of Longford, and the true founder of Bombay, which he commenced to fortify in 1669. In 1670 he helped to defend Surat against the Mahrattas, and in 1673 he defeated the Dutch attack on Bombay under Van Goen. The establishment of a Mint, the reform of the revenue system of the island, the drainage of the swamps which made the place a death-trap to Europeans, the foundation of the Courts of Justice and Police, were all his work. He died at Surat 30th June, 1677 (*Bombay Gaz.*, xxvi, Pt. I, 38 ff. ; Anderson, 149 ff. ; Douglas, *Bombay and W. India*, i, 72 ff.).

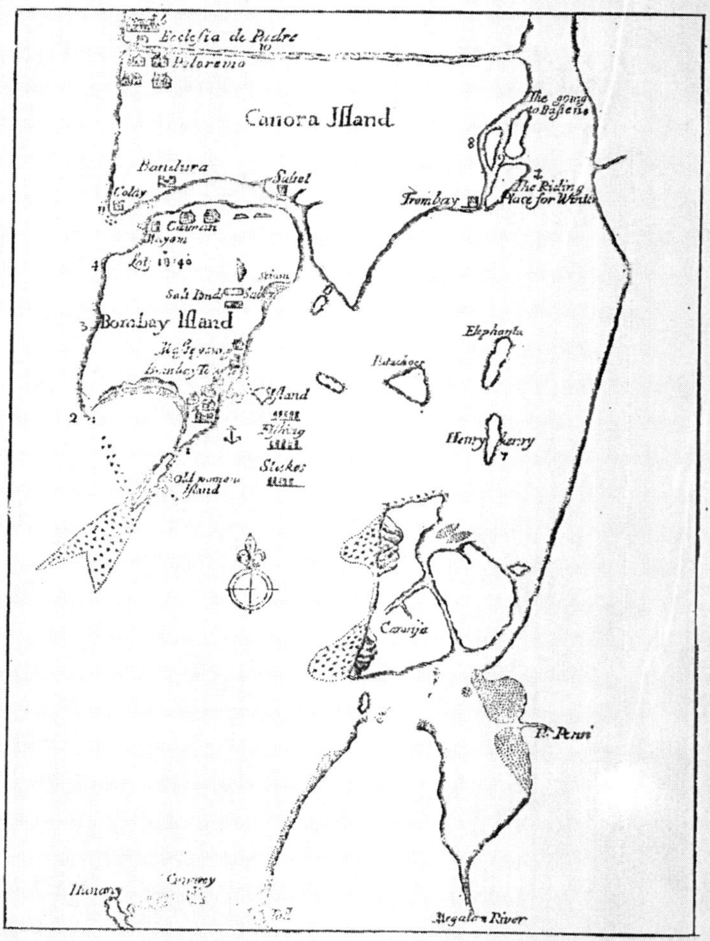

1. *Mendam's* Point. 2. *Malabar*-Hill. 3. The Great Inlett or Breach of the Sea. 4. *Verulee*. 5. *Megataim*-River. 6. *Baſſein* City. 8. *Tannaw* City and Paſs. 11. The *Agoada* or Watering-place.

(To face p. 157)

AN

HISTORICAL ACCOUNT

OF

BOMBAIM,

And the Parts Adjacent.

LETTER II.

CHAP. I.

Mentions the Island and its Possessors.

SIR,

BY the *Falcon* (in which Ship I am now taking my Passage to *Surat*) I received at once the News of your good health, and that welcome one of Peace with *Holland*;[1] the first I embrace as a Friend, the other I congratulate with all good Men.

Nulla Salus Bello, Pacem te poscimus omnes.[2]

I shall neither apologize for my long Letter, or sending this before you give me your Thoughts of the former; the Distance of Place shall excuse both: And I proceed where you left me last, at *Bombaim*, and so on till these Ships shall depart for *England*.

---

[1] It was signed in February, 1674 (Hunter, *H. of B. India*, ii, 199).

[2] Virgil, *Æn.*, xi, 362.

BOMBAIM

In *East India* is one of the Islands of *Salset*, parted from that part of the *Canarick* Coast which lies nearest *Duccan*, 60 Leagues *North* of *Goa*, and as many *South* of *Surat*. These Islands' are in number seven:[1] viz

[1] The "seven" islands in the neighbourhood of Bombay have been identified by Lassen (see his map in *Indische Alterthumskunde*) with the Heptanesia of Ptolemy (vii, I, 95); but they more probably correspond with the Sesekreienai of the Periplus (cap. 53), which have been recognised in the Burnt Islands off the coast of Ratnagiri, of which Vengurla is the chief (M'Crindle, *Ptolemy*, 187 f.; *Id.*, *Periplus*, 128 ff.). There is no definite list of these seven Bombay islands, and, unfortunately, Fryer's map is so inaccurate that it is very difficult to identify those which he names. At a later time, in Murphy's map of 1843 (*Bombay Gaz.*, xxvi, Pt. III, 649) seven islands are shown. Māhim, Vārli, Sion to the N.; Mazagon and Bombay in the centre; Old Woman's Island and Kolāba to the S. "During the last two hundred years the constant filling of small hollows, occasional large reclamations, and the building of the great Hornby (1680-1780), and several smaller sea-ramparts or vellards, have turned the seven islands into a solid belt of land, flanked by two broken ridges, which, on the south, separated about three miles by the reef-guarded waters of Back Bay, end the one in Malabar Point, and the other in Colāba" (*Ibid.*, xxvi, Pt. III, 648). Fryer's list is, however, very different from that of Murphy and other later writers. Of the identification of some of those included in his list there can be no doubt. (1) Bombaim is certainly the present Bombay. (2) Canorein, in the map Canora Island, the Canara of Grose (p. 112) is Sāshthī, from which the modern name Salsette, is derived (Yule, *Hobson-Jobson*, 786); Fryer's name for the island representing Kānheri, the site of the famous group of rock-temples which lie nearly in its centre, which Fryer visited at a later time (p. 185 ff.). (3) Trumbay is the modern Trombay, known from its shape as Neat's Tongue, about three miles E. of Bombay, from which it is separated by a creek. The name is believed to be closely connected with Mumbē or Bombay, Mumb and Trumb forming one of those jingling couplets of which the people are so fond (*Bombay Gaz*, xiv, 362). (4) Elephanto is Elephanta, of which Fryer gives an account (Letter II, chap. III). (5) Putachoes represent Hog or Butcher's Island, the former name based on the fact that ships were cleaned here ("Hog, a kind of rough, flat scrubbing broom, serving to scrape a ship's bottom under water." Smyth, *Sailor's Word-Book*, 384, where the process is described). The native name is Devdevī or Nhāvē. The Portuguese called it Ilha da Patecas, "water-melon island," from which Fryer's name is derived. Grose (p. 91) says that the name Butcher's Island originated in the fact of "cattle being kept there for the use of Bombay"; but it has been suggested this name is also a corruption of Ilha da Patecas (*Bombay Gaz.*, xxvi, Pt. I, 438 f.). (6) No satisfactory explanation of Fryer's "Munchumbay" has been found. Mr. P. B. Joshi regards it as a corruption of the Mahr. "Marumbay,"

Bombaim, *Canorein*, *Trumbay*, *Elephanto*, the *Putachoes*, *Munchumbay*, and *Kerenjau*, with the Rock of *Henry Kenry*; arising as so many Mountains out of the Sea; which accords to the Fancy of the Natives, who affirm that *Nereus* has lost these Islets, with a great deal more of the Low-Lands, from his Trident, the Earth gaining upon the Sea: And as a Remonstrance of their Credulity, they bring for proof the vast Rocks that are many Miles up the Countrey, bestuck with Oyster-shells and other Trophies of the Sea's having had once Dominion there, all which they call *Conchon*, or the *Netherlands*.[1]

In whose opening Arm, that is, from *Choul Point* to *Baçein*[2] (two famous Cities belonging to the *Portugals*)

"Murway," or "Marva"; but this island is not found in any map to which the editor has access. Dr. Codrington thinks that Fryer mixed up the seven islands of Bombay with the seven islands in the harbour, and he cannot identify "Munchumbay." Mr. A. M. T. Jackson supposes that Munchumbay was part of the islands that now form Salsette. It may be a corruption of Māne and Chembur, both places lying N. of Trombay on the E. side of Salsette. Fryer's map seems to have been based on mere hearsay. Thus he gives "Henry Kenry" inside the harbour, and "Hunarey Cunarey" at its mouth. (7) Kerenjau is Karanja or Uran Island, 18° 51′ N. lat, 73° 2′ E. long., in the S.E. of Bombay Harbour, about 6 miles S.E. of the Carnac Pier in Bombay; for a full account, see *Bombay Gaz.*, xiv, 191 ff. (8) "Henry Kenry" or "Hendry Kendry' is Mahr. Vondarī, "mouse-like," and Khandarī "sacred to the demi-god Khandērāv," mentioned in the *Bombay Gaz*, xi, 324, ff., under the names Khānderī and Underī. Khānderī lies 11 miles S. of Bombay, and 1½ miles from Underi (see Yule, *Hobson-Jobson*, 413).

[1] Fryer may have heard of the remains of crabs and sea-shells, which are still found on the summit of Matherān Hill and its neighbourhood (*Bombay Gaz.*, xiv, 240). Grose (p. 113) thinks that these hills were raised by an earthquake, "to confirme which it is pretended that there was on the top of the highest hill, not many years ago, a stone anchor, such as was anciently used for the vessels of that country." Conchon or the Konkan is the low country of W. India, lying between the range of the W. Ghāts and the sea, extending, roughly speaking, from Goa to Gujarāt; but the modern Commissionership includes N. Kanara, which lies S. of Goa (Yule, *Hobson-Jobson*, 244). In earlier times the boundaries of the tract seem to have varied (*Bombay Gaz.*, i, Pt. II, Intro. ix, f.).

[2] From Chaul Point to Bassein, as the crow flies, the distance is about 58 miles. Fryer's statement is in accordance with the identification of the place with the Simulla of Ptolemy's Tables (Yule, *Hobson-Jobson*, 210; *Bombay Gaz.*, xi, 270, *n.*). See also Letter II, chap. IV.

some 30 Leagues distance, lye those Spots of Ground, still disputable to which side to incline: For at Low Water most of them are foordable to the Main, or from one to the other; and at Spring-Tides again a great part of them overflowed.

Bombaim is the first that faces *Choul*, and ventures farthest out into the Sea, making the Mouth of a spacious Bay, from whence it has its Etymology; *Bombaim*, quasi *Boon Bay*.[1]

Beyond it lies *Canorein, Trumbay, Munchumbay*, with their Creeks, making up the *North* side of the Bay: Between whom and the Main lies *Elephanto, Kerenjau, Putachoes*, with the great Rock or barren Islet of *Henry Kenry*: These, with some part of the Main, constitute the *South-East* side of the Bay; all which together contribute to the most notable and secure Port on the Coasts of *India*; Ships of the greatest as well as smaller Burthen having quiet Harbour in it; whither if they can, they chuse to betake themselves, if they happen, as oft they do, to lose their Voyages by the *Monsoons*.

From whence these Pieces of Land receive their general Name of *Salset*, if it be worth Enquiry, I can only guess, either because it signifies in *Canorein* a Granary,[2] as they are to the *Portugals North* of *Goa*, and sometimes to *Goa* it self, as at this time, when their *Armado* of Rice was all lost, which annually used to furnish them with Provisions of Corn; or else analogically, from the fruitful

---

[1] "The grammar of the alleged etymon is bad, and the history no better; for the name can be traced long before the arrival of the Portuguese in India." It is really derived from the goddess Mumbādevī, a local form of the mother-goddess, who was worshipped here. Her shrine was on the modern Esplanade till the middle of the 17th century, when it was removed into the native town, near the Bhēndī Bāzār (Yule, *Hobson-Jobson*, 102; Edwardes, *Bombay Town and Island*, 19 f; *Bombay Gaz.*, xxvi, Pt. III, 645 ff.).

[2] Salsette is Mahr. Shashti, Shāshashtī, "sixty-six," because it was supposed to contain that number of villages (Yule, *Hobson-Jobson*, 786).

Peninsula of the same Name, near which *Goa* its self stands: But whether this be certain or not, the reason of the Denomination of *Bombaim* is convincing.

To go on then from whence we deviated, it is necessary you should be first acquainted, That after *Vasquez de Gama*, in the Year 1547, had laid open these Seas for Traffick to the *East-Indies*; the *Portugals* to their Honour took for a while sure Footing of what they had industriously so long laboured for, and brought most of the Borderers on the Sea-Coasts under their Subjection; not all *India*, as they have fondly reported. It suffices then, to avoid a Volume of Discourse, that *Bombaim* with these Islets continued still in their hands, until the Year 1661, when the Crown of *Portugal* parted with these, together with the Haven, to His Majesty of *Great Britain*, as a Portion of the Dowry of *Donna Infanta Catherina*, Sister to the King of *Portugal*, and Consort to *Charles* the Second, late King of *England, Scotland, France*, and *Ireland*.[1] A matter of great import to the Kingdom, had it been transferred according to Contract, as well in regard to the Protection of our Ships, as for the Profit of the Soil to the *English* Inhabitants; but most of all for the Awe it might impose upon them who are the Disturbers of our Trade here.

But upon what grounds they refused to surrender, may be understood, if we consider the different interests, as well as Remoteness of the *Portugueze* in *Europe* and *East-India*.[2] It is confessed they will talk big of their

---

[1] Bombay was ceded under the 11th Article of the Treaty of Whitehall, 23rd June, 1661, not merely as a wedding gift, but for the express purpose of enabling the English King to defend the Portuguese settlements in India from the Dutch (Hunter, ii, 190: Bruce, *Annals*, ii, 105). The Treaty is printed by Forrest, *Home Selections*, ii, 367 ff.; Danvers, ii, 331 f.

[2] The question at issue was whether the cession included Bombay Island alone, or extended to the adjacent Portuguese dependencies of Thana and Salsette (Anderson, 111; Hunter, ii, 192).

King, and how nearly allied to them, as if they were all Cousin-Germans at least; but for his Commands, if contrary to their Factions, they value no more than if they were merely titular; as may appear by what follows. For notwithstanding the King of *England* sent a Fleet of Five Royal Ships under the Command of my Lord of *Malbery*,[1] to waft over a Vice-Roy for them, confirmed so by their own King, and one of their own Nation; and to take possession of these Islands in the name of the King of *England*; yet they not only positively denied to surrender, but constrained the Vice-Roy to a negation; otherwise to expect never to assume that Dignity, which, by that Act they made him sensible, was more in their disposal than the King's.

Whereupon *Malbery* examining his Commission, was vexed he was pinched, and knew not how to ease himself; wearied therefore with Delays, he retreated to *Swally*, and there upon the Sands set the Souldery on Shore (himself not stirring out of the Ship) Five hundred stout Men led by Sir *Abraham Shipman*, who was designed *Generalissimo* for the King of *England* on the *Indian* Shore: Where, when in Arms, and exercised after the *English* Training, they seemed formidable to the *Moors*;[2] wherefore they are entreated by the President for the *English* Factory at *Surat*, Sir *George Oxendine*,[3] that they would

---

[1] James Ley, 3rd Earl of Marlborough, an eminent mathematician and navigator, killed in the sea-fight with the Dutch, 3rd June, 1665, and buried in Westminster Abbey (Anderson, 112 *n*; Hunter, ii, 192 f.; Bruce, *Annals*, ii, 123 ff.).

[2] The President represented "that such an application would give offence to the Mogul Governor, who, if it should be attempted, might probably seize on the Company's investment, and expell their servants from that port" (Bruce, ii, 127). Sir A. Shipman died broken-hearted in 1664. Some information regarding Sir A. Shipman's career in England is given in 10th Ser. *Notes and Queries*, iii, 197, quoting the *Ruthven Correspondence*, printed by the Roxburghe Club, 1868, and *Calendar of the Clarendon State Papers*, 1872, i, 244, 310, 323.

[3] Sir George Oxenden (for the spelling see Hedges, *Diary*, ii, 223, 241, 250, 303); born 1620, son of Sir James Oxenden, of Dene, Co.

repair Aboard; since the Jealousy of the *Moors* was such, that unless they did, they vowed the Factory a Sacrifice.

Thus bidding adieu to *Swally*, they at length arrived at *Angediva*, a Barren unhealthy and uninhabited Island, not far from the Main, and but 12 Leagues to the *Southward* of *Goa*.

Where *Malbery* left them to negotiate the right of his Master; so much of which at last they were brought to grant, as enforced them to deliver up *Bombaim*, though they capitulated for that too; parcelling it out into little Islets, made only by the inundations of the Sea: But were glad at length when they saw *Malbery* resolute, to resign the whole Island, with the Bay, into the hands of the *English*, upon the Conditions first assented to, that the Royalties should belong to the King of *England*, but every particular Man's Estate to the Right Owner, and the Liberty of their own Ceremonies in Religion, upon their Oath of Allegiance.

In the mean while Sir *Abraham*, with near 300 of his best Men, rested content without any farther Acquests, leaving their Bones at *Angediva*; poysoned partly by the noisomeness of the Air, the violence of the Rains, and the little defence against them; but chiefly by their own Intemperance.

Mr. *Cook*[1] being next to Sir *Abraham*, took up his

Kent; rose in the Company's service, and knighted at the Restoration; President at Surat, 19th March, 1662; in 1664 defended Surat from the Mahrattas; resisted the Dutch during the war of 1665-67; took over Bombay after it was given over by the Royal troops on 21st September, 1667; drew up rules for the administration of the island; died at Surat 14th July, 1669, where his mausoleum still stands (*Dict. Nat. Biog.*, xliii, 9 f.; Hedges, *Diary*, quoted above; Hunter, ii, 213 f.; Bruce, ii, 107).

[1] Humfrey Cooke, secretary of Sir Abraham Shipman, succeeded the latter after his death at Anjediva; and, in order to save the remnant of his forces, surrendered the dependencies of Bombay to the Portuguese Viceroy, on condition that the survivors might be allowed to occupy the island of Bombay. Though Charles II would not push his remonstrances against the action of the Portuguese as far as an

Commission, who with those Men that were left, was admitted upon *Bombaim* in the Year 1664, when the Royal Fleet returned.

Where at first landing they found a pretty well Seated, but ill Fortified House, four Brass Guns being the whole Defence of the Island; unless a few Chambers housed in small Towers in convenient Places to scowre the *Malabars*,[1] who heretofore have been more insolent than of late; adventuring not only to seize their Cattle, but depopulate whole Villages by their Outrages; either destroying them

---

open quarrel, he promptly disavowed Cooke's action, and, in 1666, appointed Sir Gervase Lucas to supersede him as Governor of Bombay. Lucas, on his arrival, threw Cooke into prison on charges of extortion and peculation. He escaped to Goa, and then with the assistance of the Jesuits, organised a levy for the capture of Bombay. He failed in his attempt, and was proclaimed a traitor in 1668 (Birdwood, *Report*, 85, 222; Hunter, ii, 193 f.).

[1] The northern parts of Malabar, Kanara, and the Konkan were nests of pirates from very early days down to quite modern times. Pliny (*Nat. Hist.*, vi, 23 (26)) says that "at the present day voyages are made to India every year; and companies of archers are carried on board, because the Indian seas are infested with pirates." According to Marco Polo (ed. Yule, 1st ed., ii, 324) more than a hundred corsair vessels cruised annually. "Those pirates take with them their wives and children, and stay out the whole summer. Their method is to join in fleets of twenty or thirty of these pirate vessels together, and then they form what they call a sea cordon, that is, they drop off till there is an interval of five or six miles between ship and ship, so that they cover something like a hundred miles of sea, and no merchant vessel can escape them." Mount d'Ely, according to Fra Paolino, was a haunt of them in the 17th century; and somewhat farther north Ibu Batuta fell into their hands and was stripped to his drawers (*Ibid.*, ii, 326). Linschoten (i, 73) speaks of Chale, Calicut, Cunhale, and Panana as their headquarters. P. della Valle (i, 121) found it dangerous to travel by sea from Cambay to Goa "by reason of the continual incursions of the Malabar Pirates." He describes various adventures with these gentry (ii, 201, 356, 387). Pyrard de Laval describes at length Kunhāli, the great Malabar Corsair who flourished at the close of the 16th century (i, 351, ff.; ii, 509 ff.). Dalboquerque (*Comm.*, ii, 84 ff.) was aided in the capture of Goa by the pirate Timoga. Malabar Hill at Bombay is said to have taken its name from the pirates, whom Gamelli Careri (Churchill, *Voyages*, iv, 201) describes as consisting of Moors, Gentiles, Jews, and Christians, who live in the country between Mt. Delhi (d'Ely), on the south of Kanara as far as Madraspatnam. For further accounts see Col. J. Biddulph, *The Pirates of Malabar and an Englishwoman in India Two Hundred Years Ago* (1907).

by Fire and Sword, or compelling to a worse Fate, Eternal and intolerable Slavery.

About the House was a delicate Garden, voiced to be the pleasantest in *India*, intended rather for wanton Dalliance, Love's Artillery, than to make resistance against an invading Foe: For the *Portugals* generally forgetting their pristine Vertue, Lust, Riot and Rapine, the ensuing Consequences of a long undisturbed Peace where Wealth abounds, are the only Remarkable Reliques of their Ancient worth; their Courages being so much effeminated, that it is a wonder to most how they keep any thing; if it were not that they have lived among mean spirited Neighbours. But to return to this Garden of *Eden*, or Place of Terrestrial Happiness, it would put the Searchers upon as hard an Inquest, as the other has done its Posterity: The Walks which before were covered with Nature's verdent awning, and lightly pressed by soft Delights, are now open to the Sun, and loaded with the hardy Cannon: The Bowers dedicated to Rest and Ease, are turned into bold Rampires for the watchful Centinel to look out on; every Tree that the Airy Choristers made their Charming Choir, trembles, and is extirpated at the rebounding Echo of the alarming Drum; and those slender Fences only designed to oppose the *Sylvian* Herd, are thrown down to erect others of a more Warlike Force. But all this not in one day.

It was sufficient at first for the *English* to make preparations for a growing Strength, though at present such as might offend as well as defend.[1]

[1] The changes described by Fryer in the fortifications were the result of an order of the Court that the Castle should be enlarged and strengthened. They were chiefly carried out by Philip Gyfford, to whom Fryer (p. 169) gives the credit (Bruce, ii, 226). By 1673 Gerald Aungier had so improved the defences that the Dutch Admiral was afraid to attack the place (Anderson, 59; *Bombay Gaz.*, xxvi, Pt. II, 268; Pt. III, 652 ff., where full details will be found). On later improvements of the Bombay gardens, see *Ibid.*, xxvi, Pt. III, 592 f.

Whilst things were in this posture upon some Male-administration of his Office, *Cook* was outed, and Sir *Gervis Lucas* was sent over by the King; who, had he lived, would have made the *Portugals* perform their Compact, seizing from them the *Putachos*, who to stop his Mouth, were willing to comply for the Customs of *Trumbay*.

Upon his decease Captain *Gary*[1] was impowered by the King; who began to act as Vice-Roy, carrying his Chair of State about with him; but his Majesty finding it expensive to bear out this Man's Pride, and in the casting up Accounts, not available to him, only to the Commanders of his Majesty's Ships, who by their own Adventures made good Improvements; and the *East-India*

The garden described by Fryer was attached to the houses of the Lord of the Manor, which included the Quinta or Great House. This, in 1661, belonged to Donna Ignez de Miranda, then Lady of the Manor, or Senhora da Ilha (Edwardes, 37). Ovington (p. 147) gives two drawings of the Citadel and Fort of Bombay, as they stood on 2nd April, 1668. From these it appears that the Citadel and Fort in the time of Fryer included only Bombay Castle and perhaps Fort George (Maclean, 9).

[1] Mr. or Captain Henry Gary came out as Factor attached to the ship *John*, in 1645. He subsequently held a variety of appointments, and succeeded Sir Gervase Lucas as Governor of Bombay on the death of the latter, 21st May, 1667 (Hedges, *Diary*, ii, 323; *Bombay Gaz.*, xxvi, Pt. I, 24). A. Hamilton (*New Account*, i, 192) writes: "After general Child had gotten the reins of Government again into his hands, he became more insupportable than ever. He erected a Court of Inquisition, and made an old Greek, one Captain Garey, Judge, who condemned a man to be hanged on a Tuesday, and the man suffered according to sentence; but, on Friday after, the poor dead fellow was ordered to be called before the Court, but he would not comply with the orders." In the document acknowledging the cession of the island his name appears as "Henri Gueri" (*Bombay Gaz.*, xxvi, Pt. I, 21). His name is found often in the Bombay Records—his quarrel with Widrington; his appeal for payment of arrears of salary; his deputation to Achin; his appointment, with Captain Keigwin, to be a Justice of the Peace (Forrest, *Home Series*, i, 17, 41, 136). The Council complain of his "unadvised vaine glorious boastings in his severale letters . . . seeking to magnify himself by debasing of us (soe much as in him lay)" (*Ibid.*, i, 222). Fryer speaks of him again; and it appears that he had a house at Pangim (Letter IV, chaps. I, II).

Company thereby began to be sensible that their Trade would be impaired in the vending their Commodities at home, and their Ships in *India* little bettered by the King's Port in *India*; and above all, they being liable to be Sufferers for the Hostilities committed by his Majesty's Officers on the *Indians* (who understand no distinction between King and Company) they as freely supplicated for, what his Majesty was as willing to grant, the Island: They holding it, from that time, of his Majesty about four years after the King had possessed it, they defraying all Charges.

In this Exigency on either side, the Martial as well as Civil Affairs, are wholly devolved on the Merchants; and now how they will manage the Sword as well as the Quill, concernes them.

The Old Soldiers are constrained to submit, or disband, which makes them stomach a hard Service under harder Masters: For besides that natural Antipathy betwixt the Subtilty of the one, and Generosity of the other; the stupendious elevation of their Servants on this new acquired Power thrown into their hands, Men, most of them of no Experience or Education, coming young hither, but what they learn from a Luxurious and Griping People, whose Government quadrates not with a *British* Militia: It will not be easy to conceive, as well from the incoherence of Dispositions, as the Lordly Government of a Servant, what Grudges or Miscarriages may be produced? For where the Soldiers and Generals have different Interests, and mutual Obligation is interrupted, the course of things must necessarily run-counter: Moreover, where they should be most eminent in Dangers and Assaults, and lead them on to bold Enterprizes; yet if a tenderness to Self-preservation step in between the Publick Honour and Safety, (as it always does, where that bane to Noble Actions, Covetousness, is concomitant) and which is almost essential to a Merchant, a fear of being laught at for venturing too far; the Case is desperate. For Instance, our Ten Ships, most of them hired by Merchants, and the Commanders some of them (not to say all, for there were of them as worthy Men as any in the World) Principal Owners, were more willing to shift for themselves, than to hazard a stout and unanimous Resistance: Which had they maintained boldly, as they imprudently gave the first Onset (by the *Hollanders* own confession) they had gained a Victory never to be sustained by them, nor for our Fleet sufficiently to have been recompensed; whereas for want of wise Conduct, and a joint Defence, they impressed on themselves and Nation a Blur never to be wiped off. Yet such, by the Constitution of the Company it self, is the present Misfortune, that instant Gain is preferred before Glory or a future emolument; which is the reason, why they are less solicitous for setling by Power, what they must ever be forced to beg, a Trade; and comply with Injuries, than command a Submission, as the *Dutch* do: But here also being left Tenants at will, they think it enough to leave Business in no worse plight than they found it.

And here might be considered, Whether it were not more for the Publick Welfare, should His Majesty be pleased to make it a Royal Company, or a National Concern, as the *Hollanders* is; than to let it be at the will of the Company under the forementioned Circumstances to impose Governours on the Island.

The first of which was Sir *George Oxendine*, who being President, and therefore more immediatly requisite for him to reside at *Surat*, ordered Mr. *Goodyeer*,[1] his Deputy, to

[1] When, on 1st September, 1668, the ship *Constantinople* brought to Surat the Charter by which His Majesty agreed to make over Bombay to the Company, Oxenden and his Council resolved to depute

govern *Bombaim*; but Sir *George* not long after finishing his days, together with his Presidency at *Surat*, *Goodyeer* hastens thither in hopes to succeed, when gaping for that which included this, he is excluded both: Upon which account there happened an *Interregnum* at *Bombiam*; whereby this Body Politick grew up into an Anarchy, and set upon its weak Limbs a *Quintuple* Head, called Commissioners, who were as followeth, *viz.* Mr. *James Adams*, Chairman, (outed in two days) Mr. *Sterling*, a *Scotch* Minister, Mr. *Cotes*, Captain *Burgess*, Lieutenant *Houghton*; who upon the just and happy choice of the Honourable *Gerald Aungier*, were dissolved; and Mr. *Matthew Grey*[1] nominated Deputy, till the Company sent out Captain *Young*, who had it not long before Mr. *Philip Gyfford*[2] was put in; who deserves to be remembred for his great care in raising the Bastions, and in a manner finishing, what always was still but beginning by the rest. He ruled three Years, when the Company thinking their work to go on too fast, gave the Charge of Deputy-Governour to Captain *Shaxton*,[3] and an handsome Recruit

---

Mr. Goodyer "because he had lived on terms of intimacy with Gary, and whilst on a visit to Bombay had gained the affections of the officers; which, they remarked, 'will very much conduce to their peaceable surrender, and our quiet possession of the place.' With Goodyer were associated Streynsham Master, and Cotes, members of the Council at Surat, and Captain Young, who was to be Deputy Governor." Goodyer successfully took over the place from Gary (Anderson, 118).

[1] When Gerald Aungier was appointed President of Surat, he nominated Matthew Gray to be Deputy Governor of Bombay, Young having been dismissed for gross misconduct (*Ibid.*, 119).

[2] Gray was succeeded by Philip Gyfford. He is mentioned several times by Fryer. Anderson confounds him with William Gyfford (Hedges, *Diary*, ii, 185). In a letter from Surat of 4th November, 1676, he is reported to be in a dangerous state of health, and died in the same year. William Gyfford, Governor of Madras (1681-7), was probably a relation (Birdwood, *Report*, 86).

[3] Capt. Shaxton, sent out in 1671 in command of a Company, was appointed, in consideration of his high character, a Factor, so that he might combine civil and military duties; he was also told that he continued to deserve well of the Company, he might become Deputy

of Soldiers; which revived the not yet extinguished Fewd between the Merchants and the Soldiers: Whereupon *Shaxton* was kept from it a full year; and in that Interim, the President distasted at the Insolencies of the *Mogul's* Governour at *Surat*, and fearing a second Confusion of Government at *Bombaim*, together foreseeing Clouds gathering from the *Netherlands*, not minding so much those of the Season (the *Mussoons* being about to enter) insomuch, that narrowly escaping a Dangerous Voyage, he came and took the Government himself in the Year 1671. where these three Years he has regulated Affairs with that Prudence, that whereas he found a Disaffected and Incongruous Council, he has now knit them into a Bond of at least seeming Friendship; and does daily study to advance the Company's Interest, and the good and safety of the People under him.

To this the *Hollanders* are witness; for the Spring before our Fleet arrived (the same Fleet that we unfortunately engaged) the *Dutch* attempting to surprize the Islanders,[1] found them and the Fort in so good a Condition, that they were glad to betake themselves to their Boats without any Booty, and the next day hoisted Sails (for, said they, *Bombaim* been as stark as de Deel) and not without good reason; for within the Fort were mounted 120 Pieces of Ordnance, and in other convenient Stands 20 more, besides 60 Field-pieces ready in their

Governor (Anderson, 123). There are references to his wife in the Bombay Records (Forrest, *Home Papers*, i, 82). Shaxton was accused of remissness in checking the Mutiny of 1674, was sent home, and died at the end of the voyage (Anderson, 196). In a letter of 24th January, 1676-7, the Surat Council wrote: "Herewith goes a Petition of ye widow of Captn. Shaxton deceased, he having farmed the 1 p. cent. custome for yr. ffortifications in which he pretended to have rece'd a considerable loss, in the which she begs your Honors favourable charity, etc., to weigh her present necessities and charge" (Forrest, i, 124).

[1] This refers to the attempted attack by the Dutch fleet under Rickloffe van Goen on 20th February, 1673 (Anderson, 125).

Carriages upon occasion to attend the *Militia* and *Bandarines*.[1] To the Fort then belonged 300 *English*, and 400 *Topazes*,[2] or *Portugal* Firemen: To the *Militia* out of *Portugal* musters 500 under *English* Leaders, all well armed: Of *Bandarines* (that lookt after the Woods of Cocoes) with Clubs and other Weapons, 300. Besides some Thousands more would make a Shew, but not to be relied on, should it come to the push. Moreover in the Road were riding Three Men of War, the best of 30 Guns.

Thus were they provided at our Arrival; nor were their Forces lessened by our coming. Since which a Trench out of the hard Rock the Fort is founded on, is digging to Moat it with the Sea: And they are devising Hornworks for its better security; a thing, to speak truly, of greater undertaking and expence than ever to endure accomplishing by the Company; and without it, it will prove a thing of ill contrivance, it being straitned for room to receive a sufficient number of Defendants, and worse supplied with Water for Store, or Granaries for Provision for a Siege. The first Modellers were to blame in not enlarging it to a Tank that stands without the Parade, which they might have done with almost the same Charges.

From whence let us walk the Rounds. At distance

---

[1] Mahr. *bhandārī*, people who tended the coco-palm gardens in the Island, prepared toddy, and acted as militia. Their origin is uncertain. Their services were recognised after their gallantry on this occasion, and they used to carry the Union flag and blow trumpets before the Sheriff (Edwardes, 13, 33; Anderson, 125 f.; Yule, *Hobson-Jobson*, 57).

[2] The dark-skinned or half-caste claimants of Portuguese descent and Christian profession: probably from Hind. *topī*, "a hat." Nieuhoff, in his account of Batavia, writes: "The Mardickers or Topassers are a mixture of divers Indian nations called Topassers, accomodators, because they will accomodate themselves easily to the manners, customs, and religion of such as they live among: though some will have them derive their name from a precious stone called a Topaz" (In Anderson, 122). See Yule, *Hobson-Jobson*, 933.

enough lies the Town, in which confusedly live the *English*, *Portugueze*, *Topazes*, *Gentues*,[1] *Moors*, *Cooly* Christians, most Fishermen.

It is a full Mile in length, the Houses are low, and Thatched with Oleas[2] of the Cocoe-Trees, all but a few the *Portugals* left, and some few the Company have built, the Custom-house and Warehouses are Tiled or Plastered, and instead of Glass, use Panes of Oister-shells for their Windows (which as they are cut in Squares, and polished, look gracefully enough.)[3] There is also a reasonable handsome *Buzzar*.

At the end of the Town looking into the Field,[4] where Cows and *Buffoloes* graze, the *Portugals* have a pretty House and Church, with Orchards of *Indian* Fruit adjoining. The *English* have only a Burying-Place, called *Mendam's-Point*,[5] from the first Man's Name there

---

[1] Gentiles or heathen, Hindus as distinguished from Moors or Muhammadans (Yule, *Hobson-Jobson*, 367, 581).

[2] The leaf of the palm, especially that of the Palmyra (*Borassus flabelliformis*), (Yule, *Ibid.*, 636 ; Tennent, *Ceylon*[3], i, 512 ff.).

[3] The shell of the translucent oyster (*Placuna placenta*) is still used in many places in lieu of window-glass (*Ency. Brit.*[9], xxxi, 666). It is found in creeks on the W. Coast of India, and in the Tablegam Lake in Ceylon (Tennent, ii, 492). Pyrard de Laval attests its use in Goa (ii, 15, 63); a fashion which still prevails (Fonseca, 155). A. Hamilton (*New Account*, i, 258) says that only one of the churches had glass windows, the rest being supplied with oyster-shell lights. Lockyer (*Account of Trade*, 164) says the same of Canton. Grose (p. 82) states that it was used in the European houses at Bombay. Col. Welsh (*Mil. Rem.*, ii, 149) "robbed [at Anjengo] a broken window of two or three pieces of oyster-shell, or mother of pearl, in memento of my visit to the birth-place of Eliza Draper, Lawrence Sterne's heroine."

[4] Now the eastern part of the present Esplanade (Maclean, 9 ff.).

[5] The name is spelt Mendaim in the contemporary records (Anderson, 139, 143). Hamilton (*New Account*, i, 187), criticising the position of the Fort, writes: "Had it been built about 500 paces more to the southward, on a more acute point of rocks, called Mendam's Point, it had been much better on several accounts." Prior to the opening of the present cemetery at Sonapur, known as "Padre Burrows' Godown," after Rev. H. Burrows, resident chaplain for forty-two years at Bombay, this was the burial-place of the Island. It was situated near the old Apollo Gate, not far from the site of the present Sailors' Home. Though it contained many large monuments,

interr'd, where are some few Tombs that make a pretty Shew at entring the Haven; but neither Church or Hospital, both which are mightily to be desired.[1]

There are no Fresh Water Rivers, or falling Streams of living Water: The Water drank is usually Rain-water preserved in Tanks, which decaying, they are forced to dig Wells, into which it is strained, hardly leaving its brackish Taste; so that the better sort have it brought from *Massegoung*, where is only one fresh Spring.[2]

On the backside of the Towns of *Bombaim* and *Maijm*,[3] are Woods of *Cocoes* (under which inhabit the *Banderines*, those that prune and cultivate them), these Hortoes being the greatest Purchase and Estates on the Island, for some Miles together, till the Sea break in between them: Over-against which, up the Bay a Mile, lies *Massegoung*, a great Fishing Town, peculiarly notable for a Fish called *Bumbelo*,[4] the Sustenance of the Poorer sort, who live on

---

it has quite disappeared, having been closed and the tombs destroyed in 1763, because it was considered to interfere with the military defence of the Island (Maclean, 281; *Bombay Gaz.*, xxvi, Pt. II, 292 *n.*; Pt. III, 577 ff.).

[1] Sir G. Oxenden began the work of providing a church; but on his death in 1669 efforts ceased. It was finally completed by the Chaplain, Rev. R. Cobbe, and it was opened in 1718 (*Bombay Gaz.*, xxvi, Pt. III, 579 ff.). The Surat Hospital was opened in 1676, and about the same time provision for medical relief seems to have been made at Bombay. The foundation of St. George's Hospital dates from 1672 (*Ibid.*, xxvi, Pt. III, 544 ff., 595 ff.).

[2] Bombay was provided with a good water supply in 1858, when the Behār Lake works were constructed while Lord Elphinstone was Governor. This was supplemented by the Tulsi Lake works, opened by Sir R. Temple in 1879. Mazagong, the suburb lying N. of the Fort, owes its name to the pungent odour of the fish, which its early Koli inhabitants caught, dried, and ate (*Machhlī*, Skt. *matsya*, "fish": *gānw*, Skt. *grāma*, "village"). (Edwardes, 5).

[3] Māhim, the suburb N.W. of the Island, which, like Mazagong, seems to mean "fish village" (*Ibid.*, 12).

[4] The Bummelo (Mahr. *bombīl*), a small fish (*harpodon nehereus*) which, when dried, supplies the well-known "Bombay Ducks" (Yule, *Hobson-Jobson*, 126.)

them and *Batty*,[1] a course sort of Rice, and the Wine of the *Cocoe*, called *Toddy*. The Ground between this and the great Breach is well ploughed, and bears good *Batty*. Here the *Portugals* have another Church and Religious House belonging to the *Franciscans*.[2]

Beyond it is *Parell*,[3] where they have another Church, and Demesnes belonging to the Jesuits; to which appertains *Siam*,[4] manured[5] by *Columbeens*,[6] Husbandmen, where live the *Frasses*,[7] or Porters also; each of which

---

[1] The Bombay term for paddy: probably Kan. *bhatta*; Mahr. *bhāt* (*Ibid.*, 72, 650).

[2] The Franciscan Church and Convent were erected by the aid of the Portuguese. The Manor was, when Aungier came to Bombay in 1672, the principal private estate on the Island, the Lord of the Manor being Alvarez Perez de Tavora (Douglas, i, 86 *n.*).

[3] Said to take its name from the tree-trumpet flower (Mahr. *pāral*; *stereospermum* or *bignonia suaveolens*), the N. suburb and residence of the Governor. In Fryer's time the Church and Convent of the Jesuits stood on the site of Government House. It was not till 1720 that the Church was alienated from its original use, and in 1771 it seems to have been converted into a dining-room by the Governor, W. Hornby (Maclean, 287; Yule, *Hobson-Jobson*, 678). Grose (p. 72 f.) speaks of "a place called Parell, where the Governor has a very agreeable country-house, which was originally a Romish chapel belonging to the Jesuits, but confiscated about the year 1719, for some foul practices against the English interest." For the disloyal conduct of the Jesuits, see *Bombay Gaz.*, xxvi, Pt. I, 103, 152. The revenues of the Jesuit property in Bombay used to go to their College at Agra (Manucci, iv, 149 *n.*). Bishop Heber (*Journal*, ii, 134), who visited it in 1825, says that it was purchased from a Parsi by Government about sixty years before. The garden contained a tree grown from a slip of the willow growing on the grave of Bonaparte. It has now been converted into a Plague Hospital and Laboratory for the prěparation of serum (Edwardes, 35).

[4] Sion, Mahr. *siun*, "boundary" (Maclean, 1; Edwardes, 5, 105).

[5] Cultivated.

> "Yon flowery arbours, yonder alleys green,
> Our walk at noon, with branches overgrown,
> That mock our scant manuring."
>
> Milton, *Paradise Lost*, iv, 626 ff.

[6] The Kunbi (Konkani *Kunambi*) caste of cultivators (Yule, *Hobson-Jobson*, 491). Pyrard de Laval (ii, 35) calls them Coulombins; Linschoten (i, 260), Corumbijn.

[7] Hindi *farrāsh*, "a spreader of carpets and performer of other menial duties" (Yule, *Hobson-Jobson*, 249).

Tribes have a *Mandadore*,[1] or Superintendent, who give an account of them to the *English*, and being born under the same degree of Slavery, are generally more Tyrannical than a Stranger would be towards them ; so that there needs no other Taskmaster than one of their own Tribe, to keep them in awe by a rigid Subjection.

Under these Uplands the Washes of the Sea produce a Lunary Tribute of Salt, left in Pans or Pits made on purpose at Spring-Tides for the overflowing ; and when they are full, are incrustated by the heat of the Sun. In the middle, between *Parell*, *Maijm*, *Sciam*, and *Bombaim*, is an Hollow, wherein is received a Breach[2] running at three several places, which drowns 40000 Acres of good Land, yielding nothing else but Samphire ;[3] athwart which, from *Parell* to *Maijm*, are the Ruins of a Stone Cawsey made by Pennances.

At *Maijm* the *Portugals* have another compleat Church and House ; the *English* a pretty Custom-house and

---

[1] Port. *mandador*, "one who commands."

[2] Between Mahalakshmi and Vadali the sea poured in across what are now known as the Flats, submerging the land up to Pāēdhoni (the "feet-washing place," so called because it was the last stream where travellers, before entering the Island, washed their feet), at the S. end of the Parell Road. The sea, again, flowed past Mahim and Sion into Bombay Harbour, drowning land which has since been reclaimed by the construction of the Sion Causeway (built by Governor Duncan in 1805) and the railway embankment between Sion and Kurla on the island of Salsette (Maclean, 9 ff).

[3] Sir G. Watt writes: "Samphire (St. Peter's Herb) is an expression more than a specific name, and denotes the plant or plants met with on barren and waste tracts. The locality near Bombay has been so changed that many of the wastes which Fryer must have seen have long since disappeared, and the plants formerly found on these been destroyed, so that their identification with the plants in similar localities may be questionable. Moreover, some of the more abundant plants have very possibly been introduced since Fryer's time." He is disposed to identify it with a species of *Suaeda* or other saltworts. Dr. Cook, who is preparing a Flora of Bombay, thinks it may be *Suaeda nudiflora* or *S. maritima*, which occurs in Salsette. Dr. Woodrow identifies it with *Acanthus ilicifiorus*, perhaps the most abundant and commonest plant in the marine swamps of the coasts of India.

Guard-house: The *Moors* also a Tomb in great Veneration for a *Peor*,[1] or Prophet, instrumental to the quenching the Flames approaching their Prophet's Tomb at *Mecha* (though he was here at the same time) by the Fervency of his Prayers.

At *Salvesong*,[2] the farthest part of this Inlet, the *Franciscans* enjoy another Church and Convent; this side is all covered with Trees of *Cocoes*, *Jawks*,[3] and *Mangoes*; in the middle lies *Verulee*,[4] where the *English* have a Watch.

On the other side of the great Inlet, to the Sea, is a great Point abutting against *Old Woman's* Island,[5] and is called *Malabar-hill*, a Rocky, Woody Mountain, yet sends forth long Grass. A-top of all is a *Parsy* Tomb lately reared; on its Declivity towards the Sea, the Remains of a Stupendious Pagod, near a Tank of Fresh Water, which the *Malabars* visited it mostly for.[6]

---

[1] Pers. *pīr*, a Muhammadan saint. In Letter V, chap. III, Fryer uses the word for a saint's burial-place (Yule, *Hobson-Jobson*, 692).

[2] "The island was then, and still continues divided into the Roman-Catholic parishes, or Freguezias, as they call them, and are Bombay, Mahim, and Salvaçam" (Grose, 74). In 1596 a Franciscan Church was dedicated to Our Lady of Salvation (Salvaçam). This "is now the richest of all churches, possesses landed property and several cocoanut groves, has three affiliated chapels at Parel, Worli, and Matunga, and a large house, which has served on various occasions as the Portuguese Episcopal residence" (Edwardes, 34 f.).

[3] The Jack-fruit tree, see p. 110.

[4] Worli, on the peninsula stretching out into Māhim Bay, on the N.W. of the Island: probably Mahr. *Vadalī*, "banyan-row" (Edwardes, 21).

[5] Now Lower Kolāba. The Kolāba Kolīs were, it is said, known as Al-'Omānī, that is, deep-sea fishers in the Indian Ocean, the sea of 'Omān, the southern coast of Arabia, from Muscat to Aden. The name may date from the period of the Silahāra dominion in W. India, which began about 810 A.D. The corruption of Al-'Omānī into "Old Woman" is characteristic of the early Anglo-Indians. In Fryer's time the island was used as a sort of menagerie (Edwardes, 4, 8; *Bombay Gaz.*, xxvi, Pt. III, 593, 667).

[6] Malabar Hill, the native name of which is Srī Gundī, which seems to mean "Lucky Stone," is separated from Kolāba by the shallow expanse of Back Bay. The Malabar pirates are said to have been in

Thus we have compleated our Rounds, bringing in the Circumference Twenty Miles, the Length Eight, taking in *Old Woman's* Island, which is a little low barren Island, of no other Profit, but to keep the Company's Antelopes, and other Beasts of Delight.

The People that live here are a Mixture of most of the Neighbouring Countries, most of them Fugitives and Vagabonds, no account being here taken of them: Others perhaps invited hither (and of them a great number) by the Liberty granted them in their several Religions; which here are solemnized with Variety of Fopperies (a Toleration consistent enough with the Rules of Gain), though both *Moors* and *Portugals* despise us for it; here licensed out of Policy, as the old *Numidians* to build up the greatest Empire in the World. Of these, one among another, may be reckoned 60000 Souls; more by 50000 than the *Portugals* ever could. For which Number this Island is not able to find Provisions, it being most of it a Rock above Water, and of that which is overflowed, little hopes to recover it. However, it is well supplied from abroad both with Corn and Meat at reasonable Rates; and there is more Flesh killed for the *English* alone here in one Month, than in *Surat* for a Year for all the *Moors* in that Populous City.

The Government here now is *English*; the Soldiers have Martial Law: The Freemen, Common; the chief Arbitrator whereof is the President, with his Council at

---

the habit of visiting the famous temple of Wālkeshwar (*Vāluka-īsvara*, "lord of sand"), the pagoda with its tank to which Fryer refers. Lady Falkland (*Chow-chow*[2], i, 87) gives a lively account of this place. The present temple is only about 150 years old; but remains of the ancient building are still to be seen near the Walkeshwar Reservoir. It is curious that Fryer does not mention the cleft in the rocks, known as the Yoni, or Stone of Regeneration, through which pilgrims force themselves, to show that they are "twice-born," a feat which Sivaji and Kanhoji Angria are said to have accomplished (Grose, 89; Douglas, ii, 232 f.).

Surat; under him is a Justiciary, and Court of Pleas, with a Committee for Regulation of Affairs, and presenting all Complaints.

The President has a large Commission, and is *Vice-Regis*; he has a Council here also, and a Guard when he walks or rides abroad, accompanied with a Party of Horse, which are constantly kept in the Stables, either for Pleasure or Service. He has his Chaplains, Physician, Chyrurgeons, and Domesticks; his Linguist,[1] and Mint-Master: At Meals he has his Trumpets usher in his Courses, and Soft Musick at the Table: If he move out of his Chamber, the Silver Staves[2] wait on him; if down Stairs, the Guard receive him; if he go abroad, the *Bandarines* and *Moors* under two Standards march before him: he goes sometimes in his Coach, drawn by large Milk-White Oxen, sometimes on Horseback, other times in *Palenkeens*, carried by *Cohors*,[3] *Musslemen* Porters: Always having a *Sombrero*[4] of State carried over him: And those of the *English* inferior to him, have a suitable Train.

But for all this Gallantry, I reckon they walk but in Charnel-houses, the Climate being extremely Unhealthy;[5]

---

[1] An interpreter (Yule, *Hobson-Jobson*, 517).

[2] The Chobdār, an attendant on Indian nobles.

[3] Hind. *Kahār*, the caste whose speciality is carrying palanquins (Yule, *Ibid.*, 495).

[4] See p. 134.

[5] The unhealthiness of Bombay in the early period of British rule was notorious. "Whether it be that the Air stagnates, or the Land towards the Fort lies very low, or the stinking of the Fish which used to be applied to the Roots of the Trees, instead of Dung; or whatever other Cause it is which renders it so very unhealthful, 'tis certainly a mortal Enemy to the Lives of the *Europeans* . . . which common Fatality has created a Proverb among the *English* there, that two Mussouns are the Age of a Man" (Ovington, 140 ff.). Grose (p. 48 ff.) gives similar reasons for the unhealthiness of the place, which is much debated in the correspondence of the time (Forrest, *Home Papers*, i 66, 74, 148). The question is fully discussed by Anderson, 274 ff. The use of the fish manure is considered in various official orders, *Bombay Gaz.* xxvi, Pt. I, 510 ff.

at first thought to be caused by *Bubsho*, rotten Fish ; but though that be prohibited, yet it continues as Mortal : I rather impute it to the Situation, which causes an Infecundity in the Earth, and a Putridness in the Air, what being produced seldom coming to Maturity, whereby what is eaten is undigested ; whence follows Fluxes, Dropsy, Scurvy, Barbiers (which is an enervating the whole Body, being neither able to use Hands or Feet) Gout, Stone, Malignant and Putrid Fevers, which are Endemial Diseases: Among the worst of these, *Fool Rack*[1] (Brandy made of *Blubber*, or *Carvil*,[2] by the *Portugals*, because it swims always in a Blubber, as if nothing else were in it ; but touch it, and it stings like Nettles ; the latter, because sailing on the Waves it bears up like a *Portugal Carvil*: It is, being taken, a Gelly, and distilled causes those that take it to be Fools), and Foul Women may be reckoned.

To prevent the latter of which, and to propagate their Colony, the Company have sent out *English* Women ;[3] but they beget a sickly Generation ; and as the *Dutch* well observe, those thrive better that come of an *European* Father and *Indian* Mother : Which (not to reflect on what Creatures are sent abroad) may be attributed to their living at large, not debarring themselves Wine and Strong Drink, which immoderately used, inflames the Blood, and

---

[1] The distilled "flower" (*phūl*) of arrack (Yule, *Hobson-Jobson*, 356).

[2] The jelly-fish (*medusa*) ; cf. Yule, *Hobson-Jobson*, 162. On the dangers of drinking strong arrack, cf. Bernier, 253. The Carvel or Caravel, which probably takes its name from the Span. *caraba*, had a broader beam than a galley, was provided with lateen sails, and was ordinarily of about 200 tons burthen.

[3] Gerald Aungier suggested that the emigration of European women should be encouraged, on the ground that the men, being Protestants, were in the habit of marrying Portuguese women, the consequence of which was that their offspring were, "through their fathers' neglect, brought up in the Roman Catholic principles, to the great dishonour and weakening of the Protestant religion and interest" (Anderson, 215).

spoils the Milk in these Hot Countries, as *Aristotle* long ago declared. The Natives abhor all heady Liquors, for which reason they prove better Nurses.

Notwithstanding this Mortality to the *English*, the Country People and naturalized *Portugals* live to a good Old Age, supposed to be the Reward of their Temperance; indulging themselves neither in Strong Drinks, nor devouring Flesh as we do. But I believe rather we are here, as Exotick Plants brought home to us, not agreeable to the Soil: For to the Lustier and Fresher, and oftentimes the Temperatest, the Clime more unkind; but to Old Men and Women it seems to be more suitable.

Happy certainly then are those, and only those, brought hither in their Nonage, before they have a Gust of our *Albion*; or next to them, such as intoxicate themselves with *Læthe*, and remember not their former Condition: When it is expostulated, Is this the Reward of an harsh and severe Pupilage? Is this the *Elysium* after a tedious Wastage? For this, will any thirst, will any contend, will any forsake the Pleasures of his Native Soil, in his Vigorous Age, to bury himself alive here? Were it not more charitable at the first Bubbles of his Infant-Sorrows, to make the next Stream over-swell him? Or else if he must be full grown for Misery, how much more compassionate were it to expose him to an open Combat with the fiercest Duellists in Nature, to spend at once his Spirits, than to wait a piece-meal'd Consumption? Yet this abroad and unknown, is the ready Choice of those to whom Poverty threatens Contempt at home: What else could urge this wretched Remedy? For these are untrodden Paths for Knowledge, little Improvement being to be expected from Barbarity. Custom and Tradition are only Venerable here; and it is Heresy to be wiser than their Forefathers; which Opinion is both bred and hatch'd by an innate Sloth; so that though we seem nearer the Heavens, yet Bodies here are more Earthy, and the Mind wants that active Fire that always mounts, as if it were extinguish'd by its *Antiparistasis*.[1] Whereby Society and Communication, the Characteristick of Man is wholly lost. What then is to be expected here, where sordid Thrift is the only Science? After which, notwithstanding there is so general an Inquest, few there be acquire it: For in Five hundred, One hundred survive not; of that One hundred, one Quarter get not Estates; of those that do, it has not been recorded above One in Ten Years has seen his Country: And in this difficulty it would hardly be worth a Sober Man's while, much less an Ingenuous Man's, who should not defile his purer Thoughts, to be wholly taken up with such mean (not to say indirect) Contemplations; however, a necessary Adjunct, *Wealth*, may prove to buoy him up on the Surface of Repute, lest the Vulgar serve him as *Æsop's* Frogs did their first rever'd Deity.

Thus much being premised for what concerns the Island its self, it remains to speak of it with relation to the Credit it bears among its Neighbours: The *Dutch* cast an envious Eye on it, and were it in their hands, would doubtless make it render all it is capable; and in respect of Commerce it seems to offer many Conveniences; the *Banyans* liking it better than *Surat*, living freer, and under milder Taxations, which they put the present President in some hopes of complying with, could he open the way from hence up the Country;[2] but that depending on so many

---

[1] Antiperistasis (ἀντιπερίστασις), "opposition or reaction of surrounding parts"; "the influence of circumstances in exciting opposition to, or reaction against their effects; opposition to any surrounding force or influence, force of contrast" (*Stanford Dict.*, *s. v.*). The word is used by Macaulay (*Essay on Bacon*); "he tells us, that in physics the energy with which a principle acts is often increased by the antiperistasis of its opposite."

[2] "The Gentiles, too, as well as the Christians, are permitted the Freedom of their Religion, and conniv'd at in their Heathen worship" (Ovington, 148).

Intricacies, must be not only a work of Time, but Power to bring to pass; as afterwards may fall more properly in our way to make appear.

Our present Concern then is with the *Portugal*, *Seva Gi*, and the *Mogul*: From the first is desired no more than a mutual Friendship; from the second, an Appearance only; from the last, a nearer Commerce: The first and second become necessary for Provisions for the Belly, and Building; the third for the Gross of our Trade: Wherefore Offices of Civility must be performed to each of these; but they sometimes interfering, are the occasion of Jealousies; these three being so diametrically opposite one to another: For while the *Mogul* brings his Fleet either to Winter or Recruit in this Bay, *Seva* takes Offence; on the other hand, the *Mogul* would soon put a stop to all Business, should he be denied: The *Portugal*, as in League with neither, thinks it a mean compliance in us to allow either of them Countenance, especially to furnish them with Guns and Weapons to turn upon Christians, which they wisely make an Inquisition-Crime.

CHAP. II.

Is a Survey of the Island of Canorein *near* Bombaim.

UPON these scores it was not long before I was employed to wait on the Father Superior of the *North*, a Learned Man, and a *Spaniard* by Nation, of the Order of the Jesuits.

The President commanded his own *Baloon*[1] (a Barge of

---

[1] Balloon, Balloen, "a Siamese state-barge, upwards of a hundred feet long, and richly decorated" (*New Eng. Dict.*, *s.v.*). Here a rowing vessel, the basis of which was a large canoe, or "dug-out"; perhaps Mahr., *balyānw*, "a barge" (Yule, *Hobson-Jobson*, 53). It seems to have resembled the Portuguese *manchua* (Pyrard de Laval ii, 42).

State, of Two and twenty Oars) to attend me and one of the Council, to compliment the Father on the Island of *Canorein*,[1] parted from *Bombaim* by a Stream half a Mile broad: Near our Landing-place stood a College, not inferior to the Building, nor much unlike those of our Universities, belonging to the Jesuits here, more commonly callen *Paulistines*[2] (whose Visitor was now my Patient), who live here very sumptuously, the greatest part of the Island being theirs. Our Entertainment was truly Noble, and becoming the Gravity of the Society. After I had done my Duty, the Fathers accompanied us to the Barge; afore the College-Gate stood a large Cross, thwack'd full of young Blacks singing Vespers: The Town is large, the Houses tiled; it is called *Bandora*.[3]

At our department they gave us Seven Guns, which they have planted on the Front of their College for their own Defence, besides they are fitted with good store of Small Arms: Following therein the Advice given by a Statesman to the King of *Spain*, about the *Netherlands*; That *if the Society of the* Loyolists *were multiplied, their Convents might serve for Castles.*

---

[1] The island of Salsette; the name representing the Buddhist caves at Kānheri, which are in the centre of the island, about 20 miles N. of Bombay. The caves are described by Fergusson (*H. of Ind. and East Arch.*, 129 f.), who believes they were excavated in the early years of the fifth century, A.D. Also see Fergusson-Burgess, *Cave Temples*, 348 ff.; *Bombay Gaz.*, xiv, 121 ff.; Maclean, 356 ff.; Manucci, i, 153.

[2] A title given to the Jesuits in India, because their houses in that country were in former times always dedicated to St. Paul. On the festival of his Conversion the foundation stone of the first Jesuit church in Goa was laid, probably because at his altar in the Basilica of St. Paul at Rome Ignatius Loyola took his vow to found the Society of Jesus (Yule, *Hobson-Jobson*, 688; *Bombay Gaz.*, xi, 294 *n*; P. della Valle i, 142; Tavernier, ed. Ball, i, 197).

[3] Bāndra, town and port, lat. 19° 2′ N., long. 72° 53′ E.; in the S.W. corner of the island of Salsette. The site of the Jesuit monastery of St. Anne is now occupied by the Bombay Municipal Slaughter-house. The buildings were destroyed and the place abandoned when, in 1737, the English sent a force to assist the Portuguese in defending the place against the Mahrattas (*Bombay Gaz.*, xiv, 15 ff.).

In the middle of the River we had a pleasant Prospect on both sides; on *Bandora* side, the College, the Town, the Church of St. *Andrew*[1] a Mile beyond, and upon the Hill that pointed to the Sea, the *Aquada*, Blockhouse,[2] and a Church; on the other side, the Church of *Maijm*,[3] with other handsome Buildings.

Curiosity led me a second time to visit the Island *Canorein*, having obtained leave for a longer Stay: nor went I alone, some of the best Quality on the Island being led by the same desire, joining themselves with me: We carried a Train of Servants, Horses, and *Palenkeens*, which were ferried over before us; and we coming soon after, were met by the Fraternity, and conducted to the Fathers, who detained us till Afternoon by a stately Banquet, shewing us the Civility of the Church and College, diverting us both with Instrumental and Vocal Musick, and very good Wine.

After which we were dismiss'd, and four Mile off *Bandora* were stopp'd by the Kindness of the *Padre*-Superior, whose Mandate whereever we came caused them to send his *Recarders*[4] (a Term of Congratulation, as we say, *Our Service*) with the Presents of the best Fruits and Wines, and whatever we wanted.

---

[1] The modern Church dedicated to St. Andrew stands on the sea-shore, on the site of the ancient building erected in 1575 by F. Manuel Gomez, the apostle of Salsette, Superior of the College of the Holy Name at Bassein (*Ibid.*, xiv, 22).

[2] Pathways lead down the hill as far as the Point, where are the remains of the Portuguese Agoada or "watering-place," where ships procured water, and of a block-house, which, from an inscription, seems to have been built in 1640 (*Ibid.*, xiv, 15 f.).

[3] Māhim, see p. 173.

[4] "Kind regards;" Port. *recado*, "a message;" *recados*, "compliments." "Their service only is to attend their masters and to carry messages, which they call *Racates*" (Pyrard de Laval, ii, 80). "The Negro observing it, approached him with ceremony, and gave him the Regards of the Countrey" (Ovington, 73 f.). "Pray give my recadoes to Pedro o Lavera" (Letter of 1663, in Bowrey, 75). The Span.-Port. *recado*, of uncertain origin, has no connection with our "regards" (*New Eng. Dict.*, *s. v.*, *recado*, *regard*).

Here, not adjoining to any Town, in a sweet Air, stood a Magnificent Rural Church; in the way to which, and indeed all up and down this Island, are pleasant *Aldeas*,[1] or Country Seats of the Gentry; where they live like Petty-Monarchs, all that is born on the Ground being theirs, holding them in a perfect state of Villainage, they being Lords Paramount.

From hence, when we had baited, the same Night we travelled easily to *Magatana*,[2] using our Fowling-Pieces all the way, being here presented with Rich Game, as Peacocks, Doves, and Pigeons, *Chitrels*,[3] or Spotted Deer. When we came to the Town, two several Churches strove to receive us; but having some Acquaintance with the Father of the one, and not with the other, we excused ourselves to the latter, and took up with our Friend. As soon as we came in, the Servitors fetch'd us warm Water to wash our Feet, which was very refreshing; it put me in mind of *Lot's* Courtesy to the Angels. After this, as a piece of extraordinary Civility, they showed us the Necessary House; and it is so in a Countrey where Fluxes are so common; and for that reason it is kept as neat as their Lodging Rooms, having Water to Wash after you have used a clean Towel hung there for that Purpose.

This Night we fared very well. Next Morn before Break of Day we directed our Steps to the anciently fam'd, but now ruin'd City of *Canorein*; the way to it

---

[1] Port. *aldea*, Ar. *al-dai'a*, "a villa" (Yule, *Hobson-Jobson*, 12). The pleasure-houses of the Portuguese gentry near Bassein are described with admiration by Gemelli (Churchill, *Voyages*, iv, 190). Only a few ruined walls now survive (*Bombay Gaz.*, i, Pt. II, 64 f.).

[2] Māgāthan, a place now deserted and not to be found in most modern maps, half a mile E. of the Borivli Station, on the Bombay-Baroda Railway. The private buildings and churches are no longer traceable (*Ibid.*, xiv, 216 ff.). It is chiefly remarkable for the Māgāthan or Poinsar group of Buddhist caves (*Imperial Gazetteer* (1908), xvi, 410).

[3] Hind. *chītal*; Skt. *chitra*, "spotted," the spotted deer (*cervus axis*) (Yule, *Hobson-Jobson*, 859; Blanford, *Mammalia*, 546).

is so delightsome, I thought I had been in *England*; fine Arable, Pasture, and Coppices; thus we passed Five Mile to the Foot of the Hill on which the City stands, and had passed half a Mile through a thick Wood, peopled by Apes, Tygers, wild Buffolo's, and Jackalls; here were some Flocks of Parockets: When we alighted, the Sun began to mount the *Horizon* over the Hills, and under our Feet, as if he had newly bathed his fiery Coursers, there appeared the Mouth of a *Tank*, or Aqueduct, out of a Rock, whose steaming Breath was very hot, but water cold: From hence it is thought the whole City to be supplied with Water; for as we ascend, we find such Places, where convenient, filled with Limpid Water, not over-matched in *India*: If it be so, (as I know not how to contradict it) that it should have its Current upwards through the hard Rocks artificially cut, the World cannot parallel so wonderful a Water-course!

From hence the Passage is uneasy and inaccessible for more than two abreast, till we come to the City, all cut out of a Rock; where is presented *Vulcan*'s Forge, supported by two mighty Colosses, bellied in the middle with two Globes. Next a Temple with a beautiful Frontispiece not unlike the *Portuco* of St. *Paul*'s *West Gate*: Within the Porch on each side stand two Monstrous Giants,[1] where two Lesser and one Great Gate give a noble Entrance; it can receive no Light but at the Doors and Windows of the Porch, whereby it looks more solemnly; the Roof is Arched, seeming to be born up by huge Pillars of the same Rock, some Round, some Square, 34 in number. The *Cornish* Work of Elephants, Horses, Lions; at the upper end it rounds like a Bow; near where stands a great Offertory somewhat Oval, the Body of it

[1] The Chaitya caves, the "Giants" being figures of Buddha, 23 ft. high (Fergusson Burgess, 350 f.; *Bombay Gaz.*, xiv, 166).

without Pillars, they only making a narrow Piatzo about, leaving the Nave open: It may be an 100 Feet in Length, in Height 60 Feet or more.

Beyond this, by the same Mole-like Industry, was worked out a Court of Judicature[1] (as those going to shew it will needs give Names) or Place of Audience, 50 Feet square, all bestuck with Imagery, well Engraven according to old Sculpture. On the Side, over against the Door, sate one Superintendent, to whom the *Brachmin* went with us, paid great Reverence, not speaking of him without a token of worship; whom we called *Jougy*,[2] or the Holy Man; under this the way being made into handsome Marble Steps, are the King's Stables, not different from the Fashion of our Noblemens Stables, only at the head of every Stall seems to be a *Dormitory*, or Place for Devotion, with Images, which gave occasion to doubt if ever for that End; or rather made for an Heathen Seminary of Devotes, and these their Cells or Chappels, and the open Place their Common Hall or School: More aloft stood the King's Palace, large, stately and magnificent, surrounded with lesser of the Nobility.

To see all, would require a Month's time; but that we might see as much as could be in our allotted time, we got upon the highest part of the Mountain, where we feasted our Eyes with innumerable Entrances of these Cony-burrows, but could not see one quarter part. Whose Labour this should be, or for what purpose, is out of memory; but this Place by the *Gentiles* is much adored: Some contend for *Alexander*;[3] and as a proof, think they have said enough, when it is received by Tradition, that

---

[1] The Darbār Cave, the next largest to the great Chaitya Cave (Fergusson-Burgess, 353 ff.; *Bombay Gaz.*, xiv, 172).

[2] A Jogī ascetic, see p. 138.

[3] The Portuguese, as in the case of the great ruined temples in Camboja, were accustomed to assign ancient buildings to Alexander (Yule, *Marco Polo*, i, 114.)

a great Gap out of a Solid Rock was cut by him to make this an Island: But this is contradictory to the Story delivered of *Alexander*, That he sailed up *Indus*, and encountred King *Porus*, of whom some little Remains may be collected, they speaking of that King by the Name of *Por* in *Cambaia*, where *Alexander* landed with his Army; and followed the Course of *Indus*, directly contrary to this Place, that lying *North-East*, this *South* from thence; nor do we read his stay in *India* was so long, to atchieve such Acts as these, this Place being not the only Instance of this nature; but more probable to be an Heathen *Fane*, or Idolatrous Pagod, from the Superstitious Opinion they still hold of its Sacredness: Wherefore the *Portugals*, who are now Masters of it, strive to erace the remainders of this *Herculean* Work, that it may sink into the oblivion of its Founders.[1]

Returning to *Magatana*, we spent some days in riding about the Country, which we found every-where provided with Churches.

The Chief City of this Island is *Tanaw*.[2] In which are Seven Churches and Colleges, the chiefest one of the *Paulistines*; the Houses Tiled, but low: Here are made good Stuffs of Silk and Cotton.

There is another great Town called *Mein*,[3] where is a

---

[1] On the establishment of the Inquisition at Goa, the Franciscan Fathers took possession of the caves at Kānheri and Mandapeshwar, expelled the Jogīs who occupied them, and, as at Elephanta, did their best to destroy the sculptures, on account of the superstitious feelings of the natives in respect to them (*Bombay Gaz.*, i, Pt. II, 56, quoting De Coutto, vii, 245, viii, 335, 429).

[2] Thāna, lat. 19° 11′ 30″ N., long. 73° 3′ E.; 21 miles N.E. from Bombay. Of the numerous churches and religious houses built by the Portuguese in the 16th and 17th centuries, only one now remains, the Church of St. John the Baptist, formerly dedicated to St. Anthony, built by the Franciscans about 1540 (*Ibid.*, xiv, 351).

[3] Probably Mane in Salsette, where there is an old Portuguese church (*Ibid.*, xiv, 228).

Castle and some Soldiers, towards the Sea ; over against *Baçein* there is another Fort and *Aquada.*

The *Portugals* suffer none but Christians here: It has no Rivers, but only Inlets of the Sea; but good Springs from the Rocks; the Ground excellently fertile, either of it self, or by the care of the Inhabitants; that it yields as good Cabbages, Coleworts, and better Rhadishes than ever I yet saw: Besides Garden-Fruit, here are incomparable Water-Melons, and Onions as sweet, and as well tasted as an Apple; and for the natural growth of the Soil, it is known not only to supply the adjoining Islands, but *Goa* also. It is more than 20 Miles in Length, and 70 in Circumference.

CHAP. III.

A Visit to Baçein, *a* Portugal *City in* India ; *our return by* Elephanto, *and the* Putachos, *with Observations on the Island* Bombaim.

THE several *Capitaneos* of the *Portugals* are *Triennial,*[1] which are the Alternate Governments entailed on the Families of the Conquerors, and therefore made Circular; every one in his course having his turn to rule in some Place or other for Three Years, and upon these they can borrow or take up Mony as certain as upon their Heredi-

[1] "Everie 3 yeares there is a new Viceroy sent into India" (Linschoten, i, 217). "And because their time of government is so short, and that the place is given them in recompense of their service, and thereafter not to serve any more, there is not one of that esteemeth the profit of the commonwealth, or the furtherance of the King's service, but rather their own particular commodities, as you may verie well thinke, so that the common speach in India is, that they never looke for any profite or furtherance of the Common wealth by any viceroy, as long as the Government of three yeares is not altered" (*Ibid.*, i, 221). "Every three years the King of Spain sends out one, who never makes his entry until his predecessor has made his exit" (Pyrard de Laval, ii, 76). Casualties and the exigencies of the public service prevented this regularity of succession; see the list of Viceroys in Danvers, ii, 487, ff.

tary Estates the next Incumbent being Security for the payment: Pursuant to this, a new Governour coming to *Choul*, his Honour the President sent to congratulate him; and the Admiral of the *North* coming to *Baçein*, another was sent on the same Message.

Nor could the hot Months be over, before *John de Mendos*,[1] of a Noble Family, sent for me to *Baçein* for the cure of his only Daughter, illustriously born, handsome, and on the point of Marriage with the Admiral of the *North*,[2] though not full Twelve years old.

Leaving *Bombaim*, at this time of the year, we could go either within or without; but the first being related to be pleasantest I chose that way; sailing by *Trumbay*,[3] where we receive Custom, we might see a comely Church and *Aldea*:[4] At Noon we reached *Tanaw*: Having gained our Passage over the Flats, we made no stay, but rowed streight to *Baçein*; every half Mile we were presented with fresh Prospects of delicate Country-Mansions; two of which of special note draw the Eyes of the Beholders; one of *John de Melos*, three Mile off *Tanaw*, it standing high, curiously built, has a Terras Descent with Walks and Gardens half a Mile, till it lead to a spacious Banquetting-house over the Water, with Stone-stairs for Landing:[5] Beyond it a Mile, on the side of an Hill, stands *Grebondel*,[6] a large neat built Town of *Martin Alphonso*'s;

---

[1] João de Mendonça; another officer of this name was 21st Viceroy of Goa (1564), (Danvers, i, 527 f., ii, 487.)

[2] The Admiral of the north fleet, see p. 153.

[3] See p. 158.

[4] See p. 185.

[5] Of these Portuguese country-houses nothing is known beyond the reference by Fryer (*Bombay Gaz.*, i, Pt. II, 64).

[6] Ghodbandar, "horse-port," in Salsette, 10 miles N.W. of Thāna: supposed to be the Hippokoura of Ptolemy; but this was more probably Ghoregāon in Kolāba (M'Crindle, *Ptolemy*, 44). The Church of St. John has now been converted into the residence of the Collector, having been at the time of Bishop Heber's visit an occa-

and at top of all, his House, Fort and Church, of as stately Architecture as *India* can afford; he being the Richest Don on this side *Goa.* Here we are Land-locked by the Gut; which is fabled to be made by *Alexander*; from which we have an open passage to *Baçein*,[1] it lying bare towards the Sea.

BACEIN.

Is incircled with a round Stone-wall, and has a Gate for every Wind; it is strong enough against the *Indians*, but not able to endure an *European* Foe: There are upon the Out-walls, and in the Fort, Forty two great Guns; the Fort in the middle of the City is circular; towards the Market appears a State-house Piatzed, where the Governour convocates the *Fiddálgos*[2] every Morning upon consultation, in which they all stand, a Chair not being permitted the Governour, though Gouty: Towards Evening they meet there to Game.

---

sional residence of the Governor (*Journal*, ii, 129 f.). An attack on this place by Sivaji, in 1692, led to the English Embassy to him under Mr. Ustick (Anderson, 163).

[1] Bassein, Vasāī, "the settlement": Lat. 19° 20′ N., long. 72° 51′ E.; on the coast, 30 miles N. of Bombay. The fort is now in a state of dilapidation. The great square faces the sea, and round it are the remains of some fine buildings, including the State House mentioned by Fryer. The front of the Jesuit Church is the finest piece of architecture in the city—a noble arch, columns with fluted shafts and Corinthian capitals, with the monogram I. H. S. sculptured on the lintel and above the pillars. The rest of the Church and the College, both founded in 1548 by Malchior Gonsalves, a close friend of St. F. Xavier, are in ruins. The Franciscan Church of the Invocation of Santo-Antonio is better preserved. See the excellent account of the city in *Bombay Gaz.*, xiv, 28 ff.

[2] Port. *fidalgo*, *filho de algo*, "son of something, a nobleman." ". . . some beare the tytle of Fidalgo da Caza del Rey nossas senor, that is, a Gentleman of the Kinge's house, which is the chiefest title: there are others named Mozos Fidalgos, which is also an honorable title, and they are commonly Gentlemen's sonnes, or by the Kinge's favour advanced thereunto. There are yet others that are named Cavalheiro Fidalgo, which is not so much as the other two, yet it is an honorable title, and is the title of a knight, who for some valiant act by him done is made knight, which they do for a small matter" (Linschoten, i, 188 f.). Cf. Bowrey, 194.

Within the Walls are six Churches, four Convents, two Colleges, one of the *Jesuits*, another of the *Franciscans*. It bears the Name of an Academy; the Students are instructed in the *Jesuits* College, but live in Town: Where is a Library, with Classes of Historians, Moralists, Expositors, and no more. It is a College of Polite Structure, in the *Portuco* is a Copy of *Angelos*, representing the Resurrection; above Stairs, as well as below, are fine square Cloisters, as all their Collegiate Churches have on the sides whereof are their Cells; they have a spacious Refectory, and a goodly Church; three parts of the City is devoted to their use.

The *Fidalgos* (for few Artisans are tolerated within the Walls) have stately Dwellings, graced with covered Balconies, and large Windows two Stories high, with Panes of Oister shell, which is their usual Glazing among them in *India*, or else Latised. They shew their Greatness by their number of *Sumbreeroes* and *Cofferies*, whereby it is dangerous to walk late for fear of falling into the Hands of those Pilfering Abusive Rascals. None but Christians lodge within the City, the *Banyans* repairing to the Suburbs upon *Tattoo*. The City is a Mile and half round; it stands on an Island, separated by a small Channel from the Main, as far off the Island *Canorein*, as *Canorein* from *Bombaim*, and parted after the like nature.

The Land about is plain, and fruitful of Sugar-Canes, Rice, and other Grain; a great part of which has lately been destroyed by the *Arabs* of *Muschat*, who put them to a sore fright in *Baçein*:[1] and this is done often, setting fire to their Villages, and carrying away their *Fidalgos* Prisoners, together with their Wives and Families, butcher-

---

[1] In 1674 six hundred Muscat pirates landed, and, unopposed by the garrison, plundered all the churches outside the walls, refraining from no cruelty and violation (*Bombay Gaz.*, xiv, 32, quoting Orme, *Hist. Fragments*, 46).

ing the *Padres*, and robbing the Churches without resistance, conceived on a deadly Feud, partly out of revenge of the *Portugal* Cruelties at *Muschat*;[1] but chiefly out of detestation of each other's Religion; insomuch that Quarter is denied on either side: But that on this Pretence. The *Portugals* striving to possess themselves of *Muschat*, were put to such stress, that had not their *Armado* come to their relief, they must have desisted their Enterprize: Upon the arrival whereof the new Recruits gained so much on the *Arab* Governour, that he yielded up the otherwise invincible Fort of *Muschat*; where the *Portugals* acting all nefarious Outrages, contrary to their Promise, the *Arabs* re-armed themselves with Courage and fresh Succors, and at length beat them from hence to *Ormus* in the Gulf of *Persia*; from whence also they were routed by the help of the *English* (we then being at war with them); the first blow to their Greatness in these Parts.

To check these Incursions of the *Arabs*, the *Portugals* every Year are at the charge of a lusty Squadron in these Seas, which were those we met on the Coast returning from thence; who were no sooner gone, than the *Arabs* sent their Fleet to do this Mischief here; which now 'tis done, they are again in quest of them, but they fly as often as these pursue.

And if such be the gasping Strength of the *Portugals*, to terrify the Potentest Enemies to Christianity in these Parts, what was their flourishing Estate? Whence it may easily be supposed before now all had bowed to the Cross, which yet bend under Heathenism or *Mahometism*, had

[1] The Portuguese first attacked Muscat in 1507, when Dalboquerque put to the sword all he found in the town, irrespective of age or sex (Danvers, i, 160). It was retaken by the Turkish fleet in 1550-1 (*Ibid.*, i, 497). The Portuguese erected a fort in 1586, which was unsuccessfully attacked by the Imām of Muscat in 1640-1 (*Ibid.*, ii, 69, 296). Grose (p. 64) attests the hostility felt by the Arabs of Muscat towards the Portuguese.

they not been prevented by unhappy Pretenders, that (I fear) too much preferred Merchandize and private Pieques, before the welfare of Religion : For it is morally probable, that had not the *Dutch* and we interrupted them, all might have been Christian in these parts of the World.

Having in a Week's time compleated my Business, returning the same way, we steered by the *South* side of the Bay, purposely to touch at *Elephanto*,[1] so called from a monstrous Elephant cut out of the main Rock, bearing a Young one on its Back ; not far from it the Effigies of an Horse stuck up to the Belly in the Earth in the Valley; from thence we clambred up the highest Mountain on the Island, on whose Summit was a miraculous Piece hewed out of solid Stone : It is supported with Forty two *Corinthian* Pillars, being a Square, open on all sides but towards the *East* ; where stands a Statue with three Heads, crowned with strange Hieroglyphicks : At the *North* side in an high *Portuco* stands, an Altar, guarded by Giants, and immured by a Square Wall ; all along, the Walls are loaded with huge Giants, some with eight hands, making their vanquished Knights stoop for mercy. Before this is a *Tank* full of water, and beyond that another Place with Images. This seems to be of later date than that of *Canorein*,[2] though defaced by the *Portugals*,[3] who have

---

[1] Elephanta, an island in the harbour of Bombay, also known as Ghārapurī, "cave city," or Purī, "city." The image with three heads, to which Fryer refers, is the famous Trimūrti, the central figure representing Siva as Creator, or Brahmā ; that on the left Rudra or Siva the Destroyer ; that on the right Siva as Vishnu. The elephant statue, from which the place takes its name, and which bore a smaller figure of an elephant or tiger on its back, has been removed to the Victoria Gardens at Bombay. That of the horse disappeared some time between 1712 and 1764. See Burgess, *Rock Temples of Elephanta* ; Yule, *Hobson-Jobson*, 341 ; Fergusson-Burgess, *Cave Temples*, 465 ff.

[2] Fergusson dates the temple in the eighth, Burgess in the latter part of the eighth or in the ninth century, A.D. This would make it some three centuries later than Kānheri.

[3] "These Pagodas and buildings are now whollie left overgrowne, and spoyled since the Portingalles had it under their subjections"

this Island also; but no Defence upon it, nor any thing else of Note; it may be Ten Miles round, inhabited by the *Povo*, or Poor: From hence we sailed to the *Putachoes*,[1] a Garden of Melons (*Putacho* being a Melon) were there not wild Rats that hinder their Growth, and so to *Bombaim*.

The Weather now was grown excessive hot, the Earth beginning to gape for Thirst, the Sun being in its *Zenith* with us; the *South* Winds are set in strong, and the *Toddy-Trees* ferment their Wine over the Vessels, the *Prodromi* of the ensuing Rains; which make their first shew at the first Full Moon in *May*, and continue a Fortnight, in which space it is unhealthy; till after a Fortnight's fair Weather they set in for altogether.

This Season makes the *Syddy*[2] retreat hither with his Fleet, who from a Lord of *Duccan* is promoted to be the *Mogul's* Admiral; or truer, driven to distress by *Seva Gi*, undertakes this Employment, in confidence to recover his own Dominion on the Sea-Coast, whilst the *Mogul's* General at Land is to stop his Proceedings on that side: But *Seva Gi* possessed of his Country, and bidding for his strong Castle at *Dan de Rajapour*[3] Bay, which he has been to defend this Summer, derides his Attempts, and is preparing to be install'd *Mau Raja*,[4] or Arch *Raja*, at his Court at *Rairee*;[5] for which an Embassy to keep all right must be dispatch'd.

(Linschoten, i, 291): a statement disputed by Burnell, but corroborated by the account of Coutto written early in the seventeenth century (Fergusson-Burgess, *Cave Temples*, 465 ff.; *Bombay Gaz.*, xiv, 84 f.).

[1] See p. 158.

[2] Ar. *sayyid*, "a prince": a title of the Habshī or African Muhammadans of the island of Janjira (Yule, *Hobson-Jobson*, 469, 806). Sidi Sambal was appointed Mogul Admiral in 1670, and received the title of Yāqūt Khān (Grant Duff, 110). For his visits to Bombay between 1672 and 1682, see Anderson, 169 ff.

[3] Dandā-Rājpurī, on the S. shore of the Rājpurī creek, and about a mile from the inland fort of Janjira, in which State it is now included (*Bombay Gaz.*, xi, 460 f.).

[4] Mahārājā.

[5] See p. 202.

In the mean while Nature affords us a pleasant Spectacle for this Season, as well as Matter for Admiration; whereby I know not why we should deny Reason wholly to Animals; unless it be, Man having so much, they seem comparatively to have none: For here is a Bird[1] (having its Name from the Tree it chuses for its Sanctuary, the *Toddy-Tree*) that is not only exquisitely curious in the artificial Composure of its Nest with Hay, but furnished with Devices and Stratagems to secure its self and young ones from its deadly Enemy the Squirrel; as likewise from the Injury of the Weather; which being unable to oppose, it eludes with this Artifice, contriving the Nest like a Steeple-hive, with winding Meanders; before which hangs a Penthouse for the Rain to pass, tying it by so slender a Thread to the Bough of the Tree, that the Squirrel dare not venture his Body, though his Mouth water at the Eggs and Prey within; yet it is strong enough to bear the hanging habitation of the Ingenious Contriver, free from all the Assaults of its Antagonist, and all the Accidents of Gusts and Storms: Hundreds of these Pendulous Nests may be seen on these Trees.

Here is another Tree called *Brabb*,[2] bodied like a Cocoe, but the Leaves grow round like a Peacock's Tail set upright, of the same substance with the Cocoe, only varying in figure; the Fruit of this is less than the Cocoe, and filled with a Gelly; the Wine from this is preferred new, before the other; there is a Tuft at top, cut off and boil'd eats like Colliflowers; on which Tree these Birds build also.

And now the Rains are set in, all Hostilities and Commerce cease, and every one provides for this time, as the

---

[1] Fryer seems to refer to the Weaver bird, or Baya (*Ploceus Baya*). (Yule, *Hobson-Jobson*, 928).

[2] The Palmyra tree (*Borassus flabelliformus*); Port. *brava*, *bravo* "wild" (*Ibid.*, 111).

laborious Ant for the Winter, here being no stirring out to Sea, or travelling in the Country; the best Pastime now being good Fellowship. Thus lies this place afloat, and the Rains and Thunder are violent enough to convince the incredulous of a possibility of a General Deluge. This holds with little intermission till St. *Francis*'s Moon,[1] the first Full Moon in *August*; when our *Europe* Ships, if they save their Passage about the *Cape*, venture to make in here, by the directions of the yellow Bellies of the formerly mentioned Water-Snakes,[2] who are a warning to them of adventuring too near the Shore, till this open Weather appear.

After this Full Moon, the *Banyans*, assisted by their *Brachmins*, go in Procession to the Sea-shore, and offer Cocoe Nuts to *Neptune*, that he would restore them their *Mare Pacificum*; when they make Preparations to go to Sea, and about their Business of Trade.[3]

By this opportunity our Ambassadors crossed an Arm of the Sea, and returning from *Seva Gi*, delivered the President this following Account; which I the rather insert, because the manner of dealing with these Princes and Great Men may be the better understood by this formal Address.

---

[1] See Letter IV, chap. v.

[2] See p. 127.

[3] This is a rite intended to propitiate the water spirit. Similar rites are described at the Maldives by Pyrard de Laval (i, 176 f.); at Goa by P. della Valle (i, 186 f.); by Ives (*Voyage*, 28). Ovington (p. 133 f.) says that at the close of the rainy season at Bombay "the *Bannians* endeavour to appease the incensed Ocean by offerings to its inraged Waves, and in great plenty throw their gilded Coco-nuts into the Sea to pacify its storms and Fury, and render it peaceable and calm. And after these Ceremonious Oblations are past, the Oraculous *Bramins* declare safety to the Ships that will venture upon the Ocean, before which not one of them will offer to weigh an Anchor." At the present day the rite of flinging coco-nuts into the sea at Bombay is known as the Narali Paurnima, a "Coco-nut Full Moon," held on the full moon of the month Srâvan (July-August) (Murray Mitchell, *Hinduism Past and Present*[2], 197; Maclean, 336).

CHAP. IV.

A Narrative of an Embassy to Seva Gi, *and Journey to* Rairee, *the Court of the* Rajah.

THE Ambassador having received Instructions,[1] and got all things ready for his Journey, embark'd on a *Bombaim Shebar*[2] (together with two *English* Factors, who were appointed by the Honourable the President to accompany him); and about Nine a Clock at Night arrived at *Choul*,[3] a *Portugal* City on the Main, into which he could not enter, the Gates being shut up, and Watch set; so that they passed this Night in the Suburbs, in a small Church called St. *Sebastians*; and the next day about Three in the Afternoon receiving Advice that *Seva Gi* was returned to *Rairee*[4] from *Chiblone*,[5] departed thence to Upper *Choul*, a Town belonging to the *Rajah*, about two Miles distant from the *Portugal* City; and was in former times a great Mart of all sorts of *Duccan* com-

---

[1] The instructions given to Mr. H. Oxinden were—to endeavour to settle the amount of damages sustained by the British at Rājapur, which, by a convention, had been admitted by Sivaji; to obtain permission to trade at the ports in his dominions; and that the Company's Agents might be allowed to make purchases and sales in the countries between those ports and the Deccan, particularly at the ports opposite to Bombay. The question of disposal of wrecks was also to be raised (Bruce, *Annals*, ii, 364 f., in which he quotes Oxenden's "Narrative of the Negotiations with Sevajee, 13th May to 13th June, 1674").

[2] A kind of coasting vessel (Yule, *Hobson-Jobson*, 827).

[3] Cheul or Revdandā: Lat. 18° 33′ N., long. 73° E., about 30 miles S. of Bombay. The Portuguese factory was founded in 1516 by permission of the King of Aḥmadnagar (*Bombay Gaz.*, xi, 269 f.; Yule, *Ibid.*, 210 f.). The Muhammadan town, or Upper Cheul, was reduced to ruins and occupied by Sivaji, whom Fryer calls "the Rajah." The Church of St. Sebastian is probably represented by a ruin close to the sea gate.

[4] See p. 202.

[5] Chiplun, a trading town and place of pilgrimage in the Ratnagiri District: Lat. 17° 30′ N., long. 73° 36′ E. It contains Buddhist caves and sacred Hindu tanks.

modities; but now totally ruined by the late Wars betwixt the *Mogul* and *Seva Gi*, whose Arms have plundered and laid it waste.

The *Subidar*[1] of this Town being a Person of Quality, who commands the Countries opposite to *Bombaim*, as *Magatan*,[2] *Penn*,[3] and *Tull*,[4] he thought good to give him a Visit, and to present him with a couple of *Pamerins*;[5] and the rather, because he understood by the Linguist *Naran Sinaij*,[6] he had some Aversion to our Nation, and might hinder our Proceedings at Court; from which he was willing to take him off by all fair means: He received the Visit kindly, and promised all Courtesy that lay in his Power to perform; and after some immaterial Discourse they returned to their Tents.

The Day following they took Boat, and sailed up *Choul* River, to a Town called *Esthemy*,[7] six Leagues distance from *Choul*, where they staid till next day; and set forth about six in the Morn from *Esthemy*, and about Sun-set

---

[1] Pers. *sūbadār*, governor of a Moghul province (Yule, *Hobson-Jobson*, 856).

[2] See p. 185.

[3] Pen, a town in the Kolāba District, on the Bhagavati creek, about 10 miles from its mouth: Lat. 18° 44′ N., long. 73° 11′ E. In 1668 it was a Moghul port, though it lay in Sivaji's dominions (Bruce, ii, 242).

[4] Thal, a village in Kolāba District, three miles N. of 'Alībāgh (*Bombay Gaz.*, xi, 395).

[5] Mahr. *pāmarī*, "a mantle, scarf, or turban" (Yule, *Hobson-Jobson*, 665).

[6] The "Narun Gi Pundit" of p. 200; Nārāyan Shenvi. This class of Brahmans, also known as Sārasvata, is numerous in the Konkan, Goa, and Island of Bombay, deriving their name from Mahr. *chhiānavē*, "ninety-six," probably from the number of their sections (Wilson, *Indian Caste*, ii, 29). Nārāyan Shenvī, under the name of "Narran Sunay," appears in the Bombay Records as an interpreter employed in other negotiations with Sivaji (Forrest, *Home Papers*, i, 80, 99).

[7] Astamī, a suburb of the town of Rohā, on the Kundalika or Roha river, 24 miles from its mouth, in the Kolāba District. It has a fine tank, not mentioned here (*Bombay Gaz.*, xi, 265, 378, 12). Forbes (*Or. Mem.*, i, 123 f.) calls it Ustom, where he stayed for the night in a tomb.

pitched their Tent in a Plain, six Miles short of *Nishampore*,[1] where they stayed about an hour to refresh their *Coolies*, and then set forward for *Nishampore*, and at Nine passing by *Nishampore*, arrived next Morning at *Gongouly*,[2] a little Village situated on the Bank of a pleasant Rivulet; from whence in a fair Day may be discerned the Castle of *Rairee*: The day after they proceeded on their Journy to *Rairee*, and about Nine of the Clock in the Evening came to *Puncharra*,[3] a Town at the Foot of the Hill, where they understood that *Seva Gi* was departed thence to *Purtaabgur*,[4] to visit the Shrine of *Bowany*, a Pagod of great esteem with him, and celebrated some Ceremonies there in order to his Coronation; having carried with him several Presents, and among the rest a *Lumbrico*[5] of pure Gold, weighing about one *Maund* and a quarter, which is Forty two Pounds, which he hath dedicated to the said Pagod.

In the interim, understanding they could not be admitted into the Castle till *Seva Gi's* return, they pitched their Tent in the Plain; and in order to their more speedy dispatch, make their Business known to their Procurator *Narun Gi Pundit* (whose reception was very kind) and delivered him his Honour's Letters; shewing him the several Presents they brought for the *Rajah*, and Ministers of State; of which he highly approved, and promised

---

[1] Nizāmpur, a small town in the Kolāba District, containing the ruins of an ancient Hindu temple (*Bombay Gaz.*, xi, 353).

[2] Gangāvli, not traced on modern maps.

[3] Pāchād, at the foot of the Rāygad hill (*Bombay Gaz.*, xi, 366).

[4] Pratāpgad, a fort in the Sātāra district, 8 miles W. of the modern Sanatorium of Mahābaleshwar. In 1661, precluded by its situation from worshipping at the celebrated temple of Bhawānī at Tuljapur, the family goddess of the Bhonslas, Sivaji dedicated a temple to her in the Pratāpgad fort (Grant Duff, 83, 40; *Bombay Gaz.*, xix, 545 ff.).

[5] In the "Index Explanatory" *Lumbrico* is defined to be "a Sconce or Vessel, where Lamps burn together." This word has not been traced. Mr. Ferguson thinks it may be a "ghost word," and with hesitation suggests Port. *lampadario*, "a great branched candlestick."

them to help them to the *Rajah's* presence, as soon as conveniently he could after his return from Pilgrimage to *Purtaabgur*: And bad them rest content, that his Endeavours should be totally employed in the Honourable Company's Interest, and procuring them a speedy dispatch: For which having rendered him Thanks, he presented him with the Articles which they brought for the *Rajah* to sign, translated into *Moratty* Language; which he said he would peruse, and then give his judgment of them. He then took occasion to discourse with him concerning the Conclusion of a Peace betwixt the *Rajah* and the *Syddy* of *Danda Rajapore*;[1] urging many Arguments to create in him a belief it would be for the *Rajah's* advantage, but he would not be persuaded it was for his Master's Interest to raise a Siege which had cost him so much Blood and Treasure; especially now he hath such hopes of gaining the Place: And therefore told them, it would be in vain to move it to the *Rajah*, who was resolved to take in the Castle, let it cost him what it will: And to that effect was daily sending down more Ordnance, Ammunition, Men and Money.

Our Ambassador replied, The President had no other Design in making this motion, than that of a good Neighbour; having observed the Miseries each Party endured, and the general obstruction of Trade, occasioned by the War; but since he desired him to desist mentioning it to the *Rajah*, he should not trouble him therewith; but what was more consistent with our own and his Interest; which was the encouraging Trade and Merchandise in his Country, and opening the ways to *Baligaot*,[2] that Merchants might with safety bring down their Goods to Port; which would be much to the *Rajah's* Profit, and

[1] For Syddy and Danda Rajapore see p. 195.

[2] Bālāghāt, the country above the passes of the range of the Western Ghauts (Yule. *Hobson-Jobson*, 51).

encrease of his Treasury: And this he recommended to his Prudence to persuade the *Rajah* thereto; who being a Soldier from his Infancy, its possible minded not such concerns.

To which he answered, That he doubted not but it would be effected in a short time; for that the King of *Visiapour*,[1] who is Owner of those Countries (from whence most sorts of Wares come) being weary of Wars with his Master, had sent several Embassies to conclude a peace with him; which he thought would be made up in two or three Months, and then the Ways would be free, and the Merchants have Egress and Regress as formerly. That the *Rajah*, after his Coronation, would act more like a Prince, by taking care of his Subjects, and endeavouring the advancement of Commerce in his Dominions; which he could not attend before, being in perpetual War with the *Great Mogul* and King of *Visiapour*. This is the Substance of his Discourse with *Narun Gi Pundit* who seemed to him to be a Man of Prudence and Esteem with his Master: So after a little sitting he took his leave of him, having first presented him with a Diamond Ring, for which he expressed a liking; and his Eldest Son a Couple of *Pamerins*,[2] which are fine Mantles.

They continuing under their Tent, found it very hot and incommodious; wherefore they were glad when they heard the *Rajah* was returned from *Purtaabgur*, when the Ambassador solicited *Narun Gi Pundit* to procure his leave to pass up the Hill into *Rairee* Castle:[3] The next

---

[1] Bijapur, the King of which at the time was Sultan Sikandar (1659-86).

[2] See p. 199.

[3] Rāygad or Rāiri, a famous hill fort, "a place as impregnable as Gibraltar" (Grant Duff, 679); "if reports do not bely it, it must be the most compleatly impregnable place in the universe" (Grose, 137); situated in the Kolāba district: lat. 18° 14′ N., long. 73°

day they receiv'd order to ascend the Hill into the Castle, the *Rajah* having appointed an House for them; which they did; leaving *Puncharra* about Three in the Afternoon, they arrived at the top of that strong Mountain, forsaking the humble Clouds about Sun-set.

It is fortified by Nature more than Art, being of very difficult access, there being but one Avenue to it, which is guarded by two narrow Gates, and fortified by a strong Wall exceeding high, and Bastions thereto: All the other part of the Mountain is a direct Precipice; so that it's impregnable, except the Treachery of some in it betray it. On the Mountain are many strong Buildings, as the *Rajah's* Court, and Houses of other Ministers, to the number of about 300. It is in length about two Miles and an half, but no pleasant Trees, or any sort of Grain grows thereon. Their House was about a Mile from the *Rajah's* Palace, into which they retired with no little content.

Four days after their ascent, by the sollicitation of *Narun Gi Pundit*, the *Rajah* gave them Audience, though busily employed by many other great Affairs, relating to his Coronation and Marriage. Our Ambassador presented him, and his Son *Samba Gi Rajah*,[1] with the Particulars appointed for them; which they took well

---

30′ E. From Pāchād, where the embassy halted, the ascent continues for 1½ miles to Vādī, about 600 ft. above the sea; thence to the top of the hill is a rise of about 2250 ft. in a distance of about 4 miles. The two gates through which the Englishmen passed are the Nānā Darwāza, or "Little Gate," and the Motā or Mahā Darwāza, "the Great Gate." The hill-top stretches about ½ mile from E. to W. For an account of the capture of this famous fort by the British on 14th February, 1819, see Blacker, *Memoir of the Mahratta War*, 310 ff.

[1] Sambhāji, the eldest son of Sivaji by his first wife, was born in 1657, and executed by order of Aurangzeb on 14th March, 1689 (Manucci, ii, 232, 310 ff.). The Madras Records of 27th September, 1689, state: "This evening was informed with the sad news of Haja Rajah's death; but no account who is likely to succeed" (Wheeler, *Madras in the Olden Time*, i, 213).

satisfied with them; and the *Rajah* assured them we might trade securely in all his Countries without the least apprehension of ill from him; for that the Peace was concluded. Our Ambassadour replied, that was our Intent; and to that intent the President had sent him to this Court to procure the same Articles and Privileges we enjoyed in *Indostan* and *Persia*, where we traded. He answered, it is well, and referred our Business to *Moro Pundit*,[1] his *Peshua*,[2] or Chancellour, to examine our Articles, and give an account what they were. He and his Son withdrew into their private Apartments, to consult with the *Brachmines* about the Ceremonies preparatory to his Enstalment; which chiefly consisted in Abstinence and Purifying; till which be over, he will hear no farther of Business. They likewise departed to their Lodgings.

A day or two after our Ambassador went to *Narun Gi Pundit*, and took his Advice concerning the presenting of the rest; who told him he might go in Person to *Moro Pundit*, but to the rest he should send by *Naran Sinaij* what was intended for them: Declaring likewise if he would have his Work speedily effected, and without any impediment, that it was necessary to be at some more charge to present Officers with *Pamerins*, who were not in their List of Presents; to which he assented, considering the time of the Year was so far spent, and that

---

[1] Moro Trimal Pinglē, a Deshast Brahman, came to Sivaji's notice when in charge of the erection of Pratāpgad fort in 1656. When very young he accompanied his father, then in the service of Shāhji, to the Carnatic, whence he returned to his Mahratta country about 1653, and shortly after joined Sivaji. He succeeded Shāmrāj Pant as Peshwa or Prime-Minister. In 1666 he was appointed to represent Sivaji during his absence at Delhi. He was removed from office and imprisoned by Sambhājī in 1681 (Grant Duff, 75, 95, 137). There are numerous references to him, while in command of the Mahratta forces, in the Bombay Records (Forrest, *Home Papers*, i, 67, 96, 115).

[2] Pers. *peshwā* leader; the Mayor of the Palace under the Mahratta dynasty at Poona.

if he should be forced to stay the whole Rains out at *Rairee*, the Honourable Company's Charges would be greater than the Additional Presents: He answered that two *Pamerins* were not enough for *Moro Pundit*, that we must present him with four; and *Peta Gi Pundit Vocanovice*,[1] or Publick Intelligencer, with the Diamond Ring, valued at 125 Rupees.

The *Dehir*,[2] or *Persian Escrivan*,[3] with Four *Pamerins*.
Sam Gi Nan Gi,[4] Keeper of the Seal, with Four.
Ab Gi Pundit,[5] Four.

And then he should not doubt of a speedy Conclusion; otherwise they would raise Objections on purpose to impede the Negotiation. For every Officer in Court expected something according to their Degree and Charge.

About this time the *Rajah*, according to the *Hindu* Custom, was weighed in Gold, and poised about 16000 Pagods, which Money, together with an 100000 more is to be distributed among the *Brachmines* after the day

---

[1] Petājī Pandit, the Wāqi'ah-navīs, or "newswriter." In Persia Manucci (i, 23) describes such a functionary as "Chief Secretary of State." But Bernier (p. 231) represents him in the Moghul Government as a sort of official spy, whose duty it was to report to headquarters the conduct of provincial officials. See *Āīn*, i, 251, f.; Yule, *Hobson-Jobson*, 960.

[2] Pers. *dabīr*, "a writer, secretary, notary."

[3] Port. *escrivão*, "a clerk or writer" (Yule, *Ibid.*, 804).

[4] Shāmjī Nānājī, *nānā* meaning "a respectful term of compellation, originally for a person of the name Nārāyan, and now for a person in general" (Molesworth, *Mahr. Dict.*, *s. v.*). Mr. Irvine suggests that the term "Keeper of the Seal" may mean the Nyā Shāstrī, who was "expounder of the Hindoo law, and the Shasters; all matters of religion, criminal law, and of science, especially what regarded Judicial astrology, belonged to this office," which Grant Duff (p. 105) says was held by "Sembha Oopadheea," that is to say, Sambha an Upādhya Brahman, who was possibly this officer.

[5] Ābājī Pandit, whom Mr. Irvine is disposed to identify with "Abajee [son of] Sondeo, Muzzimdar, general superintendant of finance and auditor general of accounts," who died this year (1674) (Grant Duff, 64, 81, 85, 95, 105, 117).

he is enthroned, who in great numbers flock hither from all parts of his Territories.[1]

Being earnest to press on his Errand he came for, the Ambassador sent to *Narun Gi Pundit* to know what was transacted in the Articles; but was returned for Answer. The *Rajah* stopt his Ears to all Affairs, declaring he had granted all the Demands, except those two Articles, expressing, Our Money shall go current in his Dominions, and his on *Bombaim*; and that he shall restore whatever Wrecks may happen on his Coasts belonging to the *English*, and Inhabitants of *Bombaim*:[2] The first he accounted unnecessary to be inserted, because he forbids not the passing of any manner of Coins; nor on the other side, can he force his Subjects to take those Monies whereby they shall be Losers; but if our Coin be as fine an Allay, and as weighty as the *Mogul's*, and other Princes, he will not prohibit it. To the other he says, that it is against the Laws of *Conchon* to restore any Ships, Vessels, or Goods, that are driven ashore by

[1] This rite, known as Tulā-dāna, was practised by many Hindu princes, and by the Moghul Emperors. The Rājās of Mārwār and Amber used to weigh themselves against gold, gems, nd precious cloths at the Pushkar pilgrimage, the articles being afterwards distributed among the priests (Tod, *Annals*, i, 537). Even at the present day the golden lotus through which the Mahārājā of Travancore passes, and which is broken up and given to Brahmans, must be his exact weight (Mateer, *Land of Charity*, 170; *Manual of Travancore*, i, 171, 227; Gopal Panikkar, 133 f.) Akbar was weighed twice a year against gold and other valuables (*Āīn*, i, 266 f.). The weighing of Jahāngīr is described by Sir T. Roe (i. 252) and by Terry (p. 395). The same custom prevailed in the time of Aurangzeb (Manucci, ii, 348; Tavernier, ed. Ball, i, 379 ff.; Bernier, 270). On this occasion Sivaji weighed about 10 stone.

[2] The claim to wrecks on this coast dates from very early times. "And this naughty custom prevails over all these provinces of India, to wit, that if a ship be driven by stress of weather into some other port than that to which it was bound, it was sure to be plundered" (Marco Polo, ii, 386). Abd-er-Razzak, speaking of this custom, remarks that in Calicut all ships coming into port were well treated (*India in XVth Cent.*, 14). On the custom generally see Westermarck, *Origin and Development of the Moral Ideas*, ii, 25.

Tempest, or otherwise; and that should he grant us that Privilege, the *French*, *Dutch*, and other Merchants, would claim the same Right; which he could not grant without breaking a Custom has lasted many Ages: The rest of our Desires he willingly conceded, embracing with much satisfaction our Friendship, promising to himself and Country much Happiness by our Settlement and Trade: Notwithstanding *Narun Gi Pundit* did not altogether despair of obtaining our Wrecks, because we enjoyed the same Privilege in the *Mogul*, and *Duccan* Country.

Near a Month after they had been here, *Narun Gi Pundit* sent word, That to Morrow about Seven or Eight in the Morning, the *Rajah Seva Gi* intended to ascend his Throne; and he would take it kindly if they came to congratulate him thereon; that it was necessary to present him with some small thing, it not being the Custom of the *Eastern* Parts to appear before a Prince empty-handed. The Ambassador sent him word, according to his Advice he would wait on the *Rajah* at the prescribed time.

Accordingly next Morning he and his Retinue went to Court, and found the *Rajah* seated on a Magnificent Throne, and all his Nobles waiting on him in Rich Attire; his Son *Samba Gi Rajah*, *Peshuah Mora Pundit*, and a *Brachmin* of Great Eminence, seated on an Ascent under the Throne; the rest, as well Officers of the Army as others, standing with great Respect. The *English* made their Obeisance at a distance, and *Narun Sinai* held up the Diamond Ring that was to be presented him: He presently took notice of it, and ordered their coming nearer, even to the Foot of the Throne, where being Vested, they were desired to retire; which they did not so soon, but they took notice on each side of the Throne there hung (according to the *Moors* manner) on heads of Gilded Launces many Emblems of Dominion and Government; as on the Right-hand were two great Fishes Heads of Gold, with very large Teeth;[1] on the Left, several Horses Tails,[2] a Pair of Gold Scales on a very high Launce's head, equally poized, an Emblem of Justice;[3] and as they returned, at the Palace Gate stood two small Elephants on each side,[4] and two fair Horses with Gold Trappings, Bridles, and Rich Furniture; which made them admire how they brought them up the Hill, the Passage being both difficult and hazardous.

Two days after this, the *Rajah* was married to a Fourth Wife, without State; and doth every day bestow Alms on the *Brachmins*.

Some days after, *Narun Gi Pundit* sent word the *Rajah* had signed their Articles, all but that about Money. Then the rest of the Ministers of State signed them, and they went to receive them of *Narun Gi Pundit*,

---

[1] This symbol was probably adopted from the Moghul Court. Sleeman's view that the Māhī Marātib, or Order of the Fish, was instituted by Khusrū Parvez of Persia, is denied by his editor (*Rambles and Recollections*, i, 167 ff.). It was adopted by the Shī'ah dynasty of Oudh, appears on many of their buildings, and in the names of the Machchhī Darwāza Gate and the Machchhī Bhawan Fort at Lucknow. Bernier (p. 266) describes at the Emperor's receptions "many figures of silver, beautifully made, and mounted on large silver sticks; two of them represent large fish." On the sanctity of fish in India see Crooke, *Things Indian*, 221 ff.

[2] He probably refers to the tail of the yak. In Central Asia "without it nobody goes to the wars in any good heart. For they believe that any one who has it shall come scathless out of battle" (Marco Polo, ii, 355). Hence the tūgh became the Mongol standard (Erskine, *H. of India*, i, 265); and Akbar's *chatrtoq* standard was decorated with yak tails (*Āīn*, i, 50). P. della Valle (ii, 260 f.) says that cavalry officers in S. India wore them hanging behind the saddle-bow.

[3] Shāhjahān had this symbol depicted in the Dīwān-i-Khās, at Delhi; for an illustration see Fanshawe, *Delhi Past and Present*, 36.

[4] Two figures of elephants stood at the entrance of the Delhi and Agra Forts, the latter being moved by Aurangzeb as opposed to the Muhammadan law forbidding sculptures (Bernier, 256 f.; Fanshawe, *Ibid.*, 43; *Āīn*, i, 505 *n.*). Modern Rājās, to bring luck, often keep one or two elephants at their fort gates; if taught to swing their trunks and bodies they are considered particularly auspicious.

who delivered them to the Ambassador with Expressions of great Kindness for our Nation, and offered on all occasions to be serviceable to the *English* at the Court of the *Rajah*.

I will only add one Passage during the Stay of our Ambassador at *Rairee*: The Diet of this sort of People admits not of great Variety or Cost, their delightfullest Food being only *Cutchery*,[1] a sort of Pulse and Rice mixed together, and boiled in Butter, with which they grow Fat: but such Victuals could not be long pleasing to our Merchants, who had been used to Feed on good Flesh: It was therefore signified to the *Rajah*, That Meat should be provided for them; and to that end a Butcher that served those few *Moors* that were there, that were able to go to the Charge of Meat, was ordered to supply them with what Goat they should expend (nothing else here being to be gotten for them), which he did accordingly, to the consumption of half a Goat a Day, which he found very profitable for him, and thereupon was taken with a Curiosity to visit his new Customers; to whom, when he came, it was told them, The honest Butcher had made an Adventure up the Hill, though very old, to have the sight of his good Masters, who had taken off of his hands more Flesh in that time they had been there than he had sold in some Years before, so rare a thing is it to eat Flesh among them;[2] for the *Gentiles* eat none, and the *Moors* and *Portugals* eat it well stew'd, bak'd, or made into Pottage; no Nation eating it roasted so commonly as we do: And in this point I doubt we

---

[1] See p. 94.

[2] This is an unlikely story, because almost all Mahrattas eat mutton and goat's flesh; the Kunbis, who form the bulk of them, certainly do (*Bombay Gaz.*, xviii, Pt. I, 286). Sivajī and his Court, however, under Brahman influence, may have discontinued the eating of meat, except that of sacrificed animals.

err in these Hot Countries, where our Spirits being always upon the Flight, are not so intent on the business of Concoction ; so that those things that are easiest digested, and that create the least trouble to the Stomach, we find by Experience to agree best here.

CHAP. V.

Our Passage to Swally, *and Relation of the* English *Presidency at* Surat.

AFTER the Rains were over, and the *North-East* Wind had brought in the Cool Season, by Command from the President I was sent to *Surat.*

In a Week's time we turned it up, sailing by *Baçein*,[1] *Tarapore*,[2] *Valentine*'s-*Peak*,[3] St. *John*'s,[4] and *Daman*,[5] the last City Northward on the Continent, belonging to the *Portugueze.* As also passing by *Balsore*[6] (the first Town of the *Moors* Southward of *Surat*) and eight Ships riding at *Surat* River's Mouth, we then came to *Swally Marine*,[7] where were flying the several Colours of the Three Nations, *English*, *French*, and *Dutch*, on Flag-Staffs

---

[1] See p. 191.

[2] Tārapur, a port in the Māhim subdivision of Thāna District: Lat. 19° 50′ N., long. 72° 42′ 30″ E.: about 60 miles N. of Bombay ; at present a place of no importance.

[3] The European name given to the Mahālakshmī hill, 1540 feet high, near Dāhānū in Thāna District: about 16 miles N.E. of Tārapur. ". . . . and then St. John de vacas, a Towne subject to the Portugall, at the south end especially mounting in an ambitious piramid of Natures work, named *Saint Valentin's* peake" (Herbert, 34).

[4] The Anglo-Indian corruption of Sanjān in Thāna District : Lat. 20° 12′ N., long 72° 52′ E. (Yule, *Hobson-Jobson*, 782).

[5] Still a Portuguese settlement : Lat. 22° 25′ N., long. 72° 53′ E.

[6] Balsār or Bulsār of the maps : Lat. 20° 38′ N., long 72° 58′ E. : about 40 miles S. of Surat.

[7] Or Swally Hole, the roadstead N. of the mouth of the river Tapti. The proper form of the name is Suwālī (Yule, *Hobson-Jobson*, 883 ; *Bombay Gaz.*, ii, 332 f.).

erected for that purpose, who here land and ship off all Goods, without molestation.

Here we were welcomed by the Deputy-President, Mr. *Matthew Grey*,[1] an Eminent Merchant, and by the rest of the Council, who took care for my Entertainment, which here was but rude, the place admitting of little better Tenements than Booths, stiled by the name of *Choultries*:[2] Before President *Andrew*'s[3] time they always lodged in Tents; but since, Wooden Houses tiled with Pan-Tiles have been raised in an Inclosure allotted by the Governor. In which Compound are included Warehouses, Stables, and other Out-houses, with as good a Garden as this Sandy Soil will allow; in which ours exceeds the other two, being far pleasanter seated.

To this place belong two sorts of Vermin, the Fleas and *Banyans*;[4] the one harbouring in the Sand, fasten upon you as you pass; where 'tis some Pastime to see what Shift the *Banyan* makes, being bit by them, he dare not kill them, for fear of unhousing a Soul, according to their Notion of Transmigration; but giving them a severe Pinch will put them to shift for themselves in a Nest of Cotton-Wool. The other Vermin are the *Banyans*

---

[1] He was secretary and one of the Surat factors in 1663-4 (Forrest, *Home Papers*, i, 32 f.). Gerald Aungier, President of Surat (1669-77), on his appointment, nominated Matthew Gray to the Deputy-Governorship of Bombay (Anderson, 119). He signs as Member of Council from 1671 to 1676 (Forrest, i, 47, 111).

[2] Mal. *chāwati* (Yule, *Hobson-Jobson*, 211).

[3] Matthew Andrews succeeded Nathanael Wyche as President of Surat (Anderson 88). He was succeeded by Sir G. Oxinden in 1662. His quarrel with Rolt and the charges made against him are described in Forrest, i, 30, 39.

[4] The trading caste of W. India (Yule, *Hobson-Jobson*, 63). Tavernier (ed. Ball, i, 136) gives a similar account of them; but Grose (p. 169) says that ill-repute attached only to the "under-dealers," and not to the greater merchants, "who are in general the fairest, openest, dealers in the world." Much the same may be said of them at the present day. As Jains by religion, they have an extreme regard for animal life. see p. 138.

themselves, that hang like Horse-leeches, till they have suck'd both *Sanguinem & Succum* (I mean Mony) from you: As soon as you have set your Foot on Shore, they crowd in their Service, interposing between you and all Civil Respect, as if you had no other Business but to be gull'd; so that unless you have some to make your way through them, they will interrupt your going, and never leave till they have drawn out something for their Advantage. At this time of Shipping they Present the Governor of *Surat*, to license them to keep a Mart here, which they make the *Europeans* pay dearly for: Yet such is their Policy, that without these, neither you nor the Natives themselves shall do any Business, though they are worse Brokers than *Jews*; if they be not the Spawn of them, the *Rechabites*, that would drink no Wine. These generally are the Poorer sort, and set on by the Richer to Trade with the Seamen for the meanest things they bring; and notwithstanding they take them at their own rates, get well enough in exchange of Goods with them. They are the absolute Map of Sordidness, fareing hardly, and professing fairly, to entrap the unwary; enduring servily foul Words, Affronts and Injuries, for a future hope of Gain; expert in all the studied arts of Thriving and Insinuation; so that, Lying, Dissembling, Cheating, are their Masterpiece: Their whole desire is to have Money pass through their Fingers, to which a great part is sure to stick: For they well understand the constant turning of Cash amounts both to the Credit and Profit of him that is so occupied; which these *Banyans* are sensible of, otherwise they would not be so industrious to enslave themselves.

Having viewed the Tombs by the Sea-side, and some more conspicuous at the end of the Plain belonging to the *English*; others seated behind the *Dutch Choultry*, partly *English*, partly *Dutch*: Marks set to avoid, as well the *Sylla* and *Charibdis* of *Damkin* and *Mora*,[1] two Nurseries for Stews, as to warn them of the Sands coming into the Hole where the Ships ride at Anchor very securely: We in the Company's Coaches Travelled to *Surat*, Ten Mile, brave Champion ground; but the Coach wherein I was, breaking, we were forced to mount the *Indian Hackery*,[2] a Two-wheeled Chariot, drawn by swift little Oxen. By Sun-set we entred the Company's Barge, waiting to carry us over the River; where saluted us the dreadful Noise of the *Moors* Drums and Trumpets, it being customary for them to sound at the Castle every Three hours; but chiefly at Sun-rise and Sun-set: I could think of nothing but the last Trump; so that I could persuade my self there was little Musick in it; but they say Time will bring it to be agreeable to the Ears.[3] On the other side the River, other Four wheeled Coaches expected us, and the *Moors* let us pass the Custom-house without Examination, having Women among us; which was no ordinary point of Civility, they otherwise being strict Examiners, unless the President cross the River, when they forbear also.

The Coach where the Women were, was covered with

---

[1] Mr. A. R. Bonus has kindly identified these places. He writes: "Damkin and Mora still exist. Mora is about 2 miles E. by N. of Suvālī (Swally), and Damka about the same distance N. by E. of Mora. Damka would thus be decidedly off the direct line between Swally and Surat. The two villages are no longer of universally immoral repute; presumably when sea-faring men ceased to pass by the sirens found their occupation gone." In a letter of 1623 (Foster, *English Factories*, 1622-3, p. 283) we read: "Yesterday there were no less than eighty Englishmen straggling drunck in Swally, Dampkine, and the like places." Herbert "past thorow *Swally* Town, *Batty* (famous for good Toddy), *Damkee*, to *Surat*" (p. 35).

[2] A light bullock carriage; Hind. *chhakra* (Yule, *Hobson-Jobson*, 407).

[3] This was the *naubat*, a mark of dignity with all Indian princes. Full details regarding it will be found in *Āīn*, i, 51; Tavernier, ed. Ball, i, 99; Bernier, p. 260.

Cheeks,[1] a sort of hanging Curtain, made with Bents variously Coloured with Lacker, and Chequered with Packthred so artificially, that you may see all without, and your self within unperceived: Ours was open, and guarded by such a Troop as went to apprehend our Saviour, dressed after the same manner we find them on old Landskips, and led by the same Phanatick Lights we see there Painted.

Our Reception at the *English* House[2] was Courteous and Welcome, for the Heat of the Day had tired us.

The House the *English* live in at *Surat*, is partly the King's Gift, partly hired; Built of Stone and excellent Timber, with good Carving, without Representations; very strong, for that each Floor is Half a Yard thick at least, of the best plastered Cement, which is very weighty. It is contrived after the *Moor's* Buildings, with upper and lower Galleries, or Terras-walks; a neat Oratory, a convenient open Place for Meals. The President has spacious Lodgings, noble Rooms for Counsel and Entertainment pleasant Tanks, Yards, and an Hummum[3] to Wash in, but no Gardens in the City, or very few, though without they have many, like Wildernesses, overspread with Trees. The *English* had a neat one, but *Seva Gi*'s coming,

---

[1] The modern "chick"; Pers. *chiq*, "a bamboo screen-blind" (Yule, *Ibid.*, 193).

[2] Various houses were used from time to time as the English Factory (see Foster's note on Sir T. Roe, ii, 510; *English Factories*, 1618-21, 36). "The House provided for the Entertainment of the *English* at *Suratt* belongs to the *Mogul*, and is fitted with the best Accomodation of any in the City. It is situated in the *North-West* part of it, and is able to give convenient Lodgings to forty Persons, besides several decent Apartments to the President. . . . It is built with the Convenience of several Cellars and Ware-houses, of a Tanque of Water, and an Humhum" (Ovington, 388 f.). This, or one of the other English Houses, is now situated in the Mulla Chaklo, or Mulla's Ward, N. of the Castle, and on the river-bank. It has since been used, first as a hospital, then as a lunatic asylum, and is now a private dwelling (*Bombay Gaz.*, ii, 303).

[3] Ar. *hammām*. "a Turkish bath."

destroyed it: It is known, as the other Factories are, by their several Flags flying.

Here they live (in Shipping-time) in a continual hurly-burly, the *Banyans* presenting themselves from the hour of Ten till Noon; and then Afternoon at Four till Night, as if it were an Exchange in every Row; below stairs, the Packers and Warehouse-keepers, together with Merchants bringing and receiving Musters,[1] make a meer *Billinsgate*;[2] for if you make not a Noise, they hardly think you intent on what you are doing.

Among the *English*, the Business is distributed into four Offices;[3] the Accomptant, who is next in Dignity to the President, the general Accompts of all *India*, as well as this place, passing through his hands; he is *Quasi* Treasurer, signing all things, though the Broker keep the Cash. Next him is the Warehouse-keeper, who registers all *Europe* Goods Vended, and receives all *Eastern* Commodities Bought; under him is the Purser Marine, who gives Account of all Goods Exported and Imported, pays Seamen their Wages, provides Waggons and Porters, looks

---

[1] Samples (Yule, *Hobson-Jobson*, 605).

[2] An early example of Billingsgate "in the sense of scurrilous vituperation, violent abuse." The *New Eng. Dict.* gives an example from Wycherley (1676).

[3] In 1658 the Surat Establishment consisted of—President (£500); Accomptant (£150); General Purser (£100); Warehouse Keeper (£70); these four constituting the Council; Secretary (£40); 5 Factors (£30) each; 5 Writers (£20 each); besides a Surgeon and Chaplain (£100). (Hunter, *H. of B. India*, ii, 160 f.). For the similar establishments at Bombay and Bengal, see Forrest, *Home Papers*, i, Intro. 37; Wilson, *Early Annals*, i, 62. "For the advancement of our apprentices, we direct that after they have served the first five years they shall have £10 per annum for the last two years; and having served those two years to be entertained one year longer as writers and have writer's salary: and having served that year to enter into the degree of factors, which otherwise would have been ten years. And knowing that a distinction of titles is, in many respects, necessary, we do order that when the apprentices have served their times they may be styled factors; and the factors having served their times be styled merchants; and the merchants having served their times to be styled senior merchants" (Bruce, *Annals*, ii, 374 f., 378).

after Tackling for Ships, and Ships Stores. Last of all is the Secretary, who models all Consultations, writes all Letters, carries them to the President and Council to be perused and signed; keeps the Company's Seal, which is affixed to all Passes and Commissions; records all Transactions, and sends Copies of them to the Company; though none of these, without the President's Approbation, can act or do any thing. The Affairs of *India* are solely under his Regulation; from him issue out all Orders, by him all Preferment is disposed; by which means the Council are biassed by his Arbitrament.

The whole Mass of the Company's Servants may be comprehended in these Classes, *viz.* Merchants, Factors, and Writers; some Blewcoat Boys also have been entertained under Notion of Apprentices for Seven Years, which being expired, if they can get Security, they are capable of Employments. The Writers are obliged to serve Five Years for 10 *l.* *per Ann.* giving in Bond of 500 *l.* for good Behaviour, all which time they serve under some of the forementioned Offices: After which they commence Factors, and rise to Preferment and Trust, according to Seniority or Favour, and therefore have a 1000 *l.* Bond exacted from them, and have their Salary augmented to 20 *l.* *per Ann.* for Three Years, then entring into new Indentures, are made Senior Factors; and lastly, Merchants after Three Years more; out of whom are chose Chiefs of Factories, as Places fall, and are allowed 40 *l.* *per Ann.* during their stay in the Company's service, besides Lodgings and Victuals at the Company's Charges.

These in their several Seigniories behave themselves after the Fundamentals of *Surat*, and in their respective Factories live in the like Grandeur; from whence they rise successively to be of the Council in *Surat*, which is the great Council; and if the President do not contradict, are Sworn, and take their place accordingly, which consists of about Five in Number, besides the President, to be constantly Resident.

As for the Presidency, though the Company seldom interpose a deserving Man, yet they keep that Power to themselves, none assuming that Dignity till confirmed by them: His Salary from the Company is 500 *l.* a Year; half paid here, the other half reserved to be received at home, in case of misdemeanour, to make satisfaction; beside a Bond of 5000 *l. Sterling* of good Securities.

The Accountant has 72 *l. per Annum*, Fifty Pound paid here, the other at home: All the rest are half paid here, half at home, except the Writers, who have all paid here.

Out of the Council are elected the Deputy-Governor of *Bombaim*, and Agent of *Persia*; the first a Place of great Trust, the other of Profit; though, by the appointment from the Company, the second of *India* claims *Bombaim*, and the Secretary of *Surat* the Agency of *Persia*, which is connived at, and made subject to the Will of the President, by the Interest of those whose Lot they are; chusing rather to reside here, where Consignments compensate those Emoluments; so that none of the Council, if noted in *England*, but makes considerably by his Place, after the rate of Five in the Hundred, Commission; and this is the *Jacob's* Ladder, by which they ascend.

It would be too mean to descend to indirect ways, which are chiefly managed by the *Banyans*, the fittest Tools for any deceitful Undertaking; out of whom are made Broakers for the Company, and private Persons, who are allowed Two *per Cent.* on all Bargains, besides what they squeeze secretly out of the price of things bought; which cannot be well understood for want of knowledge in their Language; which Ignorance is safer, than to hazard being poysoned for prying too nearly into their Actions: Though the Company, to encourage Young men in their Service, maintain a Master to learn them to Write and Read the Language, and an Annuity to be annexed when they gain a perfection therein, which few attempt, and fewer attain.[1]

To this Factory belongs Twenty Persons in number, reckoning *Swally Marine* into the Account; a Minister for Divine Service, a Chirurgion, and when the President is here, a Guard of *English* Soldiers, consisting of a double File led by a Serjeant.

The present Deputy has only Forty *Moor-men*, and a Flag-man carrying St. *George* his Colours Swallow-tailed in Silk, fastned to a Silver Partisan; with a small Attendance of Horse with Silver Bridles, and Furniture for the Gentlemen of the House, and Coaches for Ladies and Council.

The President besides these has a Noise of Trumpets, and is carried himself in a *Palenkeen*, an Horse of State led before him, a *Mirchal*[2] (a Fan of Ostriches Feathers) to keep off the Sun, as the *Ombrahs*[3] or Great Men

---

[1] Sir T. Roe bewails the lack of an interpreter at the Moghul Court (Foster, *Letters*, ii, 108). In 1711 the officials in Bengal recognised the importance of their officers acquiring a knowledge of the vernacular dialects; and Messrs. Crisp and Pratt were sent up country for that purpose (Wilson, *Annals*, ii, Intro. lviii). In 1766 there was no one at Calcutta who could decipher Persian documents while the English were conducting important negotiations with the Court at Delhi; but some servants were learning Hindustani (*Ibid.* ii, lxvii) In Fryer's time the business at the port towns was largely conducted in corrupted Portuguese. It is an error to suppose that the officials of early times were better linguists than their modern successors (see the instructive remarks of Sleeman, *Rambles*, i, 409 f.).

[2] Hind. *morchhal*, a fly-whisk maae of peacock's feathers (Yule, *Hobson-Jobson*, 586).

[3] Higher officials at a Muhammadan Court, especially that of the Great Moghul; Ar. *umara*, pl. of *Amir* (Yule, *Hobson-Jobson*, 637).

have, none but the Emperor have a *Sumbrero*[1] among the *Moguls*: Besides these, every one according to his Quality has his Menial Servants to wait on him in his Chamber, and follow him out.

The Presidency of *Surat* is esteemed Superior to all in *India*, the Agency of *Bantam*[2] being not long since subordinate to it, but since made independent; tho the *South Sea* Trade is still maintained from hence to *Bantam* with such Cloath as is vendible there, from thence with *Dollars* to *China* for *Sugar, Tea, Porcelane, Laccared Ware, Quicksilver, Tuthinag*[3] and *Copper*; which with *Cowreys*,[4] little Sea-Shels, come from *Siam* and the *Phillipine Islands*; Gold and Elephants Teeth from *Sumatra*, in exchange of Corn. From *Persia*, which is still under the Presidency, come Druggs and *Carmania* Wool;[5]

---

[1] Port. *sumbreiro*, a state umbrella (*Ibid.*, 851). Among the insignia of Akbar "the *Chatr*, or umbrella, is adorned with the most precious jewels, of which there are never less than seven" (*Āīn*, i, 50).

[2] The Bantam factory was founded in 1603. About Fryer's time "the Company's establishments in the E. Indies consisted of the Presidency of Bantam, with its dependencies of Jambi, Macassar, and other places in the Indian Archipelago: Fort St. George and its dependent factories on the Coromandel Coast and in the Bay of Bengal; and Surat, with its affiliated dependency of Bombay, and dependent factories at Broach, Ahmedabad, and other places in W. India, and at Gombroon in the Persian Gulf, and Bussorah in the Euphrates Valley" (Birdwood, *Rep.*, 219 f.).

[3] Port., *tutenaga*, the "white copper" of the Chinese, or zinc and pewter (Yule, *Hobson-Jobson*, 932; Marco Polo, i, 126 f.).

[4] It is curious that Fryer does not mention the Maldives as the source of these shells (Pyrard de Laval, i, 236 ff.).

[5] ". . . a sort of rare and very fine wool, which I carry'd out of *Persia* to Paris, where such wool was never seen . . . I met with one of the *Gaures* . . . who when I was at *Ispahan* in the year 1647 shew'd me a Sample of it, and informed me that the greatest part of the Wool come from the Province of *Kerman*, which is the ancient *Caramania*; and that the best wool is to be met with in the Mountains that are next to the City, that bears the name of the Province: That the sheep in those Parts have this particular property, that when they feed up on new Grass from *January* to *May*, the Fleece falls off of itself, and leaves the Sheep naked, and their Skins smooth, like a Pig's that is scalded off; so that there is no need of shearing them, as with us; After they have gather'd it, they beat it, and the course wool

from *Moco*, *Cohor*,[1] or Coffee. The *Inland* Factories subject to it, are *Amidavad*,[2] whence is provided Silks, as *Atlases*[3] wrought with Gold; *Agra*, where they fetch *Indico*,[4] *Chuperly*,[5] Course Cloath, *Siring*[6] *Chints*, *Broach Baftas*,[7] broad and Narrow; *Dimities* and other fine *Calicuts*:[8] Along the Coasts are *Bombaim*, *Rajapore* for *Salloos*;[9] *Carwar* for *Dungarees*,[10] and the weightiest *Pepper*: *Calicut* for *Spice*, *Ambergreez Granats*,[11] *Opium*, with *Salt Peter*, and no Cloath, though it give the name of *Calicut* to all in *India*, it being the

---

breaking, the fine only remains; That if you transport it, before you make it up into Bales, you must throw Salt-water upon it, which keeps the worms out of it, and preserves it from rotting. Now you must take notice that they never dye this Wool, it being naturally of a clear Brown, or a dark Ash-colour; and that there is very little of it white, which is also much dearer than the other, as well for that it is scarce, as because that the *Mufti's*, the *Moullah's* and other persons belonging to the Law, never wear any Girdles or Vails (wherewith they cover their Heads when they pray) but White" (Tavernier, 40 f.). For other references to Carmania wool, see Birdwood, *Rep.*, 27; Lockyer, *Account of Trade*, 219; Hedges, *Diary*, ii, 16, clxvii; Forrest, *Home Papers*, i, 46, 89. For later accounts, Milburn, *Or. Comm.*, i, 135; *Ency. Brit.*[9], xiv, 100.

[1] Elsewhere *coho*, "coffee," Ar. *qahwa* (Yule, *Hobson-Jobson*, 232).

[2] Ahmadābād: Lat. 23° 1′ 45″ N., long. 72° 38′ 30″ E.: the chief city of Gujarāt. The establishment of an English Agency, subordinate to Surat, was the result of Capt. Best's victory at Swallv in 1612 (Birdwood, *Rep.*, 209).

[3] A kind of satin (Yule, *Hobson-Jobson*, 39).

[4] Indigo (*Ibid.*, 437).

[5] Probably a corruption of Hind. *chaprā lākh*, "shellac." Agra in those days was a mart for lac. In 1619 the Agra factors write: "The dana [seed-lac] and the refined lac called Chupra may be procured nearer hand"; gum-lac "of the sort Choupra refined into small cakes" (Foster, *English Factories*, 1618-21, 84, 235).

[6] Pers. *shīrīnbāf*, "fine cotton stuff" (Yule, *Hobson-Jobson*, 829).

[7] Pers. *bāfta*, "woven"; a kind of cloth for which Broach was renowned (*Ibid.*, 47).

[8] Calico (*Ibid.*, 147).

[9] Hind. *sālū*, "Turkey red cotton" (*Ibid.*, 818).

[10] Coarse cotton cloth (*Ibid.*, 330).

[11] Garnets of very good quality are found in Nellore, Masulipatam, and Bezwada (Balfour, *Cycl.*, i, 1180).

first Port from whence they were known to be brought into *Europe*: All which, after the *Europe* Ships have unladen at *Surat*, they go down to fetch; and bring up time enough before the *Caphalas*[1] out of the Country come in with their Wares.

The Places about *Surat* afford variety of *Calicuts*, but not such vast quantities as are yearly exported, and moreover not so cheap; which is the reason at every place the Factors are sent to oversee the Weavers, buying up the Cotton-yarn to employ them all the Rains, when they set on foot their Investments,[2] that they may be ready against the Season for the Ships: Or else the Chief Broaker imploys *Banyans* in their steads, who is responsible for their Fidelity.

On these Wheels moves the Traffick of the *East*, and has succeeded better than any Corporation preceeding, or open Trade licensed in the time of *Oliver Cromwell*; though how much more to the benefit of *England* than a Free Commerce, may be guessed by their already being over-stocked with *Europe* Merchandise, which lowers the Price. What then would a Glut do, which certainly must follow, but debase them more, and enhance these?

But lest the New Company should be exclaimed against as too greedy Monopolizers, they permit Free Traders on their Island *Bombaim*; when, to speak truth, they are in a far worse Condition than their Servants; being tied up without hopes of raising themselves: So that in earnest they find out that to be but a Trick.

However, to confess on the Company's behalf, the Trade (I mean on this Coast) for some years lately passed has hardly ballanced Expences. They employing yearly

---

[1] Ar. *qāfila*, "a sea convoy" or "caravan" (Yule, *Hobson-Jobson*, 142).

[2] A technical term in early East Indian trade for the employment of money in the purchase of Indian goods (*New Eng. Dict.*, *s.v.*).

Forty Sail of stout Ships to and from all Parts where they trade, out and home; Manning and maintaining their Island *Bombaim*, *Fort St. George*, and *St. Helens*, besides large Sums expended to bear out the Port of their Factors; which notwithstanding by impartial Computation has been found inferior to the Costs of the *Hollanders*, and therefore more to the profit of the *English East-India* Company, than theirs, in the few Years they have adventured; so that I should mightily blame them, should they prove ungrateful to His Majesty, who by his gracious Favour has united them in a Society, whereby they are Competitors, for Riches (though not Strength) with the Noted'st Company in the Universe.

This was granted presently after the Happy Restoration of our Gracious Sovereign, when Order began to dawn, and dispel the dark Chaos of Popular Community: Then was sent out a President, to put their Charter in Force, and establish a Graduation among their Servants, which before was not observed; only for Orders sake, they did nominate an Agent; the rest being independent, made no distinction. When as now, after a better Model, they commence according to their standing, and are under a Collegiate manner of Restraint.

The last Agent was Agent *Rivinton*,[1] who was abolished by the Company's sending out President *Wych*, who lived not much more than two years: Presi-

[1] Henry Revington and Nathanael Wyche "also presided over the factory during the time of Cromwell's Protectorate. The latter was succeeded by Andrews. It has been stated that Revington was the last who was styled 'Agent,' and Wyche was the first 'President,' but this is not correct. The Principals of the factory received from the commencement the titles of President, Chief, or Agent, according as their friends or the Directors were pleased to honour them" (Anderson, 88). The Presidents at Surat about Fryer's time were Henry Revington (1657-58) Nathanael Wyche (1658-59, died 23rd May, 1659); Matthew Andrews (1659-62); Sir George Oxinden (1662-1669); Gerald Aungier (1669-77); Thomas Rolt (1677-82) sailed for England 24th January, 1682, succeeded by Sir John Child (1682-90).

dent *Andrews* took his place; and he resigning, *Sir George Oxendine* held it till his Death; in whose time *Seva Gi* plunder'd *Surat*; but he defended himself and the Merchants so bravely, that he had a *Collat*[1] or *Serpaw*,[2] a Robe of Honour from Head to Foot offered him from the *Great Mogul*, with an Abatement of Customs to Two and an half *per Cent.* granted to the Company: For which his Masters, as a Token of the high Sense they had of his Valour, presented him a Medal of Gold, with this Device:

Non minor est virtus quam quærere parta tueri.[3]

After whose Decease, the Honourable *Gerald Aungier* took the Chair,[4] and encounter'd that bold Mountaineer a second time, with as great Applause; when the Governor of the Town and Province durst neither of them shew their Heads:

Fluctum enim totius Barbariæ ferre urbs una non poterat.[5]

The Enemies by the help of an *Europe* Engineer had sprung a Mine to blow up the Castle; but being discovered, were repulsed: for though he had set fire to the rest of the City, they retained the Castle, and the *English* their house.[6]

The Extent of the Presidency is larger in its Missions than Residency; in which Limits may be reckoned an hundred Company's Servants continually in the Country; besides the Annual Advenues of Ships, which during their Stay are all under the same Command: There-

---

[1] Ar. *khil'at*, "a dress of honour" (Yule, *Hobson-Jobson*, 483).

[2] Pers. through Hind. *sarāpā*, "cap-a-pie"; a complete set of honorary robes (*Ibid.*, 808).

[3] Ovid, *Ars amatoria*, ii, 13.

[4] On October 26th, 1669.

[5] Cicero, *Ad. Att.*, vii, xi. 3.

[6] See the graphic account of Sivaji's attack on Surat, in letter of 16th February, 1663-4 (Forrest, *Home Papers*, i, 34 f.; Grant Duff, 89).

fore what Irregularities are committed against only the Presidency or Company, in case of Non-Submission, the Persons offending are to be sent home, and dismissed their Employments for Refractoriness; but if an higher Court lay hold of them in case of Murder, or any Capital Crime, then they are to be sent to *Bombaim*, there to have a Legal Trial, according to the Laws of *England*, as the President is created Governor of his Majesty's Island.

The ill managing of which Penalties formerly, or the Invalidity to inflict them, may be the true Cause of the Unprosperousness of the Ancient Undertakers; who had this Inconveniency still attending, to wit, the incorrigible stubbornness of their own Men, after they had overcome all other Difficulties, occasioned by the Grant of the *East* to the *Portugal*, and *West-Indies* to the *Spaniard*. Nevertheless this Fairy Gift was the Ground of a long and tedious Quarrel in each of the World's Ends; so that our Ships encountring with their *Carracks*,[1] seldom used to part without the loss of one or both. Nay, the long-liv'd People yet at *Swalley*, remember a notable Skirmish betwixt the *English* and *Portugals* there, wherein they were neatly intrapp'd; an Ambuscado of ours falling upon them behind in such sort, that they were compelled between them and the Ships in the Road, to resign most of their Lives; and gave by their Fail a memorable Name to a Point they yet call *Bloody Point*,[2] for this very reason. But since these Sores are fortunately bound up in that Conjugal Tye betwixt our Sacred King and the Sister of *Portugal*, laying all foul Words and Blows aside, let us see how the Affairs stand betwixt them and the

---

[1] Cargo vessels (Yule, *Hobson-Jobson*, 165)

[2] Mr. Bonus writes: "No 'Bloody Point' at Suvāli is now known; but there is still a tradition of a great fight there between the English and Portuguese." This, he thinks, may have been the action under Capt. Downton, on 20th December, 1615 (Anderson, 18 f.: *Bombay Gaz.*, ii, 77 f.)

Dutch, who followed our Steps, and got in at the Breach we made. They made them more Work, not only beating them out of their *South-Sea* Trade, but possessed themselves of all their Treasures of Spice, and have ever since kept them, with all their Strong-holds, as far as *Goa*; they only enjoying the Gold Trade of *Mosambique* undisturbed; the *Japanners* having banished both their Commerce and Religion.

Wherefore our Ships almost alone, were it not for a little the *French* of late, lade Calicuts for *Europe*: The *Dutch* have a Factory here, that vend the Spices they bring from *Batavia*, and invest part of the Money in course Cloath, to be disposed among their Planters, or sold to the *Malayans*, and send the rest back in *Rupees*:[1] So that we singly have the Credit of the Port, and are of most advantage to the Inhabitants, and fill the Custom-House with the substantialest Incomes. But not to defraud the *French* of their just Commendations, whose Factory is better stor'd with *Monsieurs* than with *Cash*, they live well, borrow Money, and make a Shew: Here are *French Capuchins*, who have a Convent, and live in Esteem.[2]

And here I might conclude, did not the Diamond Trade and other Jewels interpose; which I could wish for the Company's sake might never be struck out of their Indulgence allowed to their Servants: For it will never amount to Advantage in their hands, because the *Jews*,

---

1 "On my first visit to this port [Surat] I found there no more than two factories, one English and one Dutch, and a little church belonging to the French Capuchin fathers, whose superior was the famous priest, Brother Ambrozio. Afterwards the French came and built a handsome factory" (Manucci, i, 62). The connection of the Dutch with Surat began in 1616, when Van den Broeck attempted to open trade: but it was not till the following year that their factory was started (Anderson, 37 f.). The French factory was probably founded by Admiral Beaulieu, in 1620. In 1623 P. della Valle (i, 21) found there "Franks, who have houses there for repositing the goods, which they continually send to the Sea side to be ship'd."

2 For this establishment see the last note. A wooden post, with an inscription, now marks the site of the Altar of the Capuchin Church, behind which are the ruins of the Portuguese factory, and behind this, again, the French lodge (*Bombay Gaz.*, ii, 304 f.).

who are the chief Chapmen in *England* will blow upon them, unless they come to their Prices, when more than enough is offered them. But in particular hands the Case is otherwise, every one snatching at a Prize, which none is sensible of, but the private Buyer; but when they are publickly Invoiced, it will be at their own Wills to make their Bargains. Withal, in the Company's Servants hands, it not only keeps them Honest, but they grow Rich without wronging the Company: Whereas should they retract this, not only the *Jews* would find others to furnish them, as the *French* and *Dutch*, with their Encomiendums;[1] but other Monied Gentlemen in *England* might be tempted to set up for Interloping, who know not how better to dispose of their Monies on any Bank, than by adventuring Large Sums, that do now to my knowledge return them in a Year and a half's time from 50*l.* to 70*l. per Cent.* advance, and the Factors good Gainers too; and all this while no Prejudice done either to Freight or the Company's Trade; which if they will not believe, let them experiment to their own Cost. Nor can I say more on this Subject, than both *French* and *Dutch* Jewellers coming over Land do understand, who have made good Purchase by buying Jewels here, and carrying them into *Europe* to be Cut and Set, and returning sell them here to the *Ombrahs*, among whom were Monsieur *Tavernier*,[2] and now Monsieur *Rezin*,[3] and Monsieur *Jordan*.[4]

---

[1] A curious form, not recognised by *New Eng. Dict.* or *Stanford Dict.*

[2] Jean Baptiste Tavernier was several times at Surat—the first occasion apparently being in 1641. In 1659 he stayed there for six months. See the chronology of his Indian travels in ed. Ball, Intro. xiv, ff.

[3] M. Raisin, in whose company Tavernier dined with the Augustine Fathers residing at the Court of Golkonda (*Ibid.*, ii, 304).

[4] M. Louis du Jardin travelled in India with Tavernier. The facts of his career are obscure. He seems to have died at Surat in 1652 (*Ibid.*, ii, 159, with other references in the Index). Another person named Clement Jordan, known as Clement du Jardin, traded in India between 1674 and 1687 (Temple's note on Bowrey, 178).

Thus much may serve for this Year; by the next I may prepare a farther Account, if I live: for so long I will be

Yours,

From Surat,
Jan. 15, 167$\frac{4}{5}$.

J. F.

A

DESCRIPTION

OF

SURAT,

And Journy into *DUCCAN*.

LETTER III.

CHAP. I.

Animadversions on the City and People of Surat *in the* East-Indies.

SIR,

GOING out to see the City of *Surat*, I passed without any Incivility, the better because I understood not what they said for though we meet not with Boys so rude as in *England*, to run after Strangers, yet here are a sort of bold, lusty, and most an end,[1] drunken Beggars, of the *Musslemen*[2] Cast, that if they see a Christian in good Clothes, Mounted on a stately Horse, with rich Trappings, are presently upon their Punctilio's with God Almighty, and interrogate him, Why he suffers him to go a Foot,

---

1 "Almost uninterruptedly, almost always, mostly, for the most part" (*New Eng. Dict.*, s.v., *An-end*).

2 This abnormal plural is sometimes heard even at the present day. "And now the Moors come upon them for Satisfaction for a great number of Musslemen they had killed" (Bowrey, 188).

and in Rags, and this *Coffery* (Unbeliever) to vaunt it thus?[1] And hardly restrained from running a *Muck*[2] (which is to kill whoever they meet, till they be slain themselves) especially if they have been at *Hodge*,[3] a Pilgrimage to *Mecca*, and thence to *Juddah*,[4] where is *Mahomet's* Tomb; these commonly, like evil Spirits, have their Habitations among the Tombs: Nor can we complain only of this Libertinism, for the Rich *Moormen* themselves are persecuted by these Rascals.

As for the rest, they are very respectful, unless the Seamen or Soldiers get Drunk, either with *Toddy*,[5] or *Bang*[6] (a pleasant intoxicating Seed, mixed with Milk) then are they Monarchs, and it is Madness to oppose them; but leave them to themselves and they will vent that Fury, by breathing a Vein[7] or two with their own Swords, sometimes slashing themselves most Barbarously.

---

[1] The insolence of the "liberated" (*be-qaid*) Musalmān Faqīr is noted by many writers of the day. Manucci (i, 145) describes them as "Very rude in manner, using great liberty of speech, fearing no one and paying no one respect, whatever his rank, using much abusive language and scandalous words, or polite sayings, just as it pleases them." Of those near Surat, Ovington (p. 369) says: "If they find the People unwilling to give, they audaciously demand, and that not in the humble strain for a Picé or two, but sawcily beg a Roupie." See an earlier account in Barbosa, 51.

[2] For the custom of Running A Muck, see Yule, *Hobson-Jobson*, 18 ff.

[3] Ar. *hajj*, "pilgrimage"; Hebrew *hagg*, with the primary meaning of circular movement round a sacred object, in this case at Mecca and Medina.

[4] Jiddah, the famous pilgrim port on the Red Sea. Needless to say, the tomb of the Prophet is not at Jiddah, but at Al-Madinah.

[5] Hind. *tārī*, the fermented sap of the palmyra and other palms.

[6] Hind. *bhang*, dried leaves and small stalks of hemp (*cannabis sativa*) For a full account of the drug and of its numerous preparations, see Watt, *Econ. Dict.*, ii, 103 ff.; Burton, *Arabian Nights*, iii, 159.

[7] Lancing a vein, a use of the word classed in the *New Eng. Dict.* as archaic, the latest example being of 1836. "The natives of East India . . . make little use of physicians, unless it be to breathe a vein sometimes" (Terry, 228).

The Town has very many noble lofty Houses, of the *Moor*-Merchants, flat at top, and Terassed with Plaster. There is a *Parsy*, Broker to the King of *Bantam*, has turned the outside of his Pockets on a sumptuous House, a spacious Fabrick, but ill contrived, as are many of the *Banians*. They, for the most part, afect not stately Buildings, living in humble Cells or Sheds. Glass is dear, and scarcely purchaseable (unless by way of *Stambole*, or *Constantinople*, from the *Venetians*, from whom they have some Panes of Painted Glass in Sash Windows) therefore their Windows, except some few of the highest Note, are usually folding Doors, skreened with Cheeks,[1] or Latises, Carved in Wood, or Ising-glass, or more commonly Oister-shells.[2] The greatest Commodity here is Air, which is to be admired in the Rich *Banyans*, how they stew them-selves out of a penurious humour, crowding Three or Four Families together into an Hovel, with Goats, Cows, and Calves, all Chamber-fellows, that they are almost poysoned with Vermin and Nastiness; but surely they take delight in it, for they will fresh and fasting besprinkle themselves with the Stale of a Cow, as you behold a good Christian with Holy-water, or a *Moorman* slabber his Beard with Rose-water: Nay more, they use it as a Potion, or *Philter*, and bid the Devil do his worst after it;[3] so stupid, that notwithstanding Chints, Fleas, and Muskeeto's torment them every Minute, dare not presume to scratch where it itches, lest some Relation should be untenanted its miser-able abode.[4]

---

[1] See p. 214.

[2] See p. 172. The authorities do not now mention this use of isinglass (*Ency. Brit.*[9], x, 134).

[3] For the use of urine in W. India as a means of repelling evil spirits, see Sir J. Campbell, *Notes on the Spirit Basis of Belief and Custom*, 407.

[4] Another instance of the Jain tenderness for animal life. "If these people have lice they do not kill them, and if they worry them very much, they send to fetch some men whom they have amongst them,

The Habits and Customs of this place are reconcilable with them in the Kingdom of *Gulconda*, only the *Moguls* being more absolute, and of a more Puritanical Sect than the *Chia*'s; the Heathens are suppressed in respect of their Barbarous Rites, and reduced to a more civil Garb, being more decently Clothed.

The *Moguls*, who are Lords here, differ from them of *Gulconda* in point of their *Caliph*'s Succession, the first maintaining the Sect of the *Arabs*, the others of the *Suffean*, or *Persian*.[1]

They have Four Expositors of the Law, to whom they give Credit in matter of Ceremonies, *viz.*

Hanoffi.[2]
Shoffi.[3]
Hamaleech.[4]
Maluche.[5]

Their great scruple is about Eating together among all sorts of these *Eastern* Nations.

---

also Gentiles, whom they esteem of holy lives, like hermits, . . . and these people pick out their insects, and all those that they extract they put in their own heads, and they nourish them on themselves and on their flesh for the service of their idols" (Barbosa, 51 f.). For the precautions taken to save vermin, see Manucci, i, 156, and Ovington's (p. 301) account of the hospital for such creatures at Surat.

[1] The Sunnī contrasted with the Shī'ah sect; the latter of Persian origin, introduced into that country by Sultan Muhammad Khudābandah (1303-16), principally for political reasons, in order to attract his people to the tomb of 'Alī at Mashhad, a national shrine, instead of the Arabian holy places, then, as now, in the hands of the Turks, who are of the Sunnī sect. The Shī'ah faith was made the national religion of Persia under Shāh Ismā'īl, the first of the Sūfī monarchs in 1499. The dispute, in fact, represented the conflict between Aryan and Semite (Malcolm, *H. of Persia*, i, 278, 324, ii, 238; Pelly, *Miracle Play*, Intro., xvi).

[2] Hanafī, Hanīfī, the Sunnī sect founded by Imām Abū Hanīfah, born 702 A.D.

[3] Shāfi'īyah, founded by Imām Muhammad ibn Idrīs as-Shāfi'ī, born 767 A.D., and buried at Cairo.

[4] Hambalīyah, founded by Imām Abū' Abdū'llāh Ahmad ibn Muhammad ibn Hambal, born A.D. 780.

[5] Malakīyah founded by Imām Mālik, born A.D. 714. For these sects, see Sale, *Koran*, Preliminary Discourse, 110 ff.; Hughes, *Dict. of Islam*, 286 ff.

All *Musselmen* (true Believers) as they call themselves of this Persuasion, Communicate in that point; only some Punctilio's in respect of Marriage remain yet undecided; as for an *Hanoffi* to offer his Daughter to a *Shoffi*, is a great shame; but if the other request it first, he may comply without derogation.[1]

They are distinguished, some according to the Consanguinity they claim with *Mahomet*; as a *Siad*[2] is a Kin to that Imposture, and therefore only assumes to himself a Green Vest and *Puckery*[3] (or Turbat) none other being permitted to wear them. A *Shiek*[4] is a Cousin too at a distance, into which Relation they admit all new made Proselytes. *Meer*[5] is somewhat Allied also, and *Mussanne*.[6] The rest are adopted under the Name of the Province or Kingdom they are Born in, as *Mogul*[7] the Race of the *Tartars*, and are esteemed, as the Name

---

[1] At present, among the educated Musalmāns of Gujarāt, there is no obstacle to the intermarriage of Shī'ahs and Sunnīs; but this is not the case with the lower orders (*Bombay Gaz.*, ix, Pt. II, 175). For legal disabilities to marriage, see Hughes, *Dict. of Islam*, 316 ff. The restriction here stated rests on no legal basis. Except the Arabs, who generally belong to the Shāfi'īyah sect, most Gujarāt Musalmāns are now Hanafīs.

[2] Saiyid. They claim to be descended from the Prophet through his daughter Fātima married to 'Alī. In Persia, as in India, "their voluminous green turban seems to be an excuse for insufferable airs, gross superstition, and an indolent life" (Curzon, *Persia*, ii, 368).

[3] Hind. *pagrī*, "a turban" (Yule, *Hobson-Jobson*, 735).

[4] Shaikh, properly "an elder." Fryer correctly remarks that new converts to Islam usually claim this title. A common proverb runs: "Two years ago I was a weaver; last year a Shaikh; this year, if prices rise, I shall be a Saiyid."

[5] Mīr, for Amīr, "lord": a title of respect usually given to Saiyids.

[6] It is uncertain to whom Fryer refers. There are Mushānī Pathāns on the N.W. frontier (Ibbetson, *Punjab Ethnography*, § 403); one of the four grades of Mullās in Gujarāt is known as Ma'zūn "licensed, permitted" (*Bombay Gaz.*, ix, Pt. II, 32).

[7] Mughal, another form of Mongol, a term properly applied to the adventurers who entered India under Bābar, or were attracted there to the courts of his successors. At the present day they have become much mixed with local Muhammadans, and are popularly divided into Irānī or Persians, and Tūrānī, those from Turkistān. For a full discussion of the relation between the terms Mughal and Mongol, see Ney Elias, *H. of the Moghuls of Central Asia*, 72 ff.

imports, *White* Men; *Patan*,[1] *Duccan*; or Schisms they have made, as *Bilhim*,[2] *Jemottee*,[3] and the lowest of all is *Borrah*.[4]

These Eat highly of all Flesh *Dumpoked*,[5] which is Baked with Spice in Butter; *Pullow*,[6] a Stew of Rice and Butter, with Flesh, Fowl, or Fish; Fruits, Achars,[7] or Pickles, and Sweetmeats: If they invite a Christian, they order Dishes apart, and between Meals Entertain with *Coho*,[8] Tobacco, *Pawn*,[9] which makes a fragrant Breath, and gives a rare Vermilion to the Lips; and as a great Compliment drown you with Rosewater, Senting themselves with Essence of *Sandal*[10] and Oranges,

---

[1] Pathān, the type of the north country Musalmān, as contrasted with the Dakkhinī or South Indian class.

[2] He probably refers to the Behlīm or Bahlīm Rājputs, converted to Islām, and found in N. Gujarāt and Broach; but these do not, as he represents, form a sect.

[3] He may mean the Ahl-i-jamā'atī, "people of the congregation" (*jamā'at*), that is to say, the Sunnī sect. Jamā'at-khāna is the assembly lodge of the Khojahs or Khwājahs of W. India (*Bombay Gaz.*, ix, Pt. II, 45).

[4] Bohrā, originally Shī'ahs of the Ismā'īlī sect, the richest and most prosperous class of Musalmāns in Gujarāt (*Ibid.*, ix, Pt. II, 24 ff.; Yule, *Hobson-Jobson*, 105).

[5] Pers. *dampukht*, "steamed food" (Yule, *Ibid.*, 330).

[6] Pers. *pulāo*, *pilāv*, meat or fowl, boiled with rice and spices (Yule, *Ibid.*, 710): the standard dish of Musalmāns. According to Chardin, there were in his time in Persia twenty-four varieties, of which he gives the receipts, made up with mutton, lamb, pullets, etc. "It has," he writes, "a wonderful, sobering, filling, and nourishing effect. One eats so much that one expects to expire; but at the end of half an hour you do not know what has become of it all: you no longer feel the stomach loaded" (ed. Lloyd, ii, 226; ed. Langlès, viii, 187, quoted in Curzon, *Persia*, i, 108 *n.*). For the preparation of Pulāo see *Relation of Grand Seignor's Seraglio*, 25; Browne, *A Year Amongst the Persians*, 110; Wills, *Land of the Lion and Sun*, 296; Bellew, *Journal of Mission to Afghanistan*, 29; Schuyler, *Turkistan*, i, 125; Vámbéry, *Sketches of Central Asia*, 118; Manucci, i, 24.

[7] Pers. *āchār*, "acid and salt relishes" (Yule, *Hobson-Jobson*, 3).

[8] See p. 220.

[9] See p. 111.

[10] The produce of *Santalum album*, a small evergreen tree found in the dryer parts of Mysore, Coimbatore, and Salem Districts, as far S. as Malabar, N. to Kolhapur. The essential oil is the basis of many of the Ottos or 'Itr distilled in India, and alone has a peculiar fragrance much valued by natives for toilet purposes (Watt, *Econ. Dict.*, vi, Pt. II, 461 ff.).

very Costly, and exquisitely Extracted. They drink no Wine Publickly, but Privately will be good Fellows, not content with such little Glasses as we drink out of, nor Claret or Rhenish (which they call Vinegar) but Sack and Brandy out of the Bottle they will Tipple, till they are well warmed.

At the First entrance into their Houses, for the greater Respect, they meet at the Portal, and usher Strangers to the place of Entertainment; where, out of common Courtesy, as well as Religion, (when they enter an Holy Place) they pull off their Slippers, and after the usual *Salams*, seat themselves in *Choultries*,[1] open to some *Tank* of purling Water; commonly spread with Carpets, or *Siturngees*,[2] and long round Cushions of Velvet to bolster their Back and Sides, which they use when they ride in their Chariots, which are made to sit Cross-legg'd on, not their Legs hanging down as ours; it being accounted among them no good breeding to let their Legs or Feet be seen whilst sitting: In their *Palenkeens*, Coaches, or swinging Cotts, which they affect for Ease, are laid huge Bolsters of state, and Quilts of Cotton to lie at length, their Ceilings and Posts are Hung with *Mechlapatan*[3] *Pintado s*,[4] and adorned with other Gallantry.

They go rich in Attire, with a Poniard, or *Catarre*,[5] at their Girdle; as they are Neat in Apparel, they are Grave in their Carriage.

Their Women wear the Breeches, but in a most servile

---

[1] See p. 211.

[2] Hind. *shitranjī*, *shatranjī*, a striped or chequered cotton cloth or floor covering (Yule, *Hobson-Jobson*, 843).

[3] Masulipatam, see p. 76.

[4] In p. 51 a bird with speckled feathers: here "painted" cloth or chintz (Yule, *Ibid.*, 713).

[5] Hind. *katār*, "a dagger" (*Ibid.*, 496).

condition;[1] yet they have their Ornaments of Head, with Bracelets of Pearl, Ear-rings and Nose-rings, to which they hang Jewels, mostly set in Silver, because Gold is *Nigess*, or Unclean.[2]

They are strict observers of the Hours of Prayer, when they strip off all their Gorgeous Habiliments to their Shift,[3] and after Washing Hands and Feet, Prostrate themselves during the time of Devotion, when Rising they Salute their Guardian-Angels according to the Opinion of the Stoicks, who allotted every one his *Juno* and his *Genius*; having made their *Orisons*, and Purified themselves, they return to Company as before.[4]

They are great Revellers by Night, in the heat of the Day they sleep and dally.

They circumcise the Foreskin of the Male, which is performed by a Barber, at Eight years of Age;[5] with Feasting, and carrying the Boy about in pomp, with Musick and great Expressions of Joy. Of the Girls

---

[1] He is right in regarding the pāējāma or drawers, tight at the ankles, which are worn by Musalmān women, as perhaps the most unbecoming form of female dress in the world.

[2] Ar. *najis*, "unclean." "If by any chance as he comes out of the street, where there is some dirt, and where Horses pass to and fro, and may cast some of it upon him, he has the least spot of any daggling about him, and afterwards touch the Person whom he comes to Visit, this latter would be *Nagis*, that is to say, *unclean*, and therefore be obliged immediately to change his Cloaths; so great is the superstition of the *Persians*, as to that particular" (*Relation of Grand Seignor's Seraglio*, 41). Gold is not really impure; but sacred or under a taboo, which prevents it from being worn on the feet lest it should be defiled (Crooke, *Things Indian*, 288 f.).

[3] "The Mohammadans never address themselves to God in sumptuous apparel, though they are obliged to be decently clothed; but lay aside their costly habits and pompous ornaments, if they wear any, when they approach the Divine presence, lest they should seem proud and arrogant" (Sale. Koran, *Prelim. Dis.*, 77).

[4] Fryer is mistaken in supposing that the dawn-prayer includes invocation of guardian angels (Hughes, *Dict. of Islam*, 465 ff.). The Indian Muhammadan. however, has adopted many animistic practices from the Hindus.

[5] Gujarāt Musalmāns circumcise boys at the age of 6 or 7 (*Bombay Gaz.*, ix, Pt. II, 160).

they make small account, they being instructed within doors how to pray.

The *Cazy*[1] or Judge, after the Match is made by the Parents, marries them; from whence doubtless our Phanaticks borrowed their Custom of Marrying by a Justice of Peace: This is also a time of Solemnity sometimes kept for several Weeks together with Illuminations on their Houses, their Garments tinctured with Saffron,[2] riding triumphantly through the Streets with Trumpets and Kettle Drums; fetching the Bride from her Kindred, and they sending Banquets, Household-stuff, and Slaves their Attendants, with a great Train through their Streets, which is all their Dowry: But the *Cazy* has a Knack beyond those Couplers of *Europe*, he can loose the Knot when they plead a Divorce.[3] They have four Wives[4] if they can maintain them, and as many other Women as they please; she that bears the first Son is reckoned the Chief.

At their Labours they seldom call Midwives, being pretty quick that way, though there are not a few live well by that Profession; known by Tufts of Silk on their Shooes or Slippers,[5] all other Women wearing them plain: At the end of their *Quarentine*, which is Forty days, after the Old Law, they enter the *Hummums*

---

[1] Ar. *Qāzī* (Yule, *Hobson-Jobson*, 177).

[2] The dress is dyed with saffron to repel evil spirits (Campbell, *Notes*, 63). Compare the flame-coloured veil (*flammeum*) of the Roman bride.

[3] See Letter V, chap. XIII.

[4] "Marry what seems good to you of women, by twos, threes, or fours, or what your right hand possesses" (*Koran*, Sūrah, iv, 3).

[5] Mr. Bonus writes: "The custom of midwives, apparently Musalmāns, wearing silk tufts on their foot-gear no longer prevails, if it ever did. A shepherd class (Hindus), however, wear such tufts on days when weddings are celebrated." Fryer refers again to this custom, Letter IV, chap. VI.

to Purify;[1] and the Child, without much Ceremony, is named by the Parents.

At Funerals, the *Mullahs* or Priests, make Orations or Sermons, after a Lesson read out of the *Alchoran*,[2] and lay them *North* and *South*, as we do *East* and *West*, when they are Inhumed, expecting from that Quarter the appearance of their Prophet.[3] Upon the death of any, in the hearing of the Outcry, which is great among the Women. beating their Breasts, and crying aloud, they neither eat, nor shift their Cloaths, till the Person be interred; the Relations mourn by keeping on dirty Cloaths, and a neglect of their Apparel; neither washing nor shaving themselves: It is usual to hire People to lament, and the Widow once a Moon go to the Grave with her Acquaintance to repeat the doleful Dirge, after which she bestows *Holway*,[4] a kind of Sacramental Wafer; and entreats their Prayers for the Soul of the Departed; and for that reason the most store of Graves are in Cross-ways, or High-roads, that the Passengers may be put in mind of that Office:[5] They never Enshrine any in their *Moschs*, but in the places adjoining them; where

---

[1] At the present time, on the 40th day, grass boats are taken with music to the nearest stream, and set adrift as an offering to Khwāja Khizr or Elias (*Bombay Gaz.*, ix, Pt. II, 158).

[2] The funeral service is not recited in the graveyard, which is believed to be polluted, but in a mosque or some open space. When earth is being thrown on the corpse the invocation from the *Koran* (Sūrah, xx, 57) is recited.

[3] The head of the corpse lies N. with the face turned on the right side, in the direction of Mecca.

[4] Ar. *halwā*, "a glutinous compound of clarified butter (*ghī*), flour, sugar, and water, flavoured with grated almonds or pistachios, which resembles half-melted butter, and is greedily consumed by the Arab stomach" (Curzon, *Persia*, ii, 442). It is the "marmelades, which from Ormus is carried into India" (Linschoten, i, 48). In the time of Akbar it was made of flour, sugar-candy, and *ghī*, 10 sers each (*Āīn*, i, 59).

[5] The Musalmān, like the Roman, buries his dead near the roads, in order that the spirits may enjoy converse with the living.

they build Tombs, and leave Stipends for *Mullahs* to offer Petitions up for them.

The Duty of the *Mullahs*, besides these, is to call from the Steeples of their *Moschs* every *Pore*,[1] that is, once in Three hours stopping their Ears with their Fingers: *Allah Eckbar, Allah Eckber Eschadu ela Hale ilallah we Eschedu, Mahmed ewesul: Cuah Fleje ala Selah beie ula Felah, Alla Eckber, Alla Eckber, La Jelah Hallah*: i.e. God is Great, I profess, there is no Deity but God, and confess that *Mahomet* is the Prophet of God. Their Priests say Prayers five times a-day, and expound the *Alchoran* once a-week, and that on *Friday*,[2] which day they are not to lye with their Women, setting it apart for the Service of God.[3]

Here is a *Xeriff*,[4] who is as it were their Primate under

---

[1] Hind. *pahar*, "a watch of day or night" (Yule, *Hobson-Jobson*, 736). The five times of prayer are (1) from dawn to sunrise; (2) when the sun has begun to decline; (3) midway between 2 and 4; (4) a few minutes after sunset; (5) when night has closed in. Besides these, which are obligatory, the voluntary times are: (1) when the sun has well risen; (2) about 11 a.m.; (3) after midnight. The Azān, or prayer summons, runs thus in Arabic: "*Allāhu akbar! Allāhu akbar! Allāhu akbar! Allāhu akbar! Ashhadu an lā ilāha illa'llāh! Ashhadu an lā ilāha illa'llāh! Ashhadu anna Muhammadan rasūlu-llāh! Hayya 'ala 's-salāti! Hayya 'ala 's-salāti! Hayya 'ala'l-falāh! Hayya 'ala'l-falāh! Allāhu akbar! Allāhu akbar! La ilāha illa 'llāh!*" "God is most great! (four times); I testify that there is no god but God! (twice). I testify that Muhammad is the Apostle of God! (twice). Come to prayer! Come to prayer! Come to salvation! Come to salvation! God is most great! God is most great! There is no god but God" (Hughes, *Dict. Islām*, 28, 469).

[2] Ar. Jum'ah, "day of assembly," on which occasion the oration or sermon (*khutbah*) is recited in the mosque at the time of midday prayer."

[3] "Thursday night, preceding the day of public prayer, which can be performed only in a state of ceremonial purity. Hence many Moslems go to the Hammām on Thursday, and have no connection with their wives till Friday night" (Burton, *Ar. Nights*, i, 247 *n*.).

[4] *Sharīf*, "eminent, honourable." It is not easy to judge to which functionary he refers. In cities like Constantinople, Cairo, or Damascus, there is the Shaikh-ul-Islām. But he is not found in India, and it is not likely that there was a "Primate" at Surat. There was a chief Qāzī or Qāzī-ul-Quzzāt; but, as Mr. Irvine points out, he was probably attached to the Court, and not a local officer. For the Sharīf in Arabia, see Burton, *Pilgrimage*, ii, 3 *n*.

him the *Cazys*,[1] or Judges, are the next, then the Inferior Clergy, as the *Mullahs*,[2] and *Scribes*, or Teachers of Youth in the *Arabick* Tongue.[3]

With these, by the favour of the present *Mogul*, who lived long in that Order, till he came to the Throne, must be numbred the *Fakiers* or Holy Men, abstracted from the World, and resigned to God, for the Word will bear that Interpretation; on this Pretence are committed sundry Extravagancies, as putting themselves on voluntary Penances. Here is one that has vowed to hang by the Heels, till he get Money enough to built a *Mosch* to *Mahomet*, that he may be held a Saint. Another shall travel the Country with an Horn blowed afore him, and an Ox it may be to carry him and his Baggage, besides one to wait on him with a Peacock's Tail; whilst he rattles a great Iron Chain fettered to his Foot, as big as those Elephants are Foot-locked with, some two yards in length, every Link thicker than a Man's Thumb, and a Palm in length;[4] his shaking this speaks his Necessity,

---

[1] Under Musalmān rule the Qāzī was civil and criminal judge. Now, except that he leads the prayers of the congregation at the Ramazān and Baqarah 'Īd feasts, he is a little more than a registrar of marriage and divorce.

[2] Mullā, Pers. form of Ar. Maulavī, the law-doctor, spiritual guide, curer of disease by means of charms and amulets; the lowest of the Musalmān hierarchy. "Any one who can read the Qurān and knows his prayers may become a Mulla" (*Bombay Gaz.*, ix, Pt. II, 132).

[3] He probably refers to the Mudarris, or a Mullā or Maulavī of the lower grade.

[4] The penances of Faqīrs are elsewhere referred to by Fryer (Letter III, chap. II; IV, III). Tavernier (ed. Ball, ii, 178 ff.) saw one who "drags a heavy iron chain which he has attached to one leg: it is 2 cubits long and thick in proportion." Ives (*Voyage*, 73) describes one who "wore a sort of sandals on his feet, and loose iron chains about his legs." Terry (p. 264) saw some with "many fetters of iron upon their legs." "Several of these Fakires," says Bernier (p. 317), "undertake long pilgrimages, not only naked, but laden with heavy iron chains, such as are put round the leg of Elephants." In 1895 a Musalmān Faqīr appeared at Bombay. "This man is loaded with heavy iron chains and fetters: both his arms and legs are linked together with several heavy iron rings and chains, commencing from the ankles up to the knees,

which the poor *Gentiles* dare not deny to relieve ; for if they do, he accuses them to the *Cazy*, who desires no better opportunity to fleece them : For they will not stick to swear they blasphemed *Mahomet*, for which there is no evasion but to deposit, or be cut, and made a *Moor*.

Most of these are Vagabonds, and are the Pest of the Nation they live in ; some of them live in Gardens and retired Places in the Fields, in the same manner as the *Seers* of old, and the Children of the Prophets did : Their Habit is the main thing that signalizes them more than their Virtue ; they profess Poverty, but make all things their own where they come ; all the heat of the Day they idle it under some shady Tree, at night they come in Troops, armed with a great Pole, a *Mirchal*[1] or Peacock's Tail, and a Wallet ; more like Plunderers than Beggars ; they go into the Market, or to the Shopkeepers, and force an Alms, none of them returning without his share : Some of them pass the bounds of a modest Request, and bawl out in the open Streets for an Hundred *Rupees*, and nothing less will satisfy these.

They are cloathed with a ragged Mantle, which serves them also for a Matrass, for which purpose some have Lyons, Tygres or Leopards Skins to lay under them : The Civilest of them wear Flesh-coloured Vests, somewhat like our Brick-makers Frocks, and almost of that Colour. The Merchants, as their Adventures return, are bountiful towards them, by which means some of them thrive upon it.

---

and the two arms from the wrists up to the elbows. There is a large iron ring round his neck, with several long iron chains linked on to it, and suspending to the ground, together with several marline spikes, and a heavy iron hammer shackled on to the ends of these chains and dangling round his body. The whole of the iron chains and fetters together with his person was found to weigh over 672 lbs. ; consequently it appears the man was booked as living luggage" (*North Indian Notes and Queries*, iv, 180).

[1] Hind. *morchhal* (Yule, *Hobson-Jobson*, 586).

These Field Conventiclers at the hours of Devotion beat a Drum, from them called the *Fakiers* Drum; here ∴ of these Strolers about the City enough to make an Army, that they are almost become formidable to the Citizens; nor is the Governour powerful enough to correct their Insolencies. For lately setting on a Nobleman of the *Moors*, when his Kindred came to demand Justice, they unanimously arose in defence of the Aggressor, and rescued him from his deserved Punishment.[1]

For all the Governor comes to his Seat attended every Morning with 300 Foot with Fire-Arms, Three Elephants in their Cloathing (which is here also a principal Mark of the Greatness of these Men in place, the more Elephants they keep, they are looked on as more Honourable) Forty Horses mounted, Four and twenty Banners of State; besides a large Retinue of the *Cazy's*, who is always present to assist him in Law Points. Moreover he has Loud Trumpets made as big, and like our *Stentoro Phonica*,[2] or speaking Trumpet, with Thundring Kettle-Drums; yet neither the Formality of this Appearance, nor regard due to his Office, is terrible enough to prevail with these to submit to resign the Caitiff, and hardly is his whole Force able to keep them from bare-faced Rebellion.

But though these Outlaws (for as such they ought to be look'd on, while they disown all Subjection) behave themselves thus, the poor Inhabitants that work for their Bread, are under severer Restraints; for the Governor's Servants being upheld by as uncontrouled Licentiousness, on pretence of pressing the Craftsmen from their daily Labour into the Governor's Service, extort continued

[1] The insolence of these Faqīrs was much greater under the native government than at the present day.

[2] Στεντορόφωνος, "Stentor-voiced." "Of the stentorophonick horn of Alexander, there is a figure preserved in the Vatican" (Denham, *Phys. Theol.*, Bk. iv, ch. iii (note) (*Stanford Dict.*, *s. v.*).

Fees from them, or else they are sure to be set on work, without any thing for their Pains: Which was but even now made a Publick Grievance, by the Resistance of a sturdy *Patan*, (who is sprung from a Warlike People, of whom it is said, They never draw their Swords, but Blood must follow): And thus it happen'd; The *Patan* having employ'd a Taylor at his house, one of the Governor's Men seized him for his Master's Service; but the *Patan* rushing in to release him, the Soldier ran a young Brother of the *Patan's* through, naked and unconcerned in the Scuffle; which so enraged the *Patan*, that forcing the Sword out of the hand of this inhuman Butcher, he kill'd him and two more that came to his Rescue; and going into his house, slew his own Wife, and Sister, and a little Son of his own, that they might not fall a Sacrifice to the Governor's Rage: The wretched Taylor, animated by the Example of the *Patan* (tho but coolly), had murder'd his Wife had she not fled; but laying hold on his Old Father and Mother, he dispatched them; and bolting forth into the Street, set upon what Governor's Men he and the *Patan* could meet: Tidings whereof striking the Governor's Ears, he came with all his Power to beset the exasperated and desperate Men; but though a Thousand Men were up in Arms, and gazing upon the *Patan* standing with his Sword in his hand at the Entrance of the House, none durst venture to apprehend him; till his Fury abating, and Promises given by a Great Man, of Favour if he resigned; he attending to his Parley, in the mean while two Men with Guns from atop of the House discharged on him, and wounded him and the Taylor mortally, but not before they had carried this false Great Man with some of his Attendants along with them out of the World: So that these Curs set to keep the Sheep, are the first that worry them.

Lest therefore all Shew of Justice should be banished, now and then, when they have not Mony to buy it off, or the Emperor be informed, some Exemplary Punishments are inflicted: Some Instances whereof I shall relate.

The one was of an *Armenian*, *Chawbucked*[1] through the City for selling of Wine. The other was of a Goldsmith who had coined Copper *Rupees*; first they shaved his Head and Beard, as our Countrymen do Bayliffs when they presume to Arrest in Priviledg'd Places; then putting a Fool's Cap on his Head, they set him on an Ass, with his Face to the Tail, which is led by an *Holencore*,[2] and one of their Drums is beat before him, which is an Affront of the highest degree; thus they lead him up and down the City, where the Boys and Soldiers treat him but scurvily, pelting him all the way he passes: Being brought back to Prison they cut off his Hand, and let him lye during the Governor's Pleasure. The Third was of a Pack of Thieves that had infested the Roads a long time, and after some whiles Imprisonment the *Banyans* proffered Money for their Redemption; but the *Great Mogul* sending an Express, they were led to Execution; They were Fifteen, all of a Gang, who used to lurk under Hedges in narrow Lanes, and as they found opportunity, by a Device of a Weight tied to a Cotton Bowstring made of Guts, (with which they tew Cotton) of some length, they used to throw it upon Passengers so, that winding it about their Necks, they pulled them from their Beasts, and dragging them upon the Ground strangled them, and possessed themselves of what they had:[3] One

[1] Horse-whipped: Pers. *chābuk*, "a whip" (Yule, *Hobson-Jobson*, 185).

[2] See p. 82, Hind. *halālkhor*.

[3] An early account of Thuggee (Crooke, *Things Indian*, 473 ff.: Yule, *Ibid.*, 915).

of these was an Old Man with his two Sons, the youngest not fourteen. This being their Practice, they were sentenced, according to *Lex Talionis*, to be hang'd ; wherefore being delivered to the *Catwal*,[1] or Sheriff's Men, they led them two Miles with Ropes about their Necks to some wild Date-Trees : In their way thither they were chearful, and went singing, and smoaking Tobacco, the *Banyans* giving them Sweetmeats, they being as jolly as if going to a Wedding ; and the Young Lad now ready to be tied up, boasted, That though he were not Fourteen Years of Age, he had killed his Fifteen Men ; wherefore the Old Man, as he had been a Leader of these Two, was first made an Example for his Villany, and then the two Striplings were advanced, as all the rest were, half a Foot from the Ground ; and then cutting their Legs off that the Blood might flow from them, they left them miserable Spectacles, hanging till they dropped of their own accord.

The following Delinquents being of another kind, we shall see how they fare : The one was of a Rich Merchant of the *Moors* killing his Wife, and a Child he had by her of Three Years old, upon taking her with her Paramour in Adultery ; for which Crime a Pecuniary Mulct excused him : The other was a Boy's sticking a *Sodomitish Moor* to the Heart with his own *Catarre*,[2] while he attempted upon his Body ; which Fact was so far from being accused as a Fault, that the Boy came off with Commendation ; though there is nothing more frequently committed among them, than the unnatural Sin of Buggery.

There is another thing above all the rest an unpardonable Offence ; for a *Banyan* or Rich Broker to

---

1 Head police officer : Pers. *Kotwāl* (Yule, *Ibid.*, 265).

2 See p. 235.

grow Wealthy without Protection of some Great Person;[1] for it is so mighty a Disquiet to the Governor, that he can never be at ease till he have seen the bottom of this Mischief; which is always cured by Transfusion of Treasure out of the *Banyans* into the Governor's Coffers: Which makes them become humble Suiters for the Umbrage of any of Quality, to skreen them from this Violence.

The next in the Executive Power is the *Catwal*,[2] the Governor of the Night, as the other two Great Officers rule the Day; or nearer our Constitution, the Sheriff of the City: For after the Keys are carried to the Governor, it is the *Catwals* Business with a Guard of near Two hundred Men, to scower the Streets and Brothels of Idle Companions; to take an account of all People late out, to discover Fires and Housebreakers, and to carry all lewd Persons to Prison, which is solely committed to his Charge: So that all Night long he is heard by his Drums and Trumpets, shouting and hallowing of his Crew in their Perambulation through all Parts of the City; with Lights and Flambeaus, with some few of his Companions in Coaches or *Palenkeens*: Moreover he seizes all Debtors, and secures them, and has the care of Punishing and Executing all Offenders.

---

[1] Of the Banyans of Surat, Ovington (p. 319 f.) writes: "Their wealth consists only in Cash and Jewels, the Distinction of personal and real Estate is not heard in India, and that they preserve as close and private as they can, lest the *Mogul's* Exchequer should be made their Treasury. This curbs them in their Expences, and awes them to great secresie in their Commerce, especially in their receiving, or Payments of Money, for which they either make use of the darkness of the Night, or of the obscurity of the Morning, in conveying it the place of Payment." Bernier (p. 225) and Grose (p. 130 ff.) give similar accounts. This idea still prevails in Persia (Morier, *Second Journey*, 135; Wills, *Land of the Lion and Sun*, 76; Benjamin, *Persia*, 207; Malcolm, *H. of Persia*, ii, 378).

[2] See p. 245. Ovington (p. 229 f.) thus describes the Kotwāl of Surat in 1690. "The Catoual is another Officer in the City, somewhat

This is a Place of great Trust, but neither so Honourable or Profitable as the *Shawbunder's* is;[1] who is King of the Port, or Chief Customer, though something abated by the *Mogul's*, too fondly in a Religious Vanity granting Immunity to the *Musslemen* lately, which is no small detriment.

The Custom-house has a good Front, where the Chief Customer appears certain hours to chop,[2] that is, to mark Goods outward-bound, and clear those received in: Upon any suspicion of default he has a Black-Guard that by a *Chawbuck*, a great Whip, extorts Confession: There is another hangs up at the daily Waiters, or *Meerbar's*[3] *Choultry*, by the Landing-place, as a terror to make them pay *Cæsar* his due; the Punishment, if detected, being only Corporal, not Confiscation of Goods: This Place is filled with Publicans, Waiters and Porters, who are always at the Receipt of Custom, but are a little too tardy sometimes in the delivery of Goods, making the Merchant dance attendance, till a right understanding be created betwixt the *Shawbunder*

---

resembling a Justice of the Peace, in endeavouring the suppression of all Enormities in the City. For which reason he is oblig'd to ride the Streets for prevention of Disorder, thrice in the Night, at 9, 12, and 3 a Clock, 'till 5 in the Morning, at which Hours the Drums beat, and a large long Copper Trumpet sounds aloud. The *Catoual* is always attended with several Peons and Souldiers arm'd with Swords, Lances, Bows and Arrows, and some with a very dreadful Weapon, a Rod of Iron about a Cubit's length, with a large Ball of Iron at the end, which is able with ease to dash out the Brains, or break and shatter the Bone at once. When he meets with a Person guilty of petty Irregularities, or some trivial Offence, he confines him for some time; but if his Misdemeanour be more notorious, he must smart for it by a Chawbuck, or Bastinado."

[1] Pers. *Shāh-bandar*, "lord of the haven": harbour-master, consul, customer (an old term for head custom-house officer) (Yule, *Hobson-Jobson*, 816).

[2] Hind. *chhāp* (*Ibid.*, 207).

[3] Pers. *Mīr-bahr*, "harbour-master" (*Ibid.*, 565).

and them, which commonly follows when the Fist is mollified.[1]

Over-against the Custom-house is a stately Entrance into the Mint, which is a large Town of Offices within it self; hither repair all *Shroffs* or Bankers, for the proof of Silver, which in this place is the most refined, and purest from allay, in the World; as is also their Gold: Their lowest Coyn is of Copper.

Between these two is a crowded *Buzzar* of all those who come to sell and buy Cloath; being disengaged here, we pass the High-Streets, with Shops on each side, not like ours in *Europe*, being more like Pedlers-Stalls; we crossed several *Buzzars*, which yielded sustinence to the many Mouths we encountred.

Piercing through the City to the Walls[2] which are building to surround it, and a Ditch accompanying it, (though but shallow, yet the Wall is high, and of good well baked Brick) at length we came in sight of the Castle, having a large *Pomœrium*.

They say it has been standing ever since *Tamberlane* was here;[3] who they give out to be its Founder: It may be so, for it is old, yet bears 30 or 40 stout Pieces of Ordnance, fronts the River, and is Moated by it; to which they pass a Draw bridge, but admit no Stranger: It is

---

[1] The vexatious proceedings of these officials at Surat are noticed by Sir T. Roe and other travellers (Anderson, 158). The custom-house and the mint, mentioned later on, were situated in the Chok Bāzār Chaklo, or square market ward. The mint is now a market (*Bombay Gaz.*, ii, 303).

[2] The walls were begun after Sivajī's attack in 1664. Though the masonry has been almost completely removed, the line of the inner wall still divides Surat City from its suburbs (*Ibid.*, ii, 308).

[3] The Castle was planned and built, between 1540 and 1546, by a Turkish officer, who under the title of Khudāwand Khān, was ennobled by Mahmūd Begada, King of Gujarāt (1459-1511) (*Ibid.*, ii, 301 f.).

Manned by 300 *Luscarries*[1] or Soldiers, armed with Gun, Sword and Buckler, has a peculiar Governor independent from him of the Town or Province, being as it were confined to it, not presuming, on forfeiture of his Head, on any account to pass out of a Garden by the Bridge, it being his farthest Walk.

Up and down the City are Remains of *Seva Gi*'s Fury, the Ruins being not yet repaired; of whom they stand in hourly fear, having their Sores still fresh in their Memory: To prevent whose Rage, they are collecting an Hundred thousand *Rupees* till their Walls be finished, when we shall see how they will defend them; having 700 Men allotted for that Office, besides *Europe* Gunners at every Gate, which are Six in number, beside 36 Bastions with half a dozen great Guns apiece: Upon the top they have piled spiked Timber to annoy the Scalers.

Every Gate is barbed with Iron Spikes to break the rushing in of the Elephants; these also are under a distinct Command.

The Governor of the Town has an Army of 1500 Men in pay, with Matchlocks, Swords and Javelins; Two hundred Horse with Quivers full of Arrows at the Bow of their Saddles, Lances at their Right Stirrup, and Swords of an unweildy bulk, with Bucklers hanging over their Shoulders; their Bows are curiously and strongly made with Horn, and for that reason better in Dry than Wet Weather.[2]

---

[1] Pers. *lashkar*, "army, camp" (Yule, *Hobson-Jobson*, 507).

[2] The horn or composite bow is as old as the time of Homer, that of Pandarus being made of that of a wild goat, joined by a straight stock in the centre (*Iliad*, iv, 105-26). The pattern probably came to India from Central Asia. The "Moors" of Ormuz, in the beginning of the 16th century carried "Turkish" bows, made of stiff wood and buffalo horn; they carried far, and those who used them were excellent archers (Barbosa, p. 43), a statement repeated by Pyrard de Laval (ii. 243). There are examples of the bow of the "curved Parthian shape," made or horn coloured and lacquered, from

Among the many *Moschs* to and again, only two are famous with long Spires by the Wall, where is a stately Dwelling for the *Xeriff*.[1]

They have Three other Places for Strangers called *Caravan Serawes*,[2] or Inns, intended by the Donors *gratis*, but since perverted, and let out to Foreigners.

Near the Governor's Stables were Forty Camels housed, ready for War, and half a dozen Elephants.

These Stables are rather Sheds, or Booths of Hair-cloath, to remove on occasion, than any Building fixed for that purpose; and were it not for the manner of treating their Horses, not worth the mentioning: They have no Racks, but feed as Nature intended them, from the Ground, if they get Hay; for their Corn, it is usually *Garavance*,[3] a sort of Pease which they put into an Hair Bag, and by a String (clapping their Mouths into it) fastned behind their Ears, is kept from the Ground; out of this they have their daily Allowance; beside Butter.

Rājputāna and the Deccan, in the India Museum (Egerton, *Handbook*, 108, 115). The Tatar or Scythian bow is formed of several pieces of wood or horn, united with glue and sinews. Shorter than the long-bow, it gets its spring by being bent outside-in for the purpose of stringing it: thus the concave side of the ancient Scythian bow becomes the convex side when strung. "Bows of this class belong especially to northern regions, where there is a scarcity of tough wood suited to making long-bows in one piece" (Tylor, *Anthropology*, 195). For a full account of these bows, see H. Balfour, *Journal Anthropological Institute*, xix, 220 f., who thinks that the model was ultimately derived by the Tatar tribes from America through emigrants across Behring's Straits.

[1] There are four fine ancient mosques in Surat—that of Khwāja Dīwān Sāhib, built about 1530 A.D.; the Nāv Saiyid or that of the Nine Saiyids, erected in honour of nine martyred warriors; that of Saiyid Idrus, with a fine minaret, built in 1639; the mosque and tomb of Mīrzā Sāmī, built about 1540. It is uncertain to which of these the text refers (*Bombay Gaz.*, ii, 326).

[2] Pers. *Karwānsarāī*. In another place (Letter V, chap. II) Fryer suggests an absurd derivation for the word. The existing Sarāīs in Surat are modern.

[3] Span. *garbanzos*, the *Cicer arietinum* or gram (Yule, *Hobson-Jobson*, 144). The nose-bag is the common *tobrā* (*Ibid.*, 926).

Sugar and *Jaggaree* or Mulasso's made into Past, with the Meal of *Garavance*, which fattens all their Beasts of War, and makes them slick and fine; they cover them very warm with a kind of Felt or Flock-work, two or three double, and tye them by all their Feet stretched out at length; in which posture they always stand: When they make their Beds, they sift the Dung they make, after it is dried in the Sun, and make a soft lying for them of it;[1] they court them with all the gentleness and kind Speeches imaginable, seldom or never speaking to, or using them harshly; every Horse has one Man wholly imployed about his Service, and pretends to no other business; so that as good Horses are chargeable to purchase, they are also chargeable in keeping.

The Governor about this time taking occasion to quarrel with the *Dutch*, offering several Abuses both of Body and Purse;[2] the Commodore was resolved no longer to endure it, and therefore had sent for their Fleet, and in the mean time threatned to remove the Factory to *Gogo*,[3] a Port over-against *Swally*; which with *Diu Point* makes *Swally Hole*: To prevent which, a Deroy[4] was put upon

---

[1] This is a specially Persian habit (Wills, *Land of Lion and Sun*, 101).

[2] In July, 1671, some drunken Dutchmen insulted the attendants of Aghā Ja'far, chief officer of Surat, and after a disorderly conflict, took refuge in the English factory. The Governor ordered a boycott of the Europeans, and threatened that any of them found in arms should be slain. The President in consultation with the Dutch and French "Directores," agreed that they should show an intention of removing their factories from Surat. After some negotiations, the privileges of the Europeans were restored; but the levity of the French threatened to upset the arrangement. Finally, matters were settled on 19th August, 1671, the English obtaining a grant of one year's customs in addition to their former privileges (Bruce, *Annals*, ii, 301 f.).

[3] Gogha, a port in S.E., corner of Kāthiāwār; lat. 21° 39′ N., long. 72° 15′ E., about 40 miles from the head of the Gulf of Cambay. It was a very ancient trading port, but is now practically deserted (*Bombay Gaz.*, iv, 339 f.; Yule, *Hobson-Jobson*, 382).

[4] See p. 90.

all *Fringi*'s, that we could not go out of the Gates of the City, but by especial Commission from the Governor.

CHAP. II.

Shews the Tombs, Outwalks, Ceremonies, and Austerities of the Gentiles, *with the Ships and River about* Surat.

HAVING obtained Leave of the Governor, we went out of the Walls by *Broach*-Gate[1] (they taking Names from the chief Places they lead to), where, as at every Gate, stands a *Chocky*,[2] or Watch to receive Toll for the Emperor; and which is a Shame, a *Raspoot* also for the *Raspoots*, otherwise they would infest the Villages adjacent and drive away the Cattel; for all which it is unsafe to be far out of the Town late at Night, unless well guarded. This way was all strewed with *Moor-men*'s Tombs, and one of especial Note of a *Persian* Ambassador, who returning from *England* with Sir *Anthony Shirley*,[3] is reported to poyson himself here, rather than answer some ill Management of his Office to his Master: Not far from

---

[1] Mr. Bonus writes: "No gate of Surat is now remembered by the name of the Broach Gate. Perhaps in Fryer's day it was so known among the Europeans only. In any case, it must have been in the inner wall of Surat (the outer wall was not built till after Fryer's time): and what with fires and demolition the inner wall has now practically disappeared. The road to Broach now leads through the outer wall at a gate known as the Variav Gate: and Fryer's 'Broach-Gate' was doubtless at the point where this route issued from the inner wall, near the N.W. corner of the city as it then was."

[2] Hind. *chaukī*, "a toll-station" (Yule, *Hobson-Jobson*, 205).

[3] Sir A. Shirley or Sherley (1565-1635). He left for Persia in 1599 and returned next year. In 1613 he published "Sir Anthony Sherley: his Relation of his Travels into Persia, the Dangers and Distresses which befel him in his Passage . . . his Magnificent Entertainment in Persia, his honourable Imployment there hence as Ambassadour of the Princes of Christendome, the cause of his Disappointment therein, with his Advice to his Brother, Sir Robert Sherley; also a true Relation of the Great Magnificence . . . of Abas, now King of Persia," described as "a dull book, abounding in vapid moralising" (*Dict. Nat. Biog.*, lii, 121 ff.; [Evelyn Philip Sherley] "*The Three Brothers, or*

whence, on a small Hill on the left hand of the Road, lies *Tom Coriat*,[1] our *English Fakier* (as they name him), together with an *Armenian* Christian, known by their Graves lying *East* and *West*: He was so confident of his Perfection in the *Indostan* Tongue, that he ventured to play the Orator in it before the *Great Mogul.* In his return from him he was killed with Kindness by the *English* Merchants, which laid his rambling Brains at Rest.

From hence we passed over to the *Dutch* Tombs, many and handsome, most of them Pargetted.[2] Adjoining to which the *Armenians* have a Garden, where on a Terras (Forty Yards in Length, and Five in Breadth) are reared several Monuments Coffin-Fashion, with a place to burn Incense at the Head, like the *Moors*, only over it a Cross: One of more Eminency had an Arch over it at the upper-end.

---

the Travels and Adventures of Sir Anthony, Sir Robert, and Sir Thomas Sherley in Persia, Russia, Turkey, Spain, Etc." (1825). Herbert (p. 35) says that, "Nogdi-Ally-beg, the Persian Ambassador" was "intombed, not a stones cast from *Tom Coryat's* grave, knowne but by two poore stones."

[1] Tom Coryat, or Coryatt, born 1577: son of Rev. George Coryatt, Prebendary of York. His, "Coryatt's Crudities hastily gobbled up in Five Months' Travels in France, Italy, etc.," was published in 1611. He died at Surat in December, 1617. Terry (p. 55 ff.) says he was buried at Swally, on the sea-shore, which is more probable than the story of Fryer (following Herbert) that his tomb was in the suburbs of Surat. See Anderson (57 ff.) for an account of his curious career. Mr. Bonus writes: "A tomb still exists at Rajgari, which tradition declares to be that of Coryat; but there is no other evidence. This tomb is kept in repair by the Public Works Department. It is said that there was once a row of seven, of which this one alone remains."

[2] "The two most noted among the *Dutch*, is one, a noble Pile rais'd over the Body of the Dutch Commissary, who died about three Years ago; and another less stately, but more fam'd; built by the order of a Jovial *Dutch* Commander, with three large Punch-Bowls upon the top of it, for the Entertainment and Mirth of his sorrowing Friends, who remember him there sometimes so much, that they quite forget themselves" (Ovington, 405 f.). For these tombs, that described by Ovington having disappeared, see *Bombay Gaz.*, ii, 325 f.

Thence we took a Round, though the Inclosures are contiguous, to the *English* Tombs, short of which the *Portugals* have a Burial-Place.

The Ground the *English* Dead are inhumed in, is stocked not with so many Tombs as the *Dutch*; though in one of Sir *George Oxendine*'s it excels the Proudest.[1]

The *French* have a separate Place to deposit their Dead overagainst the *English*, with only one single Tomb, and that a small one.

In every place up and down the Fields are Tombs of *Musslemen*: A Mile from the City, buried like *Diogenes* with their Heels upwards, stand a Row of Sepulchres of the *Muttany*,[2] or *Burfta's*[3] Pilgrims, with the Soles of their Feet imprinted on the middle; some under a Foursquare, others Round rising Tombs, by the side of a Tank, on an ascending Mount.

---

[1] The Oxenden monument is made up of two tombs of the two brothers—Christopher Oxenden, died 18th April, 1659; George Oxenden, died 14th July, 1669—both with Latin inscriptions, for copies of which see *Ibid.*, ii, 323 f. "The two most celebrated Fabricks among the *English*, set off with stately Towers and Minorets, are that which were Erected for Sir *John Oxonton*, and the other for the Renown'd and Honourable President *Aungers*" (Ovington 405). This last is near the Oxenden monument, and though it has no inscription, it is believed to be that of Gerald Aungier (1677). Opposite the Portuguese chapel is a small burial ground with about twenty tombs (*Bombay Gaz.*, ii, 323).

[2] These, whom Fryer mentions again (Letter IV, chap. VI), seem to be identified by him with Jogīs. The word may possibly be Mathānī or Mathnī, residents of a monastery (*math*); or he may have confounded them with the Mastāna (Mahāsthānī, "of great territory") a name applied to cultivating Brāhmans in W. India (Wilson, *Indian Caste*, ii, 109). He probably refers to Jogīs; but if so, he seems to have been mistaken in believing them to bury their dead face downwards, a device to prevent the ghost from "walking." The Kāthiāwār Jogīs effect this purpose by branding the great toe of the right foot of the corpse; or he may have heard of the Chāran Vanjāras of Khāndesh, who cremate their dead face downwards (*Bombay Gaz.*, viii, 159; xii, 109 *n.*).

[3] This place, mentioned again by Fryer (Letter III, chap. V) is probably Barvī, three miles N.E. of Kalyān (*Bombay Gaz.*, xiii, Pt. II, 477).

A Mile and a half further is *Pulparra*,[1] a Town separated for the *Banyans* to exercise their Funeral and Festival Rites. This is a Seminary of their Heathen Doctors or *Brachmins*, many of whom were in the River doing their Devotions, which consists in Washing and Praying.

The Elder sate in a Row, where the Men and Women came down together to wash, having *Lungies*,[2] about their Wastes only, which before they put on, they select a *Brachmin* of their proper Cast to hold their Vest; which they shift so cleaverly, that the quickest Eye can discover nothing more than decent. At their coming up out of the Water they bestow their Largess of Rice or Doll[3] (an *Indian* Bean) and the *Brachmin* his Benediction, by impressing a Mark answerable to their Casts on their Forheads; which is the way they live, purely on Benevolence.

Here they have Two Pagods remaining, but defaced by the *Moors*: One of them, however, still shews a Crust of Plaster, with Images Antick enough, but of excellent durance and splendour, like Alabaster, made of a white Loam calcined, and then called *Arras*;[4] which they powder and steep in Water Three or Four Years before it be fit for their purpose; the longer the better.

---

[1] Phūlpārā, one of the Surat suburbs on the river. Ovington (p. 359) speaks of "Pulparroch, two miles distant from Suratt, a very delightful place, adorn'd with pleasant Walks and Groves of Trees, near the gentle Streams of the River Tappy." Forbes (*Or. Mem.*[2], i, 176 f.) says it was famous for its Brāhman seminaries, and that here the ashes of the Hindu dead were flung into the river. It probably represents the Poulipoula of Ptolemy, which Yule places at Sanjān (M'Crindle, *Ptolemy*, 38 f.).

[2] See p. 137.

[3] Hind. *dāl*, usually pulse of the *Cajanus indicus*, the Arhar of N. India (Yule, *Hobson-Jobson*, 312).

[4] This word, if it represents a native term, has not been traced. He seems to mean the polished plaster usually known as Chunam. It has been suggested that it may represent Mahr. *arasā*, Hind. *ārsī*, "a thumb mirror"; or that he means *Tarras* or *Trass*, a volcanic earth or sand-rock, resembling Puzzolana, used as a cement.

Here are many Monuments of their misled Zeal; the most dreadful to remember, is an extraordinary one erected by the River side, where they Burn their Dead in Honour of a Woman who Burnt her self with her dead Husband.[1] Several Corps were Flaming in their Funeral Piles; which after the Fire has satisfied its self with, they cast the Ashes up into the Air, and some upon the Water; that every Element may have a share. Some of the Devoutest desire to expire in this Water, giving in charge to their Relations to lay them up to the Chin in it at the Article of Death.

Those whose Zeal transport them no farther than to die at home are immediately Washed by the next of Kin, and bound up in a Sheet; as many as go with him, carry him by turns on a Colt-staff;[2] and the rest run almost naked and shaved, crying after him, *Ram, Ram*,[3] making all the haste they can to *Pulparra* to Burn him; which Fire is often very costly, being maintain'd with Wood of Aloes; sometimes they expend some Thousands of Rupees. The Relations exclude themselves all Society till the time of Mourning be over; the Women crying, *O Si, O Si*,[4] beating their Breasts violently, and expostulating the reason of their Departure, as if he had not a kind Wife, loving Children, good Possessions, and the like: In the time of this Mourning they bestow largely to redeem Creatures appointed to

---

[1] The common Suttee (Satī) shrines, often seen at old Hindu cremation places.

[2] An obsolete form of cowl-staff, familiar from the adventure of Sir John Falstaff: "Go take up these clothes here, quickly; where's the cowl-staff?" (*Merry Wives of Windsor*, iii, 3).

[3] The usual Hindu exclamation, an appeal to the god Rāma.

[4] This seems to be the cry of "Hasan, Husain," which accompanies the breast-beating on the 10th day of the Muharram (Yule, *Hobson-Jobson*, 419 f.). Elsewhere (Letter V, chap. xii) he speaks of "Hossy Gossy." If this be the origin of the phrase, he confounds the Musalmān rite with the wailing at a Hindu funeral.

Die, to excuse Oxen and *Buffola's* from Labour, feeding them at their own Charges, besides purchasing Milch Kine, and giving them to poor People, inviting them to Funeral Feasts, with other Largesses to the *Brachmins.*

Here are out-acted all the boasted Austerities I ever heard of; I faw a *Fakier* of the *Gentus*, whose Nails by neglect were grown as long as my Fingers, some piercing through the flesh.[1] Another grave Old Man had a Turbat of his own Hair (which they all Covet) Sun-burnt towards the ends, Grey nearer the roots, Plaited like the *Polonian Plica*,[2] but not so diseased, above Four Yards in Length.

Others with their Arms Dislocated so, that the διάρθρωσις of the Joints is Inverted, and the head of the Bone lies in the pit or valley of the Arm; in which Case they are defrauded of their Nourishment, and hang as useless Appendices to the Body; that unless relieved by Charity, they are helpless in all Offices to themselves.

Others Fixing their Eyes upon Heaven, their Heads hanging over their Shoulders, are uncapable of removing them from the Posture they are in, being accustomed to that uninterrupted Rest, having contracted and stiffned the Tendons of the Muscles and Ligaments of the Neck, that both those belonging to the Gullet, or the motion of the Head, are unserviceable; insomuch that no Aliment, not Liquid, can pass, and that too with much difficulty.

Others by continual Abstinence bring themselves into a strange Emaciated habit of Body, that they seem only walking Skelitons.

---

[1] Ovington (p. 359 ff.) gives an account of Faqīrs undergoing such penances at Phūlpāra, when Fryer may have seen them. For similar descriptions, see Tavernier (ed. Ball, ii. 196 ff.); A. Hamilton (i, 154); Bernier (317); Abbé Dubois (536 ff.); Bowrey (22, 32, with illustrations); *Bombay Gaz.*, ix, Pt. I, 544.

[2] See p. 79.

All of them go Naked (some plump young lusty Fellows) except their Privities, and bedawb themselves over with Ashes; who with their pleited Hair about their Heads, look like so many *Mægara*'s; these wait on the others. The Ancientest of them addict themselves to Reading, they live Six or Eight together, as they please; lie upon the Ground or a Matt, some of them in all Seasons abide the open Air.

At another time a *Gentu Fakier* was enjoined for Forty days to endure the Purgatory of five Fires;[1] there being a great resort by reason of a Festivity solemnized all that while: when I came early in the Morning (invited by the novelty and incredibility of the thing) he was Seated on a four-square Stage or Altar, with three Ascents, some Two Feet high, and as many Feet square, ready to shew: While he was in a musing posture, other *Fakiers* (whose Duty it is daily to salute the Sun at his Height, Rising, and Setting, with their Musick of long hollow Canes) blew them for an hour, or *Ghong*;[2] after which he fell to his Mattins, which he continued till the Sun began to be warm; then rising he Blessed himself with Holy Water, and threw himself along on the lowest square, still muttering to himself on his Knees, he at length, with one Leg bowed upright between his Thighs, rises on the other, telling his Beads (which both *Moormen* and *Gentus* wear)[3] which he had in his hands a quarter longer, and stands, like a Goose, unmoved all the time; then casting himself down, he exercised himself, as Wrastlers do here, very

---

[1] The penance of the Panchāgni, sitting between five fires, one at each of the cardinal points, and the fifth the sun. "In summer let [the Sannyāsin] expose himself to the heat of five fires" (Manu, *Institutes*. vi, 23). For the modern form of the rite, see Ward, *Hindoos*,[2] ii, 258; Abbé Dubois, 543.

[2] Gong (Yule, *Hobson-Jobson*, 385).

[3] For the Musalmān and Hindu rosary, see Crooke, *Things Indian*, 407 ff.

briskly, but guarding the position of his Leg, which he kept so fixed as if it had grown in that nature, as well when he rose as grovelled on the ground; acting thus a quarter more, it had the same operation as the *Stork*'s Bill used for a Suppository, for it brought him to a Stool; he taking his Purifying-pot in his hand, marched on one side, where he tarried not long before he returning took up his Beads he had left; and in this Interim four Fires being kindled (any of them able to roast an Ox) at each Corner of the upper and least Square, he having finished some Fopperies with his Pot, *Scævola*-like with his own hands he increased the Flames by adding combustible Stuff as Incense to it; when removing from his Neck a Collar of great Wooden Beads, he made a Coronet of them for his Head; then bowing his Head in the middle of the Flames, as it were to worship, holding the other Beads in his hands, with his Head encircled between his Arms, his Face opposite to the Sun, which is the fifth Fire, he mounted his Body with his Feet bolt upright, and so continued standing on his Head the space of three hours very steddily, that is, from Nine till Twelve; after which he seats himself on his Breech cross-legg'd after their way of sitting, and remains so without either eating or drinking all the rest of the Day, the Fires still nourished, and he sweating (being one of a good Athletick Habit, and of a Middle Age) as if basted in his own Grease.

This is imagined to be an Imposture; but if it be, it would make a Man disbelieve his own Eyes: Others more rationally impute the Heat from the Fires to be allayed by that overpowering one of the Sun; which I cannot wholly incline to, since we daily when abroad roast our Meat by Fires made in a clear Day without any shelter: But I rather conceive Custom has inured his Body to it; for the very Mountebank Tricks declare it a Practice; and the other I think as feasible as to eat Fire, tread on Hot Irons, (which is here used), or for Cooks to thrust their hands into scalding Water without Injury.

Another Devote had made a Vow not to lye down in Sixteen Years, but to keep on his Feet all that while; this came accompanied with two others under the same Oath, the one had passed Five, the other Three Years; all Three of them had their Legs swoln as big as their Bodies, with filthy running Ulcers, exposed to view for the greater Applause: Standing, they leaned on Pillows hung in a String from the *Banyan* Tree, and had a Pompous Attendance of such ragged *Fakiers* their Admirers, with Musick, Flags, and *Mirchals*:[1] The Eldest having undergone the compleat Term, to crown all, was intombed in the same standing Posture Nine Days without any sort of Food; and lest any Pretext of that kind might lessen his Undertaking, he caused a Bank of Earth to be heaped on the Mouth of his Cave, whereon was to be sown a certain Grain which ears in Nine Days, which accordingly being done, eared before his being taken thence.[2] I saw him presently after his Resurrection, in great State raised on a Throne under a Canopy, before which was a Fire made in the Pit he had been, where he put his Hands, being anointed with Oyl, untouch'd by the Flames: Which whether this may discover the Cheat of both this and the other, that such an Unction may be to resist Fire, Naturalists have not agreed in; and therefore I judge this rather a Delusion, I having not been present at this Experiment: But that this is none

---

[1] See p. 241.

[2] There are many accounts, which seem well authenticated, of Faqīrs being buried alive for considerable periods, see Elliot-Dowson, ii, 10; Vigne, *Visit to Ghazni*, 306; *Punjab Notes and Queries*, ii, 202.

I am assured, That the *Banyans* gave him Divine Honours, and saluted him prostrate, offering before him Rice, and throwing Incense into the Fire: He had a Red Trident in his hand, and is enrolled one of the Heroes or Demi-Gods in their Superstitious Kalender.

From this place of *Pulparra* to *Surat*, a Row of Trees on each hand shade the way, it being constantly filled with all sorts of People either for Worship or Pleasure.

The only thing of Grandeur extant of the Devotion of the Ancient Heathens, is a great Tank without the Walls of *Surat*, a Mile in Circumference, walled all about with descending Stone Steps: In the middle an High Place of the Heathens: Many sumptuous *Mausoleums* are erected near its Brink, with Aqueducts to convey Water, with which were it filled, the best Ship that swims in the Sea might ride in it: It looks now more like a *Circus* or *Gymnaseum*, able enough to contain as many as such Spectacles would delight. In their great Solemnities it is usual for them to set it around, with Lamps to the Number of two or three *Lecques*, which is so many Hundred thousand in our Account.[1]

The Citizens by the King's Favour have good store

[1] The Gopī Talāv, W. of Salābatpura, and N. of Rustampura wards, with an area of 58 acres, partly the bed and partly the banks of the ancient reservoir. P. della Valle (i, 32) writes: "The Diametre of this Artificial Lake is good two furlongs, which in our parts would seem a competent largeness, but here 'tis not much; and this Fish pond of *Surat* is not accounted among the greatest, but the least in *India*; where indeed they are numerous, and the most magnificent, and goodly structures, or rather, the only structures in this Country which have anything of magnificence, or handsomeness." "Only adjoyning *Nancery* gate, I saw a Tanck or Magazon of water, a brave work and worthy the noting. It is of good free stone, circling in above 100 sides and angles; eight and twenty Ells between every angle, in compasse very neere a thousand paces. It diminishes its largeness gradation by 16 degrees or steps towards the bottome, of most use to receive a great quantity of raine water, to quench the flagrant thirst of the sunne-burnt *Indians*" (Herbert, 36 f.). It is also described by Sir T. Roe (i, 112). The tank was ruined about 1717 (*Bombay Gaz.*, ii, 312). Leques = lākhs, or 100,000.

of Gardens neighbouring *Surat*;[1] the biggest of all is the Queen's, though some Private Men have neater, where we often go to take the Air, and feast in pleasant *Choultries* or Summer-Houses, spread after the *Moors* manner with Carpets, refreshed with various Figures of the Rising Water, out of several Spouts from square Tanks Pargetted. All the time of our durance here Water is sprinkled, to mitigate the Fieriness of the Sun.

Here are Grottoes descending also under Ground by huge Arches and Stone Steps shaded by Trees on each hand, till it come to the deep Well at bottom, from whence by Leathern Bags drawn upon Wheels by Oxen, the Water is carried up, and in Gutters streams about the Gardens.[2]

In these by the help of a *Brachmin* skilled in Simples, I have found the Silk Cotton-tree,[3] distinguished by us from the Vulgar beneficial one, by its being a Tree, the other a Shrub; it is most like a Maple in Leaf and Branch, only the Bark is not furrowed; it brings forth between three Leaves, first a Bud or Button, then a white Flower, last of all Seed about which the Cotton grows, in three distinct Cells, answering the three Leaves.

As also the Plant of which *Bang*[4] is made; it grows as our Hemp, the Juice of whose Seed ground in a Bowl like Mustard-seed, and mixed with any other Liquor, is that they equivocate with their Prophet instead of the

---

[1] The gardens in the suburbs are now cultivated fields.

[2] This is a Bāolī, one of the step-wells, for which Gujarāt is celebrated (Yule, *Hobson-Jobson*, 108).

[3] *Bombax malabaracum*, the Semal of N. India. "There is also another kind of cotton that comes from a tree larger than the preceding, like an ash: this tree produces certain pods full of cotton, which, by reason of its short staple, is good for nothing but to make pillows for their beds" (Pyrard de Laval, ii, 364). See Watt, *Econ. Dict.*, i, 487; Fra Paolino, 396 ff.; Yule, *Hobson-Jobson*, 807.

[4] See p. 92

Grape; and that which follows agrees to what Mr. *Ray* notes out of *L O B in Ado*: *Lacustris aqua cui cannabis intabuerit tantopere viru nocet, ut epotasit præsentissimo sitientibus veneno*; this with *Dutry*[1] (as has been said) is the inebriating Confection of the Post.[2]

Here he discovered to me his beloved *Alluh*,[3] the Bark of a Tree, the present remedy against all manner of Fluxes.

Though these People delight much in Gardens, yet are they but rude, compared to ours of *Europe*; they make a noble Entrance, a Banquetting-house in the middle eying the four Quarters of the Garden, beset with Trees like Wildernesses in every Quarter, or else planted with *Potatoes*, *Yawms*,[4] *Berenjaws*,[5] all hot Plants, and their Coolers, as *Pompkins*, *Cucumbers*, *Gourds* and such like; they are only divided by Gravelly Walks and Water-courses; not curiously adorned with Flowers; *Bismalvas*[6]

---

[1] See p. 92.

[2] See p. 92.

[3] Sir G. Watt writes: "As to the 'beloved Alluh' bark I am at a loss to reply. There is no Indian plant with that name, and I do not think *Vengueria spinosa* would do. But there are two plants, the barks of which were much prized in India before the introduction of Quinine. I suspect one of these may have been playfully called *Alluh*. These are: (1) *Holarrhena antidysenterica*; both the bark and the seeds are much valued, the latter being known as *indarjau*; (2) *Soymida febrifuga*, the *rohun*, which even to this day holds a high place in the opinion of native physicians." For these plants see Watt, *Econ. Dict.*, iv, 255; vi, Pt. III, 318. One of these may have been the Macir of Pliny (*N. H.* xii, 16 (8)), a red bark used in dysentery.

[4] The Yam (Yule, *Hobson-Jobson*, 977): also mentioned in Letter VIII, chap. I.

[5] The Baingan or Brinjal (*Solanum melongena*) (Yule, *Ibid.*, 115).

[6] Sir G. Birdwood conjectures that this may be a corruption of the Ar. *bismillāh*, "in the name of God," an expression of wonder at its beauty. Lt.-Col. Prain identifies it with a species of *Althaea* (*e.g.*, *Bauhin*), and Fryer, he thinks, may refer to *Althaea officinalis*, the marsh mallow, or *A. rosea*, the hollyhock (see Watt, *Econ. Dict.*, i, 199 f.). Sir G. Birdwood suggests *Abutilon indicum*; but is on the whole disposed to identify Fryer's *Bismalvas* with *Bixa orellana* (Watt, *Ibid.*, i, 454 f.), or with Arnotto, "which is not a Malvad, but it has a specious resemblance to that Order. It is a great favourite with Indians, and is always found in the old native gardens of W. India, where it was, presumptively, introduced by the Portuguese very shortly after its discovery in the Isthmus of Darien."

and some Wall-flowers or *Stock-Gillyflowers*[1] being the height of what they aim at: Only the *Culga*,[2] so famed for the Silk, in imitation of its Paint, I take it for our *Amaranthus*; and Δενδρομαλάχη, or the Tree *Mallow*,[3] which is red as Scarlet in the Morning, and at Noon faints into a pale Colour, and towards the Evening is pure white; some few *Lysimachias*,[4] which besides their several sorts of *Jessamins*,[5] is all the choice: Roses would grow here if they would but cultivate them.

---

[1] Sir G. Birdwood writes: "The Gillyflower of Shakespeare, Spenser, and Chaucer is *Dianthus caryophyllus*, and it is the July-flower of Abraham Cowley. The Gillyflowers of later writers were both the *Cheiranthus cheiri*, or wall-flower, and the *Matthiola incana* or Stock; but to-day *Dianthus caryophyllus* is distinguished as the Clove Gillyflower, and *Matthiola incana* as the Stock Gillyflower. Fryer cannot possibly have meant either the wall-flower or the stock; but may well mean *Dianthus caryophyllus* and *Dianthus chinensis*, both of which are cultivated in Bombay Gardens, the latter being a great favourite with Indian ladies for the decoration of their head-tire."

[2] Hind. *kalghā*, "a spire, crest, comb of a cock"; hence applied to the *amaranthus tricolor*, or cock's comb, "a most beautiful species of *sāg*, bearing at the top a head or cluster of leaves of three colours, red, yellow, and green, which have the appearance of the flower; it is very ornamental, and used as spinach (*sāg*). If the head be broken off, similar clusters form below" (F. Parkes, *Wanderings of a Pilgrim*, i, 314).

[3] Sir G. Birdwood and Lt.-Col. Prain identify this with *Hibiscus mutabilis*, the "Changeable Hibiscus" of Watt (*Econ. Dict.*, iv, 242), who describes it as "a small tree without prickles, which has flowers that change in colour, almost white in the morning and red at night. It is a native of China, but is now largely cultivated in gardens all over India from the Panjab to Burma and Madras." Sir G. Birdwood adds that it is "the *Rosa mutabilis* of Anglo-Indians, the *Inconstante Amante* of the Indo-Portuguese."

[4] Lt.-Col. Prain writes: "Lysimachia in pre-Linnean times was frequently applied to *Oenothera* and *Jussiaea*; here possibly for *Jussiaea villosa*. No true Lysimachia is likely to have been grown in the Surat gardens in Fryer's time." Sir G. Birdwood says: "No true Lysimachias, of which our Creeping Jenny and Yellow Loosestrife are examples, are to be found in any part of W. India. Guessing, I would say that Fryer has applied this term to some species of herbaceous *Cassia* or arborescent *Cassia*. *C. alata* is a conspicuous ornament in Indian gardens after the Great Rain from June to September."

[5] Sir G. Birdwood writes: "All the well known species of Jessamine are natives of India, and from India have spread into every tropical, sub-tropical, and temperate country of the world. It is from

A Mile from the City grows the humble Sensitive Plant,[1] common in the Fields; *Eastward* of *Surat*, two Courses,[2] *i. e.* a League, we pitched our Tent under a Tree, that besides its Leafs, the Branches bear its own Roots, therefore called by the *Portugals*, *Arbor de Rais*:[3] For the Adoration the *Banyans* pay it, the *Banyan Tree* (by whom it is held as sacred as the Oak to our Old *Druids*); who paint it daily, and make Offerings of Rice, and pray to it: It has Leafs like an *Ivy*, and is the same with that at *Johanna*, only that was incorporated into one Body, and this by often taking Root is capable of overspreading a whole Field, so that it is said there are of them able to shade an Army of 30000 Horse and Men singly; however it is possible to be so contrived, if it be lookt after, to make a Wood alone of it self.[4]

The Hedges and Lanes are chiefly set with two sorts of Bushes, called by us Milk-Trees,[5] because of a succulent Juice like *Spurge*, white, and of the consistency of the best Milk; but if it comes near the

---

Arabic name, *Yāsmīn*, we derive the scientific generic names, and the popular English names, Jessamine, Jesse, Jeshamy. The W. Indian names of these lovely and delightfully fragrant wild creepers and scandent shrubs and trees are *mogrā* and *chambelī*."

"And luxuriant above all
The Jasmine, throwing wide her elegant sweets,
The deep dark green of those unvarnish'd leaf
Makes more conspicuous, and illumines more
The bright profusion of her scatter'd stars."

(Cowper, *Task*, Bk. VI, "A Winter's Walk at Noon," lines 173-6.)

[1] *Mimosa pudica* (Watt, *Econ. Dict.*, v, 248).

[2] The Kos.

[3] Port. *arvore de râiz*, "tree of roots," *ficus bengalensis* or *indica*.

[4] This is probably the celebrated Kabīr Bar, or fig-tree of the Saint Kabīr, which is described by P. della Valle (i, 35). Cf. the account of one at Gombroon by Herbert (p. 122) and Yule, *Hobson-Jobson*, 277.

[5] *Euphorbia tirucalli*, abounding in acrid, milky juice (Yule, *Ibid.*, 565).

Skin or Eyes it is not so benign, according to the Experience of the Famous *Verulam* [*Nat. Hist. Cent.* 7. *Exp.* 39. *Omnem succum lacti similem ex plantis incisis acrem esse*,] and my Observation here; for if by chance it stick upon any part of the Body, it frets like an *Escarotick*; and I have seen an unruly Horse, rushing through it, both blind himself and Rider, both their Heads being swoln to an extraordinary bigness. I believe it to be a kind of *Tithymal*,[1] *quod tenerum lac non secus ac Mamma effundit*; the first sort of which has broader and jucier Leafs, and has four or five together; not jagged, but somewhat oval, a Finger's length, and half as broad; one only thick Stalk arises from the Root, and several Branches proceed from thence; they are all Green and Tender, springing up a Man's height, full of Prickles as our *Carduus*, of whose Milk inspissated is made *Euphorbium*. The other grows up into the Body of a Tree, and is Woody; above which it sends forth several tender smooth Stalks, which sprout out into Boughs seeming almost naked, because its Leafs are small, and come out at its Joints, sometimes singly; it is most like a Privet, very quick of Growth, and each of them make good Fences. The Goats despise it not, feeding, though very cautiously, on the Leafs and Branches of the latter, when the Heats have parched up the Grass and other Plants.

Before we leave the pleasant Fields for the dusty stinking Town, Sugar-Canes and Tobacco would deserve our Remark, which are both plentifully thriving here; had not these been already the Subject of other Pens.

The next diverting Prospect must be that of the River; it glides by the Town in swift Tides, and at Spring-Tides (which it would always do, were they industrious to keep

---

[1] Τιθύμαλος, spurge, euphorbia.

it in its Banks) it bears Ships of 1000 Tun Burthen up to *Surat* Walls; but they unlade first, because of the Sands, occasioned by their Sloth. They lye very thick a Mile together, and scattering down to the River's Mouth, reckoning more than an Hundred Sail of good Ships, besides small Vessels: For all which they were beholden to the Poverty of some *English* Shipwrights, the first of whom received the deserved Reward of his Officiousness (being *Scutica dignus*) from the *Moors*, who apprehending him stealing Customs, *Chawbucked* him handsomly.

The *Dutch* never permit the Natives to be taught any Eminent Art whereby they may become their Competitors: Nor is it, I think, better Policy to instruct them in any beneficial Science, as that of Navigation, no more than one would an Adversary how to use his Weapons; which these, had they equal Courage to their other Advantages of Strength and Nature, might easily thereby turn the Points of their Weapons upon us.

But for all these great Preparations, as yet they dare not venture out without *Europe* Passes, or Pilots; though some of their Ships carry 30 or 40 Pieces of Cannon, more for Shew than Service. Besides these Merchant-Men, here are Three or Four Men of War as big as Third Rate Ships: The other are Frigats[1] fit to Row or Sail, made with Prows instead of Beaks, more useful in Rivers and Creeks, than in the Main. The Emperor also has four great Ships in Pay always, to carry Pilgrims to *Mæcha* on free Cost and bring them back from *Hodge*,[2] where they prove a Crew of sanctified Varlets.

---

[1] This word had not at this time acquired its modern signification. It represents the development of the Port. *fragata*, Ital. *fregata*, or row-boat, into the war-ship. See Hedges, *Diary*, ii, 52; Forrest, *Home Papers*, i, 68; Sir T. Roe, i, 94.

[2] See p. 230.

The Heir of *Bantam*[1] is now here to take his Passage thither in one of them, with his Retinue, which are some of the *Pengrims*[2] or Lords of the Country, his Unkle and others, which were about Twenty, with their Wives: He was first at *Bombaim*, where he was entertained like a Prince, for the Obligation the Company have to their Trade there, he having been disobedient to the King his Father, and has not yet shewed any kindness to the *English*, siding rather with the *Dutch* Interest to undermine the Old King, and settle them in the Pepper-trade, which afterwards will not be in his Power to redeem out of their hands: Here little notice is taken of him, they all being in miserable poor Habits and he of little Credit, being a Giddyhead, were it not for the *English* Captain that brought him, a Confident of the Old King's, who furnishes him with Money but sparingly, he being indiscreet in his Expences. He is of the *Java* Extraction, short of Stature, broad-fac'd, little Eyes, and less Beard, a mere Boy; the rest wear their Beards like the *Chineses*, which is comparatively like a Cat's; their Heads shaved, covered only with Skull-Caps of Knit-Work, their Upper-Garments loose like a Frock: When they appear before him, they prostrate themselves along, then rising up with Respect,

---

[1] Surat was the centre of the pilgrim traffic to Mecca from India and E. Asia (Terry, 130 f.). Nothing is known of this Bantam prince, but the Bombay Factory Records of 29th September, 1674, state: "The Heir of Bantam is now here [Surat] . . . he was first at Bombaim."

[2] Mr. W. W. Skeat writes: "If the word is Malay, the nearest form in that sense is *Penglima* (derived from *lima*, the old Malayan word for 'hand,' now meaning 'five'). It might easily be shortened to *Penglim* or *Pengrim* by Europeans. It means 'a Rājā's executive officer' or 'right hand,' as we should say, as distinguished from *Penghulu*, 'head man' or 'consultative officer.'" Bruce (*Annals*, i, 239) speaks of the "Pangram of Bantam"; "the Pengram, Protector of Bantam, understanding thereof, seems to be very angry" (Foster, *Letters*, ii, 276).

sit crouching on their Heels: Their Women were covered with dark Blue Sheets.

The Old King had retired from the Cares of Government, and committed all to this his Son; but the *Pengrims* soon tired with his exorbitant Sway, made intercession for the Old King's reassuming his Authority; whereupon this Voyage was framed as an Expedient to settle his Mad Temper, being intrusted to the sober Conduct of the King's Brother.

These Vessels that are for this Voyage are huge unshapen things, and bear both the Name and Model of their old Junks: They return usually very Rich, and are at their Arrival adorned most abundantly with Streamers. Their way of Salutes are with Even, as ours with Odd Guns.

The Seamen and Soldiers differ only in a Vowel, the one being pronounced with an *u*, the other with an *a*; as *Luscar* is a Soldier; *Lascar*, a Seaman.[1] The Captain is called *Nucquedah*,[2] the Boatswain *Tindal*.[3]

CHAP. III.

Of their Solemnities, Sports and Pastimes; their Marriages; of the Parseys, *their Strength by Land and Sea, their abundant Wealth, and Fitness for Trade.*

AND now having entertained you thus far, I shall continue to you the Circumstantial or Accidental Shews, together with their Sports and Exercises.

---

1 Pers. *lashkar*, "army." "All the mariners and pilots are Indians, either Gentiles or Mahometans. All these seamen are called *Lascar*, and the soldiers *Lascarits*" (Pyrard de Laval, i, 438). See Yule, *Hobson-Jobson*, 508.

2 Pers. *nā-khudā*, "ship-master" (Yule, *Ibid.*, 612).

3 Mal. *tandal*, "leader of a body of men" (*Ibid.*, 923).

The first depends on the New Moon,[1] when, all Malice apart, the *Moors* embrace one another, and at the sight thereof make a Jubilee, by firing of Guns, blowing of Trumpets, Feasting and Praying very devoutly.

The next is the Day of the Week observed for the *Great Mogul's* Advancement to the Throne;[2] which is not so generally kept, only by the Soldiers and Officers.

But that which affects them all, is at the end of their *Ramazan*[3] or *Lent*, which is always the first New Moon in *November*; which as it is observed with the greatest Strictness, not swallowing their Spittle all the Day of its Continuance, so is it celebrated when it concludes, with the highest Expression of Joy and Solemnity.

The Governor goes in Procession, and bestows his Largess in his Passage to the Chief Place of Devotion, liberally scattering Rupees as Kings do Medals at their Coronations, waited on by all the Gallants of the Town: His Son first leading a Body of Horse of the Cavalry of the City; himself beginning the first File on the Left-hand, the place of highest Honour, it was as deep as the Street would admit, observing no Rank: After whom followed the *Cazy*, with Green Banners, with a Band of Foot of 100 Men; then the Customer with his Men and Colours, both carried in *Palenkeens*; whom followed the *Mullahs* and Merchants, without any distinction, some

---

[1] It is doubtful to which feast Fryer refers. He may refer to the Ramazān, which ends with rejoicing, when the new moon is first seen (Hughes, *Dict. of Islām*, 533 ff.), Cf. Bowrey, 96.

[2] The *Jashn* or *Jashan*, kept annually on the anniversary day (*Julūs*) of the Emperor: curiously enough, it does not seem to be mentioned in the *Āīn*. Humayun observed it in 1531 (Erskine, *Hist. of India*, ii, 10). Special coins, known as *nisār*, were scattered amongst the crowd on such occasions (Lane-Poole, *H. of the Moghul Emperors*, lxxxv, ff.).

[3] The ninth month of the Muhammadan year. Owing to the fact that the calendar is lunar, it does not always fall at the same time of our year. When it occurs in the hot season the fast is exceptionally severe.

in Coaches, others in *Palenkeens*, with their large Troops of Servitors: Then five Elephants in Armour, with Banners supported by those that were in their Seats, capable of a dozen Sitters; they manage them by one Rider sitting near his Neck, with an Iron Instrument a Cubit in length, the Point bended downwards as long as a Finger, ascribed by *Livy*[1] to the Invention of that famous Leader's Brother *Asdrubal*, who seeing these Creatures of great Terror to the Enemy, but if taking an heedless Course were as liable to damage Friend as Foe, found out this Remedy; delivering a Graver to their Masters with an Hammer, ordered them to strike it with their main strength on the Juncture where their Head was fastned to their Neck, if they were unruly, whereby the great Bulk fell to the Ground. *Magister fabrile scalprum, cum malleo inter aures positum, ipsâ in compage quâ jungitur capiti cervix, quanto maximo poterat ictu adigebat*, But afterwards they learned by striking on the Vertebra's of the Neck, to rule them; which Custom I see here maintained. After these came a Dozen Leopards on State-*Hackeries* with their Keepers, who train them up to hunting.[2] At convenient distances the Trumpets sounded, and Camels of War with *Patereroes*,[3] on their Saddles, marched with a Pace laborious

---

[1] Livy, xxxvii, 47, 1; xxvii, 49.

[2] Akbar used to have his hunting leopards (*chītā*) carried on horses, carts, or in litters (*Āīn*, i, 287). In Manucci (iv, 302) there is a drawing of a leopard carried on a sort of shelf behind the saddle of a horseman. Mundy (*Pen and Pencil Sketches*, 24) gives a drawing of a cart such as Fryer describes. Fanny Parkes (*Wanderings*, i, 398) gives a lively account of her adventure, when she sat on the leopard's cart and accidentally interfered with his tail.

[3] Span. *pedrero*, an engine for flinging stones: later, a piece of ordnance for discharging pieces of broken iron, etc., and for firing salutes. "We saw one small Iron gun mounted and an Iron Pateraro" (Hedges, *Diary*, i, 67). "Prows, each to carry 10 gunns and Pattareros" (Bowrey, 254). Herbert (p. 127) speaks of "pedroes," and in a Portuguese indent of 1530 we have "camellos pedreiros

to the Guiders, giving them a Disease not much different from a *Gonorrhea.* Here nothing was seen but Banners and Streamers, nor heard but Kettle-Drums and Trumpets; after which followed the Governor in the middle of a Troop of Soldiers, all in Coats of Mail and Head-pieces, armed at all Points, both themselves and Horses; himself mounted on a little She-Elephant, with all the Trappings and Accoutrements of State. *Et ad morem antiquum quo puberes filii & jam in virili togâ, comitabantur triumphantem patrem, quod etiam ex Livio appareat de Paulo loquente.*[1] Two or three Striplings (his own Children) rode smiling with him, who were very White respectively; the Governor himself being a *Mogul,* which is as much as *Suffet*[2] in *Arabic,* from whence the *Persian* Emperor is called *Suffee,* and this, *Mogul,* as being derived from the same Parent; as also are all those descended from them. In this State he rode to a Place set apart for this Day's Solemnity, out of the Walls, to the Queen's Garden-Gate, before which it stands, where after Prayers he receives the Compliments of the Grandees, and return to Feast.

At this time the Walls of the City, and Towers of the Castle, wanted not their Adornments, being bestuck with bloody Ensigns, and smoking with Guns of Jubilee, as well as tooting with their Trumpets, and beating with their Drums; as the *Jews* on their Sabbaths, or their solemn Feast days were wont.

The New Moon before the New Year (which com-

(swivel-guns)" (Danvers, i, 410). They are mentioned by Manucci (ii, 100, iv, 430). Commodore Trunnion (*Peregrine Pickle,* ch. ii) "planted his courtyard with patereros continually loaded with shot."

[1] The custom of the General's children sitting, on his triumph, in his chariot, or riding with him is attested by Livy, xlv, 40, 8; and see Tacitus, *Ann.*, ii, 41.

[2] The Sūfī, Safavī, or Safī dynasty, which ruled Persia, 1449-1722 A.D., and nominally till 1736 (Yule, *Hobson-Jobson,* 855).

mences at the *Vernal Equinox*) is the *Moors Æde*,[1] when the Governor in no less Pomp than before, goes to sacrifice a Ram or He-Goat, in remembrance of that offered for *Isaac* (by them called *Ishauh*);[2] the like does every one in his own House, that is able to purchase one, and sprinkle their Blood on the sides of their Doors.

About this time the *Moors* solemnize the Exequies of *Hosseen Gosseen*,[3] a time of ten days Mourning for two Unfortunate Champions of theirs, who perished by Thirst in the Deserts, fighting against the Christians: Wherefore every Corner of the Street is supplied with Jars of Water; and they run up and down like Furies in quest of these two Brethren, laying about with Swords, Clubs, and Staves, crying with that earnestness upon their Names, and dancing in such Antick Dances as resemble the *Pyrrhical* Saltation. *Hæc Celebratio non omnino dissimilis ei generi exerceri solita à juvenibus armatis Lacedemoniæ cum Patris Achillis rogum celebraret*;[4] that a sober Man could make no other judgment on them, than that they were distracted. This is done through the Streets, where if two Companies encounter, they seldom part without bloody Noses; which Occasion being given like *Esau*'s Intentions on the Day of his Father's Lamentation, to revenge himself on his Brother *Jacob*, has been the Cause why the *Mogul* has restrained it for the prevention of Outrages;[5] but yet his Mandate is not so valid to

[1] I'du'l-Azhā, Baqarah 'Īd, or the cow festival, celebrated on 10th Zū'l-Hijjah: known to Europeans in India as the Bakri 'Īd, or goat festival (Hughes, *Dict.*, 192; Yule, *Ibid.*, 336).

[2] Ishāq.

[3] Hasan-Husain, the names of the martyrs; the cry at the Muharram festival, corrupted by the earlier Anglo-Indians into "Hobson-Jobson" (Yule, *Ibid.*, 419).

[4] For *solita* read *solito*: for *Patris filii*. The worship of Achilles in the Peloponnesus is discussed by Frazer, *Pausanias*, iii, 367.

[5] Mr. Jadunath Sarkar refers to Khāfī Khān (*Muntakhab-ul-labāb*, *Bibliotheca Indica*, ii, 213 f.), where it is stated that in 1669, on account of a fatal riot arising from the celebration at Burhānpur, Aurangzeb

S

make them forsake it here: After Sun-set they eat, and fall to singing the Psalms of *Doud*, or *David*, in the most consonant Tone I have heard.

The last Day they prepare a couple of Coffins,[1] and have a Man or two on Horseback all bestuck like our Man in the Almanack,[2] with Arrows; these ride reeling, and ready to drop off their Horses for Faintness, till they come to the River, where they put the Coffins afloat with a loud Cry, and then returning, repeat with great Veneration their Names, and after this trim their Beards, wash and shift their Cloaths, (all this while worn negligently, as Mourners) and return to their most beastly Vomit of Luxury, than this of more than Manly Fury.

This Religious Bigot of an Emperor *Auren Zeeb*, seeks not to suppress it utterly, but to reduce the Celebration, to preserve their Memories by a pious Respect, suitable to the Gravity of the *Moors*: For, says he, hereby Opportunity is offered to the *Caiphers*[3] (Unbelievers) to think

---

ordered that letters should be sent to all the district Governors forbidding the making of the tombs of the martyrs and carrying them in procession. This passage is omitted by Elliot-Dowson (vii, 284). As a strict Sunnī, Aurangzeb detested the Shī'ahs who celebrate the Muharram. At a much earlier period Sikandar Lodi prohibited the celebration (Elliot-Dowson, iv, 448 *n*).

[1] These are the *ta'ziya*, models representing the tombs, made of a bamboo framework covered with paper (Yule, *Hobson-Jobson*, 904). For an illustration see Broughton, *Letters from a Mahratta Camp*, 55; for the celebration Herklots, *Qanoon-e-Islam*, 112 ff.

[2] This alludes to the woodcuts in the ephimerides of 17th and 18th centuries, illustrating the supposed effects of the planets, etc., on the diseases in various parts of man's body, over which they were imagined to preside. The arrows are merely lines pointing to the various organs of a naked figure, sometimes seated and sometimes erect, each line being characterised by the respective sign of the Zodiac (10th Ser., *Notes and Queries*, ix, 475 f.). "A Fellow with a terrible pair of Whiskers and a Wooden Leg, being stuck round with Pistols, like the Man in the Almanac with Darts, comes swearing and vapouring upon the Quarter-Deck" (Capt. Edward England, *History of the Pirates*, 1726, i, 123; *Ib.*, 10th Ser., x, 118).

[3] Ar. *Kāfir*, an unbeliever in Islām (p. 62).

Musslemen favour the Lewd Worship of the Heathens; which is not only a Scandal to the *Mahometan* Religion, but an Encouragement to the Enemies thereof to persist in their own, whilst such Licentiousness is connived at in that which should be set as a Pattern for them to imitate: For even at this instant he is on a Project to bring them all over to his Faith, and has already begun by two several Taxes or Polls,[1] very severe ones, especially upon the *Brachmins*, making them pay a Gold *Rupee*[2] an Head, and the inferior Tribes proportionable; which has made some *Rajahs* revolt, and here they begin to fly to the *Portugal* Countries, and *Bombaim*; though should they make a joint Resistance they are a thousand to one more than the *Moguls* can with an unanimous Contrivance fairly muster.

On an Eclipse of the Sun or Moon, the *Moors* are in a lamentable Plight, making a great noise with Pots and Pans, and other noisy Instruments; not omitting their Prayers, fancying them prevalent to deliver them from their Travel.[3] When the Heathens, instructed by their *Brachmins*, by a better Philosophy, declare to them the Day before the two great Luminaries are obscured by the Interposition of the Moon's, or Earth's Globe, that

[1] The Jizyah imposed on Hindus by Aurangzeb in 1679-80. The rates, according to Manucci (ii, 234) were: 13⅓ rupees on great merchants; 6½ middle class; poor 3⅓ *per annum*. See Elliot-Dowson, vii, 296; Tod, *Annals*, i, 426 f.; Yule, *Hobson-Jobson*, 460.

[2] The Ashrafī or Gold Mohur. "The Gold Moor, or Gold Roupie, is valued generally at 14 of silver" (Ovington, 249). "The gold rupee of Bengal, Surat, and Bombay, is worth sixteen silver rupees, or eight Roman scudi" (Fra Paolino, 87).

[3] Special prayers, consisting of two *rak'ahs*, are enjoined by the traditions at eclipses (*Mishkāt*, iv, c. 51, tr. Matthews, i, 325). At the present day Muhammadans, as well as Hindus, shout and beat brass vessels, to scare the demon which is swallowing the moon. Bernier (301, 339) and Tavernier (ed. Ball, ii, 247 ff.) give lively accounts of these observances at the eclipse of 1666. The same custom prevails in Persia (Browne, *A Year Amongst the Persians*, 117).

they may Fast, Wash, and Purify themselves for Twenty four Hours before the Eclipse happens, and all the time of its lasting; after which is past, they feast and bestow their Benevolence freely on the *Brachmins*, holding them for this their profound Knowledge, in mighty Admiration.

And though the Jollity and Pomp of the Heathens is much allayed by the Puritanism and unlimited Power of the *Moors*, insomuch that they are wholly forbidden to Burn their Wives with the Husbands; yet must not the *Indians* be totally denied their Feasts, and chiefly that of their publick Nuptials,[1] which comes in twice a Year: as the *Atticks* in their γαμηλιὼν in *January* and *October*, so these in the Months *Fulgannau* and *Puxu*, in *January* and *March*; to enjoy which times of Festivity, the Governor expects large Gratuities, which they collect as every one can afford; All which times they make Processions, and appear, (especially the Children and Young Folks) in rich Dresses of Gold and Silver, Mitres on their Heads, and weighty Sashes about their Middles bedawbed and stained all over with Saffron Colour; the Married Folks riding on Horseback, *Palenkeens*, and Coaches, splendidly adorned, drawn by Oxen, Goats, and Elks, Painted over with Saffron, their Horns tipped with Silver; Musick, Streamers, and Banners going before them, the Women Singing *Epithalamiums*, the Men following, and a great Attendance with Pageants, *Mirchals*,[2] and *Kitsols*,[3] giving *Pawn* and Coco-Nuts frankly, as they pass.

[1] It is not easy to understand exactly what Fryer means. Possibly he was told that the months Phālguna (Feb.-March) and Pūs or Pushya (Dec.-Jan.) were lucky months for marriages, which is not exactly correct. Gujarāt Brahmans marry in any of the five months—Māgh (Jan.-Feb.); Phālguna (Feb.-March); Chaitra (March-April); Baisākh (April-May); Jyestha (May-June), when Jupiter and Venus are in conjunction with the Sun (*Bombay Gaz.*, ix, Pt. I, 40).

[2] See p. 218.

[3] Port. *quitasol*, "bar sun": a Chinese paper umbrella (Yule, *Hobson-Jobson*, 487).

The Ceremonies after Washing and Cleansing, conclude by their Sitting Two Hours Tied by the Neck, while the Priest Prays, the Woman being then Manacled with Gold or Silver Shackles about her Wrists and Ankles, a white Sheet being held over them Unvailed, a Coco-Nut exchanged to confirm the Bargain, and Corn scattered upon them; all Emblems of the Matrimonial Bands, Chastity and a firm resolution to comply with one anothers Fortunes; and then dismisses them, by sprinkling Water on the Married Couple, that they may Increase and Multiply. The Women are never Married more than once, the Men are under no such Obligation.[1]

The first New Moon in *October*, is the *Banyans Dually*,[2] a great Day of Celebration to their *Pagan* Deities, when they are very kind-hearted, presenting their Masters with Gifts, as knowing they shall be no Losers, and Entertain one another with mutual Mirth and Banquetting.

The next Moon their Women flock to the Sacred Wells;[3] where they say, it is not difficult to persuade them to be kind, supposing their Pollutions not to remain after their Washing in these Holy Waters.

March begins with a Licentious Week of Sports and Rejoycing, wherein they are not wanting for Lascivious Discourse, nor are they to be offended at any Jest or Waggery.[4] And to shew their Benificence at the begin-

---

[1] For a full account of a high-caste Hindu wedding in W. India, see *Bombay Gaz.*, ix, Pt. I, 39 ff. The rule against the remarriage of Hindu widows applies only to the higher castes; among those of lower rank the levirate and remarriage of widows are permitted.

[2] Divālī or feast of lamps, celebrated on the new moon day of Kārttik (Oct.-Nov.)

[3] The days on which bathing is auspicious in W. India are so numerous that it is impossible to fix any particular date for this rite (*Bombay Gaz.*, ix, Pt. I, 29).

[4] The Holī, or feast held at the vernal equinox, the full moon of the month Phālguna (Feb.-March): accompanied by much licentiousness.

ning of the Rains, they Treat the Ants and Flies with Sweatmeats and Wafers, studiously setting Hony, Syrups, or any thing that may entice them to their own death, out of their way; allowing them Sugar, or any other dried Confects for their Repast, instead of them.[1]

They are constant Benefactors to the Dogs, which are many, the Bitches littering in the Streets; but avoid touching them, as they would an *Holencore*,[2] whom if their Garments chance to brush, they hie them home, Shift, and Wash.

And now we enter upon the *Agonalia*, first of the *Moors*: They love to outdo one another in Feats of Activity, as Riding full speed, and to stop with a Jerk, or motion of the Body, their Horses being well managed.; Tilting and *Gereeding*,[3] that is, Casting of Darts, both for Utility and Recreation; Shooting with Bows and Arrows, which is near at hand, not far off, as we at Rovers; Running on Foot, which belongs to the *Patta-*

---

[1] The feeding of ants in W. India is done chiefly by pious Srāvaks or Jains, and Vāniyas, the merchant classes (*Ibid.*, ix, Pt. I, 380). "They have a custom in Cambaia, in the high wayes, and woods, to set pots with water, and to caste corne and other graine upon the ground to feed beasts withall" (Linschoten, i, 253). In the Central Provinces at the present day, "when women go out to the fields they take a little sugar and put it on an ant-hill to feed the ants. It is considered a virtuous act to satisfy the *atma* or spirit which resides in all animals; and as there are so many ants, large results can be obtained in their case for a trifling outlay" (Russell, *Census Rep.*, 1901, i, 93). In Madras offerings of milk are made at white ant-hills when people are afflicted with ear-ache and other diseases (Thurston, *Ethnographic Notes*, 295). The custom prevails in many other parts of India (Ralph Fitch, in Pinkerton, ix, 409; *Punjab Notes and Queries*, ii, 115).

[2] See p. 82.

[3] Ar. *jarīdah*, the palm-frond stripped of its leaves, used as a javelin. "They have amongst them [at Cambay] the game of the Jerid, as in Spain" (Barbosa, 56). "The Great Persons of the Court come to the Exercises of the *Girit*, or the Dart, which is perform'd most commonly on Fridays, immediately after their comeing out of the Mosquey" (*Relation of Grand Seignor's Seraglio*, 22). Pyrard de Laval (ii, 110) describes the Portuguese at Goa, "making, on Sundays and holidays, a thousand parades and careers on their horses, during

(*To face p. 279*)

mars,[1] the only Foot-posts of this Country, who Run so many Courses[2] every Morning, or else Dance so many hours to a Tune called the *Patamars* Tune, when they labour as much as a *Lancashire* Man does at *Roger of Coverly*, or the *Tarantula* of their Hornpipe; these wear Feathers in their Turbats.

The Wrestlers Anoint with Oil, and are Naked, only a Belt about their Wastes, in which they weary one another only by pure Strength and Luctation, not by Skill or Circumvention; these two last use Opium to make them perform things beyond their strength; and it is incredible to think how far these will Travel before the virtue of it be worked off.

Hunting of Tigers is sometimes a Pastime, at others a Tragy-Comedy; for besetting a Wood where Tigers lurk, with Men and Horses, and putting a Set of their loud Musick to strike up in the middle of it; they rouze at the unaccustomed Noise, and rushing forth seize the first in their way, if not Shot or Launced, to prevent them: Wild Bulls and *Buffola's* are as dangerous, nor is the Boar less fierce than any of them.

Antilopes are set upon by Leopards on this wise; they carry the Leopards on *Hackeries*, both for less suspicion, and to give them the advantage of their Spring;[3] which if they lose, they follow not their Prey, being for a surprize; wherefore the *Hackeries* wheel

---

which they throw oranges, canes, and reeds." In more modern times, Malcolm, (*Sketches*, 200) writes: "They threw the jerreed (a wooden javelin) at each other with excellent aim; and it was only avoided by extraordinary activity, the horseman sometimes to all appearance throwing himself from his horse, while the jerreed whizzed over him." Herbert (p. 124) calls the game "Giochi di Canni." For other accounts see Lady Sheil, *Glimpses of Life in Persia*, 79; Lane, *Modern Egyptians*, ii, 5.

[1] See p. 102.

[2] Kos, a measure of distance, about 2 miles.

[3] See p. 271.

about at a distance, till they come near enough to apprehend them, they feeding fearless of the *Hackeries*; then with three or four Leaps, after a small Chace seize them, and easily become their Masters.

The Great Men have *Persian* Greyhounds,[1] which they Cloathe in Cold Weather, and some few *Hawks* ; a *Colum*[2] may be Hunted with a Greyhound, as we do Bustards, being a great Fowl and long in Rising.

Buffola's animated by their Keepers, fight with great fury ; their Horns, being reversed, are useless ; but they knock Foreheads with a force adequate to such great Engines, till they are all of a gore, and follow their blow with such vigour, that the strength of their Backs exert themselves into their Natural Parts, which they brandish as if stimulated to Venery ; the stronger will hardly permit the weaker to go back to return with his force, but pressing on him, endeavours to bear him down ; thus foiling one another, they are a long time before they will yield.[3]

Persian Rams set together in this manner, are not parted without a Bloody Catastrophe, which are kept on purpose for the sport of their Great Men ; as likewise are Elephants, who engage at the Will of their Masters.

---

[1] Persian greyhounds are still imported and naturalised in India. "Their coats are ragged and their forms lack symmetry ; but some of these animals recall Sir Walter Scott's 'Maida' of beloved memory" (Kipling, *Beast and Man*, 273). Their blood can be traced in the native breeds known as the Rāmpur and Banjārā hounds. Akbar used to import hunting dogs from Kābul, and especially from the Hazāra country (*Āīn*, i, 290).

[2] The Coolong or great grey crane (*Grus cinerea*) (Yule, *Hobson-Jobson*, 249).

[3] These animal fights, which in India date from the Maurya period, were a favourite amusement of the Mughals (Tavernier, ed. Ball, i, 106). They survive in some of the Native States, as, for instance, at Jodhpur and Baroda ; and they were common at the Court of Oudh (Prinsep, *Imperial India*, 168 ; Rousselet, *India and its Native Princes*, 101, ff. : Lord Valentia, *Travels*, i, 153, 159 ; Arnold, *India Revisited*, 92 : Lady Dufferin, *Viceregal Life in India*, 147).

Here are no Gladiators, but at Cudgels[1] they will play as at Backsword, till they warm one another.

The chief Pleasure of the *Gentiles*, or *Banyans*, is to Cheat one another, conceiving therein the highest Felicity, though it be Cuckolding, which they are expert at. They will play at Chess, or Tables;[2] but their utmost Fewds are determined by the dint of the Tongue, to scold lustily, and to pull one anothers *Puckeries*,[3] or Turbats off, being proverbially termed a *Banyan* Fight.[4]

Nevertheless they are implacable till a secret and sure Revenge fall upon their Adversary, either by maliciously plotting against their Life, by clancular Dealings, or Estate, by unlawful and unjust Extortions: Then you shall have them with this Prayer in their Mouths,

> ——— ——— *Pulchra Laverna*
> *Da mihi fallere, da justum sanctumque videri;*
> *Noctem peccatis & fraudibus adjice nubem.*[5]

Example is more than Precept, and the Youth have no other Education besides their Parents, more than some mean Pedagogue's, who teaches the Children first their Letters or Cyphers on the Ground, by writing on the Dust with their Fingers, which is their Primer; where when they are perfect, they are allowed a Board plastered over which with Cotton they wipe out, when full, as we do from Slates or Table-Books; when they arrive to Paper,

---

[1] The *lāthī* or brass-bound bludgeon of bamboo, commonly carried by men.

[2] Backgammon. "This is the ape of form, Monsieur the nice; That when he plays at tables, chides the dice" (*Love's Labour Lost*, v, 2; Nares, *Glossary*, *s. v.*). See Brand, *Observations on the Popular Antiquities of Great Britain* (1849), ii, 353.

[3] See p. 233.

[4] "This Tongue Tempest is termed there a *Bannian Fight*, for it never rises to Blows or Bloodshed" (Ovington, 275). "The Persians are mightily addicted to ill language, and foul mouth'd reproaches. So that when two men fall out, instead of fighting with their fists, they fight with their tongues, and curse one another" (Tavernier, 235).

[5] Horace, *Epist.*, I, xvi, 60 ff.

they are presumed to be their Crafts-masters, and to earn it.[1]

The *Moors*, who are by Nature slothful, will not take pains; being proud, scorn to be taught; and jealous of the Baseness of Mankind, dare not trust their Children under tuition, for fear of Sodomy; whereby few of their Great Men or Merchants can read, but keep a Scrivan of the *Gentues*: On which account it is the *Bunyans* make all Bargains, and transact all Money-business; and though you hear, see, and understand them, yet you shall be choused, they looking you in the face; for as a piece of Superstition, they must put their Hands under a *Ramerin*,[2] or Mantle, when by their Fingers they instruct one another, and by that slight often contradict their Tongues:[3] Such a subtile Generation is this, and so fitly squared a Place is *Surat* to exercise their Genius in.

In *February* the *Bussorah* Ships, and in *August* the *Juddah* Fleet from the *Red Sea*, each of which, beside our *Europe* Ships, export vast quantities of *Indico*, *Cotton*, *Cotton-Yarn*, and *Silks*; and vend them to the *Caphalay*, waiting on them over-land; so that returning, they are forced to ballast their Ships with *Dates*, *Persian* and *Arabian* Drugs; and freight with Horses from each Place: But the main is brought back in Gold, Silver and Pearl, which does in a manner center here: For

---

[1] This is exactly the mode of instruction in village schools at the present day.

[2] Pamerin; p. 199.

[3] The practice of silent bargaining in India has been noticed by many writers (Varthema, 169; Pyrard de Laval, i, 179; Tavernier, ed. Ball, ii, 68; and see Yule, *Hobson-Jobson*, 849 f.). At the present day in the Bombay opium market "the broker will take the hand of the seller, and throwing a sort of cloak over the two clasped hands so as to effectually conceal them from any standing by . . ." He does the same with the buyer. "The secret is all under the cloak, the prices being determined by signs that are understood by the mere pressure of the fingers" (Maclean, *Guide*, 131).

though it circulates all the World over, yet here it is hoorded, *Regis ad exemplum*, both by King and People, he having Tanks thereof unsealed for many Ages, and the *Gentiles* hide it for Eternity.[1] So that though it be not of the growth of this Country, yet the innate Thrift of the *Gentiles*, and the small occasion of Foreign Expences, and this humour of laying up their Talent in a Napkin, buries the greatest part of the Treasure of the World in *India*:[2] There being a far greater urgency for Cloathing, than that of Superfluity; which is the Spice-Trade of the *South Seas*, which only pays for what it carries off here, all the rest loading their Beasts without the Money returned in their Sacks Mouths; and for all that the *Hollanders* return Money from hence, yet it is swallowed up again by the Trade of the Bay, and a great deal more consumed there for their fine Cloath.

This Year the *Bussorah* Fleet brought the *Bassa* of that Place hither, who is now encamped on a pleasant Green by the River's side; the *Great Mogul* condescending to have the Title of *Sanctuary to the Distressed* inserted among his other Aiery ones, as *King of the World where-ever the Sun shines*, being the Inscription on his *Rupees* in *Persian* Characters (the Court Language.)

---

[1] The complaint that India hoards the gold supply of the world is as old as Pliny (*Hist. Nat.*, vi, 26). The early Muhammadan historian, Shahābu-d Dīn, notices it (Elliot-Dowson, iii, 583). "Gold and silver, after circulating in every other quarter of the globe, come at length to be swallowed up, lost in some measure, in *Hindustan*" (Bernier, 202, 222 ff., 473 ff.). Tavernier (ed. Ball, ii, 205) attributes it to the desire of Hindus to bury treasure for use in the next world. It attracted the attention of the early Anglo-Indian officials (Foster, *Letters Received*, iv, Intro., xxxiii). For the present aspect of the question, see *Imperial Gaz.* (1907), iii, 269, 291 f.

[2] This is a curious remark in the light of modern discoveries and the statements of ancient writers (Herod., iii, 106; Ktesias, *Indika*, 12). But in Mughal times the main source of gold was the Himalaya (*Āīn*, i, 37). For the present supply, see *Imperial Gaz.*, iii, 141 ff.; Watt, *Econ. Dict.*, iii, 519 ff.

Dergs hau sic casud chubadera moneir
Paudshaw Aureng zeeb Allum Geir.[1]

For which sake he dispatched Five hundred Horsemen, and Three hundred *Camels*, to receive the *Bassa*, his Family and Retinue, ashore; who being Governor in *Mesopotamia* for the *Grand Seignior*, grew powerful, and was therefore suspected; which drew the forces of the *Sultan* his Master upon him; but knowing the Sea open, he sues to the *Mogul* for Protection, who promised not only to receive him, but imploy him honourably; and as a Testimony of his sincere Intentions, has sent these to attend him in Court.

The Trade of Jewellers is no small addition to the Profit of this Town, which I shall not now specify, intending to treat of them apart, both for yours and my own satisfaction, together with a general Collection of Coins and Weights, as time and opportunity shall make me better acquainted: In the mean time, telling you what I saw at the House of an *Hindu* that wrought in Coral, where was to be wondred the Tools he worked with, more than his Art, because we see it surpassed in *Europe*; but with far more invention of Instruments: Here Hands and Feet being all the Vice, and the other Tools unshapen bits of Iron: From whence I went the same day to a *Moorman* that cuts all sorts of Stones, except Diamonds, with a certain Wheel made of Lacre[2]

---

[1] Fryer's reading runs: *Dar jahān sikkah zad chū badr i munīr; Pādshāh Aurangzīb 'Ālamgīr*. The better reading is given by Manucci (i, 339; ii, 131): *Sikkah zad dar jahān chūn badr-i-munīr, Shāh Aurangzīb-i-'Ālamgīr*. "Struck coin in the world like sun and moon, Aurangzīb, the conqueror of the world." Lane-Poole (*H. of Mogul Emperors*, cli) gives *Sikkah zad dar jahān chū muhr i munīr, Shāh Aurangzīb 'Ālamgīr*. Also see Bernier, 149.

[2] Lac (Yule, *Hobson-Jobson*, 499). The stone now used with the melted lac is powdered corundum (see Baden-Powell, *Handbook of the Manufactures and Arts of the Punjab* (1872), p. 193.

and Stone ground and incorporated, only to be had at *Cochin*, and there the Name is known.

They cut Diamonds with a Mill turned by Men, the String reaching, in manner of our Cutlers Wheels, to lesser that are in a flat Press, where under Steel-wheels the Diamonds are fastned; and with its own Bort are worn into what Cut the Artist pleases: These are sold most in the Country, they coming short of the *Fringies* in Fancy; wherefore they are sent rough into *Europe*, where they are both set and cut to more advantage.

A *Banyan* that seemingly is not worth a *Gosbeek*[1] (the lowest Coin they have) shall pull out of his *Puckery*[2] some thousand Poundsworth of these for sale; when all the Wariness in the World is required, and so I dismiss them.

This City is very nasty by their want of Privies, and their making every Door a Dunghill; yet never had they any Plague, the Heats evaporating, and the Rains washing this Filth away.[3]

The Diseases reign according to the Seasons; the *North* blowing, Bodies are rendered firm, solid and active by exhausting the Serous Humours, *ad Hyp.* 17. *Aph. Lib.* 3. for which cause Dry Weather is more healthy than Moist, it hastening Digestion, and facilitating Excretion, when no Fevers that are treacherous root themselves in a deep Putrefaction. About the Variable Months they are miserably afflicted with Coughs and Catarrhs, Tumors of the Mouth and Throat, Rheumatisms, and intermitting Fevers; Also Small Pox invades the Youth, as in all *India*, so here: In the extreme Heats, *Cholera Morbus*,

---

[1] A coin, which Herbert (p. 231) values at a penny (Yule, *Hobson-Jobson*, 389).

[2] See p. 233.

[3] Ovington (p. 316) refers to the filth of the Surat streets. Fryer's reference to plague was ominous. Soon after his visit, in 1684, it broke out, and raged for six years (*Ibid.*, 347 f.)

Inflammation of the Eyes by Dust and the fiery Temper of the Air: In the Rains, Fluxes, Apoplexies, and all Distempers of the Brain, as well as Stomach; to correct which, the Natives eat *Hing*,[1] a sort of liquid *Assa Fœtida*, whereby they smell odiously. For all Lethargick Fits they use Garlick and Ginger, given in Oyl or Butter.

To Cup they use *Ventosoes*,[2] without Scarifications. They have good Escaroticks and Vesicatories, made by a certain Nut, the same they chop or mark their Calicuts black with instead of Ink,[3]

They apply Cauteries most unmercifully in a *Mordisheen*,[4] called so by the *Portugals*, being a Vomiting with a Loosness; the like is done in a Calenture.[5]

Physick here is now as in former days, open to all Pretenders; here being no Bars of Authority, or formal Graduation, Examination or Proof of their Proficiency; but every one ventures, and every one suffers; and those that are most skilled, have it by Tradition, or former Experience descending in their Families; not considering either alteration of Tempers or Seasons, but what succeeded well to one, they apply to all.[6]

In Fevers their Method is to prescribe Coolers, till they have extinguished the Vital Heat; and if the Patients are so robust to conquer the Remedies used to quench the Flame of the Acute Disease, yet are they

---

[1] Hind. *hīng* (Yule, *Hobson-Jobson*, 418).

[2] Port. *ventosa*, "a cupping-glass."

[3] Probably the Marking-nut tree (*Semecarpus anacardium*). The pericarp of the fruit contains an astringent principle, used as marking-ink, and giving a black colour to cotton fabrics, while it is a powerful vesicant (Watt, *Econ. Dict.*, vi, Pt. II, 498 ff.).

[4] Mort de chien, Mahr. *modachī*, cholera (Yule, *Ibid.*, 586).

[5] See p. 48.

[6] Fryer's remarks, in a measure, still apply to native methods of medicine and surgery. Compare the account given by A. Hamilton, *New Account*, i, 153. Still the Portuguese preferred natives to their own physicians (Linschoten, i, 230; Pyrard de Laval, ii, 70).

left labouring under Chronical ones, as Dropsy, Jaundice, and Ill Habits, a long while before they recover their Pristine Heat.

They are unskill'd in Anatomy, even those of the *Moors* who follow the *Arabians*, thinking it unlawful to dissect Human Bodies; whereupon Phlebotomy is not understood, they being ignorant how the Veins lye; but they will worry themselves Martyrs to death by Leeches, clapping on an hundred at once, which they know not how to pull off, till they have filled themselves, and drop of their own accord.

Chirurgery is in as bad a plight, Amputation being an horrid thing: Yet I confess it is strange to see, that what Nature will effect on such Bodies, Intemperance has not debauch'd.

Pharmacy is in no better condition; Apothecaries here being no more than Perfumers or Druggists, at best; for he that has the boldness to practise, makes up his own Medicines, which are generally such Draughts, that if their own Energy work not, yet the very Weight must force an Operation.

They pretend to understand the Pulse, but the Urine they will not look on.

I have seen a Barber undertake the Cure of a Bloody Flux, by pretending the Guts were displaced, and laying the Patient on his Back, and gently tickling his Reins, thrust on each side the *Abdomen* with all his strength; then placing a Pot filled with dried Earth, like that of *Samos*,[1] upon his Navel, he made it fast by a Ligature; and on some Bodies thus treated he had gained Credit,

[1] The virtues of the earth of Samos are described by Pliny (*Hist. Nat.*, xxxv, 53 (16)). For a good account of the *terra sigillata* or "holy earth" of Lemnos, see H. F. Tozer, *Islands of the Ægean*, 257 ff.

but this died. *Prosper Alpinus* mentions something like this among the *Egyptians*.

Here they will submit to Spells and Charms, and the Advice of Old Women.

Here is a *Brachmin* Doctor who has raised a good Fortune; they pretend to no Fees, but make them pay in their Physick; and think it Honour enough if you favour them with the Title of your Physician only.

This *Brachmin* comes every day, and feels every Man's Pulse in the Factory, and is often made use of for a Powder for Agues, which works as infallibly as the *Peruvian* Bark; it is a Preparation of Natural *Cinnaber*.[1] Midwifry is in esteem among the Rich and Lazy only; the Poorer, while they are labouring or planting, go aside as if to do their Needs, deliver themselves, wash the Child, and lay it in a Clout or Hammock, and return to work again.

The Mixture of Casts or Tribes of all *India* are distinguished by the different Modes of their binding their Turbats; which cannot be found out presently, there being such variety of Observation.[2]

Amidst which it is time to return, to see what Grace we are in among this divided Multitude: Our Usage by the *Pharmaund*[3] (or Charter) granted successively from their Emperors, is kind enough, but the better, because

---

[1] Four preparations of mercury are still largely used by native physicians: the black sulphide; cinnabar; an impure sulphide; and the perchloride. They are prescribed for fever, lung, and skin diseases (Watt, *Econ. Dict.*, v, 235).

[2] In W. India, "the Konkani Brahmin has on his head a disc of artfully-folded red calico, three or four feet in diameter: the Bhatia has the top of his turban curled up above his forehead, like a rhinoceros' horn; the Sikh has a closely-fitting and neatly-folded turban; the fishermen's turban is usually made out a piece of old fishing-net; and a Mahratta's head-dress looks like a bundle of tightly-twisted snakes" (Balfour, *Cycl.*, iii, 78).

[3] Pers. *farmān* (Yule, *Hobson-Jobson*, 354).

our Naval Power curbs them ; otherwise they being prone to be imperious, would subjugate us, as they do all others that are harness'd with the Apron-strings of Trade :[1] Supposing us then to bear the Face of Ministers of State, as well as the sly Visage of Mechanicks, they depose something of their Ferity, and treat with us in a more favourable Stile ; giving us the Preference before others here resident, and look on us with the same Aspect as they do on their great *Ombrahs*.[2]

In Town there are many private Merchants that bear a Port equal to our *Europe* Companies, being only *Vockeels*[3] or Factors for money'd Men up the Country, that drive as great a Trade as the Company, yet dare not assume that Liberty allowed us : We fortify our Houses, have *Bunders*[4] or Docks for our Vessels, to which belong Yards for Seamen, Soldiers, and Stores : To that which belongs to the *Dutch* is a sweet Garden, shor'd up with Timber from the incroaching River, with Arbors and Beds after the *Europe* Mode.[5]

Among the Rarities of our own House I saw an Unicorn's Horn, not that of the *Rhinoceros*,[6] of which

---

[1] An interesting anticipation of modern views on the command of the sea. Fryer refers to the subject, p. 118. Compare Dalboquerque's answer to the terms of "the Adil Khan" (Danvers, i, 195).

[2] Ar. *umarā*, "the Amīrs" (Yule, *Ibid.*, 631). For the position of the Ombrahs in the time of Aurangzeb, see Bernier, 211 ff.

[3] Ar. *wakīl* (Yule, *Ibid.*, 961).

[4] Pers. *bandar*, a quay, seaport (*Ibid.*, 127).

[5] "Upon the sea-shore, on the other side of the river, the Europeans have their gardens, to which they can retire should at any time the Mahomedans attempt to attack them" (Manucci, i, 62).

[6] The horn of the rhinoceros gained this reputation from being identified with that of the unicorn. The belief that it is useful in detecting poison was, and is, common in the East. "Their hornes in India are much esteemed and used against all venime, poyson, and many other diseases : likewise the teeth, clawes, flesh, skin, and blood, and the very dung, and water, and all whatsoever is about him, is much esteemed in India, and used for the curing of many diseases and sicknesses, which is very good and most true, as I my selfe by experience have found" (Linschoten, ii, 9 f. : cf. i, 96). Also see P. della Valle, i, 5; Stevens, *H. of Persia*, 128; Ovington, 267 ; Barbosa, 101 ; Forbes, *Or. Mem.*[2], i, 438.

Cups are made and profered for Sale here, and are relied on to discover Poyson, if poured into them.

> —*Quod Reges Indorum protinus aureis*
> *Orbibus includunt, & vina liquantia potant,*
> *Actum nec morbos tuti sentire feruntur,*
> *Nec quæ inter mensas occulta hausere venena.*[1]

As also two Skins of *Sabæan* Asses, highly valued among the *Eastern* Princes both for their Swiftness and Beautifulness, being streaked with a dark Grey upon a White Ground, upon the Back direct, in other Parts waving towards their length:[2] As also Pigeons tumbling in the Air, attributed to the Indisposition of their Brain; but to me it appears a voluntary Action, they not falling at all upon it, but after three or four Turns would fly, and repeat it as often as they listed, without any interruption in their Course, and when they seemed to direct themselves to any place, without any Inclination to it, as an Irregularity, but rather out of Affectation; which notwithstanding cannot be taught any, but only those of this kind; no more than any other besides Carriers, (which were here with blubber'd Noses, and of a Brown Colour) to carry Letters: Others walked on the Ground, with their Breasts bearing out, and the Feathers of their Tails spreading like Turkies, bridling their Heads so that they were even with their Rumps; this also is a peculiar Species, and not Artificial; they propagate their own kind, and are of a pied Colour.

From *Siam* are brought hither little *Champore*[3] Cocks

---

[1] In line 3, for "actum," read "ac tum."

[2] This was probably a zebra skin. The Abyssinian embassy to Aurangzeb brought "a small species of mule, whose skin I have seen; no tiger is so beautifully marked, and no *alacha* of the Indies, or striped silken stuff, is more finely and variously streaked" (Bernier, 135).

[3] Bantam fowls, perhaps from Champa, a kingdom of Indo China (Yule, *Hobson-Jobson*, 62, 183).

with ruffed Feet, well armed with Spurs, which have a strutting Gate with them, the truest mettled in the World; they are generally White, with an Eye of Yellow. Here were Milk-White Turtles[1] from *Bussorah*, *Cockatoos*[2] and *Newries*[3] from *Bantam*, as also a *Cassawar*[4] that digests Iron.

From *Amidavad*[5] small Birds, who, besides that they are spotted with White and Red no bigger than Measles, the principal Chorister beginning, the rest in Consort, Fifty in a Cage, make an admirable Chorus.

And also for Vermin, the strongest huge Rats, as big as our Pigs, which burrow under the Houses, and are bold enough to venture on Poultry, and make them their Prey:[6] A *Mongoose*[7] is a-kin to a Ferret: Squirrels delicately streaked White and Black, run about the House, and on top of Terrasses.[8] Musk-Rats of the same Colour, short-feeted, but a Span in length, their Bodies no thicker than a Mouse; they infest the Houses and Water-Jars with their Scent; from which last all Care is taken to preserve them. *Guiana*, a Creature like a Crocodile, which Robbers use to lay hold on by their Tails when they clamber Houses.[9]

---

[1] Turtle doves.

[2] Malay *kākātūwa* (Yule, *Ibid.*, 227).

[3] The Lory parrot (*Ibid.*, 521).

[4] Cassowary (*Ibid.*, 170). "It eats voraciously, and, like the ostrich, will swallow whatever comes in its way" (*Ency.-Brit.*[9], v, 186).

[5] The so-called Avadavat (*Estrelda amandava*), which took its name from Ahmadābād in Gujarāt (Yule, *Ibid.*, 41).

[6] The Bandicoot (*Nesocia bandicota*). It was the habit of the early travellers to exaggerate its size (Blanford, *Mammalia*, 425; Yule, *Ibid.*, 58).

[7] *Herpestes mungo* (Blanford, 119 ff.; Yule, 596).

[8] The pretty palm, or common striped squirrel (*Sciurus palmarum*).

[9] The Iguana, Mahr. *ghorpad*. "The Ghorepurays were originally named Bhonslay, and their ancestor acquired the present surname, according to their family legend, during the Bahminee dynasty, from having been the first to scale a fort in the Concan, which was deemed mpregnable, by fastening a cord round the body of a *ghorepur*, or guana" (Grant Duff, 39; Yule, *Hobson-Jobson*, 397 f.).

For Insects, *Centipedes*, Scorpions, and vast Spiders; these lye perdue, and often set upon People unawares; for the Venom of the two former, they have Oyl made of each;[1] the first is the worst, and often deadly; the other works off after a burning Fit of Four and twenty hours. Abroad in the Fields and Rivers are poysonous Snakes; and here was lately a Woman, as she went to fetch Water at the River, devoured by an Aligator or Crocodile, though the *Brachmins* pretend to Charm them that they shall do no Mischief in this their Sacred River; and this was given out to be a Judgment not otherwise to be expiated.[2]

And now the *Dutch* Fleet being arrived at the River's Mouth (after having demolished the City St. *Thomas*, near *Fort St. George*, the *French* yielding on Discretion), they restored us the Prisoners taken in the Engagement, having treated them very civily: And the Governor was forced to go from *Surat* to *Swally* (to the *Dutch* Commodore, removed thither) to intreat an Agreement; the Clamours of the Merchants being instant, the *Bussorah* Fleet was in jeopardy, which they threatened to seize; but on his Appearance, and Assurance of Satisfaction, all was salved.[3] Lest therefore this should be judged too mean a Compliance, he paid a Visit with all his

---

[1] In Persia this remedy was, and is, popular. Olearius, the secretary of the Holstein embassy in 1637, was bitten by a scorpion at Kashan, and derived great relief from this oil. The same notion prevailed in Europe. Madame de Sévigné, in a letter dated 8th July, 1672, writes: "Je vous prie, quoiqu'on dise, de faire faire de l'huile de scorpion, afin que nous trouvions en même temps les maux et les médicines" (quoted by Curzon, *Persia*, ii, 15 f.).

[2] For charming of crocodiles, see p. 146. Compare with this the account given by Marco Polo (ii, 332) of the S. Indian pearl fishers, who get an "Abraiaman" [Brahman] to charm the sharks. "And their charm holds good for that day only; for at night they dissolve the charm, so that the fishes can work mischief at their will." Tennent (*Ceylon*,[3] ii, 564 f.) says that this custom still prevails.

[3] The French surrendered St. Thomé to the Dutch on 26th August, 1674 (Wheeler, *Madras in the Olden Time*, i, 79).

Pomp to our Deputy-President, still at *Swally*, though the *Europe* Ships were gone, others from the *South*-Seas being expected.

Thus repassing the River after this Great Man, in order to repair aboard Ship, I beheld whole Droves of all Sexes and Ages coming to wash in the River, which is done twice a day; and the Finest Dames of the *Gentues* disdained not to carry Water on their heads, with sometimes two or three Earthen Pots over one another for Household service; the like do all the Women of the *Gentiles*.

On this side the Water are People of another Offspring than those we have yet mentioned; these be called *Parseys*, who were made free Denizens by the *Indians* before the *Moors* were Masters, and have continued to Inhabit where they first set Footing, not being known above Forty Miles along the Sea-coast, nor above Twenty Mile inland.[1] It is likely these upon the overflow of the *Scythians*, and their Irruption into *Persia*, were driven from thence as Fugitives to seek fresh Habitations; which, those furnished with Boats from the *Persian* Gulf, might easily escape hither; where they complying with some Propositions, as not to Kill any Beasts or living Creatures, and Conform to many of the *Gentue* Ceremonies, were Entertained and allowed to live among them.

Since the *Moors* have Subdued the Country, they think themselves not obliged by the former Capitulation, they Feeding on both Fish and Flesh; and for that reason were in hopes of exemption from the present Poll, pretending their Law agreeable to the *Moors*, but that would not free them from the Tax. These drink Wine and are of the Race of the Ancient *Persians*.

---

[1] The Pārsīs are said to have landed at Sanjān A.D. 716. Their compromise with the Hindus of the place is described by Dosabhai Framji Karaka, *H. of the Parsis*, i, 30.

They Worship the Sun, and keep at *Nunsarry*.[1] a Delubrium, where is always a Fire (first kindled by the Sun) kept alive as the Holy Vestal Nuns were wont; they Adore all the Elements, and if at any time they go a Voyage, will not exonerate in the Sea, or on the Water, but have Jarrs on purpose; if their Houses be on fire, they quench them not with Water, rather chusing to load them with Dust or Sand.

These Bury not their Dead, but expose them in round Tombs made on purpose, (open on top, and walled high around, in distinct Apartitions) to the Vultures and ravenous Fowls to Entomb them; and to that end, in the middle of this Enclosure is a Well for the Filth to drain away; the next of Kin, after the Body is put in, Watch aloof, to know what Part these Birds of Prey lay hold on, and from thence make their report of the future Bliss, or ill State of the Deceased.

These are somewhat Whiter, and, I think, Nastier than the *Gentues*;[2] and Live, as they do, all of a Family together; as if the Father be Living, then all the Sons that are Married, and Men grown, with their Wives and Children, house it with the Father, and have a Portion of his Stock; if he die, or be absent, the Eldest Brother

---

[1] Navsārī, lat. 20° 55′ N., long. 73° 10′ E., 18 miles from Surat, where the Pārsis settled in 1142 A.D. Their chief fire temple is now known as the Ātish Bahrām, to which it is said the sacred fire was brought from Vāsenda after the troublous times in 1507. Efforts are made to procure new fire from a tree which has been struck by lightning, the fire thus obtained being purified by holding sandalwood chips over it in an iron sieve, four fires in succession being lighted in this way (*Bombay Gaz.*, vii, 562 ff.; ix, Pt. II, 213; Dosabhai Framji, ii, 213).

[2] Fryer's rather contemptuous account of the Pārsīs, here and at Letter IV, chap. VI, shows that at this time they had gained no commercial importance at Surat. This dates from their settlement at Bombay, which commenced under Portuguese rule, and became more considerable after the transfer of the place to the British. Ovington (pp. 370 ff.) a few years after gives a better account of their condition.

has the Respect of the Father shewn, and so successively; they all Rising up at his Appearance, and Sit not till he be Seated.

These are rather Husbandmen than Merchants, not caring to stir abroad; they supply the Marine with Carts drawn by Oxen, the Ships with Wood and Water; the latter of which is excellent, drawn out of a Well at old *Swally*; where, and at others, the Women put me in mind of *Jacob's* Well, and the Custom of old for them to draw Water, which though here it is fetch'd up by Oxen, yet elsewhere the Women draw in Jarrs, or Earthen Pots. The *Moors* have it brought on *Buffola's* Backs, or else on Oxen; which here also they use, as all over *India*, instead of Pack-horses, their greatest *Caphala's* consisting of them, Horses being only for War or Pleasure, and the best of them Foreigners, and of great Prices; so that 300*l*. is but an easy Rate for a good *Persian* or *Arab*.[1]

Here are brought up large gallant Milk-White Oxen[2] with Circling Horns, artificially Modelled in Cases, which

---

[1] The price of Arab or Persian horses, owing to losses in the sea voyage, was very high. Thus Tavernier (p. 65) writes: "Having spoken of the *Arabian* horses, I must needs say, that there are some that are valu'd at a very high rate. The Mogul's Ambassador gave for some three, four, and six thousand Crowns, and for another he offer'd eight thousand Crowns, but the Horse would not be sold under ten, and so he left it." On his return the Emperor was angry, "upbraid'd the poorness of his spirit, and banish'd him for ever from his presence unto a Province far distant from the Court." Pyrard de Laval (ii, 67) says that Arab and Persian horses sold at Goa from £104 to £112. Linschoten (i, 54) says that good horses cost £224. Tavernier (ed. Ball, i, 102, 385) states that the least valuable of the Mogul's horses cost £875; the best were worth £2250.

[2] The milk-white oxen of Gujarāt have long been famous. "The Gujarāti oxen are good draught cattle; they are of a pure white colour, and handsome; indeed their beauty is the wonder of all beholders" (*Mirāt-i-Ahmadī*, Bayley, *Local Muhammadan Dynasties*, 2). P. della Valle describes them as "fair, large, white, with two bunches like some camells, and run, and gallop, like Horses" (i, 21). Similar accounts are given by Grose, 250; Ovington, 259; Forbes, *Or. Mem.*[2], ii, 184.

they Tip with Silver, Gold, or Brass, and make them shine like Jet; putting a Rope through their Nostrils, and an Headstal on them of *London* Cloath, surrounding their Necks with Collars for Bells, Feeding them delicately as their Horses; and one of these fitted for a Coach, will Sell for 30 or 40*l.* The other Oxen are Little, but all have a Bunch on their Neck; and how they become Oxen is on this manner; Their Religion not allowing them to Castrate them, they Bruise their Testicles, not Geld them by Cutting them off when Young; which answers the intention as fully as the other. This kind of restraint upon Nature is exercised on no Brutes but these, they never offering to deprive their Horses of their Stones or Tails, which they always suffer to grow; a Bobtailed Nag, or Gelding, being as rare here, as a Crop-eared Horse, which never was seen.

A *Buffola* is of a Dun Colour, and are all as big as their largest Oxen; they love to wallow in the Mire like an Hog; there are of them Wild, which are very Fierce and Mischievous, Trampling a Man to Death, or Moiling him to Pieces with their Foreheads; their Horns are carelessly turned with Knobs around, being usually so ordered, or rather disordered (for they retain no certain Form) that they lie too much over their Heads to do any harm with them. Their Flesh is reckon'd Hotter and Courser than Beef, which is the most common Sustinence of the *Moors*;[1] as their Milk and boiled Butter is of the *Gentues*; for did they not boil their Butter, it would be Rank, but after it has passed the Fire, they keep it in Duppers[2] the year round: On which Dr *N. G.* in

[1] Buffalo beef is rank and coarse. Tavernier (ed. Ball, ii, 37) says that it causes dysentery. Now-a-days it is cheap, but none, except the poorest classes, knowingly eat it (*Bombay Gaz.*, xiv, 20).

[2] Hind. *dabbā*, a vessel made of green buffalo hide, which, when dried and stiffened, is used for holding and transporting *ghī*, oil, etc. (Yule, *Hobson-Jobson*, 328).

his Account of the Rarities of the Royal Society, has sufficiently enlarged.

Here in the Marshes are brought up great store of Cattle of all sorts; and though there lie store of *Aligators* to and again, they are seldome known to Prey either on them or their Young; so that what stir they make of Charming them, is but a pious Fraud of the *Brachmins*, they being a lazy sort of Amphibious Creature, feeding on Grass as well as Fish, and I question whether ever their Appetite stand towards Flesh.[1]

The Mutton here is not much inferior to the Mutton of *England*, for the Pallat, though as to its Wool, there is no compare. Cows Butter sometimes will be hard in the Cold Season, and look yellow, but they arrive not to the making of Cheese, unless it be Soft Cheese, which pickled, our Seamen keep a good while, as they do their *Achars*.[2]

Here grow Carrots, Turnips, Rhadishes; Cabbage rarely, though Coleworts frequently; Melons of all sorts, and Betes: Wheat as good as the world affords; Rice, Barley, Millet, and Nuchanny;[3] Pease and Beans; Oyl-Trees,[4] and Rape[5] for Lamp Oyl; (only Wax Candles for the Rich, by reason of the warmth being to be used).

Herbs for Salading are Purslain, Sorrel, Lettice, Parsley, Tarentine, Mint, and Sog,[6] a sort of Spinach.

---

[1] The Magar or snub-nosed alligator is certainly a cattle-eater. For charming them, see p. 292.

[2] Pers. *āchār*, acid and salt relishes, pickles (Yule, *Hobson-Jobson*, 3).

[3] Mahr. *nāchanī*, *nāchnī*, the Raggy millet (*Eleusine coracana*) (Watt, *Econ. Dict.*, iii, 237)).

[4] He may refer to the castor-oil plant (*Ricinus communis*), which, on rich soil, grows to a considerable height (*Ibid.*, vi, Pt. I, 506).

[5] *Brassica campestris*, of which there are at least three varieties (*Ibid.*, i, 522).

[6] Hind. *sāg*, pot herbs.

Here Asparagus[1] flourish, as do Limes, Pomegranates, Genitins;[2] Grapes in abundance; but the *Moors* suffer no Wine to be made.

Fish, Oisters, Soles, and *Indian* Mackerel,[3] the River yields very good, and the Pools and Lakes store of Wild Fowl; peculiarly Brand Geese, Colum, and Serass, a Species of the former; in the Cold Weather they shunning the *Northern* rigid Blasts, come yearly hither from Mount *Caucasus*; what is worth taking notice of, is their Aspera Arteria, wound up in a Case on both sides their Breastbone in manner of a Trumpet, such as our Waits use; when it is single it is a Serass, when double a Colum, making a greater Noise than a Bitte n, being heard a great while before they can be seen, flying in Armies in the Air.[4]

As we came nearer *Swally*, Groves of *Brabb*[5]- *Trees* present themselves; from whence the *Parseys* draw Wine a-kin to Toddy, which after the Sun is up, contracts an Eagerness with an heady Quality; so that these places are seldom free from Soldiers and Seamen of the *Moors*, which sometimes meeting with ours, there happen bloody Frays, especially if the Quarrel be about Strumpets, who here ply for their Fares: The like disputes are sometimes among the *Europeans* themselves, and then they

---

[1] For the numerous varieties of Indian asparagus, see Watt, *Econ. Dict*, i, 343.

[2] Pomme de St. Jean, varieties of the apple or pear.

[3] The Horse Mackerel (*Caranx affinis*, Day, *Fish, Ind.*, 219) or the mackerel (*Scomber micrclepidotus*, *Ibid.*, 250) is perhaps meant.

[4] Hind. *sāras*, the great grey crane (*Grus antigone*) (Yule, *Hobson-Jobson*, 289). "The Crane's power of uttering the sonorous and peculiar trumpet-like notes is commonly and perhaps correctly ascribed to the formation of its trachea, which on quitting the lower end of the neck passes backwards between the branches of the furcula, and is received into the hollow space formed by the bony walls of the carina or keel of the sternum. Herein it makes three turns, and then runs upwards and backwards to the lungs" (*Ency. Brit.*[9], vi, 546).

[5] See p. 196.

make sport for the *Parsèys* upon the Trees, who have the diversion of the Combatants; as Boxing among the *English*; Snicker-Sneeing[1] among the *Dutch*; ripping one anothers Bellies open with short Knives;[2] Duelling with Rapiers among the *French*; Sword and Dagger among the *Portugals*.

Coming to the Marine, beside the *Dutch* Fleet and *English* Ships, were Four *Arabs* with Red Colours, like Streamers, Riding in the Hole. These are true Rovers both by Sea and Land; they are constantly upon the Plunder with the *Portugals*, but care not to engage where nothing is to be gotten but Blows, wasting those Places that lie most open on the Sea-coast and Unguarded.

These have lately fitted themselves with good stout Ships at *Surat*, their own Country supplying them with no Materials for Building; the non-payment whereof, according to the Contract with the Governor, at present has put a stop to their increase that way in Shipping; and has kindled matter for farther alarming the Merchants: For the Governor, for his security, has seised the *Imaum's Vockeel*,[3] nor intends he to enlarge him till the uttermost *Gosbeek*[4] be paid.

On this Pretence they begin to interrupt the Merchants on the Seas, seising their Vessels, and furnishing themselves at cheaper Rates.

Nor does their late Enterprize over the *Portugals* make them less formidable; so that if they be not checked by

---

1 "Snick-a-snee, fighting with knives, a Dutch word apparently [Icelandic *snikka*, "to nick, cut"], and used generally when speaking of Dutchmen. In Norfolk, a sort of large clasp-knife is still called a "*snickersnee*" (Nares, *Gloss.*, *s. v.*)

2 Compare the Japanese Harakiri (Yule, *Hobson-Jobson*, 411). As a punishment, it is referred to by Herbert (p. 172). Muizzuddin at Patna in 1712 was charged with ripping up women in child (Wilson. *Early Annals*, ii, 50).

3 Ar. Wakil, "an attorney" (Yule, *Ibid.*, 691).

4 See p. 285.

these Knights of *Lisboa*, they will infest this Ocean, no less than the *Moors* of *Algiers*, *Tunis* and *Tripoly*, do the *Narrow Seas* in the *Mediterranean*, especially the *Gulf* of *Persia*, in whose Mouth they are conveniently seated, and villainously inclined; in which it concerns them to omit no Diligence.

Having staid here since the close of the Rains, all the Cold Season, and beginning of the variable Winds, which are sent hither to qualify the Heats before the fall of the Rains (they blowing very high) I left the most frequented Port in *India*, and the only one on this Coast the *Mogul* has.

It is a Corporation exempt from any Jurisdiction but the Emperor's; though it be but the second City of the Province, and within this last Century, by the concourse of the *Europeans*, advanced from a Fishing Town to be so great an Empory.

Ro Neal,[1] a Mile beyond it on *Swally* side, was once before it, now abandoned to Seamen and Washermen: The Customers then paid half to the *Portugals*, who once a-year came with their Provoes[2] and received their Levies; since this is become of more note, it is better looked after by the *Mogul*, than that was by the Emperor of *Cambaia*.

It has for its Maintainance the Incomes of Thirty six Villages; over which the Governor sometimes presides, sometimes not, being in the *Jaggea*[3] or Dioces of

---

[1] Rānder, Lat. 21° 13′ N., long. 70° 51′ E., a place on the right bank of the Tapti, about two miles above Surat. It is the Ravel of Barbosa (p. 67). In contemporary records it appears in various forms—Roan, Raneill,' Raneale (Anderson, 375; *Bombay Gaz.*, xxvi, 122; Foster, *English Factories*, 1618-1621, 130, 137, 158). It was once a place of importance, but declined from the end of the 16th century owing to the growth of Surat (*Bombay Gaz.*, ii, 299; *Āīn*, ii, 243).

[2] See p. 65.

[3] Pers. *jāgīr*, "place-holding"; an assignment of rent-free land (Yule, *Hobson-Jobson*, 446).

another; who fail not once a-year to send to reap the Profit, which is received by the Hands of the *Desie*[1] or Farmer, who squeezes the Countryman, as much as the Governor does the Citizen: Corn being distributed among them for so much Earth as they Till, which at the time of Harvest is not carried home, before the *Desie* hath taken Three parts, leaving no more for their pains, and to sow the Land again, than One.

The Business of the Customs, as we have already said, is ordered by the Chief Customer, who has *Chockies*[2] in all Inland Parts to receive Toll, and is responsible to none, only the Emperor.

To govern the Province, *Mahmud Emir Caun*[3] is entrusted, the Son of *Emir Jemla*, who established *Aurenzeeb* in his Throne.

His Metropolis is at *Amidavad*,[4] the Chief City of *Guzerat*: Who notwithstanding he has vast Forces, Wealth and Territories, is not able to quell the *Coolies*[5] from pilfring, *Seva-Gi* from plundring, and the Outlawed *Raspoots* from dispoiling, where-ever they please to descend in Companies from the Mountains, or Troops out of the Desart of *Sinda*: Though none of these, nor

---

1 Mahr. *desāī*, head-man of a district, or petty chief (*Ibid.*, 306).

2 Hind. *chaukī*, a custom-station (*Ibid.*, 205).

3 Muhammad Amīn Khān, son of Mīr Muhammad Sa'īd Ardastānī, surnamed Mīr Jumla. In 1674 he succeeded Mahārājā Jasvant Singh as thirty-sixth Viceroy of Gujarāt. He died at Ahmadābād on 4th June, 1683 (Grant Duff, 68; *Bombay Gaz.*, i, Pt. I, 285; Manucci, ii, 203). Mr. Irvine points out that the references in Elliot-Dowson (vii, 108 f., 517) apply to two different persons, the former to this man, the second to the Wazīr, a Tūrānī and cousin of Nizām-ul-Mulk, Asaf Jāh.

4 Ahmadābād, capital of Gujarāt.

5 The Kolīs, a famous predatory tribe in Gujarāt, who though they have unwillingly taken to husbandry, still are thieves (*Bombay Gaz.*, ix, Pt. I, 237 ff.; Bayley, *Gujarat*, 86; Elliot-Dowson, v, 446 f.) "Others that yet dwell within the Countrie called Colles which Colles, Venesares, and Reysbutos of Cambaia doe yet live by robbing and stealing" (Linschoten, i, 166).

all joined together, can cope with him in a pitched Field, but only by Thievery and Surprise: Wherefore when any *Caphala*[1] or Treasure passes, they hire Soldiers to guard it, otherwise they are liable to be made a Prey.

Where these Difficulties removed, *Surat*, as if Nature had designed her both by Sea and Land the Seat of Traffick, would have nothing to hinder her from being the compleatest Mistress thereof in the whole World: If the Disposition of the People be considered, what Masters they are of this Faculty, of Buying at small, and Vending at great Rates, both Native and Exotick Wares! The sordid Penury of the *Banyans* that live poorly and meanly, yet worth a King's Exchequer; and notwithstanding the Governor often finds occasion to fleece them, yet by the quickness of Merchandise passing thorough this City, they recruit on a suddain.

The commodiousness of the River serving to bring Goods in from *Europe, Asia, Africa* and *America*; the long continued Current from the *Inland* parts through the vast Wildernesses of huge Woods and Forests, wafts great Rafts of Timber for Shipping, and Building; and *Damar*[2] for Pitch, the finest scented *Bitumen* (if it be not a Gum or Rosin) I ever met with.

And if the King's Fleet be but ordinary, considering so great a Monarch and these Advantages, it is because he minds it not; he contenting himself in the enjoyment of the *Continent*, and styles the Christians Lions of the Sea; saying that God has allotted that Unstable Element for their Rule.

They have not only *Cair*[3]-*Yarn* made of the *Cocoe* for

---

[1] See p. 221.

[2] Malayo-Javanese *damar*, a term used for various resins employed as pitch (Yule, *Hobson-Jobson*, 294).

[3] Coir, Tamil *kayiru*, the fibre of coco-nut husk made into rope. (*Ibid.*, 233).

Cordage, but good Flax and Hemp; and Iron from the Mountains of the *South*:[1] So that it may be concluded, for the Benefit of an Harbour, for the Dispositions of the Natives, for a convenient Supply (or more truly Abundance) of all things, for a due imployment of them; but above all, for the Commodities Exported, and the Riches Imported, *Surat* cannot be fellowed in *India*.[2]

CHAP. IV.

Brings me with a New Deputy-Governor from Surat *to* Bombaim, *and sends me to the* Mogul's *General at* Jeneah.

THE Fourth of *April* 1675, arriving at *Bombaim* with Mr. *Gyfford*,[3] he was reinstated Deputy-Governor of that Island; Captain *Shaxton*[4] in this interim having his Sword demanded from him by the Governor, and had been under Confinement; being bound to answer

---

[1] For the production of iron by native methods in Central and S. India, see Watt, *Econ. Dict.*, iv, 499 ff.

[2] During the 17th and 18th centuries Surat ranked as the chief import and export centre of India. The transfer of trade to Bombay, the famine of 1813 in N. Gujarāt, fire and flood in 1837, all greatly depressed it. Its condition is now fairly thriving (*Imperial Gazette*, xxiii, 165 f.)

[3] Philip Gyfford was Deputy-Governor of Bombay from 1670-1 till his death in 1676. Birdwood (*Report*, 86) suggests that he was a connection of William Gyfford, Governor of Bombay, 1681-7. On this see Hedges, *Diary*, ii, 185, and Anderson, 119. The Council of Surat, in a letter dated 4th November, 1676, wrote: "In persuance of o'r former intentions we have considered ye necessity of resettling the Government of Bombay, and though our worthy ffreind, Mr. Phillip Gysford [? Gyfford], be still in being . . . yett seeing his condition is such yt promises little hopes of life"; they nominate John Pettit to succeed in the event of his death (Forrest, *Home Papers*, i, 108).

[4] Captain Shaxton was sent out in 1671 in command of a Company, and afterwards, in consideration of his high character, was appointed Factor. He was suspected of abetting the Mutiny of 1674. Fryer takes his side in the matter. At any rate, he was obliged to give up his sword; was tried; the case referred to the Court of Directors; and he was sent to England, where he died at the end of his voyage (Anderson, 219 f.; Bruce, *Annals*, ii, 367 f.; Hunter, *H. of B. India*, ii, 204). A Madame Shaxton, perhaps his wife, seems to have remained in India, where the authorities commend her case to the consideration of the Directors (Forrest, *Ibid.*, i, 82, 124).

an Indictment, wherein he was accused of Abetting the Mutinous Soldiers.

For whose Trial, after a long endeavour to bring him to acknowledgment, was erected a select Court of Judicature, and an Attorny ordered to impeach him, who with some borrowed Rhetorick endeavoured to make him appear a Second *Catiline*; but he cleared himself so handsomely of all Objections (being sick at that time the Stirs were, and having no reference to him, their Complaints being of another nature, as the taking Money for more than could be passed current again, and other like pretended Exactions) that they had no more to answer, than that it should be referred to the Company; before whom he must personally appear, and therefore was ordered home, but was prevented by Death at the end of his Voyage: Otherwise he would have made it plain, Envy had underhand worked, what she durst not attempt boldly on a Man of Honour; and for no other Reason, than that he understood himself as a Soldier, and in that point would be known.

By this Man's Misfortune might have been seen the dislike that the Company's Servants bear towards any of equal poise with themselves, and not of that Rank; for thereby they count they are injured, having others put over their heads, as 'tis termed; but if by chance they convince them of their Folly, it becomes a Crime unpardonable: The first ground of this Quarrel being upon unnecessary Appendices to the Fort, as Pallisadoes in Mud, so contrived, that they were rather a means to take than defend it, which afterwards were all washed away by the Rains; to these some Despight being added (he being a Man sharp in his Jests, and blunt in Counsel) it never ended, till it proved as fatal as *Remus's* leaping over his Brother *Romulus* his Ditch, cast for a Trench about Old *Rome*.

Few days had been spent afore a *Sea Tortoise*[1] was brought to the Fort, in Length Six Feet, the content of his Hut near two Bushels, reckoning only that part with which his Back is shielded, being an huge Shell of a brown Colour; never to be made transparent as those come from the *South-Seas* are, nor easily to be crackt by any weight; for Experiment I and two more got upon it, and the *Tortoise* unconcerned carried us: Its Head is loricated with Scales, the Neck reaching as far as the Hut, soft and undefensible; the Fins are four, placed instead of Legs, by which it crawls as well as swims; the Belly is covered with a Breast-plate called the *Callapee*, soft and whitish in respect of the Back-piece or *Callipei*;[2] its Tail is short and wreathed like a Serpent's; altogether it is as lovely as a Toad: It sighs like a Woman, and weeps like a Child; being taken and turned on its back, it is shiftless.

I caused it to be opened, and examined its Heart, which (contrary to the Opinion of the Vulgar) is but One, they affirming it to be Three, grounded on this Mistake; the Auricles being larger than in other Creatures, equalling almost the Ventricles and whole Body of the Heart, which is bigger in proportion than belongs to such an Animal, being as large as an Ox's; which might be the reason of its Pusilanimity: The Veins and Arteries were filled with Currents of cold black Blood: It participates more of Flesh than Fish, of a viviparous than oviparous Offspring, yet lays imperfect Eggs without a Crust (only covered with a Membrane, being most Yolk) buried by it in the Sands, to receive from the

---

1 Probably *Chelone imbricata*, the Hawk-bill Turtle, or Indian Caret, which is the chief source of the tortoise-shell of commerce (Watt, *Econ. Dict.*, vi, Pt. I, 433).

2 Calipash, the upper shell or carapace: Calipee, the lower shell or plastron; both probably adoptions of some West Indian words (*New Eng. Dict.*, *s.v.*).

Sun's heat the perfection of their Hatching (as the Eggs of *Egypt* from Furnaces, or others from Dunghills): It spawns them as Fish do, in huge quantities, as much at one time as will more than fill a Seaman's Bonnet (every one being as big as an Hen's Egg). By them aboard Ship they are ordered like buttered Eggs of a Fowl, though nearer akin to a Serpent's, hanging together as those do.

For this end they come ashore, and when pursued, cast up with their Claws a Cloud of Sand to blind their Enemies; when overtaken some are so big, four men can hardly turn them.

It is supposed they feed on the Grass or Oaz on Land, or at the bottom of the Ocean; and from the Fable of the Three Hearts, springs the Conceit of its Tripartite Community, of Fish, and Flesh, and Fowl; the Outward Covering being Shelly, the inner Meat Carnous, its way of preserving its kind being by Eggs, as the Feathered Fowl do: To me it seems (though the Flesh be highly extolled for the taste and colour of Veal) neither Fish, nor Flesh, nor good Red Herring.

It bears the Vogue for altering the Blood; wherefore good in Scurvies got by bad Air and Diet in long Voyages, and for the Running of the Reins by impure Copulation; for which 'tis used as an undoubted Cure, purging by the Genitals an Oily viscous Matter of a Yellow hew, if fed upon constantly for thirty days; restoring the decayed Vigour of the Body, and giving it a grace and lustre as elegant, as Viper Wine does Consumptive Persons, or worn-out Prostitutes.[1]

About this time the President put in execution a Project for the advancing the Island *Bombaim*; wherefore

[1] In India the medicinal properties of snakes are recognised. In Burma the gall-bladder and fat of the boa-constrictor are prized, the fat being esteemed a sovereign remedy for rheumatism and strains (Shway Yoe, *The Burman*, ii, 324). In N. India the skin of a

an Envoy was sent to explore the Passage through *Seva Gi*'s Country into the Confines of *Duccan*; but returned with a fruitless Account, only making farther work for me.

One of the *Mogul*'s Generals over Seventeen thousand Horse, and Three thousand Foot, and Governor of *Jeneah*[1] (the Chief City of that Kingdom) having occasion for one of my Function, on St. *George*'s Day I was commanded by the Honourable *Gerald Aungier*, with only Oral Instructions, to embarque on a *Bombaim* Boat of Twelve Oars and a Steer's-man, waited on by two of the Governor's Servants, four *Moor. Peons*, a *Portuguez*, my own Servants, a *Brachmin* for Linguist,[2] an Horse-keeper, eight Coolies to my *Palenkeen*, a dozen *Frasses*[3] for Lumber, and one Horse.

Thus equipped, I left *Bombaim* about Three in the Afternoon, and the same Night about Nine Anchored on this side *Tanaw*,[4] where in our passage were visible a great way off, on the tops of the Mountains, several Fortresses of *Seva-Gi*'s, only defensible by Nature, needing no other Artillery but Stones, which they tumble down upon their Foes, carrying as certain destruction with them as Bullets where they alight: The next Morning, with only sending my Servant ashore to acquaint the *Rendero*,[5] I

---

snake is worn as an amulet against disease. Fryer may have known the theories of Pliny (*Nat. Hist.*, xxix, 20, 21, 22) on the various medicaments prepared from the dragon, viper, and other snakes. For similar beliefs, see Black, *Folk-Medicine*, 155 f.

1 The famous hill and fort of Junnar in the Poona District: Lat. 19° 12 N., long. 73° 56′: 56 miles N. of Poona. It is described in p. 321.

2 Interpreter (Yule, *Hobson-Jobson*, 517).

3 See p. 174.

4 See p. 188.

5 Port. *rendeiro*, "a tax-gatherer or farmer." "So it is with merchandize of every craft, trade, or kind, however small, the power of dealing in it, making or selling it, is farmed out to the highest and last bidder. They call these farmers *Renderes*" (Pyrard de Laval, ii, 178). "However, this has made Volup Venny the Rendere of ye customs very uneasy . . . Your Ex^cy^ &ca are no strangers to ye Rendeiroes of ye last years Tobacco stand" (Forrest, *Home Papers*, i, 154 f.).

quitted the Pass; and a Mile beyond the City deserted *Baçein* River on the left, and took our Course up a spacious Navigable River, which makes the Island of *Baçein*,[1] the Banks of which are low and fruitful; on both sides are placed stately *Aldeas*,[2] and Dwellings of the *Portugal Fidalgos*; till on the Right, within a Mile or more of *Gullean*,[3] they yield possession to the Neighbouring *Seva Gi*, at which City (the Key this way into that Rebels Country) Wind and Tide favouring us, we landed at about Nine in the Morning and were civilly treated by the Customer in his *Choultry*,[4] till the *Havaldar*[5] could be acquainted of my arrival; who immediately ordered me a great *Mosch*[6] for my reception, whence I sent the *Brachmin* to complement him, and deliver the Presidents Letter.

Who understanding my Business, desired the favour of me to visit him, and there should attend on me some of his Friends that were diseased; I easily condescended, thinking to procure my Dispatch with more speed; which succeeded alike, I received his *Chitty*[7] or Pass, with two Guides to direct us through the Country.

Early therefore the next Morning I left the most Glorious Ruins the *Mahometans* in *Duccan* ever had occasion to deplore: For this City, once the chief Empory, excelled not only in Trade, but the general consequent, Sumptuousness, if the Reliques of the Stately Fabricks may add Credit to such a belief; which Reliques, not-

---

[1] See p. 191.

[2] See p. 185.

[3] Kalyān in Thāna District: Lat. 19° 14′ N., long. 73° 12′ E., 33 miles N.E. of Bombay.

[4] See p. 108.

[5] Hind. *hawaldār*, *hawāldār*, a sergeant of a native regiment (Yule, *Hobson-Jobson*, 412).

[6] Mosque.

[7] Hind. *chitthī*, a letter (Yule. *Ibid.*, 203).

withstanding the Fury of the *Portugals*, afterward of the *Mogul*, since of *Seva Gi*, and now lately again of the *Mogul*, (whose Flames were hardly extinguished at my being here, and the Governor and People on that score being prepared more for Flight than Defence at present) are still the extant Marks of its pristine Height:[1] The remaining Buildings having many Stories of square facing Stones, and the Mosques, which are numerous, of the same, abating little of their ancient Lustre, being all watered with delicate Tanks; about which are costly Tombs with their distinct Chappels or Mosques, where formerly the *Mullahs*[2] had fat Pensions to pray for the departed Souls, which is maintained by them as efficacious; wherefore they covet Funerals in the most conspicuous Places, which the Pleasant Summer houses hanging over here, cause these Places to be; the unemploy'd People of the Town daily wasting their time in these inviting Varieties; which is the only thing pleads for their continuance, *Seva Gi* as a *Gentu* being otherwise inclinable to raze them; yet purposely to pervert them from the use of the Donors, and Intention of the Founders, orders them to be converted into Granaries, especially those within the City.

The Houses the present Inhabitants kennel in are mean, the People beggarly, by reason of these Hostile Incursions.

---

[1] Fryer, who never saw any of the great native cities, rather exaggerates the importance of Kalyān. Sir James Mackintosh, who visited it in 1810, says that Fryer, whose description of the splendid ruins and stately fabrics had tempted him to go there, ought to have been hanged (*Life*, ii, 19). At the same time, it was a fine city. In 1636 it passed from the rule of Ahmadnagar to that of Bījapur. In 1648 the Mahrattas surprised it; the Mughals recovered it in 1660, but lost it again in 1662. At the time of Fryer's visit in 1675 it was a mass of ruins. Its trade had departed to Thāna, as the increased burden of ships made it difficult for them to pass up the river (Maclean, 100 f.; *Bombay Gaz.*, xiv. 113 ff.).

[2] See p. 240.

By Twelve at Noon having journey'd over Rocky, Barren, and Parched Ways, I came to *Intwally*,[1] Three Course, or Seven Mile and an half; the Season of the Year (the Heats being now most violent) as well as the time of the Day not permitting us any longer to endure their Extremity, I never staid for License, but shaded myself under a Wooden Mosque, the only Structure standing in the Town, it suffering the same Fate with *Gullean*, and was then reaking in its Ashes, the *Moguls* Army laying Waste all in their Road, both Villages, Fodder, and Corn; and for their Cattel they drive them along with them, and take them, their Wives and Children for Slaves; so that none escape, except those that can fly fastest, or hide themselves in the Woods, which they also set on fire, to leave them destitute of those Recesses. This *Gom*[2] or Town stood in a large Grove of *Mangoes*, on the Bank of a deep Creek, which though at this time fordable, yet I believe the Rains may swell into a Torrent.

Having refreshed my self and *Coolies*, I hired an Ox, they complaining they had too much Burthen, travelling more advisedly by Moonshine, (through a better Soil, and more exchange, as Arable Ground, Heaths, Forests, and Woods, some of which were on Fire two or three Miles together) from Six till Twelve, when we took up our Rest at a poor Village called *Moorbar*,[3] six Course from *Intwally*: This place was not able to afford us an House or Shed, but we were forced to creep into one of their Cottages, half finished, they thatching it with Bents

---

[1] Titvālā, a small village, 7 miles N.E. of Kalyān (*Bombay Gaz.*, xiv, 361).

[2] Hind. *gānv*, *gāon*.

[3] Murbād in Thāna District, 14 miles S.E. of Titvālā. It is now a place of greater importance than in Fryer's days (*Bombay Gaz.*, xiv, 285).

shelving from the Ridge down to the Bottom on both sides, no bigger than a Man might carry.

I kept the *Coolies* to their Watch, notwithstanding their hard Days labour, as well to keep Tigres and Wild Beasts from us, as Thieves and Robbers: The day following I staid here till Four in the Afternoon to avoid the Soultriness of the Weather, which I could hardly do where I was lodged, there being no Air; which caused me to remove out of the Town at Sun rise to the least of two pitiful *Tanks* belonging thereto; they being all here ignorant Idolaters, and Husbandmen, every one chusing his own God; no Family being without some *Pan Dæmon*, or *Incubus*; which they paint with hideous Forms, bedaub with stinking Oil, and offer the Fruits of the Earth to: Most Abominably Superstitious, that an ill *Augury* shall detain them idle a whole day, though they and their Household must starve, if they work not; such as an Hare crossing the Way, or a Crow on the Left hand.[1] They have no publick *Pagod*, or Place of Worship, besides these *Tanks*, where they wash and burn their Dead, giving me a Nosegay of one of their Carkases, before I got my Breakfast, as I lay to repose under a Tree; which made me range for Game, and disperse my Servants for Provant, being otherwise likely to go without; they living upon *Batty*,[2] or Seeds of Grass, eating neither Fish nor Flesh, neither indeed have they any unless by chance; for after my Purveyors had made diligent search, with much ado they purchased one Hen, tho several Villages were in sight, and all of them greedy enough to take Money, had they had Provisions. It is all Plowed Land hereabouts, but *Seva Gi* commonly

---

[1] For meeting omens in India, see Crooke, *Popular Religion*², ii, 47 ff.

[2] See p. 174.

reaps the Harvest, leaving hardly so much to the Tillers as will keep Life and Soul together.

And now going to set out, I began by the murmurings of the *Coolies* to understand that the Guides, being jealous of falling into the Enemy's hands, had a design to lead us about; (but every one besides the *Launs*[1] *Peons* being Strangers, and they fearful to discover themselves, we were persuaded to resign our selves to their Conduct) over Hilly, but none of the worst Ways; two or three Miles together they are all burnt, bearing nothing but withered Benty-Grass, which burning afore the Rains, benefits the Ground much; and are now out of distrust the *Moguls* should Forrage their Army here.

Below this, we passed over a fine Meadow checquered with Purling Brooks, and three Villages, much about an equal distance one from another: And now the broken Ribs of these lofty Mountains seen so far off at Sea all along from *Cape Comory*, as if founded for an Ascent unto the Skies, begin to be discovered by our near approach; when Night interposing her black Vail between our Eyes and them, they became vested with a more benighted Darkness than hung over us; which served as a sable Cloud to direct us to *Dehir*,[2] by Eleven a Clock at Night, nine Course from our last Stage, seated at the end of a large Plain, at the foot of that Chain of Hills supposed to cross the *Taurus*, through the Continent *North* and *South*,[3] as that does *East* and *West*; it is by

[1] Khān, the Persian title of nobility: in India especially applied to Pathāns.

[2] Dhasāī in Thāna District (*Bombay Gaz.*, xiii, Pt. II, 477). Mr. Rieu, however, informs me that it is more probably Dehirī at the foot of the Sahyādrī Ghāt

[3] The range of the Western Ghāts. They certainly do not cross the Taurus.

most Geographers concluded to be Mount *Sephir*,[1] here called the *Gaot*.

We found them all in Arms, not suffering their Women to stir out of the Town Unguarded to fetch Water, being accustomed to continual Alarms; which cautiousness obliged them to usher me into the Market-place, by a small Party which lighted on me in their Rounds; when I sent my *Gulleon Peon*, one of our Guides, with his Masters *Chitty*, or Pass, to the Governor, who received it kindly, and gave me leave to be my own Quartermaster (little Complements being expected from Soldiers).

My Company, as well as my self, being Tired, and now stiff with a little Rest allowed them till the return of the *Peon*, we were not willing to be at more pains to seek for a better Inn, than what a *Fakier* had taken up before us; but we rouzed a Lion, who had just been lain asleep with *Bang*, who opened with such a Clamour, that I was afraid it would have brought all the Watch about us, had they not been in the same tune, calling on one another, as Children when the Light is out, do for fear; beating their Drums, and sounding their Trumpets (Shriller than the *Moors*, and more Tuneable) all Night long; by which means, and my Quarrelsome Inmate, I could compose my self to no Quiet; though for the latter, at length I thought of an Expedient plying him with *Arack* till his Tongue resolved its self in Silence, which was much more grateful than his Bawling.

The next Morning when Day had cleared our Eyesight, I saw the Idol, this Drunken Priest Adored, hard by me; it was thick and short, Carved in Stone, of a Monstrous

---

[1] Sephar of Genesis (x, 30); the Saphar of the Periplus (23); Sapphar of Pliny (*Hist. Nat.*, vi, 26); generally identified with Dhafār in S. Arabia (Yule, *Marco Polo*, ii, 445; Keane, *Gold of Ophir*, 70). It is referred to in p. 147.

Visage, whisking his Tail over his Head; the upper Parts to the Waste, were Painted with Red; it insulted over another ugly Creature it trod on; it was of a Sooty Colour, and Swam in streams of Oil; yet it called in a great many *Devotes*, who came to pay their *Salams*.[1]

I sent to the *Havaldar*, to know when he would Pass us up the *Gaot*; word was brought he was not awake, having been up all Night; in the interim therefore, I Walked about the Town, which is Crowded with People, but miserably Poor, and of no Note, were it not that *Seva Gi* Stables his choicest Horses here, for the conveniency of this Plain to supply them with Hay and Corn, which causes them to have the greater Force, and makes it the Residence of an *Havaldar*, who is a kind of petty General: Changing the Town for the open Fields, I was led to a Grove of *Mangoes* and *Thamarinds*, at the end of which, was a Mosque, and a great many Tombs of excellent Stone, Demolished; one of which they remember with Respect, by the Name of *Melech-Bury*, a great Warrior;[2] however, that which pleased me most of all, was a sudden surprize, when they brought me to the wrong side of a pretty Square Tank, or Well, with a Wall of Stone, Breast high; where expecting to find it covered with Water, looking down five Fathom deep, I saw a clutter of Women, very Handsome, waiting the distilling of the Water from its dewy sides; which they catch in Jarrs, and constantly carrying it away, leave it only weeping: It

---

[1] An image of Hanumān or Māruti, the Monkey God, the protecting deity of village sites in the Deccan and N. India.

[2] Mr. Rieu informs me that there are three or four old tombs at Deherī, and one at Dhasāī; but they are not now held in special reverence, nor attributed to any particular person. Possibly Fryer may have heard of Malik Ahmad Bhairī, the founder of Ahmadnagar (1490-1508). But he was probably buried at his capital.

is cut out of a firm Black Marble[1] Rock up almost to the Top, with broad steps to go down.

Now we could not only see their Forts, but hear also the Watchmen from their Garrisons aloft, some Five hundred, some more, some fewer Men, to and again among the Hills, the main strength of this Prince consisting in these; coming back I found my troublesome Comrade very Merry, and packing up his Housholdstuff, his *Bang*-bowl, and *Hubble Bubble*, to go along with me, before I had gotten leave from the *Havaldar*, who had newly sent word he was ready to receive me.

I made him not tarry long, following the Messenger, who brought me into the middle of a ragged Regiment, distinguishable from the *Mogul's* on that score, but more peculiarly by their Hair appearing on both Ears under their *Puckeries*; their Weapons are much alike, though to me they give more cause of Laughter, than Terror (considering the awkwardness of their wearing them) notwithstanding they are the Instruments of Death.

When I came before the Governor, I found him in State, though under an Hovel; where were many *Brachmins* with Accompt Books, writing at some distance; nearer, his Privy-Council, with whom he seemed to Advise: I was placed on his Left hand, and desired my Interpreter to acquaint him my Errand, withal intreating his Favour for my secure passing the Hill: He made it a piece of difficulty, and told me I must return to *Bimly*[2] for Orders, to whose *Havaldar* he was account-

---

[1] Limestone, but not marble, is found in many parts of the Bombay Presidency (Watt, *Econ. Dict.*, ii, 145). Fryer was vague in his identification of marble. For instance, he wrongly states that the buildings at Persepolis are built of this stone (see Letter V, chap. IV).

[2] Bhiwndī or Bhimdī in Thāna District. Lat. 19° 19′ N., long. 73° 9′ E. (*Bombay Gaz.*, xiv, 45). It must be distinguished from the port of Bimli or Bimlipatnam, on the E. Coast, in the Vizagapatam District (Manucci, ii, 387; Bowrey, 123).

able, not to him of *Gulleon*; which was within half a days Journy from whence I set forth. Hearing this I bore my self as sedately as I could, having been informed of the advantage they take of a disturbed Countenance; and sweetned him with his own Authority being sufficient, telling him of his Master's Kindness to the *English*, and their Friendship towards him; which worked him to a yielding Temper; yet he scrupled my *Canister*,[1] or Trunk, might be lined with Pearl, my Horse sold to the Enemy, hoping to suck somewhat out of me; I replying, What I had brought were at his liberty to search, and that I went only on an amicable account to Cure a Sick Person, and should be as ready to serve him, if required, his Fury was quite pawled; but perceiving an hungry look to hang on them all, and suspecting lest they should serve me some Dog-trick, I made a small Present, and he signing the Pass, dismissed me with a Bundle of *Pawn*, the usual Ceremony at Parting.

Being clear, I could not so readily shake off my *Fakier*, he would march with me; when we were not gone above two Course, or three Miles, the Liquor working out by his Walking, he began to grow weary, and called out for the Horse, which I had caused the *Portugueze* to Mount, which he took in such dudging, seeing himself on Foot, and him on Horseback, that he turned Tail, and went back again to his Vomit, without bidding adieu.

And now our mighty Task began to try our Feet, as well as weary our Eyes:[2] I not caring to hazard my self longer in my *Palenkeen*, alighted, and though I thought

---

[1] Properly a basket trunk; it was probably like the modern *pitārā* used by native travellers (Yule, *Hobson-Jobson*, 715).

[2] Fryer's route was along the Avāpā footpath, about 6 miles S. of the Nānā pass. This road was closed in 1826 (*Bombay Gaz.*, xiii, Pt. I, 316).

it a work impossible to conquer, I put the best face on it I could, tarrying till they were all together, the better to chear them. The *Coolies* providing themselves with Staves, distrusted not only their own Legs, but the Ground they went on, it having forsaken many a tall Tree around us; some holding by the mouldring Earth with half their Roots bare, others half buried in Pits they never grew in, lay expecting their *quondam* Neighbours downfal.

The busy Apes, the Forlorn hope of these declining Woods, deeming no place safe where they beheld us, made strange Levaltoes[1] with their hanging Brats from one Bough to another, Chattering an Invasion; but these saw us presently exalted beyond their Bowers, and feared us from above, as much as we to salute them below: Thus far was passable enough, when the Sun levelled himself unto our Steps, and we looked for Day beneath us. Here I made a second pause, and promised them Nectar in the Skies; this proved but a faint Cordial to the *Frasses*, who failed afore they got a quarter up; for whom after I had provided (the Moon assisting us with a less parching Light) I found my Hands as necessary to Clamber as my Feet, Travelling on all Four; the Stones were laid step by step, but in little order; and now so steep, that it differed little from Perpendicular, only by the winding of the Mountain; and so Narrow, that Two Men could not pass abreast; where chiefly were laid Trees and Timber to make work for the Army, should they attempt this Way; which sorely increased our trouble, being the first Adventurers, beside the danger we incurred of being Assaulted from above, they not yet

---

[1] *Lavolta*, Ital. *la volta*, "the turn," "a lively dance for two persons, consisting a good deal in high and active bounds" (Nares, *Gloss. s. v.*).

knowing who we were. To look down made my Brains turn round; over my Head pendulous Rocks threatened to Entomb me.

We had not gone long thus, before the Cry came, the Ox was fallen; 'twas well he chose not the place where I was in, for the least lapse had irrecoverably whirled him to the bottom: Arguments were too weak to persuade the *Coolies* to go back to him to help him; I therefore proceeded to Threats, which made Two of them return to his Aid: I confess the sense of their hard Labour urged me to pity; the Anguish of which extorted Tears from some, unseasonable at this time to take notice of to them; we had only this Comfort, the Even was Calm and Serene, and we were mounted beyond the humble Mists, which we could discern fluctuating against the impenetrable Promontories; which may be the reason sometimes (they say) Men and Oxen are hurled down the Precipice by sudden Gusts, when they are exalted to the Clouds, and they break with too great an Impetuosity: For all this Light we seemed Obscured, the splendour of the Moon being shaded by the sides of the Mountains, which appeared here all Marble.

The Horse (being a *Turky*[1] one) made the best shift of all, and was more forward than convenient, pelting us with great Stones his Hoofs had removed, which caused us to retard his haste, and leave him to come last.

About Nine a Clock at Night the Moon shone over our Heads, more joyful at her presence, than her feignedly beloved *Endimion*: An hour after we came tired to the Brow, through a narrow Cavern cut out of the main Rock; here being no Guard, the noise of the Army being over, I was the second Man Trampled on the Top, half an hour after the *Palenkeen* came, and all the

[1] Turkoman.

rest within two hours more: Here I was as good as my word, and distributed *Arack* among them, which made them, for all their tedious Tug, run amain to the next Town *Oppagaot*;[1] where early in the Morning I crowded under an Old Shed.

This *Gur*[2] or Hill is reckoned four Course up (every Course being a Mile and half): From whence is beheld the World beneath all furled with Clouds, the *Cærulean* Ocean terminating the Horizon, the adjacent Islands bordering on the Main, the Mountains fenced with horrible Gulphs, till strange Vertigoes prejudicate Fancy, not daring longer to be made a Spectator: The bandying Eccho still persecutes with terrible repeated Sounds, meeting fresh Objects to reundulate it, though at the greater distance, being yet enclosed with Mountains, which they maintain as Fortresses; and I can give no reason why they do not this Entry also, unless because it is so contrived that Ten Men may keep down Ten thousand.

Here is a sensible alteration of the Air: The Dawn of the Morning, and latter part of the Night, 'twas sharp, cold, and piercing; so that all I gathered about me would scarce keep me warm; and all the Day there were fine cool Briezes, though below we were almost choaked with soultry Heats: The Reason whereof I judge to be, because the High Mountains reverberate the flowing Particles of the Atmosphere; as we see the Rocks do Water more strongly, by how much more force the Waves assail them; so here the Air (which is thicker below) driven against these Hills breaks off in Flurries, which seeking to retire into their own Ocean, mitigate the violence of the Heat in their passage, by fanning as it were the Air; by which

[1] Fryer probably gives as the name of the place the words of his guide, who here announced that he had reached the top of the hill —*ūpar ghāt*.

[2] Hind. *garh*, a fort (Yule, *Hobson-Jobson*, 404).

means, and the Sun's rarifying the Misty Vapours, they are left pure, and fall at Night in more limpid Dews to cool and refresh the Earth: To which Sense sings *Lucan*,

> *Fulminibus proprior terræ succenditur aër,*
> *Imaque telluris ventos tractusque coruscos*
> *Flammarum accipiunt: Nubes excedit Olympus.*[1]

Moreover, Bogs and Fens are rarely found to soil the Air, or pen in the Heat for want of ventilation.

This is a sad Starvling Town; to it belongs a *Subidar*, or Customer; who blown up with the confidence of half a dozen Bill-men, thought to have compell'd me to stay till the Governor of the Castle should examine my *Cocket*,[2] which he had sent him by the *Havaldar*: I ordered him to send it with one of the *Gulean Peons*; but he made Answer, the Governor having been up all night, was not then at leisure. While we were talking, a drove of *Combies*[3] (Hinds) passed with Provisions on their Heads for the Castle; and I having staid till Three in the Afternoon, not getting any other Answer, I commanded the *Coolies* to march, though the *Subidar* prohibited and kept them from following them with my Men and Arms, as Carbines and Blunderbusses; and the Governor not coming as he told my *Peons* he would, by Four, I dismissed the *Gulean Peons*, they daring to go no farther; and if there were farther occasion for a Pass, to bring it after me; thereby frustrating their Intention, which was to retard me, whereby to make their Booty of me.

They durst no more than curse, for all I departed without leave, taking my Course into a deep Valley, which winded and turned like a River, and I believe is one in the Rains: Half way we met another *Caphala* of Oxen laden with

---

[1] Lucan, *Pharsalia*, ii, 269 ff.

[2] Certificate of payment of duties.

[3] The Kunbī, an agricultural caste in the Deccan (Yule, *Ibid.*, 491).

Provisions, hardly escaping the *Mogul*'s Army, which they told us was not far afore us: My *Coolies* more jealous of the Villany of *Seva Gi*'s People than my self, made haste, and by Ten at Night arrived at *Aumbegaum*,[1] Ten Course.

From whence *Mucklis Caun*'s[2] Men had driven all away with a Party of his Horse, only one *Fakier*, who had set up his Standard in a Shop in the *Buzzar*, next to whom I shrowded my self under one of the same Stalls: Before Five in the Morning, for fear of farther Interruption, I posted hence, up Hill and down Hill, not having Rice for my People to eat (all being fled) we came to a neat Stone Well of Good Water; hard by which was an excellent Fig-tree, on whose Fruit, yet Green, my *Indians* fed heartily, and trouped by three or four wretched Towns, up another Mountain, not altogether so bad as the first, yet on account of their wanting their wonted Food, it went hard with the *Coolies* to foot it to *Beelseer*,[3] two Course short of *Jeneah*, where we baited; it being high time, they having gone near Fifty Miles without eating more than a few squashy Figs: They unloaded at Noon under a Row of spreading *Mangos*, on the side

---

1 Ambegāon, in the Poona District, on the left bank of the Ghod river (*Bombay Gaz.*, xviii, Pt. III, 102).

2 Mr. Irvine believes that he was the Mughal commander at Jenneah (Junnar) to whom Fryer had been sent. Probably the man meant is Qāzī Nizāmā Mukhlis Khān, who entered the Imperial service late in Shāhjahān's reign, and was appointed to Balkh about 1647. About 1658 he was posted to the Deccan, took the side of Aurangzeb, by whom he was promoted, and given the title of Mukhlis Khān, "loyal lord." He was placed in temporary charge of Akbarābād, and about 1660 transferred to Bengal. About 1667 he was placed under Sultān Mu'azzam, sent with him to Lahore, and thence to the Deccan. Nothing is known of the rest of his career.

3 Mr. E. Carmichael, Collector of Poona, identifies this with Belsar, W. by S. of Junnar, and at the distance stated by Fryer. It is situated on the S. bank of the Mina river, two miles up from the village of Kusur, which appears in the S.W. corner of Mr. Cousens' sketch of the environs of Junnar.

of a Brook; and provided themselves with Victuals in an adjacent Village, liable to continual pillaging on both sides; but being reduced to the Condition of having little or nothing to lose, it is the better born.

Hence it is plain to *Jeneah*, the Hills keeping their distance from its Invincible *Gur*: The length of whose Bottom fills most of the space from this Place to the City, which is the Frontier of the *Mogul*'s Territory this way; and has been for many Years the Seat of War to the *South*, which is the signification of *Duccan*.[1]

I sent the Governor's *Peon* to acquaint him of my approach (I not arriving till Sun-set) which he met me with others that were appointed at a Garden short of the Town,[2] with the Governor's Complement; and conducted me to a Palace in a Compleat Garden, adorned with *Cypress* Trees[3] (not usual in *India*) *Hummums, Tanks, Choultries* and *Walks*, with *Water-Courses*: When I was asleep, the *Nabob* or Governor sent me a Service in Plate covered with Embroidered Velvet over Noble *Surpooses*[4] or Covers, ushered with two Silver Staves, and a Trumpet sounding afore it; which Course was observed as long as I remained there.

The last day of *April*, being *Friday*, and the next

---

[1] Skt. *dakshina*, south (Yule, *Hobson-Jobson*, 301).

[2] Mr. Cousens identifies this with the present Afiz Bāgh. "It is not known for certain," he writes, "what 'Afiz' means; but it has been supposed to be a corruption of 'Habshī' [Abyssinian]. In this place is the old house, built some two or three hundred years ago, with a jungly Garden and ruined tank around it. There are signs that it was a fine, extensive place at one time. Near by, on the west of the Garden, is the largest mausoleum at Junnar, said to be that of the builder of the Mansion. The Afiz Bagh is about a mile east of the city, the only side from which a traveller could have come, save by the terrible Nānāghāt pass on the west." Also see *Bombay Gaz.*, xviii, Pt. III, 152.

[3] *Cupressus sempervirens*, only a garden tree in N.W. India (Watt *Econ. Dict.*, ii, 646).

[4] Pers. *sarposh*, "head-cover." The silver staves were carried by a Chobdār (Yule, *Ibid.*, 877, 204).

after my arrival, he sent to excuse myself, because it was his day of Devotion; when after a Princely manner he rides on an Elephant to the *Mosque*; and thence divertises himself in some place of Delight within his *Seraglio* till high Night.

CHAP. V.

Introduces me into the Nabob's *presence*; *my Business with him; a Prospect of the* Gur (Seva Gi's *Birth place*); *the Army and Country of* Duccan: *Of the Pass of* Tanaw, *and benefit thereof, were it in the hands of the* English.

It was the first of *May* therefore before I waited on him; when he ordered a Guard of Horse to attend me to the Castle, which was large, but rude, and the Wall of raw Brick; serving as well to secure Cattle as Men from the Enemy.[1]

His own Apartments in the middle encompassed a verdent Quadrangle of Trees and Plants; in whose chief *Choultry* were assembled all his Great Men on his Right hand, he being enclosed in a Seat of State, boulstered up with Embroidered Cushions, smoaking out of a Silver *Hubble bubble*; afore whom lay a rich Sword and Buckler, with a Crescent Moon instead of Bosses,[2] his Page bearing his Bow and Arrows, much after the *Turkish* manner, as *Busbequius* reports of the *Grand Segnior*, *Sedebat in Solio humili instrato*; *juxta autem arcus & sagittæ*. All the Floor was spread with a soft Bed, over all a fine white Calicut;[3] the Pedestals were Massive Silver, where I put off my Shooes, and after Respect paid, delivered

---

[1] The city fort (*kot*), in which the office of the local officer, or māmlatdar, is now situated.

[2] Shields decorated with the Turkish symbol of the crescent, which is little used among Indian Muhammadans, are in the India Museum (Egerton, *Handbook*, 48 ff., 133 f.).

[3] White calico; see p. 90.

the President's Letter, and was received immediately next to him on his Left hand,[1] all that side being kept void for my entertainment: The result of this Visit was, after he had acquainted me who were to be my Patients, to tell me I must be patient till a good day presented, and then I should be called again; it remaining a Custom still in the *East* to defer important Affairs till a Lucky Day, *totis hœrentia fastis.* I only intreated he would be mindful the Rains were at hand, falling earlier here than in the Low Countries.

Our Discourse being ended, a Couple of Singing-men[2] began their Songs of Praise, which they pride themselves in, not being content with moderate Flattery; a thing odious to a generous Spirit, accounting those that do it, servile; and those that admit it, imprudent to be deluded by Fawning Knaves: But here are not only those that profess it for Lucre, but it is the general strife who may impose most obsequiously. *Adulandi certamen est, & unum amicorum omnium officium, quis blandissimè fallat*; as *Seneca* observes in the corruption of his Age, *de Benef. Cap. XXX.*

Such as appear before him make a *Salam* or Bow before they ascend the *Choultry*, when if he allows them Conference, leaving their Slippers below, they mount the *Buchanna*;[3] where they bow, by first putting their Hands to their Heads, then to their Feet, which Salute they call *Pervenau*, used to *Cauns* or Dukes. Above their Head, cross their Breast to the Foot is *Pharmau*, only for Kings; the most familiar is a Bow with the Head:[4]

---

[1] The place of honour in the East.

[2] Like the Bhāts, who recite songs of eulogy at Hindu Courts.

[3] Hind. *bichhaunā*, bedding: here the thick padded cotton floor-covering of the Darbār hall.

[4] The rules of salutation at the Mughal Court were fixed by Akbar. "Some kings have adopted the bending down of the head. His Majesty has commanded the palm of the right hand to be placed

If they are permitted to sit in his Presence, those only of Consular Dignity have Liberty to sit (as they call it at ease) cross Legged; but an *European*, before he is accustomed, will not be reconciled to that Term: Others of Inferior Rank kneel, sitting on their Heels, to which Posture, though I was not tied, I was thankful when he sent me a Bundle of *Pawn*, and I had leave to make use of my Legs; being led out, as I was conducted in, by Two Virgers,[1] and a large Train following, with a Master of Ceremonics accompanying.

In my passage through the Castle they seemed rather Encamped than Fortified; wherefore if *Seva Gi* brings any Power, they betake themselves to speedy Flight, or retire to the Body of the Army under *Badur Caun*[2], Generalissimo in these Marches; being ill provided to endure a Siege, and more able to defend themselves, joined to an Host of Forty thousand Horse always at *Pergom*,[3] three Days Journy hence.

Curiosity invited many Spectators, and Courtesy some of Quality to be my Harbingers at my Lodgings; which at my return I found pestered, as I had the Streets all

---

upon the forehead, and the head bent downwards. This mode of salutation . . . is called *Kornish* . . . The salutation, called *taslīm*, consists in placing the back of the right hand on the ground, and then raising it gently till the person stands erect, when he puts the palm of the hand upon the crown of the head" (*Āīn*, i, 158). The terms used by Fryer have not been conclusively traced. Mr. Irvine thinks he may have confounded *farmān*, "an order," with *parwānagī*, "an order or commission"; perhaps here permission to take a seat at the Darbār.

[1] Perhaps he means Chobdārs; see p. 178.

[2] In 1672 Aurangzeb superseded Mahabbat Khān and Sultān Mu'uzzam, appointing in their stead as Viceroy of the Deccan Bahādur Khān, afterwards known as Khān Jahān Bahādur (Manucci, ii, 222, 231; Grant Duff, 113, 121).

[3] Pedgāon, on the river Bhīma, about 40 miles S. of Ahmadnagar, which from 1672 to 1700 was one of the chief stations of the Mughal army. It is the Pairgaom of Grant Duff (p. 114). Khān Jahān renamed it Bahādurgarh (*Bombay Gaz.*, xvii, 732).

the way I came: They were very Civil, making no Intrusion before they had requested leave; and then interrogating the State of *Europe*, the Government, Policy, and Learning; nodding a satisfaction in the account I gave them: Nor were they less communicative in their Relations, of those Occurrences which wheeled in their Sphere, being highly concerned to shew they had Bookmen as well as Sword-men.

A good Day coming, the Governor sent for me to Visit his Lady in the *Haram*, which was opposite to a Chamber he sate in, accompanied only with one pretty Wanton Boy, his Only Son by this Woman; upon which account he had the greater kindness for her: An old Gentlewoman with a Tiffany Vail, made many trips, being, I suppose, the Governant of the Womens Quarters; at last I was called and admitted with my Linguist.

At our being ready to enter, she Clapped with her Hands to give Notice; when we were led through a long dark Entry, with Dormitories on both sides, the Doors of which Creeked in our passage (but I was cautious of being too Circumspect) till we came to an aiery Choultry; where was placed a Bed hung with Silk Curtains; to which being brought, I was Commanded to place my self close by it, from whence I might conveniently Discourse and Feel her Pulse, putting my Hand under the Curtains. It was agreed among them to impose upon me; wherefore at first they gave me a Slaves Hand, whom I declared to be Sound and Free from any Disease, nothing contradicting the true Tenor and Rythme of Pulsation;[1] when they began

[1] Shāh 'Ālam played a similar trick on Manucci, by pushing his own arm through the curtain; but Manucci found it thick, muscular, and hairy, and detected the stratagem (ii, 398). When Bernier was called in by a lady of the Court, he was blindfolded with a Kashmīr shawl on entering the Zananah (p. 267). De Lan bled the Queen of Golkonda, by operating on her arm passed through a hole in the

to be more ingenuous, telling me, it was done to try me: Then was given me another Hand, which demonstrated a weak languid Constitution; and collecting the Signs and Symptoms, I feared not to give Sentence; which met with their Approbation, and so I was sent back the same way I came.

The *Caun* had been acquainted with what had passed, and seemed pleased; whereupon I must visit the *Haram* again the next day to Bleed another of his Wives, he being tolerated Four,[1] though he keeps more than Three hundred Concubines.

And now the Curtain was extended athwart the *Choultry*, and an Arm held forth at an hole; but this was a slight fence for such Animals, who leaning too hard as they peeped, pulled it down, and discovered the whole Bevy, fluttering like so many Birds when a Net is cast over them; yet none of them sought to escape, but feigning a shamefacedness, continued looking through the wide Lattice of their Fingers: The Lady I had by the Arm was a Plump Russet Dame, summoning the remainder of her Blood to enliven her Cheeks (for among the darkest Blacks, the Passions of Fear, Anger, or Joy, are discernible enough in the Face) and she bearing a command, caused it to be hung up again; pouring upon her extravasated Blood a Golden shower of Pagods, which I made my Man fish for.[2]

In this interview they appeared to me not altogether unimployed, there lying pared Mangoes, and other Fruits for Confection, and Achars, or Pickles; some Samples

---

curtain (Tavernier, ed. Ball, i, 303). Forbes (*Or. Mem.*[2], ii, 324) says that a similar custom prevailed in his time at Cambay, when European physicians attended on noble ladies.

[1] The legal number (Herklots, *Qanoon-e-Islam*, 95).

[2] When Manucci bled Shāh 'Ālam's ladies they gave him Rs. 200 and a suit of robes (*sarāpā*), (ii, 355).

of good Housewifry in Needleworks; and no indecent decorum in managing their Cloystered way of living, making it agreeable to the choice of Custom rather than Restraint: But here are foulmouthed *Homers* that Stigmatize them, how deservedly I dare not say.

> Ὡς οὐκ αἰνότερον καὶ κύντερον ἄλλο γυναικός.[1]
>
> *Nil gravius nil improbius quam fœmina vivit.*

And a Man would guess no less, to see the number of Spies upon them, of Toothless Old Women, and Beardless Eunuchs, that they are incontinent in their Desires, for which reason they debar them the sight of any thing Male, but their Lord; they Waiting, as well to hand them Necessaries, as Wood, Water, Meat, and the like, taking them at the Door, as to prevent unlawful Intruders.

These have their Singing Wenches; exercise their Ears and Noses with weighty Jewels, as the Gipsy of Old did her Hair and Neck.

> ———Colloque comisque
>
> *Divitias Cleopatra gerit, cultuque Laborat.* Lucan.[2]

And are Cloathed like the Men, only they go in their Hair within, and abroad with Vails.

Gaining by these steps a nearer intimacy with the *Nabob*, he cut me new Business out every day; he advised me of the intention of the Governor of the Castle on the Hill, to commit his Brother to my Care; and I in a private Conference, according to my Instructions, propounded the Commodity might arise from an intercourse of Commerce between this place and *Bombaim*, from thence to *Bussorah*, *Persia*, and *Mæcha*, for to provide the Army with Horses;[3] in return of whom

---

[1] Homer, *Odyssey*, xi, 427.

[2] *Pharsalia*, x, 139 f.

[3] In this reference to horses he was following the precedent of the Portuguese, who used the control of the sea trade to extend their influence over the kingdoms of the Deccan (*Dalboquerque*, ii, Intro., 65).

might be exchang'd the same Goods procurable at *Surat* and better Cheap, should they succeed in their Conquests over the Low Countries; which is not a matter of such impossibility should they earnestly set about it, considering the Avenues are open: But by that proceeding, it would take away a powerful obstacle to the maintaining so vast an Army as is always in *Duccan*, whereby a main Body of the Soldiery would be out of pay; which is absolutely against the Generals interest, and therefore he would never consent: This I soon saw was the main Argument, though he coloured it with pretext, that 'twas a work of more pains to reduce *Seva*, than was represented, in respect of his Situation, being impowered not only to make Excursions, but to bid them Defiance.

Whereupon I told him, if the latter was not feasible, it was in vain to propose any thing in relation to the former, for that all access was stopped if the Low Lands were not cleared; the *Havaldars* being unconscionable in their Customs, and without doubt would interrupt what might be serviceable to their Enemies, or bring prejudice to their Prince; whereas were the Ways free it would enrich his *Jageah*[1] beyond the *Bunder* at *Surat* and tie the *English* to a perpetual Truce, who were known in these Parts addicted to Traffick, and Friends to Peace: He asked further, How far we desired to extend this Liberty? I replied, beyond the *Portugal* Dominions, which would front the Island of *Bombaim* about *Tull*;[2] otherwise we must be at the charge of double Custom, to them as well as the *Mogul*. He said all this had been moved to *Badur Caun*, but those to whose hands the Presents for him had been entrusted, had defrauded him of them, on whom nothing was to

[1] See p. 300.

[2] Thal in Thāna District, 3 miles N. of 'Alibāgh (*Bombay Gaz.*, xi, 395).

be wrought without liberal *Piscashes*,[1] he bearing it as high as the King himself, and at this juncture he was an unfit Mediator to him, having lately had some jarrs with him (the Governor of *Jeneah* undervaluing his Authority in an Expedition, not long enough ago to be thoroughly forgot); however did the President immediately apply himself to him, he was inclinable enough to let him Settle Factories; which I gave him to understand, without a mutual Benefit on both sides, was not the present Design; but for the esteem we bore to Men of Honour, and that made account of their Word, it was wished the *Moguls* were possessed of those Parts; which was never to be cultivated, either with good Manners, or Profit, whilst Perfidy reigned there.

This being the substance of our Discourse, after he had related the Business to his Council (he replied) he would intimate what might be effected in it, to the President, in answer to his Letter.

At Night it was dismally Tempestuous, Killing Two of the Watch on Duty, and carrying a Tower off the Hill at one Clap; below, it brake one Man's Arm, the Prologue to the Rains.

The Day after the *Nabob*'s Brother, of the Castle, was received kindly here, bringing a noble Train, and *Piscash* to bespeak his Welcome; he was Lodged in a Palace adjoining that where I was.

The Eleventh of *May* I went abroad to a Garden left by a common Strumpet. in which was a noble

---

[1] Pers. *pishkash*, "what is first drawn, firstfruits": then "a present to a superior." There are three Persian terms for a present—*ta'aruf*, *pishkash*, *in'ām*. The first means a gift to some one of about the same rank as the donor, in which case no return is expected, at any rate in money. When an inferior offers a gift to a superior it is *pishkash*, or "offering"; and he usually expects at least its money value. *In'ām* is a gratuity, a "tip," from a superior to an inferior (Browne, *A Year amongst the Persians*, 68; Curzon, *Persia*, i, 445; Yule, *Hobson-Jobson*, 701).

Tomb built in remembrance of her, with a Well belonging to a lovely Spring, which by Aqueducts supplied the City with Water.[1]

Who when she died, like Flora *Fair*,
Did make the Commonwealth her Heir.[2]

Hence we went to a ruined Palace, where *Auren Zeeb*, the present Emperor, was hospitably received in his Father's Reign, and lived a pretended *Fakier.*[3]

Cotton in its season is Planted all hereabouts: The Fields produce Wheat in abundance, and other Grain; but are often served as the *Philistine's* were by *Sampson*, the Foxes from the Mountains with Firebrands consuming them; which made us bethink of retiring, they descending sometimes in Parties to Prey on Straglers, that often Troopers are sent home disrobed and dismounted, to be laught at for their Misfortune.

Having tarried now till the Rains had made their first onset Fourteen days together, with horrid Thunder; at the end thereof I set apart a day to take notice of the adjacent Rarities; among which is a City called *Dunge-*

---

[1] Mr. Cousens writes: "About a mile and a half from Junnar, along the road going to Kusur, to the S.W., is a mango grove or garden, still known as Umā's gardens (Umāvana in the inscription). In it is an inscribed stone, which I copied, which tells us that the garden was given to the public by Umā, threatens those who should alienate it with a curse, and promises blessings to those who respect the gift and keep it up. She is said to be of the family of Kubera. This, I think, must be the garden left by the common strumpet."

[2] "Flora was a rich harlot in Rome, and for that she made the Common-wealth her heir; her birth-day was solemnised long after; and to make it a more plausible holiday, they made her goddess of flowers, and sacrificed to her amongst the rest" (Burton, *Anatomy of Melancholy*, ed. Shilleto, iii, 407 f.). He got the story from Lactantius (I, 20). The source of Fryer's verses has not been traced.

[3] Fryer again (Letter IV, chap. IV) refers to this palace where Aurangzeb was hospitably received. "In 1643, when only twenty-four, he [Aurangzīb] announced his intention of retiring from the world, and actually took up his abode in the wild regions of the Western Gháts (where Dr. Fryer was shown his retreat) and adopted the vigorous system of self-mortification which distinguished the fakír or mendicant friar of Islám" (S. Lane-Poole, *Aurangzíb*, 48).

ness,[1] of like Antiquity and Workmanship, as *Canorein*,[2] cut out of a Mountanous Rock, with a Temple and other Spacious Halls, by no means inferior to it both for Water and other Refreshments, and much more entire; Time having not dealt so cruelly with it, but the Lines of its ruined Beauty are still legible, though in old Characters; however it is left a desolate Habitation for Batts and Wasps; to disturb which it is dangerous, being overgrown and desperately revengeful, following their Aggressors till they have Whealed them into Contrition for their unadvised Provocation: To be out of the Noise of these buzzing Hornets, and to secure our selves from the surprize of any disturbed Idolator, who might bellow the report of our being here, we hasted to the safer Plain, and ended the rest of the day in a pleasant Garden, on the brink of the River which glides hence to *Surat*.

The Governor of the *Gur* hearing I was preparing for to return to *Bombaim*, requested before my departure to accept of my choice, either to ascend the *Gur*, or else to meet him at his Garden below, being the prescribed Limits of his Walk: I signified my readiness to comply with the former, wherefore he sent Four *Palenkeens*, his Kinsman, an Ingenuous *Mogul*, and his Brother to attend me.

We Travelled Two Miles before we came to the Foot of it, where is a Garison, or Fortified Town, walled with strong *Chockies*, or Watches, and a Troop of Five hundred Horse, and as many Camels of War; here are

[1] A good example of a corruption in the "Hobson-Jobson" manner. The name of the hill is Ganesh Dongar, "hill of the god Ganesa." The scarp of the range that bounds Junnar to the N. has been excavated in a line of caves, one of which has been converted into a temple of Ganpati or Ganesa, and gives the name to the Ganesh Lena or Ganesh Caves (*Bombay Gaz.*, xviii, Pt. III, 204; Fergusson-Burgess, *Cave Temples*, 248 ff.).

[2] Kānherī, see p. 158.

great Stacks of Hay and Corn, all their Droves of Beasts being sheltered here anights.[1] *Seva Gi* has distressed this often, and put them to the rout; but that, whose Top we are endeavouring to gain, is inaccessible, unless by Seven winding Gates,[2] which are very strong, and able to clear one another as they rise, the Way being lined with Murtherers,[3] and they themselves defended with good Pieces of Ordnance: The last is a Piece of excellent Work and Strength, and the place filled with Soldiers.

Hence it is painful Riding, and requires a strong Back to keep State in a *Palenkeen*, it being carried almost bold upright, over slippery Marble steps, cut out of the shining Rock, as smooth as Glass, and reflecting the Sun-beams as much: After we had mounted near an Hundred Stairs, we were received into the Neck of the Castle, which is collared about with a Wall, rather to keep them from falling down, than needful to prevent Assailants; from whence an easy Ascent leads to a Level, which is the Circus to train the Infantry; where are conspicuous Tombs of their former Kings, being firmly Built, and a Mosque of polished Marble, which on Festivals only they repair unto:[4] No Houses here are able to resist the Storms of Wind, or the Sun's Heat, for which conveniency they have made the *Eastern* side of the Hill most Inhabited, it serving instead of a Bank; where they live in little low Huts, the Governor's not, exceeding in height, (though a pretty neat Dwelling,

---

[1] This is the Shivner hill, which rises to a height of about 1000 feet half a mile W. of Junnar.

[2] For details of these gates, see *Bombay Gaz.*, xviii, Pt. III, 155.

[3] "A very destructive piece of ordnance, calculated to do much execution at once, having a wide mouth, and discharging large stones" (Nares, *Gloss.*, *s. v.* Murdering Piece). Cf. the Paterero, p. 271.

[4] On the hill there is still a mosque with fine flying pointed arches between its minarets (*Bombay Gaz.*, *Ibid.*, 159).

fenced with Trees, no where else to be found) who had expected me Two whole Hours; but being impatient of delay, and the Sun growing too hot, he betook himself to his *Haram*, having ordered his Kinsman (whose Civil Deportment met with his Commands) to Entertain me; he is but Poor (so that he threatens the *Nabob* to turn *Fakier*) yet Generous, of a free open Temper, neither Jealous nor Lazy, as the *Moors* most are; but applying himself to several Handicrafts, which he has learned of the *Europeans*; he is learned too in the *Persian* and *Arabick* Languages, though not to Vain-glory; being so Humble, Facetious, and Merry, that nothing but Spight and Envy can disagree with him: His Name is *Nishambeak*;[1] such another I have not met with, so general a lover of *Franks*; which he specified in an especial manner to me, receiving me in an Airy Banquetting-house, Embellished and Adorned on purpose; and notwithstanding the Governor's Son was to pay his Compliments, would not suffer me to give him Place, but diverted me with several Interludes of *Morisco* Dancing. That which took most with them I perceived, was a Jester, or Mimick, the Ancient Salt at publick Banquets, as we may gather from *Statius*:[2]

Non ego Mercatus Phariâ de puppe Loquaces
Delicias, doctumque sui convicia Nili
Infantem, Linguâque simul salibusque protervum.

And from *Lucan* to *Piso*:[3]

Sed Miserum (clientem) parvâ stipe numerat
——ut pudibundas
Exercere sales inter convivia possit.

---

[1] Nizām Beg, who was apparently Qila'hdār or governor of Junnar. Mr. Irvine cannot trace this officer. "Shaikh Nizām (Khānzamān Dakkhinī) is well known; but he did not leave the Haidarābād and enter the Mogul service until 1687; and he was too big a man to be Qila'hdār of a second-rate fortress."

[2] *Silvae*, v, 5, 66 ff. In the last line read *linguâ nimium*.

[3] *Auctor Panegyrici ad Pisonem*, 114 ff.

Having feasted the Fancy, he contends to cloy the Stomach, with loads of *Viands*, stowed in Plate, serving me with his own Hands, his Friends and he being content to feed on the desire they had to satisfy me, not being to be courted to fall to till I had done; they served me with variety of Stews and Baked Meats, but offered me *Sherbet* only for Drink; I had provided against this chance by filling my *Metarrah*[1] with Beveridge, which passed for Water, being drunk out of a Leather Bottle Tipped with Silver, for Travel.

After Dinner they made their loud Musick proclaim my going to the Governor (whereat flocked all the *Gur*) and after formal Salutes, I presented him with a Glass of Chymical Spirits. As the *Parthians* were wont not to receive Visits without a Gift; *Et exempla in Oriente plura sunt, interea & Magorum in sacris qui Christum adoraturi, munera attulerunt.* So here the like Custom prevails.

I was placed close by him, he like an Hermit, having the Court brought to him, admired the Splendour as well as the Novelty of our *Europe* Dress; asking my Servant if I lay in them, because it is their fashion not to undress to go to Bed, but lye in the same Clothes they wear in the day; he made me declare the use of my Rapier, at first not apprehending it so

---

[1] In Letter V, chap. II, *metarrah*; in V, chap. IX, *metarrha*; Pers. *maṭārah*, "a flexible leathern drinking-bottle or cup used by travellers: an ewer from which they pour water when performing ablutions" (F. Johnson, *Pers. Dict.*, s.v.). "Before you set out, you must provide your self of several Houshold Goods, especially of those Bottles that are call'd *Matures*, which are made of *Bulgary*-leather: every man carries his own at the Pummel of his Saddle, or else fasten'd to the Crupper of his Saddle behind. Besides that you must buy Borracho's; the most serviceable things in the World; for they will never break, and will hold above fifty Pints at a time. The smaller Bottles serve to put *Aqua-vitae* in; and the Leather whereof they are made has that peculiar to itself, that it keeps the Water fresh" (Tavernier, 47). Manucci (i, 14) advises similar bottles, but does not name them.

serviceable as their Broad Two-handed Swords; 'twas a Question out of my road, yet I made him understand our Custom in War was to appear all armed Cap-a-pee, where there Broad Swords would find a rebate; whereas these Sharp-pointed Weapons would pierce the Junctures of the Harness, or the Pleats of a Coat of Mail (they denying a Stab to be more mortal than a Slash).[1] He was very inquisitive about our Military Discipline; and heard it with pleasure. He called all his Male Children about him, who sate at his Feet, and gave me an History of their Maladies; as most here did that durst speak, there being an infinite number of Captains and Grave Fellows: The Old Men mended their Eyes with Spectacles, the young marred theirs with staring.

The *Choultry* was hung with Green and Red Velvet checkered; his Pawn Boxes were large, and of Massy Gold; his Retinue brave, his Carriage affable; he gave me a Bow-Ring[2] off his Thumb, of Cashmire (of equal value as Vertue, being a Charm against Thunder) and the liberty to take a Round about the Castle, never

---

[1] At Golkonda "they do not have a sabre like the Persians, but they carry a broadsword like the Swiss, with which they both cut and thrust, and they suspend it from a belt" (Tavernier, ed. Ball, i, 157). At a later date Forbes (*Or. Mem.*[2], i, 337) says that the Mahrattas "are not as fond of curved blades as the Turks or Persians, but prefer a straight two-edged sword, and will give a great price for those they call Alleman, or German, though formerly brought from Damascus." Various Mahratta swords are illustrated and described by Egerton, *Handbook of Indian Arms*, 117 f.

[2] "The morowe aftre the King sent for me, and tolde me that he wolde make me a little passetyme in shewing me the Jewells that were sent him out of India, and first caused to be deliured vnto me a rynge (that serveth to drawe their bowe) of gold wth a rubie in the myddest of twoo carretts, and some dyamands about it" (Josafa Barbaro, 56). Herbert (p. 128) says that at Lar "upon their thumb they commonly wear a ring of horne which makes the arrowes go off strong and easily." In Akbar's time such rings were made of rhinoceros horn (*Āīn.*, ii, 281). P. della Valle (i, 119) speaks of flamingos, "of whose beaks *Mir Mahammed* in *Spahàn*, makes bow-rings for the Kings." Hooker met a headman with "a broad ivory ring over the left thumb, as a guard when using the bow"; and remarks that a broad ring of

before granted any not listed in his Service: A *Portuguez Mestizo*,[1] Chief Gunner of the Castle, was very officious, though I was entrusted to the charge of his prime Eunuch.

The first Object busied me, was a place *Seva Gi*'s Men had attempted to scale, by me esteemed a desperate Design, and very improbable; yet two Men got up, and a Stone casually tumbling, deterred their Accomplices, leaving them a Sacrifice to the Governor and Women, who being left alone to the defence of the Castle (all the Men deserting on the approach of a vast Army of *Seva Gi*'s) hurled them down the Mountain for their rash Adventure; confirming to me by a great Stone let fall, the unavoidableness of their destruction; it running with that force where-ever it came, that it beat all a-fore, till it rested in the middle of the Valley.

It is stored with Granaries hewed out of Stone, I suppose for Religion's sake at first, being too delicately engraved for the present use; though there be several *Tanks* filled with Butter of 400 years standing, prized by the *Gentiles* as high as Gold, prevalent in Old Aches, and Sore Eyes, one of which was opened for my sake, and a Present made me of its black stinking and viscous Balsom:[2] There are other *Tanks* or Cisterns for Water, which look nastily, Green, Yellow, and Red, being distilled in the Rains, and in the Heats evaporated to a Consistency; in some of these *Gurs* the Water is so bad,

---

this material, agate, or chalcedony is a mark of rank here, as among the Manchus and throughout Central Asia (*Himalayan Journals*, 150). For a discussion on the origin of the thumb-ring, see *Man.*, vii, 133 ff., reviewing Sir R. Payne-Gallwey, *Projectile-throwing Engines of the Ancients* (1907). Kashmīr is the home of sorcery, and charmed rings naturally came from there.

[1] Port. *mestiço*, a half-caste (Yule, *Hobson-Jobson*, 604).

[2] Old Ghī still maintains its reputation in native medicine (Watt *Econ. Dict.*, iii, 495).

that they use Onions to correct its unsavoriness. (Garlick indeed with us is called the Countryman's Treacle).[1]

They have Provisions for a Seven Years Siege for a Thousand Families, but no other Ammunition than Stones, excepting two unshapen *Sakers*[2] of Two and twenty Foot long, with a narrow Bore of Brass of *Gentu* Mould, at each end one, on huge winding Carriages; one of which at random killed a *Rajah* some four Months ago, when *Seva* was encamped about *Jeneah* slinging a Bullet two Course off; which Shot caused a Bonfire of a couple of his Ladies, beside other Domesticks, one of each sort to attend him in another World, as his Chief Physician, Barber, Washerman, Horse-keeper, and the like, to the number of Twenty odd; a thing as customary at the death of any great *Rajah*, as 'tis for the Wife of every *Gentue* of note at the death of her Husband.

By this fatal Instrument of Mortality stood the remaining part of the Tower the Thunder had cleft in twain: Near where a *Dutch* Apostate has a wretched Dwelling, enjoying a Pair of Wives, the miserable Tools who induced him to this lamentable Condition, that he is despised and slighted by them all; few of those that endure Circumcision meeting with better fortune.

Having taken my full view, and returning to give the Governor Thanks for this freedom, I met him as he came from Prayers through a Lane of Soldiers, followed by a Crowd of his Domesticks, when taking my leave, he

[1] Lyte, in his *Herbal*, published in 1578, speaking of garlic, says: "It is good against all venome and poyson, taken in meates or boyled in wine and dronken, for of its owne nature it withstandeth all poyson: . . . Therefore Galen, prince of Physicians, called it poore men's Treacle. . . . It is also good to keepe such from danger of sicknesse, as are forced to drinke of divers sortes of corrupt waters." In provincial England it is called "poor-man's treacle" or "churl's-treacle." Also see M. L. Lemery, "A Treatise of all Sorts of Foods," 3rd ed., 1745, p. 145 (10th Ser., *Notes and Queries*, xi, 173).

[2] A small piece of ordnance, taking its name from *saker*, a species of hawk (Nares, *Gloss*, *s. v.*).

ordered my release, being ushered with the same State down as I came up, leaving him Prisoner in his strong Hold.

Hence might be beheld many Dens and Caverns,[1] fondly believed to be carved and cut out of the Rocks by some Divine Power; having no account of their original. Indeed they are miraculous; And I am apt to judge, the pious Zeal of former Ages, when undisturbed in their Tranquility, thinking the greatest labour too little to express their love to a Deity, set them upon such imployments, more than that they could promise to themselves any security from these Places; which though the Passages to them be difficult, yet they are generally unprovided of Human Necessaries; This Hill being only independent, whereby it stands out against all the opposite Forts of *Seva Gi*, many of whom in a still Night may be heard by Voice, but more by Trumpets.

Here are a Thousand Sword-men in pay, no Horse or Elephant being able to climb it: It was never fairly taken, the Governor is one of approved Fidelity; the *Mogul* having not the like Fort in all his Kingdoms, and is of main concern to the *Frontiers*; putting a stop to *Seva Gi*'s progress, otherwise likely to overrun *Duccan*. His name is *Hagiess Caun*,[2] originally a *Brachmin*, now a strict *Musleman*; some years past Governor of the City, when oppressing the Poor, their Cries reaching the King's Ears, he was translated hither, in consideration of his good Service; where he receives a liberal Pension, and is at no Expence, which agrees well enough with his covetous Humour; which Humour of his *Seva Gi* being

[1] A full account of the Buddhist Caves in the neighbourhood of Junnar will be found in Fergusson-Burgess, *Cave Temples*, 248 ff.

[2] This may represent Hāfiz or Hājī Khān; but Mr. Irvine knows of no one, of either name, who would suit.

informed of, left no means unattempted to gain the Surrender of his Trust; promising Mountains of Gold in exchange of this, which he scrupled not to receive; appointing a day for the delivery of it to *Seva Gi*, if he sent 7000 horse to take possession; who keeping touch, met with the same measure he had meated to others, they being all surprised by an Ambuscado from *Badur Caun*, whom the Governor had advertised of all the Transactions.

That which makes *Seva Gi* so intent on this more than the forementioned Advantages, is, because it was his Birth-place; to whom that of *Virgil* is applicable,.

Non tibi diva parens generis, nec Dardanus author
Perfide: *Sed duris genuit te cautibus ingens*
Jenneah; *Duccanæque admôrunt ubera tigres.*[1]

What makes it more famous, it was anciently the Seat Royal of the *Duccan* Kings, under whom *Seva Gi*'s Father was Keeper; but *Aurenzeeb* in his Conquest of this Kingdom (after he had fled hither for protection) had it surrendred unto him: It is reckoned two Course and an half in height; is surrounded, though a good way off, with Hills, all but towards the *North*, where it seems to stand Captain of the Mountains.

The *Moguls* I perceive are inclinable to the like Credulity the *Gentues* are, pointing out a Mount where undoubtedly *Solomon* gave Audit to the Two Women claiming the same Child, and pronounced Judgment in favour of the true Mother; and it still bears the name of *Tocta Schelimon*, *Solomon*'s Throne;[2] I brought Night

---

[1] *Nec tibi diva parens, generis nec Dardanus auctor, Perfide*; *sed duris genuit te cautibus horrens Caucasus*; *Hyrcanaeque admorunt ubera tigres* (Virgil, *Æneid*, iv, 365 ff.).

[2] Takht-i-Sulaimān, a common name for mountains. That in Kashmīr is mentioned by Bernier (p. 399). Another, more famous, is the chief peak of the Sulaimān range, on the Punjab frontier, nearly due W. of Dehra Ismāīl Khān, the higher of the two peaks being 11,317 ft.

with me to *Jeneah*, being too well guarded to suspect any Attempt; though notable enough by the multitudes of Oily Flambeaus.

This Day gave me occasion to take notice of the sneaking Officiousness of the *Banyans*, who pressed on my Heels, and where-ever I went, waited like Lacquies, which put me in mind of that Distich of *Martial's*,

Lecticam sellamque sequor, nec ferre recuso
Per medium properans, sed prior ire tutum.[1]

The New Moon brought the Soldiers to their several Standards, against the Governor's House, by their *Salam* to refresh his Memory of their Pay, being Fourteen Months behind-hand. Pay, says *Tacitus*,[2] is the Cause of Soldiers, and Money is the Cause of Pay; which is not wanting to the Muster-masters, who abuse the common Troopers in retarding it; to the end, that having run into debt, they might compound for half their Wages in ready Money;[3] for all which they leave not often their Side, for they are sure of something with ease, whereas *Seva Gi* is a kind of Free-booter, whose Maxim is, No Plunder, no Pay; which comes with pain and hazard: Yet it is common for him to have *Moors* in his Army; for the Liberty of their Country is not stood

---

above sea level. There are at least three of the name in Persia (Curzon, *Persia*, i, 568, ii, 59 72); and one in Turkistan (Schuyler, *Turkistan*, ii, 43). The "Judgement of Solomon" is a familiar theme in Eastern folk-lore (Burton, *Ar. Nights*, xi, 51; Rhys Davids, *Jataka*, i, xiv ff., xliv ff.; Clouston, *Popular Tales and Fictions*, i, 15 f.).

1 *Epigr.*, x, 10 f.

2 *Nam neque quies gentium sine armis, neque stipendia sine tributis habere queunt* (*Hist.*, iv, 74).

3 "The King himself regulates as well the effective number [of troops] that each *Omrah* is to maintain, as the nominal number which he need not keep, but which is also paid for, and usually forms the principal part of his salary. His salary is increased by the money that the *Omrah* retains out of every man's pay, and by what accrues from his false returns of the horses he is supposed to provide" (Bernier, 212 f.)

so much upon, as *Whose Salt they eat*[1] (their own Phrase); so that you may see *Gentues* in the *Mogul's* Army, as well as *Moguls* among the *Gentues*: For the most part of the Body of the Cavalry consists of *Moguls*, the Infantry of *Gentues*, with Match-Lock Muskets.

In order to this Convention every Petty Officer brings the number of his Men and Horse along with him, who first salute him, and he the Governor, owning none else for their Commander, though they fall off under such an Ensign as they are ordered to march with: They are taught little more than the Grand Paw,[2] and to make a Salam: They ride in wide Saddles as our War Saddles. but hold with the Calves of their Legs, not fasten themselves to their Saddles by their Thighs, as we do;[3] by which slight they raise themselves to mow down their Enemies, and will cast a Spear, and take it up from the Ground on full speed: They stop with a jerk, not taking their Horses up by degrees, which they laugh at us for, as well as our riding with our Feet at length: They have no Spurs to their Heels, but in their Bridle-bit is one to stop the most untamed Horse, or bore his Mouth through, pointing out of a Circle upon their Tongues.[4]

They have other excellent Qualities; as he that runs fastest, is the best Soldier: Besides, their Arms are kept so bright, they are afraid to handle them for fear of

---

[1] *Namakhwār*, "eating salt," a dependent; *namakhalāl*, "one true to his salt"; *namakharām*, "untrue to his salt."

[2] Fr. *grand pas*, *pas*, "step."

[3] See drawing of a man on a Deccan pony in Kipling, *Beast and Man*, 183.

[4] The "thorny" bit is still in common use with natives. For illustrations, *Ibid.*, 173. So in Persia the bit has a terribly high port, while in addition there is a strong ring attached to the cross-bar. As a result, horses fear to lengthen their stride, and "star-gazing" is common (Sykes, *Ten Thousand Miles*, 147 *n.*).

soiling them: Their Leaders are good Carpet-Knights, loving their *Buchannos* better than the Field.

The old *Roman* Discipline takes place, *viz.* Commanders of Tens, so of Hundreds, thence to Legions;[1] and accordingly receive their Salary, making their own Terms with those under them: The Governor distributing to the Officers, and they to the Soldiers, every one having their Snips; that never was more truly verified that Proverb, *Half the King's Cheese goes away in Parings.*

The Grandees of the Army appear with their Furniture of Silver and Gold, on *Persian*, *Arab*, or *Turkish* Steeds; the rest rarely get any other than the Race of the Country, which are Fiery and Mettlesome, but very Flashy, probably because they pinch their Bellies to put into their Own.

And now the Rains began to urge me to take my Leave of the *Caun* of *Jeneah*, which I did in a full Assembly convocated for the purpose; where I was informed Two hundred of *Seva Gi*'s Men had pursued me almost to *Ambegaum*,[2] with a resolution to have carried me back, but durst come no further, for the Report of the Army being in Motion; wherefore the *Naibob* advised me to take another way, and a select Guard of his should attend me to the utmost Extent of his Territories; after which he dismissed me very honourably, with a Letter to the President, which is not sealed on the Paper, but in a Neat Bag of Cloath of Gold or Silver.[3]

This *Naibob Mucklis Caun* lives not in that Splendor the Governor of *Surat* does, though he have ten times the Salary, being liable to the daily Assaults of *Seva Gi*;

---

[1] See Letter V, chap. XII.

[2] See p. 321.

[3] This is the Kharīta; see Yule, *Hobson-Jobson*, 475.

but he exceeds in Command, being Absolute, without any Dependance on the General; which causes an Emulation on either side, and the more, because the *Mogul* has lately heaped new Honours on *Badur Caun*, doubling his Stipend, and giving him the Title of Foster Brother, his Mother nursing the King.[1] But this Governor, to equalize him in Wealth, keeps but half the alotted Number in Pay, and lives sparingly, which makes him take Sanctuary with regret sometimes under *Badur Caun*, he being always upon the Forlorn Hope.

This Cheat is practised all over the Realm, notwithstanding here are Publick Notaries placed immediately by the *Mogul*, to give Notice of all Transactions; which they are sure to represent in favour of the Governors where they reside, being Fee'd by them, as well as Paid by the Emperor; so that if a Defeat happen, it is extenuated; if a Victory, it is magnified to the height: Those in this Office are called *Vocanoveces*.[2]

The Government of this Place is as in all other Cities of the *Moguls*. The Walls are broken down, but the Gates are still remaining: With the City's Safeguard Trade is fled, though it be commodiously seated, and furnished with course Chints, fine Lawn, and plenty of Cotton-Grounds; but the Plowmen and Weavers have followed the Merchants, a Rich one not being to be heard of in seven or eight days Journy from hence.

The Buzzars therefore consist chiefly of Provisions, which they compel the Country to bring in, and some-

---

[1] Manucci (iv, 124) names Qamar-ud-dīn Khān as foster-brother of Aurangzeb, a statement which Mr. Irvine informs me is doubtful. He thinks that, even it be correct, it may be accounted for by the fact that ladies who were in a physical condition to do so were often given leave to suckle a royal infant, and thus became, as it were, honorary foster-mothers. Bahādur Khān's mother may have been, he thinks, the real wet nurse of Aurangzeb.

[2] See p. 205.

times take them by Force, by reason of the general Poverty reigning among them.

Wherefore the 22[d] of *May* I left them, and took my Way by *Nunny Gaot*,[1] or the Little Hill in respect of the other, which we saw mounted a prodigious height above us: Hither I came by twelve a Clock at Noon, a far shorter and easier Way than the other: It is ten Course from *Jeneah*, wherein we travelled between a Couple of *Seva Gi's* Castles; and overlooking the *Gaot*, is a third very like *Jeneah Gur*, which hailed us; I sent one to answer them, but kept on my Course till I came to the *Gaot*, where I was constrained to bestow more time than I was willing, 300 Oxen laden with Salt (which is so precious up the Country, as to be proverbially preferred to Bread, they saying, *Whose Salt they eat*, as we, *Whose Bread*,) stopping the Gap; but with a little Intreaty, after an hour's standing still in the Sun, I got them, by sending my *Peons*, to desist below, till we had widen'd the Pass above; after which it is feasible, being supplied at fit distances with charitable Cisterns of good Water, and towards the bottom adorned with beautiful Woods, delighting as well as refreshing us with the Shade: By Sunset I was in the Plain, where an honest *Subidar* that took off his Liquor,

---

[1] Fryer having been misled into crossing the difficult Avāpā pass on his way to Junnar, returned by the Nānā Ghāt, in Thāna District, which lies about 70 miles N.E. of Bombay. It shares with the Tal pass to the N. and the Bor pass to the S. the bulk of the trade between the Deccan and the coast: it is still used for grain and salt traffic. He interprets the name to mean the "little" (*nanhā* or *nannahā*) pass; but native tradition connects it with a man named Nānā (*Bombay Gaz.*, xiv, 286 ff.) Ptolemy's Nanagouna is perhaps due to his confusion of the place with a river (M'Crindle, *Ptolemy*, 48). The Pilee of Nikitin (*India in XVth Cent.*, 9) was perhaps Pilu at the foot of the pass. The cisterns mentioned by Fryer still exist; but he makes no references to the remarkable figures and inscriptions. One of the "castles" may have been Bahirugad or Bairāmgad, a few miles N.E. of the pass (*Bombay Gaz.*, xiv, 14).

let me pass without trouble, being more like a Scout than a Set-Watch.

Nor do I believe the *Mogul's* Army dare venture to advance between these Streights, which are so well maintained; but farther *North* the Hills seem to stoop more to the Plain, and it may be that Way they may Pass; though this way be tolerable for *Caphala's* and Merchants who have their Passports.

We reckon to have measured this Day Fifteen Course, most in the Heat of the Day, to the side of a poor Village called *Wesnure*,[1] where we rested under a Tree, the *Coolies* being unprovided for; nor could they purchase any thing here, the Inhabitants being hared out of their Wits, mistrusting even their own Countrymen as well as Strangers, living as it were wildly, betaking themselves to the Thickets and Wildernesses among the Hills, upon the approach of any new Face; for my Horse by chance breaking loose, set a whole *Gom* or Town upon the hoof, they thinking *Auren Zeeb's* Luscarry at hand; thus unhappily live these, a Prey to every one.

The Clouds had spread themselves over the Tops of the Hills, that they seemed to make a *Ne plus ultra*, or the World's-End.

The next Day at Twelve a Clock at Noon we struck into our old Road at *Moorbar*,[2] from whence before we were misguided; we packed hence by Five in the Afternoon, and left our Burnt Wood on the Right-hand, but entred another made us better Sport, deluding us with false Flashes, that you would have thought the

---

[1] The Collector of Thāna informs me that there is no place of this name on Fryer's route. He is disposed to identify it with Vaishākharē, the largest place between Nānā Ghāt and Murbād, with a bazar, at which Fryer would be likely to halt. It is 3 miles from the foot of the pass and 20 from Murbād. The name is usually interpreted to be derived from Vaisya-griha: but the latter part is more probably Mahr. *ākhara* or *akhara*, meaning "the village outskirts."

[2] Murbād; see p. 310.

Trees on a Flame, and presently, as if untouch'd by Fire, they retained their wonted Verdure.[1] The *Coolies* beheld the Sight with Horror and Amazement, and were consulting to set me down, and shift for themselves; whereof being informed, I cut two or three with my Sword, and by breathing a Vein,[2] let *Shitan*[3] (the Devil) out, who was crept into their Fancies, and led them as they do a startling Jade, to smell to what their Wall-Eyes represented amiss; where we found an Host of Flies, the Subject both of our Fear and Wonder, which the sultry Heat and Moisture had generated into Being, the certain Prodromus of the ensuing Rain, which follow'd us from the Hills.

This gave my Thoughts the Contemplation of that Miraculous Bush crowned with Innocent Flames, that gave to *Moses* so pleasant and awful a Prospect; the Fire that consumes every thing, seeming rather to dress than offend it.

Thus we came to *Barfta*,[4] a despicable Country Town Seven Course more; it is in possession of the *Combies*, who are not strong enough to aid their Herds against the devouring Jaws of the Wild Beasts, a young *Buffola* being seized the Night before, out of the Tabernacle they lodged me in; wherefore they cautioned me to keep Fires all Night, lest the Horse might lose one of his Quarters, or our Oxen might serve them for a Supper; I added to the Fires a strict Watch, whose mutual answering each other in an high Tone, was deafen'd by the Roaring of Tigres, Cries of Jackals, and Yellings of

---

[1] This was due to fire-flies, which it is curious the coolies did not recognise (Yule, *Hobson-Jobson*, 351).

[2] See p. 230.

[3] Ar. *shaitān*, Heb. *sātān*, "an enemy"; Satan.

[4] See p. 254.

Baloos, or over-grown Wolves:[1] At Cock-crow (the Lions Charm) we parted hence, and observed the Sheds here were round, thatch'd, and lined with broad Leaves of *Teke*[2] (the Timber Ships are built with), in fashion of a Bee-hive: These *Combies*[3] are the Wood-men. About Seven we overtook our deep Creek, and being somewhat swelled by the Rains, we followed its Current till we found it passable; about Eleven we returned to *Gullean*.[4]

The Hardship these poor *Combies* undergo was obvious to the sense of the very *Cooties*, who often in this Journy would reflect on their own Happiness under the *English* Government; those being all so harass'd, that they dare not Till the Ground, never expecting to reap what they sow, or remain in their Houses, but seek lurking-Places in Deserts and Caverns, being naked to the Violence of the Plunderer, and therefore both unsafe and uncomfortable Journeying for Travellers. I took up my Station where I was before, and sent my Man to the *Havaldar* to complain of the Treachery of the Guides; he professed he was asham'd, but a new Governor being since put over his Head, with the Command of a Party of Horse, he was incapable of punishing them; yet for what further Courtesy he was able to do he was ready, and to that end sent to the *Subidar* for his License for a Boat, which now are all pluck'd up and housed ashore, the Rains more than approaching, so that it was troublesome procuring one; but by their joint Power it was at last atchieved; which a cross-grain'd *Brachmin*,

[1] The Hind. *bhālū* means properly a bear. Here it may refer to a hyæna. In W. and S. India the term *bhālū* or *kol bhālū* is applied to the half-legendary *phiāl* or jackal, which is believed to utter a peculiar cry when a tiger or leopard is in the neighbourhood (Blanford, *Mammalia*, 141 f.).

[2] The teak tree (*tectona grandis*).

[3] See p. 320.

[4] See p. 308.

supported by an outlaw'd *Portugal*, contradicted in despight of both, seizing it by Force with Three Files of Soldadoes.

For which cause I was tied to the Consort of cröaking Frogs, making so hideous a Noise, that I took little Rest this Night: When Day broke I could hardly believe my Eyes, for Bulk,[1] or Ears, for Sound, exceeding ours incredibly; and to raise the Wonder, this Night was the first of the Rains, before which none were heard: Wherein *Pliny*[2] may be trusted, better than in some other Reports; for speaking *de Ranis*, he says, *Mirum semestri vitâ resolvuntur in limum, nullo cernente, & rursus vernis aquis renascuntur, quæ fuere natæ, proinde occultâ ratione cum omnibus annis id eveniat.* Et Aristot. de Gen. Anim. cap. 4. *Generantur autem in terrâ & humore animalia & plantæ; quoniam humor in terrâ, spiritus in humore, calor animalis in universo est, ita ut quadammodo animarum plena sunt omnia.*

Sic Ovidius,

Semina limus habet virides generantia ranas.[3]

Who all consent to the possibility of the thing, the prolifick Virtue lying hid in the slimy Matter, till a conjunction of fit Causes dispose it for suddain Action.

Walking the Quarters of my Lodgings, a more delightful, and as unusual a Prospect attracted my Animadversion; a great Tree full of stringy red Flowers, set in open Calices upon a long Stalk, like budding Grapes;[4]

[1] Some Indian frogs attain a considerable size. Ovington (p. 145) describes toads at Bombay "not of a much less size than a small Duck." Any one who has heard the croaking of frogs which accompanies the first break of the rains, will recognise the truth of Fryer's description.

[2] *Hist. Nat.*, ix, 74.

[3] Ovid., *Metam.*, xv., 375.

[4] Probably the *Hibiscus mutabilis*, a native of China, now cultivated in gardens throughout India. Its flowers are almost white in the morning and red at night (Watt, *Econ. Dict.*, iv, 242). Ar. *nūr*, "brightness, splendour" is possibly the origin of the name.

which before the Sun had collected much force, I saw begin to fall in showers upon the Ground; desiring to handle one Bough, I observed them fixed; still they upon the Tree dropped till all was shedded, and the Ground strewed with them, which a *Brachmin* carefully gathered up to reserve for a Physical use; but more truly out of Superstition, paying Rent for the Privilege: This Wonder is renewed daily, they Blossoming in the Night, and contrary almost to all other Plants, are disgusted with the Sun-beams, drooping in the day; which is like the *Arbor Tristis*[1] at St. *Thomas* his Mount, only the Flowers of that are White and Sweet, and this Red and indifferently Scented; the Leaves of the Tree resemble those of a Walnut; in the Country *Nomenclature* it is called. *Nure*: of what Virtue I cannot learn.

Discharging here my Oxen, which I hired of a *Gentue*, who though they will not Kill their Neat, make no Conscience to Work them to Death, allowing them hardly Food to keep them alive.

Neither are they less Inhuman towards their Sick, a Woman being brought to die among the Tombs in my sight; pretended to be done to avoid the Governor's troubling the Family (where she lived a Dancing Wench) for Money; they making themselves Heirs to their Estates when they die: *Non ad eundem finem quem Herodotus ait, uti Antiquiores Ægyptii ægrotos suos non ad medicos, sed in compita, & publicas vias deferebant, populum prætereuntem pro morborum curatione consulturi*: Not for that purpose, as *Herodotus* presumes; the *Egyptians* brought not their Sick to Physicians, but laid them in the Streets and Publick Passages, that the People passing by might be consulted for their Cure.[2]

---

[1] See p. 116.

[2] Herodotus attributes this custom to the Babylonians, not to the Egyptians (i, 197); Burton (*Anatomy of Melancholy*, ii, 242 f.) makes

Every Third Hour I had the din of a Man of God of the *Moors*, permitted to come hither to call them to Prayers; as he cried aloud he stopped his Ears with his Fingers, that he might emit his Voice with the more strength, and less disturbance to himself; experience thereby directing us to hear our own Sounds the better; and some Anatomists tell us, Nature has framed a Cartilaginous passage from the hollow of the Drum of the Ear, to the process of the outward part of the cuneal Bone reaching to the Palat, which being open may possibly divert the Noise; but whether this do help, or is understood by them, yet this they do Practise; and this Afternoon their *Sanctum Sanctorum* was open, the Priest entring in Barefoot and Prostrating himself on the Mats spread on the Floor, whither I must not have gone, could his Authority have kept me out; the Walls were white and clean, but plain, only the Commandments, wrote in *Arabick* in the *West-end*, were hung on a Table over an Arched Place, where the Priest Expounds on an Ascent of Seven Steps, railed at top with Stone very handsomely:[1] It is supported within with Four substantial Pillars of Timber well carved, the Roof all Wood, with a square Hole over the Pulpit: Underneath are fine cool Vaults, and Stone Stairs to descend to a deep Tank,

---

the same statement: "The most rational of them [physicians], and skilful, are so often deceived, that as Tholosanus infers, I had rather believe and commit myself to a mere Empirick than to a mere Doctor, and I cannot sufficiently commend that custom of the Babylonians, that have no professed Physicians, but bring all their patients to the market to be cured; which Herodotus relates of the Egyptians, Strabo, Sardus, and Aubanus Bohemus, of many other Nations." Also see Strabo, xvi, 348.

[1] The Mimbar or mosque pulpit has three steps, and is sometimes a movable wooden structure, sometimes a fixture of brick or stone built against the wall (Hughes, *Dict.*, 349). No "commandments" seem ever to be inscribed in a mosque. The Musalmān creed—*La Ilāha illa 'llāhu: Muhammadun Rasūlu 'llāh*—"There is no deity but God; Muhammad is the Apostle of God" may have been written over the Mimbar.

where this Priest was following the Occupation of making such Paper as they use; which after he had steeped Çotton Rags in Water, he by beating brought it into the form of Paper; and cutting them, or slicing the Mass into Sheets, was pasting them up on the Stone-sides of the Mosque, next the Sun, to dry; after which they are polished and glazed, and so made fit for their use.[1]

In the Evening I saw the reason of our stay this day; a Pragmatical *Portugal* fled to this Place, for designing the death of a *Fidalgo* in the front of 40 Men marching to the Governor's; his Name *Pedro Sylvio*, a Rich Lout, no Gentleman: Besides these he keeps as a Guard to his Body, he has a Bloudy Leash of *Cofferies*[2] imployed to be revenged on his Antagonist at *Baçein*; here he acts without Controle, and is about to accept of Pay under *Seva Gi*, he being courted thereto, because he is a bold desperate Fellow, the fitter Instrument to ruin his Nation.

In the mean time here arriving a *Bombaim* Boat, she was presently disburthened of her Lading, and I Embarqued, and the 26th of *May* came abreast of *Tanaw*,[3] the Pass here being another main Impediment to the intended Trade up the Country with the *Moors*; which, had we in our possession, according to the Contract with *Portugal*, we might the easier make *Seva Gi* comply; and more than that, find Lordships for *Englishmen*, where they might live contentedly, and not be beholden to Foreign Supplies for Provisions: By Three the next Morning I Anchored against the *Bunder* at *Bombaim*, and Landed presently after Travally-Beat, delivering my Letter from the *Caun* to the President.

---

[1] Paper is made in the same fashion at the present day; see Baden-Powell, *Handbook*, 91 ff.

[2] See p. 62.

[3] Thāna.

Here rode an *Europe* ship called the *Fleece*; which lost her Passage last Year, coming too late out of *England*: and about Noon the *Rainbow* arrived, they being forced to put in at *Bombass*,[1] an Island of the *Portugals* on the Coast of *Melinda*, which produces excellent Ivory, and other Miracles, from whence they sailed together; till just on this Shore a Storm separated them, the *Fleece* gaining this Port; the *Rainbow* fell first in with *Surat*, and to Day came to an Anchor here.

Thus if I have been too prolix in this Narrative, I must beg your pardon for endeavouring to satisfy you on two Scores, which none but one of my Profession must pretend to; the one relating to the Women, and the other to their Fortified *Gurs*[2] or Castles; and if it find your Acceptance, it is all the Aim I have, and my Pains is thereby sufficiently rewarded.

Bombaim 1675.
Sept. 22.

---

[1] Mombasa, the island off the coast of E. Africa; the Mombaza of Barbosa (p. 11). See Gray's Note on Pyrard de Laval (ii, 236), where Burton's description of the place (*Zanzibar*, ii, 28) is referred to.

[2] Hind. *garh*, Mahr. *gad*.